A Therapist's Guide to EMDR

Tools and Techniques for Successful Treatment

Also by Laurel Parnell

EMDR in the Treatment of Adults Abused as Children

Transforming Trauma: EMDR

A Norton Professional Book

A Therapist's Guide to EMDR

Tools and Techniques for Successful Treatment

Laurel Parnell

W. W. Norton & Company
New York • London

For additional information about Laurel Parnell's workshops and trainings, readers may contact her by visiting www.emdrinfo.com.

Manufacturing by LSC Harrisonburg
Production Manager: Leeann Graham

Library of Congress Cataloging-in-Publication Data

Parnell, Laurel, 1955–
    A therapist's guide to EMDR : tools and techniques for successful treatment /
Laurel Parnell.
        p.   cm. — (A Norton professional book)
    ISBN-13: 978-0-393-70481-5
    ISBN-10: 0-393-70481-5
        1. Eye movement desensitization and reprocessing.   2. Psychic trauma—
Treatment.   I. Title.
RC489.E98P36   2006
616.85'21—dc22   2006049496

    ISBN-13: 978-0-393-70481-5
    ISBN-10: 0-393-70481-5

W. W. Norton & Company, Inc., 500 Fifth Avenue, New York, N.Y. 10110
www.wwnorton.com

W. W. Norton & Company, Ltd., 15 Carlisle Street, London W1D 3BS

9 0

This book is dedicated to the EMDR therapists and clients
who have had the courage to open to the unknown
and find their way to healing.

May you be peaceful
May you be happy
May you be free from suffering
May you be liberated

—*Loving-kindness meditation*

BRIEF TABLE OF CONTENTS

Acknowledgments   xiii
Preface   xv
Introduction   3

PART I: EMDR THEORETICAL OVERVIEW

1. EMDR Refresher   27
2. Essential EMDR Protocol   36

PART II: USING EMDR WITH CLIENTS

3. Evaluation and Preparation for EMDR   47
4. Tools and Techniques for Ego Strengthening   79
5. Case Formulation   119
6. Reevaluating the Therapy   140
7. Target Development   148

PART III: THE EMDR SESSION

8. The Procedural Steps   193
9. Tools and Techniques for Processing Difficulties   224

PART IV: CLINICAL APPLICATIONS

10. Working with Phobias   293

11. Recent Traumas and Critical Incidents   309

12. Care for the Caregiver   320

Appendix 1: EMDR Procedures and Checklists   325
Appendix 2: Trauma Exposure and Crisis Intervention with CIPBS   339
References   345
Index   353

EXPANDED TABLE OF CONTENTS

Acknowledgments   xiii
Preface   xv
Introduction   3
   What EMDR Does and How it Works   3
   Neurobiology of Trauma and Recent Brain Research 14
   The Discovery of EMDR and its Development   18
   Organization of Book   22
   Conventions Used Throughout the Book   23

PART I: EMDR THEORETICAL OVERVIEW

1. EMDR Refresher   27
   Review of Basic EMDR Protocol and Procedure   27
   Rationale and Application of Interweaves   33
   EMDR Resource Development and Installation (RDI)   34
   Three-Phase Trauma Therapy Model   34
   EMDR as a Stand-Alone Therapy vs. EMDR as a Therapeutic Method
      That Is Integrated into a Treatment 35

2. Essential EMDR Protocol   36
   Modifications of the Standard Procedural Steps   36
   How to Modify the Standard Procedural Steps   39
   When to Modify the Standard Procedural Steps   42
   Modifying the Procedural Steps for Clients with Complex Trauma 43

PART II: USING EMDR WITH CLIENTS

3. Evaluation and Preparation for EMDR   47
   Take a History of the Presenting Problems   47

Assessing Readiness for EMDR   57
Integrating EMDR into Clinical Treatment: How to Introduce EMDR
  to Clients   65
Explanation of Theories   66
Informed Consent for EMDR   67
Set Up Signals for "Stop" and "Keep Going"   68
Types of BLS   68
Establishing a Metaphor to Use   70
Treatment Issues   71

4. Tools and Techniques for Ego Strengthening   79
Identification, Development, and Installation of Inner and Outer Resources   80
Other Coping Skills   110
Techniques for Creating Distance and/or Containment   116

5. Case Formulation   119
Using the Standard Protocol for Current Anxiety and Behavior   121
How to Determine a Target from a Current Issue or Problem   123
Longer-Term Therapy with Multiple Complex Issues   135

6. Reevaluating the Therapy   140
Functioning   143
Check the Log or Journal   143
Symptoms   145
Behavioral Shifts   145
Dreams   146
Insights   146
New Memories   146
System Changes   146
The Target   147

7. Target Development   148
Targeting Single-Incident Traumas   148
Targeting for Clients with Multiple Traumas   149
Tips for Target Development   151
Targeting Triggers and Flashbacks   153
The Bridging Technique for Target Development   154
Using Art for Targets   184
Dreams as Targets   187

PART III: THE EMDR SESSION

8. The Procedural Steps   193
    Installing or Evoking Resources   193
    Identifying the Presenting Issue or Memory   193
    Creating an Image   193
    NC (Negative Cognition)   197
    PC (Positive Cognition)   198
    VoC (Validity of Cognition) Scale   200
    Emotions/Feelings   201
    SUDS   201
    Location of Body Sensations   202
    Desensitization   203
    Installation of the PC   211
    Body Scan   211
    Close and Debrief the Session   212
    Suggestions for Helping Clients Manage Between Sessions   222

9. Tools and Techniques for Processing Difficulties   224
    Working with Abreactions   224
    Dissociation During EMDR Processing   229
    Client Sleepiness   231
    Client Numbness   233
    Clients with Body Memories without Visual Memories   233
    Memory Chaining   235
    Using Interweaves and Other Strategies to Release Blocked Processing 236
    Implementing Noninterweave Strategies   248
    Implementing Interweave Strategies   251

PART IV: CLINICAL APPLICATIONS

10. Working with Phobias   293

11. Recent Traumas and Critical Incidents   309
     Protocol for Recent Traumatic Events   309
     Modified Protocol for Recent Traumatic Events   314
     Using the Recent Traumatic Events Protocol with Critical Incidents   317

12. Care for the Caregiver   320
     Suggestions for Therapist Self-Care   320
     How to Be the Best EMDR Therapist   323

Appendix 1: EMDR Procedures and Checklists   325
     EMDR Procedural Steps Checklist   325
     Sample Vignette of the Procedural Steps   326
     Modified EMDR Procedural Steps Checklist   328
     Sample Vignette of the Modified Procedural Steps   329
     Clinical Signs of Dissociative Disorders   330
     Quick Assessment for EMDR Readiness in an Outpatient Setting   332
     Summary of Resources, Coping Skills, and Techniques for Creating Distance
          and/or Containment   333
     Protocol for Development of the Positive, Conflict-free Image   334
     List of Negative and Positive Cognitions   335
     Summary of What to Do If the Processing Is Looping or Stuck   336
     Summary of Noninterweave Strategies   336
     Important Concepts for Adaptive Information Processing   337
     Summary of Interweave Categories and Subcategories   337

Appendix 2: Trauma Exposure and Crisis Intervention with CIPBS   339

References   345
Index   353

ACKNOWLEDGMENTS

FIRST OF ALL I WANT to thank Francine Shapiro, brilliant pioneer and mother of eye movement desensitization and reprocessing (EMDR), who has worked tirelessly to bring EMDR to those in need of healing. I appreciate my clients who had the courage to face their fears and come out the other end free to live more fully. My deep appreciation to my friends and colleagues who have facilitated at my trainings and have given me encouragement through the years as well as a wealth of ideas to expand the use of EMDR: Linda Cohn, Harriet Sage, Alison Teal, Christie Sprowls, Susan Tieger, Lynn Dixon, Philip Manfield, and Cynthia Kong. A special thanks to Christa Diegelmann and Margarete Isermann who brought me to Germany and shared laughter over pretzels as well as their innovative work with cancer patients. Thank you to Brooke Brown for reading through the manuscript and giving me helpful suggestions. My appreciation to Maggie Phillips for her expertise in resource development, energy psychology, and somatic psychotherapy. I want to thank Deborah Malmud, editor at Norton Professional Books, for her confidence in me and excellent feedback. Thanks to Sheryl Fullerton for her advice in early stages of this project.

Many thanks to Nischala Devi, dear friend with whom I have shared writing and walks on the beach, and to John Prendergast for our weekly meetings that have enriched my life.

I appreciate my husband, Pierre Antoine Blais, whose love has sustained me through this process, and my sons Catono Perez and Etienne Perez-Parnell. I will try to wait a bit before I take on another project of this magnitude. Thanks to Jean Pumphrey, lifelong friend, mentor, and aunt.

I appreciate all the therapists worldwide who have contributed to the growth and development of EMDR over the years, working to make this planet a saner, more peaceful place to live. I feel myself part of a greater whole. Together we are making a difference.

PREFACE

SINCE MY TRAINING in 1991, I have been immersed in EMDR, using it extensively in my clinical practice, providing consultation, and training thousands of therapists in the United States and internationally. I felt a desire to write a book that allowed me to share my knowledge with a wider audience. The purpose of this book is to help EMDR-trained therapists be able to use EMDR skillfully and successfully with a range of clients.

Like many of us who have been using EMDR for years, I continue to have a passion for the work. Coming from a background that was primarily psychodynamic, I have found ways to integrate EMDR into a psychodynamically informed approach. Although I was trained by Francine Shapiro and the EMDR Institute in 1991, I have worked independently since 1995 under the auspices of the EMDR International Association. Therapists who are trained by me learn to integrate EMDR into a broader treatment approach that honors the therapeutic relationship, finding ways EMDR can be modified to fit the client, rather than forcing the client into a rigid technical mold. And, having practiced meditation for over 32 years, I bring a transpersonal approach to the work emphasizing nonjudgmental listening, attunement, and presence. I believe that using EMDR is an art, requiring flexibility, creativity, and the use of intuition.

From my teaching and consultation work, I have found four areas where most EMDR-trained therapists need help: case formulation, ego strengthening, target development, and the ability to work with processing difficulties. Since 1999 I have taught an advanced EMDR workshop that focuses on these areas. Material from my trainings as well as these workshops is included in this book. I wanted to write a book that would review the basic information from the training but then add onto that foundation with new information. Too often therapists leave the EMDR training enthusiastic, desiring to use it in their practices, but then lose their nerve when they come upon a difficulty with a client. My hope is that this book can support you in your work, providing you with practical information. If you have a problem, look it up in the Contents or Index. Hopefully you will find something that will be of use to you.

The book reviews the theoretical basis for EMDR and new information on the neurobiology of trauma. It provides a detailed explanation of the procedural steps along with helpful suggestions and modifications. Areas essential to successful utilization of EMDR are emphasized. These include: case conceptualization; preparation for EMDR trauma processing, including resource development and installation; target development; methods for unblocking blocked processing, including the creative use of interweaves; and session closure. Case examples are used throughout to illustrate concepts. The emphasis in this book is on clinical usefulness, not research. In *A Therapist's Guide to EMDR*, you will be able to find helpful suggestions in simple, easy-to-understand language.

A Therapist's Guide to EMDR is meant to supplement Shapiro's basic EMDR text, *Eye Movement Desensitization and Reprocessing* (2001). This book builds on Shapiro's text, providing information that is accessible and easy to use. It breaks down the steps to using EMDR in a way that is clear and understandable. I have included illustrative case material throughout the book that I hope helps makes the work come alive. From my teaching experience, I believe that the stories and vignettes will help you to remember the points I am trying to teach. From the case examples you will be able to see what I was thinking and why I did what I did. This book does not include a thorough review of the literature. For that information please refer to Shapiro's text (2001). It also does not go into all of the technical detail contained in her book. This book is for EMDR-trained therapists who want to know more about how to integrate EMDR into their psychotherapy practices. It is a practical book that gives valuable information clinicians can use immediately. It will help therapists trained in EMDR to weave this treatment into their practices and serve as a bridge between the training and the use of EMDR in clinical practice. *This book is not intended as a substitute for training in EMDR. In order to use EMDR in clinical practice, you must complete training with an EMDRIA (EMDR International Association)-approved instructor.*

I have written two other EMDR books, *Transforming Trauma: EMDR* (1997a) and *EMDR in the Treatment of Adults Abused as Children* (1999). The first book was meant to introduce EMDR to the general public, whereas the second, like *A Therapist's Guide to EMDR*, was written for EMDR-trained therapists, but focused on treatment of adult abuse survivors. *A Therapist's Guide to EMDR* shares some of the material found in *EMDR in the Treatment of Adults Abused as Children*, but I have expanded some areas, added new information, and included tools and techniques for working with a range of clients.

This book was written for therapists newly trained in EMDR as well as the old-timers. There is something for everyone. I have collected tools, techniques, and tips from conferences, workshops, consultation with colleagues, and my own clinical experience. You can read it from beginning to end, or use it as a reference when you want information on a particular area.

EMDR is constantly evolving. We learn from one another, sharing our successes and learning from our mistakes. As a result, EMDR grows. Each of us who uses EMDR uses it in our own way. Just as our clients have their own unique processing styles, we as therapists have our own ways of integrating and using EMDR in our practices. This is exciting, cutting-edge work. I continue to feel awed by the power of it to transform lives and am deeply grateful for the privilege of being part of the evolution and development of this wonderful therapeutic method.

A Therapist's Guide to EMDR

Tools and Techniques for Successful Treatment

INTRODUCTION

THE FOLLOWING ARE important theories and general principles to keep in mind when using EMDR with traumatized people. This overview will help to guide your EMDR work. I have drawn this information from Francine Shapiro's basic text (2001), my two previous books (Parnell, 1997a, 1999), and research on the neurobiology of trauma. After this overview I review EMDR's discovery and development, and explain the organization of the book. This introduction is meant to refresh and renew your memory and understanding, providing the background and foundation for the more complex information that follows.

WHAT EMDR DOES AND HOW IT WORKS

The theoretical model and key concepts used to guide EMDR treatment will be reviewed in this section, followed by a brief discussion of the theories about how EMDR works.

ACCELERATED INFORMATION PROCESSING

In its broadest definition, a trauma is an experience that causes one to develop erroneous beliefs about oneself or the world and to behave in ways that are not skillful. For example, a child who is abused may come to believe she is bad and the world isn't safe. She may have difficulty in intimate relationships. These experiences also become fixed in the body-mind in the form of irrational emotions, blocked energy, and physical symptoms.

Shapiro describes two types of traumas: major traumas, or "big T" traumas, and minor traumas, "small t" traumas. The "T" traumas are those that affect one dramatically, such as war, assaults, rape, childhood physical and sexual abuse, disasters, accidents, and losses. They jolt one out of one's usual perspective on life, causing one to question oneself and the order of one's world. These traumas often lead to debilitating symptoms of posttraumatic stress disorder (PTSD), like nightmares, flashbacks, anxieties, phobias, fears, and difficulties at home and work. Research has shown that EMDR is effective in healing the psychological damage caused by these traumas (Feske, 1998; Spector & Read, 1999; Van Etten & Taylor, 1998; Waller, Mulick, & Spates, 2000). The "t" traumas are those experiences that give one a lesser sense of self-confidence and assault one's sense of self-efficacy. Like a perceptual filter, they cause one to develop narrow and limiting views of oneself and the world, keeping one from living to one's full potential and causing suffering. An example of this kind of trauma is a woman who sought therapy because she was suffering from a feeling of chronic alienation and low self-esteem. She traced these symptoms to her childhood. As a child she had extremely poor vision but did not know it. She had difficulty in school and was socially ostracized. Before her vision problem had been properly diagnosed and treated, significant emotional damage was done. She viewed herself as not good enough, incompetent, and flawed. Despite years of talk therapy and much insight, her symptoms remained. Small "t" traumas, like "T" traumas, can be effectively cleared with EMDR.

It seems that when a person experiences a trauma, either a "t" or "T," it becomes locked into its own memory network as it was experienced—the images, physical sensations, tastes and smells, sounds, and beliefs—as if frozen in time in the body and the mind. Consequently, a woman who has been in a car accident may avoid driving. She may develop fears of other things as well that in any way remind her of the accident. Her entire sense of self-confidence may be shaken. Reminders of the accident trigger an emotional response because all of the memories related to the accident are locked in her nervous system and she is unable to process them. Internal or external reminders of the accident cause the experience to flash into her consciousness in its original form.

Ordinary daily events seem to pass through us without leaving a mark. Traumatic events, however, often get trapped and form a perpetual blockage. Like a broken record, they repeat themselves in our body-mind over and over again. Nightmares may actually be the mind's attempts to process this trapped information, but the trauma memory always lasts beyond the dream. Perhaps this mechanism that freezes traumatic events was an adaptive device in early humans, helping to protect them from repeating mistakes. But now this mechanism has become maladaptive; rather than protect us, it obscures our perceptions and emotions. For example, a young boy who was sexually abused by his mother may distrust all women when he is an adult. This fear can impede his ability to form a close relationship with a mate, prevent him from having female friendships, and cause problems for him with female coworkers in the workplace. His anxiety around women may be very high, and he may have no idea why.

In theory, the body-mind has a *natural information processing system* that works to process and integrate information. This system is likened to the healing system in the body that goes into action to heal a wound. When confronted with a trauma, the information processing system gets inter-rupted—like a blocked wound in the body—causing an ongoing array of PTSD symptoms. Just as the body is not able to heal a wound when there is debris in it, the brain often cannot process a trauma memory. In order for a wound to heal, we must clean it so the body can do its job.

In EMDR, in order to activate clients' information processing systems, we ask them to focus on a "target" related to the trauma, such as a memory with the image, emotions, body sensations, and negative beliefs associated with it. Through this target we are attempting to stimulate the memory network where the trauma is stored. After stimulating the memory network, we add alternating eye movements or other bilateral stimuli (BLS) that stimulate *accelerated information processing* (Shapiro, 1995, 2001). Accelerated information processing is a rapid free association of information between memory net-works that enables clients to draw on information where they find insight and understanding. Each set of BLS further unlocks the disturbing informa-tion and accelerates it along an adaptive path until clients return to a state of equilibrium and integration. Some clients process so rapidly that it is hard for the therapist to believe they have cleared the material so quickly. One woman cleared in a few minutes a molestation that happened to her as an adult in a movie theater. Another woman cleared hundreds of abuse memo-ries in moments, telling me she saw glimpses of images pass by like a flip book. Clients process at different rates, but one of the hallmarks of EMDR is the accelerated information processing. Thoughts, feelings, fantasy images, and body sensations pass through rapidly. Everyone has his or her own unique processing style. Different memories also seem to be held by the body-mind in different ways—some more cognitively, others more somatically.

As clients process with EMDR they go down different channels of associ-ation. The term *channel* is a metaphor that refers to expressions of stored information experienced by the client and expressed as emotions, physical sensations, images, and cognitions. According to Shapiro, a channel contains information that is associated by a thread such as a setting, an image, a belief, a physical sensation, or an emotion.

ADAPTIVE INFORMATION PROCESSING MODEL

Another important concept is that EMDR moves information from dysfunctional to functional. The end result of successful EMDR is adaptive resolution of the trauma. This means that the emotional charge is reduced or eliminated and there is an objective view or understanding of the incident. Just as the river flows to the sea and the body heals the wound, EMDR clears the trauma and brings integration and wholeness. This humanistic ideal is what we observe with all complete EMDR sessions. When the body-mind is allowed to heal, the end result is wisdom, compassion, empowerment, and a sense of wholeness.

In my experience training EMDR therapists, one of the hardest things for therapists to do is to stay out of the client's way and to trust the process. The process has its own intelligence. Just keep it moving and it will lead to healing. Trust it and stay out of the way. You may not be able to imagine how that will be possible in the beginning, but it will find its way there. Don't interfere, interpret, or derail clients unless they are stuck. Trust that it knows where to go. This is the beauty of EMDR. Be open to the miracle of the mind.

A very important related concept is that EMDR will not remove anything that is useful or necessary. EMDR will clear what is dysfunctional, but it will not remove anything the client needs for functioning. A rape victim, for example, may no longer be plagued by nightmares and flashbacks of the traumatic events, but she will not forget that it happened. Instead of being consumed by anger, she will feel powerful. Instead of believing that no man can be trusted, she will believe that *some* men can be trusted. She will also learn better what she needs to be safe and take the necessary precautions. An underlying principle of EMDR is that basic health resides within all of us. What EMDR does is remove blockages caused by negative images, beliefs, and body sensations, allowing one's natural state of well-being and emotional balance to come through.

EMDR unlocks what is natural within each of us. It is our innate healing process that has been blocked and can be unblocked with EMDR. There is an inherent wisdom within each person that is already whole, it is just obscured by the traumas. Our job as therapists is to help clear the blockages so that our clients can have access to their own innate wisdom. Because I believe this is so important and fundamental, I will return to this concept throughout this book.

As an EMDR consultant, I have found that many EMDR therapists have difficulty trusting that their clients can process to completion if they keep them going beyond where they believe it is possible. For example, one EMDR therapist believed a rape victim needed her anger in order to protect herself. Instead of processing until the client no longer felt any disturbance, the therapist closed the session, leaving the client still feeling angry. Another therapist I observed while I was facilitating at a training was working with a client who was processing the death of a parent. Believing that it was as far as anyone could go, the therapist wanted to close the session with the client feeling sad. After I encouraged the therapist to keep going, the client went beyond his therapist's expectations, to an experience of spiritual release and elation. I trusted that if sadness was as far as the client could go, then she would not have cleared it after more BLS.

EMDR will not clear what Shapiro (1995, 2001) called *ecologically appropriate emotions*. These are the emotions at a level of resolution suitable for a given individual, time, and situation. For example, if a battered woman is still in danger from her abuser, her fear may not be cleared to neutral or no disturbance. Though she may feel more empowered, she is still not safe. Disturbances can only be considered to be ecological after the therapist has continued the appropriate reprocessing. This is important, because therapists will too often believe that clients have reached an endpoint, and not encourage them to go further. Many times while facilitating at trainings or consulting with EMDR therapists, I will see the therapists keeping their clients from full resolution of their traumas. *When in doubt, go a little further.* It is essential that therapists encourage their clients go do one or more sets of BLS to see if their level of disturbance can decrease more.

A related idea is that EMDR cannot clear anything that is true. With EMDR, clients come to what is true for them, even if it is something they are unhappy to discover. One woman I worked with sought treatment because she wanted to be more physically intimate with her partner. By the end of our work together she realized that the reason she was not intimate with her partner was because she was not attracted to her. As a result of her realization, she ended the relationship.

PSYCHOLOGICAL MEMORY TO OBJECTIVE MEMORY

EMDR transforms psychological memory to objective memory (Parnell, 1997a). Psychological memory (Klein, 1988) is memory that feels emotionally charged, alive in the present, and self-referential. Enormous energy and tension are employed thinking about and maintaining a psychological past, and these memories form the basis of our personal identity: we believe we are our history. Our bodies and minds hold these memories and they imprison us. By identifying with them we cannot live fully in the present. Objective memory is memory that is functional, devoid of emotional charge, and not self-referential. Often after EMDR sessions clients will report that long-term disturbing memories (psychological memories) no longer belong to them and they'll say, "It's over" or "It's like reading about it in the newspaper." Old memories, including memories of terrible abuse, cease to feel personal to the client. Instead of feeling like "it happened to me," a client will feel like "it happened." The shift is from "These are my memories" to "These are memories." Clients can simply acknowledge that these things happened (objective memory) and release them rather than identify with their histories. The memories are no longer alive in the present; rather they are experienced as belonging to the past, remembered simply as facts.

Often at the end of an EMDR session clients view the image of the original traumatic event as if from above the scene, dispassionately seeing all of the components as a whole. They are part of the scene but no longer the center of it, they are just one part of a complex picture.

OBJECTIVE FORGIVENESS

A concept related to objective memory is that of objective forgiveness (Parnell, 1996a, 1997a). Commonly, objective forgiveness results from the complete reprocessing of a traumatic event and signifies that the psychological memory has shifted to objective memory. Objective forgiveness is not a sentimental kind of forgiveness but rather an unemotional comprehension of why someone harmed the client. Often, understanding and peace replace the desire for revenge. At this point the person feels that the past is indeed in the past. In objective forgiveness, objectivity prevails. It is acceptance, not resignation, and this kind of forgiveness creates a kind of inner peace. For example, at the completion of an EMDR session a woman who was sexually abused by her brother when she was a small child realized that her brother was himself a victim of their father. She saw that there had been a chain of abuse going back generations. This understanding brought her peace and forgiveness, along with the understanding that her brother, who had not undergone psychotherapy, was not safe for her or her children to see.

Objective forgiveness applies to clients as well as to others. So often clients suffer with lifelong regret and feelings of self-blame: the veteran who killed a comrade accidentally in friendly fire, the mother who did not protect her children from her abusive husband, the police officer who could not protect his own family, the rape victim who against her better judgment got into the rapist's car, or the adult who as a child sexually abused his younger sister. Self-hate, guilt, and condemnation impede emotional healing; with the full clearing of traumatic events, clients understand why they acted as they did, experience it in the past, and then experience themselves more fully in the present.

For example, a woman was suffering from guilt because she survived a car accident as a teenager but her older sister did not. In therapy she realized it was her sister who had made her change places in the front seat minutes before the accident. With that realization, her guilt evaporated and she understood that she had done nothing wrong. Relief coursed through her and she felt at peace for the first time since the accident. She felt she had a right to live, and could move on with her life. She could forgive herself for living.

In the case of perpetrators, or people who have knowingly caused harm to others, it is important that they take responsibility for their past actions and express a desire to make amends. Perpetrators recognize that they cannot change the past but can do positive things in the present.

I do not emphasize objective forgiveness as a goal of therapy. I believe it can be a natural by-product of healing. To force it creates the danger that clients will bypass their anger or feel that they are doing something wrong. Objective forgiveness should not be imposed on the client. Remember the adaptive information processing model. Clients will go where they need to go when they can go there. For example, my client Melanie whose treatment I wrote about in Chapter 10 in *Transforming Trauma: EMDR* (Parnell, 1997a), told me early in therapy that she would never forgive the aunt who abused her. I told her that was fine, she didn't need to forgive her. Then, years after she had finished therapy, she told me that she was beginning to feel forgiveness for her aunt. "My child hates this, but my adult can't help it," she told me.

EMDR AND A FELT SENSE OF TRUTH

EMDR helps clients get in touch with a bodily sense of rightness or truth (Parnell, 1996a, 1997a). They learn to *feel* what is true for them. During EMDR processing they sort through what others have told them about themselves, what they believe they should think or feel, and then arrive at what they *feel* to be true. For example, a woman who had been sexually abused by her brother was confused about her feelings. Suddenly she saw the scene from outside herself and realized unequivocally that it was wrong.

She said, "No, this is no! What he is doing is wrong. This is what is true for me." Sometimes the truth is that she was abused as a child. She was powerless then, but as an adult she has power now.

During EMDR clients develop an attunement to their own inner wisdom, which they had been taught to censor or discount as children. The EMDR process supports and nurtures the development of this suppressed body-centered knowing. EMDR clears away the clutter so that clients can see what is in the room.

In EMDR the therapist follows and facilitates the clients' process without interpretation or criticism. This in turn enables clients to observe and report on their experiences with less judgment and aversion, listening to themselves. They are thus able to base their actions on information that arises for them out of their processing, rather than from preconditioning. In this way clients learn to be attuned to their bodies and minds and to feel what is true for them. In EMDR therapy clients develop and strengthen their sense of truth or inner wisdom. For example, a woman who was processing a disturbing situation with her elderly father reported after a set, "The truth is he is dying. Seeing that, I know what I have to do now. I feel more distant, more objective about the situation."

EMDR clients learn to integrate this felt sense of rightness into their daily lives. They develop an inner sense of whom they can trust and a feeling of correct judgment. They become more sensitive to a bodily sense of right and wrong and learn to trust and listen to their body wisdom.

MEMORY NETWORKS

As EMDR therapists we work with *memory networks*. These networks have also been called neuronetworks, complexes, and schemas. These networks are webs of associations radiating from key experiences called *nodes*. The strands that make up the web can be smells, sounds, cognitions, body sensations, and emotions. Shapiro (1995, 2001) refers to the strands as *channels*. A simple example of a memory network is one developed after a single-incident trauma. A client who has been in a car accident might have in his memory network the sound of breaking glass, screeching brakes, forward movement of his body, the sensation of his hands gripping the steering wheel, clenched stomach, feelings of powerlessness and fear, and the belief "I'm going to die." As a result of the experience he may be afraid of driving because it triggers the memory network from the accident. According to Hebb (1949), "Neurons that fire together wire together." The patterns of neuronal firing form circuits of simple to complex neuronetworks.

Experiences from childhood create memory networks that affect how we view ourselves and our world in the present. A self-structure is created from interpretations of experiences. For example, a child who is abused by her father believes she is bad and to blame for the abuse. That belief in her inherent badness, along with the associated body sensations and emotions, forms a foundation for how she views herself throughout her life. Later experiences of harm from others serves to further reinforce the negative view of herself.

Ego states are also memory networks. These states can range from well integrated to disassociated. The typical ego states that we work with in EMDR are child self and adult self. In the child ego state are the thoughts, feelings, body sensations, and self-referencing beliefs associated with the age of the client when the ego state developed. For example, someone who has activated a child ego state from sexual abuse at the age of three will have the body perception of a small child, simple black-and-white thinking with regard to herself and her world, and a feeling of powerlessness with regard to her affect on her environment. The adult ego state with current information about her self-efficacy along with coping skills she has learned in therapy may be disassociated from the child ego state. When she is triggered, the child ego state will be activated, causing her to feel the powerlessness she felt as a small child. The goal in ego state therapy as well as in EMDR is to increase healthy integration between ego states.

The following is an example of how a client might present with symptoms from early memory networks. Imagine that you are working with a woman who comes to see you because she is being triggered at work by her boss. Whenever he comes up to her desk to ask her a question she becomes speechless, feels powerless and small, and believes she is stupid. When this happens she feels out of control, not in her competent adult self. She tells you she doesn't understand why this is happening because her boss is actually a nice guy. He has done nothing to cause her to feel this way. When you take her history you discover the memory networks that have linked together to cause her current difficulty with her boss. In her childhood her father was overbearing and very critical. He would oversee her homework and always find fault with it. When he criticized her she felt powerless and stupid, her heart beat rapidly, her stomach clenched, and she felt small. This early memory network also linked to other networks of experiences with overbearing and critical teachers, boyfriends, and employers. When her boss comes up to her desk the early memory networks are stimulated, causing her to feel and think about herself the way she did as a child.

The concept of memory networks is key in EMDR work. When clients come to see us we listen to their symptoms and their life story, looking for the memory networks at the root of the problem. Very often experiences from childhood are kept in memory networks that have not integrated with adult networks, causing clients to act in seemingly irrational ways. These networks create a perceptual filter through which they view the world and themselves. Acting like blinders, they prevent clients from being able to see the full picture.

Not only does EMDR clear the charge from traumatic experiences, it also *integrates networks*. When traumas occur the information gets locked into its own memory network with the thoughts, feelings, and body sensations associated with the experience. Other information is not integrated. What EMDR seems to do is to integrate information held in different memory networks so that a broader, more complex understanding emerges. Many clients describe this as puzzle pieces coming together to form a complete picture. For some it can seem as if they are viewing the scene from above, with all the parts there. This idea of integrating networks is key to utilizing EMDR successfully with clients having complex problems. There are times when it is helpful for the therapist to ask questions that aid the client in linking networks that are not linking on their own, using what are called *interweaves*. I will explain this more fully when I discuss interweaves in Chapter 9.

Another result of the integration of neuronetworks and right and left hemispheres is the development of a *coherent narrative* and a *coherent sense of self* (Siegel, 2002). Clients can reflect on what happened to them in the past, understand how the past affected them in the present, and have a sense of a positive future. Emotions, body sensations, cognitions, and sensory information from the past and present are integrated and made sense of. As a result clients *feel* whole. "Now I understand what happened to me and why I acted as I did." It is a body-mind integrated understanding of their life. For example, after a particularly powerful EMDR session a client who had been tortured and sexually abused as a child and whose memories of the abuse had been fragmented told me, "I feel a release of stress and panic. I can feel a sense of joy coming into my core. I feel a slow opening to this connection, integration of myself like I've kept the pieces separate. I can have my life and be happy. I can feel my chest knitting together. I can feel my left and right sides knitting together. I can feel my body coming together, I can feel my body!"

For many clients this integration of information allows them to make decisions in their lives that come from their whole, rather than from fragments that cause them to react. They develop the ability to respond to situations flexibly. This "response flexibility," as described by Siegel (1999), refers to the capacity of the brain to respond to the environment with a range of responses that are adaptive. Instead of always reacting to a stimulus in a rigid manner, clients have choices about how they will respond.

EMDR can also be used to *differentiate networks*. When a person is traumatized, a typical response is to avoid that which has caused the trauma. In order to protect the organism, the body-mind generalizes. For example, a woman who was bitten by a dog as a child may fear all dogs. She may have difficulty feeling safe even with small, gentle dogs. With EMDR she can learn to differentiate dogs that are safe from dogs that are not. I will also return to this concept in the interweave section.

KEY CONCEPTS OF EMDR

Accelerated Information Processing
    "T" and "t" traumas
Adaptive Information Processing
    Moves Information from Dysfunctional to Functional
    Clears Emotional Charge
    Transforms Psychological Memory to Objective Memory
    Fosters Objective Forgiveness
    Creates a Felt Sense of Truth
    Reveals Memory Networks
    Integrates Networks
    Differentiates Networks

HOW DOES EMDR WORK?

There are several different theories about EMDR, but it is not known how it works. Theories about how EMDR works are based primarily on observed clinical effects.

EMDR practitioners integrate patterned eye movements or other BLS with talk therapy techniques to clear emotional, cognitive, and physical blockages. In theory traumas leave unprocessed memories, feelings, and thoughts that can be reprocessed or "metabolized" with BLS. Similar to the way rapid eye movement (REM) or dream sleep works, the eye movements help to process this blocked information, allowing the body-mind to release it.

Dreams each night cleanse the body-mind of the day's residues. It seems that some particularly strong dreams that are related to past events are the body-mind's attempt to heal. The problem is that during disturbing dreams the eye movements are often disrupted and one wakes up, thus not allowing the REM sleep to complete its job. With EMDR, which is different from dreams, the therapist keeps the eyes moving back and forth and guides the client into focusing on the traumatic event. This allows the event to be fully experienced and reintegrated.

EMDR clinicians have found that hand tapping and bilateral sounds are also effective in stimulating the reprocessing of material. Perhaps the stimulation of the two hemispheres of the brain causes the reprocessing effect of EMDR. There is also a theory that the eye movements are linked with the hippocampus, which is linked to the consolidation of memory. Another theory is that the dual attention the client maintains with EMDR, focusing simultaneously on the inner feelings and the eye movements, allows the alerted brain to metabolize whatever it is witnessing.

At the 2002 EMDR International Association Conference, Bruce Perry presented his theory that it is the rhythm used in EMDR that causes the observed effects. He explained that cultures all over the world use drumming and dancing to process traumatic experiences. He postulated that hardwired into the human nervous system is the calming affect rhythm has on us. The fetus in utero floats in a safe, calm environment with all of its needs taken care of and hears the rhythm of its mother's heart. The sound of the heartbeat is linked somatosensorily to calm in the developing nervous system. Because of that early association, when the EMDR client lights up the memory of a traumatic experience, activating the base brain and midbrain, and then adds the rhythm of the eye movements or other BLS, the calming response short-circuits the trauma response, creating reciprocal disinhibition. His theory might help explain the desensitization we observe with EMDR, but it does not adequately explain to my satisfaction the accelerated information processing.

I have heard anecdotal accounts of eye movements being used for hundreds of years by yoga practitioners to calm the mind, as well as by Latin American shamans. It may be that Shapiro not only rediscovered a basic biological mechanism for clearing the body-mind of present-time disturbances but also ingeniously made the leap to linking the eye movements with stored psychological material.

NEUROBIOLOGY OF TRAUMA AND RECENT BRAIN RESEARCH

It is useful to know something about the neurobiology of trauma when working with trauma clients. There has been an explosion of research in the past 10 years that has greatly increased our understanding of how trauma affects the brain and human behavior. One of the preeminent researchers in this area is Bessel van der Kolk, whose edited book *Traumatic Stress* (1996) contained much of the research cited here. This advancement of new knowledge has been made possible by the development of neuroimaging devices including the single photon emission computed tomography (SPECT) scan, which allows us to view pictures of the brain under different conditions. This information has revolutionized the way we view how traumatic memory is encoded and the long-term consequences of trauma. Trauma, particularly during the early stages of brain development, impairs mental and emotional functioning and affects physiology far more than we realized and for a much longer time. Trauma memory is stored differently than ordinary memory—in the right hemisphere in fragmented unintegrated form, separate from the brain's language center—which explains why traditional talk therapy is inevitably limited and inadequate to effectively resolve early trauma.

MEMORY DEVELOPMENT

When we are born we have *implicit* memory. This memory is stored in the right hemisphere of the brain and it is emotional, behavioral, somatosensory, perceptual, and nonverbal. The infant has no concept of time. When he is hungry, he wants to be fed; when he is wet, he cries. There is no concept of past and future. There is also no self-concept. The locus of me or I has not yet developed as a concept that is experienced as ongoing over time. Focal attention is not required for encoding of this memory. Sensorimotor schemas are developed in early childhood, which create a template of schemas of the self and world.

Later, we develop *explicit* memory. Explicit memory or narrative memory is semantic and autobiographical—one has a sense of self in time: "I did this" and "I felt that." In explicit memory, which requires conscious awareness and focal attention, there is hippocampal processing. Information is consolidated into working memory and then moved to long-term permanent memory.

From birth to 3 years old the hippocampus is not mature so memory is left in implicit form in the right hemisphere and not encoded into explicit memory. This is referred to as "infantile amnesia." People can remember early childhood events implicitly with somatic responses but not explicitly in a narrative. For example, the smell of warm milk might elicit feelings of happiness and comfort with no narrative memory accompanying them (Siegel, 1998).

PSYCHOLOGICAL TRAUMA IN CHILDHOOD

Psychological trauma causes *disassociation of hemispheric processing*. The left hemisphere—which is responsible for verbal and motor control, the manipu-

lation of words and symbols, and the sequential processing of information—is locked out, and memory is encoded only as implicit memory in the
right hemisphere. Memory remains in fragmented form as somatic sensations
and intense affect states and is not collated and transcribed into personal
narratives. It appears that terror blocks the hippocampus so that information
will not go to explicit memory. Researchers have found that there is diminished hippocampal volume in chronic PTSD (van der Kolk et al., 1997). If a
person is triggered by something in her life that activates her implicit memory,
it feels "timeless"—like it is happening now. This is what we find so often
when using EMDR while working with adults traumatized as children. The
feelings aroused in their bodies feel current, and clients lose the sense that
what they are experiencing now comes from something that happened in the
past.

Early abusive experiences are stored in the right hemisphere of the brain
separately from the language centers of the left brain; the right side of the
brain holds the negative affective states. Early trauma causes what Schore
(1998) called "synaptic pruning" in the orbital frontal cortex and creates a
disturbance in the sympathetic-parasympathetic systems that results in hyperarousal, the misreading of external cues, and difficulty with self-soothing
or calming. Children who have been abused have problems with affect regulation. They become easily overstimulated and have trouble calming themselves. They also have difficulty coping with stress. Early trauma creates a
predisposition to the development of PTSD. Synaptic pruning also affects
the person's ability to experience positive emotional states and predisposes
them to depression (Schore). When there is excessive pruning of the
synapses in the orbital frontal cortex, it affects attachment, empathy, and
the capacity to regulate body pain. People with childhood trauma *do* hurt
more.

TRAUMA AND THE BRAIN

Traumatic memories lodge in the brain in different ways than other memories. The moment a trauma takes place, the pieces are not put together:
trauma freezes the integrative process, and the information is not integrated
into schemas like ordinary memory. *Trauma interferes with the evaluation, classifi-
cation, and contextualization of experiences.* Memory remains as implicit memory
stored in the limbic system, which is responsible for fleeing, fighting, feed-
ing, and reproduction. In the limbic system the *amygdala* attaches emotional
meaning to incoming information. It passes the information on to the hippocampus, which is the brain's early warning system, telling it whether the

information is dangerous or not. The *hippocampus* filters out irrelevant information, evaluates what goes on, and files it.

For traumatized people, because the amygdala-to-hippocampus connection is disrupted, the information is not integrated and filed. Information is left in fragmented form. The different fragments include visual, affective, tactile, olfactory, auditory, and somatosensory information.

When a person experiences a trauma, the left anterior frontal lobe known as Broca's area—the language part of the brain—is deactivated. This deactivation of Broca's area causes "speechless terror" for many traumatized people and they can't talk about or understand their experience with words. They feel intense emotions without being able to put a label on what they are experiencing. Although they may be feeling intensively, they are unable to communicate what they are experiencing (van der Kolk et al., 1997). In working with traumatized people, we must activate the right side of their brain where the trauma is stored. Art, EMDR, movement, and sand tray work activate the right hemisphere.

The following are important things to keep in mind when working with traumatized people:

1. *People with PTSD don't attend to neutral stimuli: their brains are geared to traumatic stimuli.* Their lives are fixated on the trauma; they live in the past. Because their brains don't attend to neutral stimuli, they don't take in new information. Real life loses its meaning on a daily level; they only process and pay attention to threatening stimuli. This causes a lack of engagement in the world (McFarlane, Weber, & Clark, 1993).

2. People with PTSD have more active limbic systems and *ordinary talk psychotherapy does not decondition the limbic system.* The part of the brain that holds the traumatic memory continues to be triggered, acting as if present-time nonthreatening internal or external stimuli are dangerous, even if they *understand* that the stimuli are not dangerous and the reasons for their responses. They still have the same somatosensory or emotional responses to the old cues. You can't reason the body out of reacting to stimuli that causes a reaction in the limbic system. Stimulation of this part of the brain causes a nonverbal response that is not changed by intellectual understanding. The limbic system continues to respond as if there were present dangers (van der Kolk, 1994). This is why so many clients who have been abused as children or traumatized as adults do not change their behavioral responses to triggers even after years of insight-oriented psychotherapy.

3. *With PTSD there is a loss of the capacity to analyze and categorize arousing information.* People with PTSD cannot talk about their experience. The left

hemisphere is locked out. Reason is absent, and there is an increased emotional response (van der Kolk, McFarlane, & Weisaeth, 1996).

4. *People with PTSD are not able to utilize language to gain distance from the offending stimulus.* Therefore, therapies that depend on language are not able to help traumatized clients (van der Kolk et al., 1996).

5. *Fragmented or misclassified sensations are reactivated in state dependent form with PTSD.* Traumatized people are "triggered" by internal or external reminders of the original trauma (van der Kolk et al., 1996).

According to van der Kolk (1998), part of the treatment for PTSD is to teach clients to pay attention to nontraumatic stimuli as a way of deconditioning the limbic system. Mindfulness training can help activate the frontal lobes and enhance the left hemisphere. In conjunction with mindfulness practices, EMDR helps people process the specific traumas and to integrate the memory fragments by activating the frontal lobes, thus moving memory from implicit to explicit. After the fragmented memory is made into narrative form and the traumatic event successfully processed with EMDR, the person can tell the story of what happened.

THE DISCOVERY OF EMDR AND ITS DEVELOPMENT

The use of eye movements to affect psychological disturbances was discovered in 1987 by Francine Shapiro, who at the time was a graduate student in clinical psychology. While walking through a park in Los Gatos, California, she noticed that disturbing thoughts she was having were disappearing. Intrigued, she began to closely watch her thought processes and noticed that when a disturbing thought came into her mind, spontaneously her eyes began to move very rapidly. The eye movement seemed to cause the thought to shift out of her consciousness. When she made the thought resurface, it had lost much of its negative charge. Then she began doing this experiment deliberately. She thought about things that bothered her and moved her eyes in the same way. Again the thoughts went away. She then tested this process with some older memories and some present problems. They all reacted the same way. Curious to know if this discovery would work on other people, she tried it on her friends. She found that most of them couldn't sustain the eye movement for any length of time so she began to direct them to follow her finger with their eyes.

After testing this process on about seventy people, Shapiro came to believe that the eye movements were causing a desensitization of the disturbing material. She developed a more refined method, which she called eye movement desensitization (EMD). (In 1990 she expanded the name to EMDR to include the concept of reprocessing. Further experience with the method convinced her that the eye movements reprocessed traumatic memories into something more adaptive and functional.) In 1988 Shapiro tested her new therapy in a research study conducted in Mendocino, California, with twenty-two subjects: Vietnam vets, victims of rape, and victims of sexual abuse. All were suffering from persistent symptoms of PTSD including nightmares, flashbacks, intrusive thoughts, low self-esteem, and relationship problems. The participants were divided into two groups and measured on their symptoms as well as on their anxiety and beliefs about the traumatic event. Participants in the treatment group had one EMD session ranging from 15 to 90 minutes. Those in the control group did not get EMD but instead were asked to describe their traumatic experiences in detail. After a single EMD procedure, the treatment group showed a marked decrease in anxiety, a more objective assessment of the trauma, and a reduction in symptoms. The control group showed no or minimal changes. For ethical reasons, the control group was then given an EMD session, and they, too, experienced a significant decrease in their symptoms. The treatment group was measured again 1 and 3 months later. Shapiro (1989a) reported that EMDR led to significant and enduring positive behavioral changes, as rated by the participants and their significant others.

Since Shapiro's initial efficacy study, EMDR has had more published case reports and research to support it than any other method used in the treatment of trauma. Positive therapeutic results with EMDR have been reported with combat veterans (Blore, 1997; Carlson, Chemtob, Rusnak, & Hedlund, 1996; Carlson, Chemtob, Rusnak, & Hedlund, 1998; Daniels, Lipke, Richardson, & Silver, 1992; Lipke, 2000; Lipke & Botkin, 1992; Silver, Brooks, & Obenchain, 1995; Thomas & Gafner, 1993; White, 1998; Young, 1995), phobias and panic disorder (De Jongh & Ten Broeke, 1998; De Jongh, Ten Broeke, & Renssen, 1999; Doctor, 1994; Feske & Goldstein, 1997; Goldstein & Feske, 1994; Kleinknecht, 1993; Nadler, 1996; O'Brien, 1993), crime victims and police officers (Baker & McBride, 1991; Kleinknecht & Morgan, 1992; McNally & Solomon, 1999; Page & Crino, 1993; Shapiro & Solomon, 1995; Solomon, 1995, 1998), phantom limb pain (Tinker & Wilson, 2005), people suffering from excessive grief (Puk, 1991; Shapiro & Solomon, 1995; Solomon, 1994, 1995, 1998; Solomon & Kaufman, 1994), children traumatized by assault or natural disaster (Chemtob, Nakashima, Cocco, & Sharpe, 1993; Hamada & Carlson, 2002; Lovett, 1999; Pellicer, 1993; Puffer, Greenwald, & Elrod, 1998; Tinker & Wilson, 1999), sexual assault victims (Edmond, Rubin, & Wambach, 1999; Hyer, 1995; Parnell, 1999, Puk, 1991; Rothbaum, 1997; Scheck, Schaeffer, & Gillette, 1998); people suffering from addictions (Henry, 1996; Popky, 2005; Shapiro, Vogelmann-Sine, & Sine, 1994), people experiencing performance anxiety (Crabbe, 1996; Foster & Lendl, 1995, 1996; Maxfield & Melnyk, 2000), as well as for many other problems.

One of the most significant EMDR research studies was done by EMDR-trained researchers Sandra Wilson, Lee Becker, and Robert Tinker (1995). Wilson and colleagues sought to replicate the findings of Shapiro's original study while improving the research method addressing issues raised in critical reviews (Aciereno, van Hasselt, Tremont, & Meuser, 1994; Herbert & Meuser, 1992; Lohr, Kleinknecht, Conley, dal Cerro, Schmidt, & Sonntag, 1992). In order to address the issues raised, a large and diverse sample was employed ($N = 80$); participants were randomly assigned to treatment or control conditions and to one of five EMDR-trained therapists; evaluations were conducted by an independent assessor using objective and standardized measures; subjects participated in no other therapy while in EMDR treatment; PTSD diagnoses were objectively made; and all subjects' treatment was monitored by the principal investigator. The participants were 40 men and 40 women with traumatic memories. Very few of the participants had heard about EMDR before the study. Their traumas occurred from 3 months to more than 50 years prior to the beginning of the study. The volunteers were suffering from anxieties, phobias, sleep disturbances, intimacy problems, and depression and had been experiencing these symptoms since the traumas had occurred. Participants were randomly assigned to either a treatment or a delayed treatment group. All of the treatment subjects were given a pretest, three EMDR sessions, a posttest, and a follow-up test 90 days later. The nontreatment group was given the pre- and posttests and follow-up test without any treatment.

The results were impressive. The EMDR group showed significant improvement in all areas and maintained relief from their symptoms over the 90-day period. No improvement was observed in the untreated group. After these delayed-treatment participants received their EMDR sessions, they also improved on all measures.

Fifteen months after the EMDR therapy, another follow-up study was conducted, which demonstrated that the volunteers continued to benefit from the treatment. Many of the participants said their self-confidence had increased and the positive treatment effects generalized into more aspects of their lives (Wilson, Becker, & Tinker, 1997).

Therapists who use EMDR find it to be more effective than other therapeutic methods they have used. Success rates with previously difficult cases have been quite high, and clients are getting better much more quickly. In a survey of 445 EMDR-trained clinicians who together had treated more than 10,000 clients, 76% of the respondents reported EMDR to be more effective than other treatments they had used, and only 4% found it less effective (Lipke, 1994).

EMDR has come a long way since Shapiro's 1987 walk in the park. Thousands of therapists have been trained worldwide, EMDR courses are being taught in psychology graduate school programs, there has been increased acceptance by managed care companies and HMOs (Kaiser Hospital in California), and there is an international EMDR professional organization (EMDRIA). The EMDR Humanitarian Assistance Program (HAP) is currently training Department of Defense therapists who work with military personnel traumatized by the wars in Iraq and Afghanistan. Furthermore, in 1995 the American Psychological Association division 12 (Clinical Psychology) initiated a project to determine the degree to which extant therapeutic methods were supported by solid empirical evidence. Independent reviewers (Chambless, Baker, Baucom, Beutler, Calhoun, Crits-Christoph, et al., 1998) placed EMDR on a list of "empirically validated treatments," as "probably efficacious for civilian PTSD." In addition, the practice guidelines of the International Society for Traumatic Stress Studies has chosen EMDR as an effective treatment for PTSD (Chemtob, Tolin, van der Kolk, & Pitman, 2000; Shalev, Friedman, Foa, & Keane, 2000). Since Shapiro's original study, more than a dozen controlled studies of EMDR have been published supporting its efficacy with PTSD (Feske, 1998; Marcus, Marquis, & Sakai, 1997; Spector & Read, 1999; Van Etten & Taylor, 1998; Waller, Mulick, & Spates; 2000). Although there are reports in the literature of EMDR's effectiveness for the amelioration of a range of different problems, it is only for the treatment of PTSD that there is substantial support for its efficacy (Shapiro, 2001).

EMDR practitioners who have used EMDR extensively in their clinical work have expanded EMDR beyond Shapiro's original protocols and have developed protocols and procedures for working with a wide range of client populations. Those of us who have used EMDR with clients with complex issues and multiple childhood traumas have found that Shapiro's original protocols often weren't enough for successful healing. So we have taken the basic EMDR premises and added techniques from hypnotherapy and guided imagery to increase the efficacy. The use of interweaves has become more sophisticated than what was originally described in Shapiro's textbook (1995). I expanded this area in my book *EMDR in the Treatment of Adult Abused as Children* (Parnell, 1999) and will expand it further in this book.

ORGANIZATION OF BOOK

A Therapist's Guide to EMDR has twelve chapters and is divided into four parts.

Part I, "EMDR Theoretical Overview," reminds EMDR therapists about the basics. This section contains two chapters, which provide the theoretical and practical foundation for the rest of the book. In Chapter 1, "EMDR Refresher," I review the basic EMDR protocol and procedure, the rationale and application of interweaves, resource development and installation, and the three-phase model for complex trauma treatment. Chapter 2, "Essential EMDR Protocol," presents ways to simplify and adapt the standard protocol according to the needs of different clients.

Part II, "Using EMDR With Clients," contains five chapters that provide information on how to think about your EMDR clients and prepare them for treatment. Chapter 3, "Evaluation and Preparation for EMDR," teaches how to take a thorough history, assess readiness for EMDR, integrate EMDR into clinical treatment, and handle common treatment issues such as resistance, countertransference, the pacing of treatment, and session length. Chapter 4, "Tools and Techniques for Ego Strengthening," provides a wealth of information on ways to prepare clients for EMDR trauma processing work, including resource development and installation.

Chapter 5, "Case Formulation," provides guidelines and case examples for creating treatment plans. Chapter 6, "Reevaluating the Therapy," explains how to begin a session following a session of EMDR. Chapter 7, "Target Development," covers how to develop and use specific targets for EMDR processing; tips for target development; targeting triggers and flashbacks; the bridging technique for finding targets from symptoms, issues, or current problems, physical symptoms, negative cognitions, and emotions; targeting dreams; and the use of art for targets.

Part III, "The EMDR Session," provides the reader with practical detailed information about how to navigate individual EMDR processing sessions. Chapter 8, "The Procedural Steps," takes the reader through each of the steps and explains in detail how to navigate them. Chapter 9, "Tools and Techniques for Working With Processing Difficulties," offers advice about how to work with different issues that come up during EMDR processing sessions. Topics covered include working with abreactions, dissociation, sleepiness, numbness, body memories without visual memories, memory chaining, and blocked processing. A large part of the chapter is dedicated to working with blocked processing including noninterweave and interweave strategies illustrated with case material.

Part IV, "Clinical Applications," contains Chapters 10, 11, and 12. Chapter 10, "Working With Phobias," presents information on how to work with simple and process phobias, illustrated by case examples. Chapter 11, "Recent Traumas and Critical Incidents," presents protocols and case material covering work with these kinds of clients. Chapter 12, "Care for the Caregiver," offers advice for therapists doing trauma-focused work.

CONVENTIONS USED THROUGHOUT THE BOOK

I have used fictitious first names for clients throughout the book. All of the identifying details of the cases have been changed in order to protect the privacy of the clients. I have changed names, professions, family constellations, races, and specific life events, and some cases represent composites of more than one client.

I have used the word *client*, a term I prefer over *patient*. All clients are referred to by first name, which I feel creates a more personal feeling about the people whose lives I describe. Most of the case examples in the book are my clients, although some are from EMDR colleagues.

In my EMDR work I use eye movements directed by a light bar as well as alternate tapping on the hands or knees, auditory stimulation, and tactile stimulation created by a device called the tac-audio. In the book's transcripts you will see the ">>>>>>" sign, which indicates a set of reprocessing stimuli that may take the form of alternating eye movements or alternating auditory or kinesthetic stimuli. Unless otherwise indicated, assume that the client was directed by the therapist to focus on whatever material had just come up, and that at the end of BLS, the therapist asked the client a question like, "What came up for you?" or "What do you get now?" to elicit information about the client's experience during the set of BLS.

PART I

EMDR THEORETICAL OVERVIEW

1

EMDR REFRESHER

REVIEW OF BASIC EMDR PROTOCOL AND PROCEDURE

Eye movement desensitization and reprocessing (EMDR) therapy typically begins with a client's desire to heal from a trauma, overcome a performance problem, or deal with a troubling aspect of life. Shapiro (1995, 2001) divided EMDR into eight phases of treatment. I will briefly review the basic information and then, in the chapters that follow, go into more detail with case examples. The first two phases are history-taking and preparation.

It is essential that before EMDR processing begins, therapists take a thorough *history* (phase 1). This enables them to establish hypotheses about the origins of the presenting problems so that the appropriate clinical interventions are used, safeguards are established, and the best targets for EMDR processing can be selected. Also during this time, therapists and clients are establishing a therapeutic relationship within which the reprocessing work can take place.

During phase 2, the *preparation phase*, therapists give clients specific instructions about what they will be doing with the EMDR processing along with a summary of the theory about trauma and what the eye movements or other bilateral stimulation seem to be doing. The therapists inform clients about the possibility that distressing unresolved memories could come up, they may experience disturbing emotions or sensations, and that after EMDR processing sessions some people have dreams or nightmares, new memories, or flashbacks. Therapists let the clients know that it is important to give accurate feedback about what they are experiencing during the processing and to let whatever happens happen without censoring it. Therapists tell clients that there are no right or wrong feelings and that everyone processes things differently. Clients are told that they are in control and that they can stop the processing whenever they feel a need to. A signal for stop is established, such as raising a hand or closing the eyes.

An important part of the preparation for many clients, especially those with early childhood abuse and complex posttraumatic stress disorder (PTSD), is to establish an inner safe place where they can go if they want to stop the processing and take a break or close the session. I will discuss the use of the safe place in more detail in Chapter 4.

It is essential that a feeling of connection, caring, and safety be established between therapists and clients. Clients are ready for EMDR processing when there is a feeling of safety and trust established in the therapeutic relationship, clients understand what the processing entails, and both therapists and clients feel prepared.

Phase 3 of EMDR is *assessment*. Ninety minutes or longer is the recommended length of time for a session targeting a significant traumatic incident, especially if it is an early childhood abuse memory. During the assessment phase therapists and clients identify and focus on a *target* related to the trauma.

Targets in EMDR are the entryways to memory networks and EMDR processing. They are the nodes selected as the focus for EMDR processing sessions. Targets contain the image, emotions, body sensations, and erroneous beliefs associated with traumatic memories. Target memory networks must be activated in order for processing to occur. The target for a single incident trauma is the most disturbing part of the incident. I would ask the client, "When you think of the accident, what is the worst part of it?" Targeting the most charged part of the incident creates a generalization effect through the entire memory, often making it possible for clients to process all of it without having to direct them to different parts. It is like beginning in the center of the web with the different associative strands radiating out from the center. The most charged part is most likely to affect all of the strands.

When working with an issue or behavior, we want to target the *earliest or strongest* memory associated with it. In the example of the woman who is afraid of dogs, we would look for the earliest traumatic encounter with a dog, or the worst. Sometimes the first was not very significant and did not lead to symptoms; a later experience was much more frightening and symptoms developed subsequently. When we target the first or worst experience, we get the most comprehensive generalization effect throughout the memory network. The charge from the early incident often will light up the network all the way through time, clearing many incidents with one session of EMDR. Target development is one of the most important steps for successful utilization of EMDR. For that reason I will detail methods for finding the best targets in Chapter 7.

After the targets have been chosen, therapists ask clients for pictures that represent the most charged part. "What picture represents the worst part of the incident?" A man who is working on a memory of a serious car accident might choose as his target the *image* of his car spinning out of control on a slick country road. Next, the client is asked for a *negative cognition* (NC)—an erroneous, self-referencing belief associated with the incident that has carried over to the present. He might be asked, "When you bring up the picture, what do you believe about yourself now?" His belief might be, "I'm powerless." The therapist then asks the client for a positive cognition (PC), a positive self-referencing belief that corresponds with the NC. What would he like to believe about himself when he brings up the image? In this case such a PC might be "I am powerful." Therapists then ask clients to rate the validity of the positive statement on a scale from 1 (completely false) to 7 (completely true). "When you bring up the image of your car spinning out of control, how true does 'I'm powerful' feel to you now on a scale of 1 to 7, where 1 feels completely false and 7 completely true?" Shapiro (1995, 2001) originally developed the validity of cognition scale (VoC) for the purposes of her dissertation research.

Next, therapists ask clients what *emotions* they feel. "When you bring up that incident and the words 'I'm powerless,' what emotions do you feel *now*?" In this example, the client might report fear and anxiety.

At this time the therapist takes a SUDS (subjective units of distress scale) reading, a scale developed by Wolpe (1991) to determine the degree of disturbance. A SUDS reading is taken at different times during the processing to measure progress. "On a scale of 0 to 10, where 0 is no disturbance or neutral and 10 is the highest disturbance that you can imagine, how disturbing does it feel to you *now*?" In this case the client may report that he feels it is an 8.

Therapists then ask clients for the *location of the body sensation*. "Where do you feel the disturbance in your body?" He may feel tension in his stomach and a knot in his throat.

Phase 4 is the *desensitization*. During this phase the target is activated and reprocessed. Clients are asked to bring up the disturbing images, emotions, body sensations, and NCs. When the targets are activated, the alternating bilateral stimulation (BLS) is added to begin the reprocessing. The BLS may include eye movements, auditory stimulation, tactile stimulation, or others. Clients are instructed to let whatever comes up come up without censoring it. "I'd like you to bring up that picture with the words 'I'm powerless.' Feel the fear and anxiety, the sensations in your chest and throat. When you have it let me know. Now, follow my fingers." If you are using eye movements directed by the therapist's fingers, begin slowly, increasing the speed to a pace that is comfortable for the client. After about 24 saccades (1 saccade is equal to 1 left-right eye movement) or when there is an apparent change, therapists stop and instruct clients to "let it go and take a deep breath."

Do not count eye movements. The number 24 is only a suggestion or a ballpark estimate for the first set. Look at the client and watch for change. The therapist asks, "What do you get now?" or "What are you noticing now?" Clients may experience images, body sensations, a range of emotions, insights, ordinary thoughts, or nothing much at all. After clients report their experience, the therapists say, "Go with that," and begin another set of eye movements or other BLS.

When clients are processing with EMDR, they maintain a *dual focus of attention*. As they focus on the traumatic memory, they are receiving BLS and are reminded that they are safe in the present as they process the past. For many clients the EMDR process is likened to watching a movie. For those familiar with Vipassana meditation and mindfulness practices, the witness awareness is cultivated. There are times when EMDR therapists will need to use techniques to help clients maintain this dual focus. I will discuss these techniques later in this book.

It is important that therapists pay close attention to their clients' experiences and be present with them. The therapists keep the clients' eyes moving until there is an indication that the clients have finished processing a piece of information. If they are very emotional, therapists keep clients' eyes moving until they become calm, allowing them to fully clear a part of the traumatic event. Different clients prefer different speeds and numbers of BLS. Some do best with only 10 or 15 saccades at a time, whereas others like to go on for hundreds. After each round of BLS clients are asked, "What is happening now?" or "What do you get now?" The clients report their experiences and then continue with more BLS.

Some clients like to talk during the EMDR processing. For many, this is very useful for keeping them in contact with their experience and allowing therapists to better track them. During the BLS clients go through a multi-dimensional free association of thoughts, feelings, and body sensations. Some people go through an enormous range of experiences including intense sensations, horrific images, and strong emotions such as intense rage, overwhelming terror, grief, love, and forgiveness; possible memories including descriptions attributed to prenatal and infancy experiences; and dreamlike imagery rich in detail and symbolism. Throughout all of these experiences clients are told to "let it all just pass through," and they are reassured that "this is old stuff." Therapists can use the metaphor of riding in a train and tell the clients that their inner experiences are like scenery they are passing. Many clients experience a kind of witness awareness or observing ego that enables them to observe their experiences as if they were watching a movie. It is as if they are both *in* the experience and *observing* it simultaneously. For clients who lose their observing egos and become overwhelmed by the old traumatic memories, it can be helpful for therapists to encourage and strengthen the observing parts. This process of BLS and check-ins continues during the sessions, with therapists occasionally rechecking the original images and measuring the SUDS. It is important during the processing to keep clients from becoming too dispersed. Some clients can go down many different associated channels that get further and further away from the original issue or memory. In these cases it can be helpful to return to the target images and check in.

When clients return to the images and report that they don't disturb them anymore, therapists do SUDS readings. "Bring up the original incident. On a scale of 0 to 10, where 0 is no disturbance or neutral and 10 is the highest disturbance that you can imagine, how disturbing does it *feel* to you *now*?" When clients feel free of the emotional charge, reporting a SUDS of 0 or 1, it is time to proceed to phase 5: *the installation of the PC*.

First clients are asked to bring up the original images and then asked what they believe about themselves now, thus eliciting PCs. It may be that clients come up with the same PCs identified in the beginning of the sessions, or they may be new PCs that have arisen spontaneously as a result of reprocessing the memory. These PCs fit the clients' subjective experiences. They can include statements such as "I am safe now," "I did the best I could with what I knew at the time," and "It is in the past." In the case example of the man who had a car accident, the PC might be, "I survived." After the PCs have been identified, the VoCs are then checked. "When you bring up the accident and say to yourself 'I survived,' how true does it feel to you now, on a scale from 1 to 7 where 1 is completely false and 7 is completely true?"

If clients report that they feel completely true—6 or 7—the therapists *install* the PC by asking the clients to hold that statement with the previously distressing image (which often changes by becoming smaller or dimmer, black and white rather than color, or less threatening in some manner) and do a few sets of BLS. With the installation, the PCs and reprocessed incidents are linked and integrated. After a set of BLS, the therapists again check to see if the targets have remained the same or changed. Sometimes new material emerges that needs to be reprocessed; a new associated memory network may have opened. If so, therapists can either try to clear it in the same session if there is time, or make a note of it and return to it next time, making sure to close down the clients as much as possible before ending the session.

If clients report the VoC to be a 6 or less, there are a number of things therapists can do. First therapists can check the appropriateness of the PCs. Perhaps the PCs just don't fit the situation and a better one would be more exacting. There may be a blocking belief that clients are holding that need to be addressed and possibly reprocessed. Clients may have additional memory links that keep the PCs from being completely true. For example, the abuse survivor may not be able to feel a 7 on "I'm safe now" if there are more memories of abuse that have not yet been reprocessed. Oftentimes, by adding the word *can* to make it a process PC enables the VoC to increase and the PC successfully installed. For example, "I can be safe," "I can be powerful," "I can be in control."

Phase 6 in EMDR is the *body scan*, which clients do after a memory or incident has been reprocessed and the installation of the PC has been completed. In this case clients would be instructed: "Close your eyes, bring up the incident and the thought 'I survived,' and mentally scan your entire body. Tell me where you feel anything." If the clients report any sensation, they do more BLS. If they are positive sensations, the BLS will strengthen the feeling. If they are sensations of discomfort, therapists should reprocess until the discomforts clear. The body scans alert therapists to unprocessed memories. In our example, the client may find that in doing the body scan he has pain in his arms. This could be a body memory linked to this accident or another memory. If there isn't time left in the session to reprocess this, the client should be properly closed down and debriefed. The therapist notes that this body sensation remained and may return to it in the next session.

Phase 7 of EMDR is *closure*. If the processing has cleared the disturbances from the original incidents, the closure is rather simple. Therapists and clients may talk for a while about the processing session and the insights that emerged. Therapists advise clients that the processing of material may continue on its own between EMDR sessions and that any new material that arises between sessions can be worked on in the next session. Clients can help to facilitate this natural processing by recording their dreams and insights in a journal, as well as drawing, painting, or engaging in other kinds of artwork. To help clients cope better with their stress between sessions, it is useful to teach clients meditation and stress reduction techniques. Clients are told that they can call the therapists if they need to.

Often the problems are not cleared during the EMDR processing session, and the sessions are incomplete. Clients still feel upset, or the SUDS is above 1 and the VoC is less than 6. If this is the case, body scans are not done, especially if it is obvious that there is still material to be processed.

There are many methods to close down such sessions and they will be covered in Chapter 8. Creating a sense of closure is crucial for the clients' wellbeing because EMDR brings up highly charged material that can leave clients open and vulnerable. Some people should be advised to walk around the block before driving and perhaps not return to work for the day. (See Appendix 1, pages 325–327 for EMDR Procedural Steps Checklist and Sample Vignette of the Procedural Steps.)

Phase 8 of EMDR treatment is *reevaluation*. When clients come in for the next session, the therapists inquire about anything of importance that has come up related to the issues that were worked on in the previous sessions. The clients may have had dreams, insights, memories, thoughts, or flashbacks, or they may have noticed some new physical sensations. Therapists ask clients to refer back to the targets that were worked on in the previous sessions to check to see if anything new arises. For example, the client may have another memory associated with the one that was cleared, and that new memory now feels upsetting. Therapists and clients then decide what the next targets for EMDR processing will be, depending upon what has come up during the week.

RATIONALE AND APPLICATION OF INTERWEAVES

There are times when using BLS and following clients' processes are not sufficient to keep the information flowing to a positive resolution. Clients sometimes enter into cognitive or emotional loops, repeating the same images, thoughts, emotions, and body sensations without a reduction in the SUDS level. This looping is like a broken record, with the clients stuck in a groove going over and over the same material.

Processing can also be blocked without the high emotional intensity of looping. There is no change, and the disturbances are not being processed. At these times therapists can use creative means, called cognitive interweaves, to continue the release and reprocessing of the traumas. Cognitive interweaves are a proactive EMDR strategy that serves to jump-start blocked processing by introducing information from therapists, rather than depending solely on what arises from clients. The statements therapists offer weave together memory networks and associations that clients were not able to connect. Interweaves introduce a new perspective, new information, or information that clients "know" but do not have access to in the states of mind that are activated. Traumatic experiences often seem to be stored in one part of the bodymind without being affected by more current information. Interweaves bridge the parts of the clients' minds that have been separated. After an interweave is introduced, BLS is added and the processing begins to flow again. Interweaves are particularly effective with adults traumatized as children, who often seem to relate to the experience completely from the child's perspective, without the observing ego and adult perspective. Interweaves can also be used to help close sessions. Types of interweaves and interweave strategies will be presented along with case material in Chapter 9.

EMDR RESOURCE DEVELOPMENT AND INSTALLATION (RDI)

In theory, when a traumatic memory is targeted with EMDR, what is dysfunctional from the system is cleared, allowing what is adaptive to come to the foreground in awareness. We have also found that when memories or experiences that were positive or adaptive are activated and BLS is added, these resources become stronger and more available to clients and are experienced as more integrated. This is what is called resource installation. Resource development includes identifying resources, talking about them, and helping clients find new resources and coping strategies. Resource development is common to many types of therapies, including hypnotherapy.

RDI can be used in the preparation phase of treatment to help emotionally fragile clients with affect tolerance and ego strengthening prior to beginning EMDR trauma processing. Examples of resources that can be developed include safe place and conflict-free images; positive memories of being loved, nurtured, empowered, and supported; people or animals from the past or present; and spiritual figures and experiences. Resources are installed by activating the sensory information associated with the resources and adding short sets of BLS to strengthen it. The number of saccades can range anywhere from 6 to 12 or more depending upon the clients. The idea is to begin with short sets in order to focus clients on the resources and to avoid association to traumatic material.

The use of RDI with EMDR was first suggested by Foster and Lendl (Foster & Lendl, 1996; Lendl & Foster, 1997) for performance enhancement. It was applied to the treatment of addictions by Popky (1997, 2005), and to childhood trauma by Wildwind (1993), Parnell (1995–1998; 1997a; 1998a,b; 1999; Parnell and Cohn, 1995; Thompson, Cohn, & Parnell, 1996), and Leeds and colleagues (Leeds, 1997, 1998; Leeds & Korn, 1998; Leeds & Shapiro, 2000). I have written extensively about RDI (Parnell, 1999) and have included additional information in Chapter 4.

THREE-PHASE TRAUMA THERAPY MODEL

For many clients with severe childhood trauma suffering from complex PTSD, therapy typically proceeds over three phases (Parnell, 1999). The phases are (a) the beginning phase; (b) the middle phase; and (c) the end phase. The beginning phase, comprised of assessment, preparation, and ego strengthening, includes Shapiro's phases 1 (history-taking) and 2 (preparation). In this phase clients are assessed for appropriateness for EMDR and are sufficiently stabilized, inner and outer resources are developed and installed, the therapeutic relationship is well established, and coping skills are learned. The therapeutic container must be strong enough, which means that clients need to be able to tolerate high levels of affect prior to beginning intensive trauma work in the middle phase of treatment. The middle phase of processing and integration is where EMDR trauma processing work is done extensively. In the end phase of creativity, spirituality, and integration, less EMDR is done, and there is more talking. Questions such as "Who am I?" and "What do I want to do with my life?" arise, which need to be addressed. I have found it is helpful to think in terms of these three phases when working with complex clients. Talk therapy is typically integrated throughout the work. Transference and countertransference issues are addressed, as is resistance. EMDR is integrated into an overall treatment plan that can include many other therapeutic modalities.

EMDR AS A STAND-ALONE THERAPY VS. EMDR AS A THERAPEUTIC METHOD THAT IS INTEGRATED INTO A TREATMENT

Shapiro (1995, 2001) describes EMDR as an eight-phase therapy. This model is most applicable to work with single-incident traumas, PTSD, phobias, and presenting complaints that are specific and for which targets can be found. The more structured and goal oriented the treatment, the better this model fits.

EMDR can also be used as one method among many that are *integrated* into psychotherapy. Therapists and clients who are accustomed to talk therapy with an emphasis on the therapeutic relationship may choose to use EMDR at different times in the treatment to target areas where clients feel stuck. Many of these therapists would probably describe themselves as psychotherapists who integrate EMDR into their work. They would not consider everything they do within their therapy to be EMDR. Many therapists who work with trauma use EMDR along with other methods. Somatic experiencing, thought field therapy, guided imagery and hypnosis, sensorimotor therapy, art therapy, sand tray work, movement therapy, and different types of talk therapy along with EMDR are therapeutic methods trauma therapists use according to the needs their clients.

2

ESSENTIAL EMDR PROTOCOL

IN CHAPTER 1 I described the standard EMDR protocol and procedural steps as outlined by Shapiro (1995, 2001). Since EMDR's inception many clinicians have found it necessary to modify these steps according to the needs of their clients (Cohn, 1993a, 1993b; Diegelmann, 2006; Diegelmann & Isermann, 2003; Lovett, 1999; Parnell, 1999; Shapiro, 2001; Shapiro & Silk-Forrest, 1997; Tinker & Wilson, 1999). This chapter explains those modifications.

MODIFICATIONS OF THE STANDARD PROCEDURAL STEPS

EMDR sessions can be quite successful by using a simplified procedure that uses the most essential elements. According to Shapiro, "flexibility and creativity on the part of the clinician are often central to clinical success" (2004, p. 311). From my experience as therapist, consultant, and EMDR trainer, and from a review of the literature, I have found that EMDR can be distilled into four essential elements that I call the essential EMDR protocol. In order to work clinically it is important to understand this conceptual model, within which you can creatively adapt the different elements according to the needs of the client. These adaptations should be done according to the client's age, intellectual ability, education, culture, type of trauma, psychological makeup, and issues.

THE ESSENTIAL EMDR PROTOCOL

1. Create safety
2. Stimulate the memory network
3. Add BLS and process
4. End with safety

CREATE SAFETY

Safety can be created in a variety of ways. First of all, the therapeutic relationship must be established and a bond created between therapists and clients. Clients must trust therapists and therapists must trust that clients will tell them the truth. Safety also includes client stabilization with regard to emotional disturbance, suicidality, substance abuse, and medical condition. Can clients install resources for ego strengthening? Are they able to find a safe or comfortable place, nurturing, or protector figures? Drawing pictures, creating sand trays, or playing in a playroom can establish safety for child clients. For some clients it does not take long to establish safety, whereas for others it can take months or years before they are sufficiently stabilized. Clients who are in residential settings require less stabilization because the setting itself helps with safety.

STIMULATE THE MEMORY NETWORK

The memory network where the trauma is stored can be stimulated in a variety of ways. Asking the client for a picture that represents the worst part of an incident, and the associated negative beliefs, emotions, and body sensations can activate the memory network. Drawing a picture of the conflict or problem can also stimulate memory networks, as can creating a sand tray. Sometimes a smell, sound, or taste can stimulate a network. Moving in a particular way can activate networks. EMDR therapists have used a variety of creative methods to activate memory networks.

ADD BLS AND PROCESS

A wide variety of types of BLS can be used to activate the adaptive processing system. Shapiro (1995, 2001) first developed EMDR using eye movements, but many other types of BLS have been used successfully with the EMDR protocol: therapists using alternate tapping on the hands, knees, shoulders, or backs; machines producing alternating bilateral vibrations in handheld devices; bilateral auditory stimulation heard through headphones; drumming; stamping the feet right and left; scribbling back and forth across a page. With the BLS clients process the disturbing memory. For some clients the processing moves very quickly, especially for young children; for others it takes longer.

END WITH SAFETY

It is important that EMDR sessions end with safety. Clients should feel safe and contained before they leave the session. The standard EMDR procedure includes installing the PC, body scan, and closure, all important steps in creating safety at the end of sessions. For some clients the standard procedure is not appropriate, and modifications can be used. For young children, playing in the playroom after the session may be enough. For others, drawing a picture without the use of a PC may be sufficient. The important point here is that the clients leave feeling safe at the end of the session, however that is created within the context of the therapeutic relationship.

A case reported by the child therapist Robert Tinker (Shapiro & Silk-Forrest, 1997) illustrates the most simplified use of these essential elements. When little Davy, aged 2, was referred to Tinker, he was suffering from severe trauma. Born with a cleft palate and fetal alcohol syndrome, he was in the middle of surgery to correct the cleft palate when he awoke. Though he was quickly put back under, he suffered serious emotional trauma. As a result, he could no longer sleep through the night, waking every hour screaming from night terrors. His grandparents, who were his guardians, were at their wits' end. They didn't know what to do. Exhausted and hopeless, they were on the verge of sending Davy to foster care when they met with Tinker. Tinker had never done EMDR with a hyperactive traumatized 2-year-old who had delayed language ability. He had to be creative in working with the boy, improvising using essential EMDR elements.

Tinker began by establishing safety. After meeting with the grandparents and Davy, he let Davy play in the playroom, exploring the toys and surroundings. He then directed Davy to play patty-cake with him, getting him to slap Bob's open palms alternately, a form of BLS. In the second session Bob decided that he would stimulate Davy's memory network that held the surgery trauma by using three key words he believed were associated with it: mouth, pain, and bright lights. After Davy explored the room for a while, Bob coaxed him to sit down and play patty-cake. Davy began to slap Bob's hands a few times, right left, right left. Then as the patty-cake continued, Tinker said the trigger words out loud. When Davy heard one of the words he slapped Bob's hands harder. Then, after just a few minutes of processing in this way, he lost interest and took off to explore the room again. In this way he ended with safety. The following session the grandparents reported that Davy's symptoms had been eliminated. He was sleeping through the night without night terrors and was calmer, less agitated. It should be noted that Bob used no cognitions or scales with Davy. He created safety, activated the network, added BLS, and ended with safety.

Another colleague, Maureen Mahoney, also improvised her EMDR work using the essential EMDR protocol with a traumatized 2-year-old with attachment disorder. One day while playing with the boy in the therapy room, a female therapist walked down the hall with very heavy footsteps, causing the child to startle with fear. The next time Maureen heard the woman coming down the hall, Maureen suggested to the boy that they play "stomp" and march in place stamping their feet left and right. They did this for a few minutes, making a game out of it. Maureen's idea worked. When the woman stomped down the hall again, the boy didn't even notice it. He never startled to her footsteps again. The essential EMDR protocol included: the safe relationship Maureen had established with the boy, the memory network that was stimulated by the woman's footsteps, BLS in the form of left-right marching, and the session ending with the therapist and boy playing safely together.

HOW TO MODIFY THE STANDARD PROCEDURAL STEPS

I have found that for many clients it is most helpful to skip the steps that are not clinically useful. Steps that are not clinically useful create an empathic break in the therapeutic relationship, activate memory networks other than those that are the focus of treatment (e.g., perfectionism), confuse the client, and deactivate the memory network.

Fundamental to EMDR and all good therapy is the therapeutic relationship. If you feel that asking for one of the procedural steps will negatively impact the relationship, it is better to move on to the next step. For example, many of the therapists working with firefighters in New York City after 9/11 did not ask them for the NC, PC, or VoC because they did not want to harm the fragile therapeutic alliance. They knew that the NC, "I am powerless," would be so dystonic that the clients would not have remained in the room to process the traumatic memories. Even without the cognitions, the firefighters were able to successfully reprocess the disturbing memories (Colelli, 2002). Lovett (1999) does not recommend asking children for a NC because she is concerned that the power differential will affect the child, disrupting the therapeutic relationship and possibly adding more distress. Diegelmann and Isermann (2005), who work extensively with cancer patients, do not ask them for NCs and PCs, believing they would affect the therapeutic relationship and are not clinically helpful.

For many clients the standard procedural steps are cumbersome: the PC and scales take them out of their experience, making it difficult to reactivate the memory network in order for them to process the memory. The standard protocol takes clients from right brain to left brain to right brain, back and forth. For some clients this is helpful and containing, but for others it feels as if they are being manipulated, which can disrupt the therapeutic relationship. Many clients who have difficulty connecting with their feelings in the first place cannot find them after naming the PC and VoC. Clients (and therapists) with perfectionist tendencies can become stuck with the cognitions, spending too much time trying to find the correct ones. Sometimes memory networks associated with punitive teachers or parents become activated, taking clients away from the issues they came to work on.

It is important to remember that the memory network must be activated in order for processing to occur. Therefore if the standard procedural steps *deactivates* the memory network, the steps should be modified in order to *activate* the network.

Many clients have difficulty coming up with a PC. They often feel so utterly terrible with the traumatic memory activated that trying to think of something positive feels preposterous and frustrating and can cause them to feel like failures. They may also feel that the therapists are not sensitive to their present pain. The struggle to find a PC, for many adults with childhood trauma, can also pull them out of the child self's experience and take them from the right hemisphere to the left, for an adult intellectual response.

To ask clients to then rate their PCs can also feel like a useless exercise. The number rating challenges the adult self (left hemisphere), who cannot even imagine a VoC above a 1 for the PC. For instance, it is very difficult for a client who has activated a memory of being orally raped and threatened with death to rate the PC "I am safe" above a VoC of 1. This whole process can derail the flow of the therapy. Insisting on getting a VoC can harm a fragile therapeutic alliance. In retrospect, this whole process has been a waste of precious processing time when at the end of the session an entirely new belief has emerged that is a perfect fit for where the client has arrived. Taking a VoC at the end is also not necessary if clients come up with a PC that they report is true for them. To ask them to rate their belief on a scale is splitting hairs and does not serve the therapy. For some clients it can feel as if you are doubting their response, causing confusion, and taking away the positive statement they have just made.

As an EMDR trainer and consultant I have found that therapists have the most difficulty learning and understanding the VoC. If these highly educated professionals have a difficult time understanding it, then it must be even more difficult for clients. The rationale for the VoC according to Shapiro (2001) is that it helps the therapist and client assess the validity of the PC. It serves to give feedback about the change that has occurred during the session. But, because of its subjectivity, it is not really a valid measurement. And, since the PC that arises at the end of the session is often different from the one chosen in the beginning, the client is measuring the validity of two *different* cognitions. What does this mean? In my experience clients can express in words the change they have experienced without the use of the VoC. Many well-educated American clients have difficulty understanding the VoC scale, but this problem is amplified tenfold for clients from different cultures, clients who are not well educated, and clients for whom numbers and scales are unfamiliar and alienating. Because of these problems, the VoC is one of the first steps that can be omitted. In my opinion, the cost-benefit ratio justifies this.

For some clients, the SUDS can also be omitted. This is the case if the memory is so obviously distressing that asking them for a SUDS reading creates an empathic break that disrupts the therapeutic alliance. If your client is crying, don't take a SUDS reading. Start the BLS and help the client process through the memory.

Targets do not have to have all of the components in order for EMDR processing to be successful. Modifications can be made in the target by eliminating components that you either cannot find or are not clinically appropriate or necessary for the client. This is a clinical decision and relies on the therapist's empathic judgment. The most important elements are an image, body sensations, and emotions, along with some kind of cognitive component combined with the BLS. It is possible to begin processing with only body sensations, but the processing is more likely to be diffuse and go into many different channels. Well-developed targets that include the image, NC, emotions, and body sensations set the stage for more thorough and complete processing and increase the likelihood of successfully resolving the target. The idea is to activate as much of the memory network as possible and then process it with the BLS. Therefore, it is best to have some kind of image, emotion, body sensation, and negative belief to most vividly stimulate the memory network.

It is important to develop the target in a fluid, easy way that is attuned to the client. Do your best to help your clients come up with each of the target components but move on to the next one if too much difficulty arises. Do not struggle with the components. If you sense it is getting frustrating, move on to the next part. You don't want the setup to traumatize you or your clients. You can guide them, offer suggestions, and do your best to come up with the parts.

The steps that can be most readily omitted are: the PC (in the initial setup), the VoC, and the SUDS. The PC that arises after the reprocessing of the memory can be ascertained and installed. This is similar to the protocol modifications used for EMDR with children (Tinker & Wilson, 1999), except that they recommend taking a SUDS with children. (Adults, in contrast to young children, show their emotions more visibly and can tell the therapist how distressed they feel.) The image and NC can also be eliminated if clients cannot come up with them without it becoming frustrating or if it is deemed clinically detrimental by the therapist.

WHEN TO MODIFY THE STANDARD PROCEDURAL STEPS

Omit the NC

- if it causes an empathic break
- if clients struggle too much to find it
- if it takes too much time
- if it is not clinically appropriate
- if it is inappropriate for some children

Omit the PC and VoC

- if they will cause an empathic break
- if clients are struggling to find them
- if you are short on time
- if it will cause the client to intellectualize too much
- if it causes clients to lose the charge
- if it is too confusing for clients
- if it is not helpful
- if clients are children

Omit the SUDS

- if clients are clearly distressed
- if it will cause an empathic break
- if clients have told you in words that they are distressed
- if it takes clients out of their memory network
- if it is not clinically helpful

Children and some adult clients can indicate by other means the level of distress (e.g., showing with their hands, pointing to pictures, drawing a picture)

I have found that by changing the order of the procedural steps and omitting some of the elements, clients can quickly activate the memory network and seamlessly enter into the processing. The modified procedural steps are streamlined and efficient, taking very little time to activate the memory network and ready clients for the desensitization. This is especially helpful when you are limited to 50-minute sessions. I have found this modified procedure to be smooth and easy for clients. They are able to get an NC quickly from the emotions and body sensations and are in the memory network, ready to process.

In this procedure after we have determined what memory we are going to target I ask clients to close their eyes and go inside. Then I ask them what picture represents the worst part. Next I ask them what emotions they feel. Then I ask what they notice in their body. I then ask for what they believe about themselves now. After the NC I may or may not ask for the SUDS.

This procedure goes directly into the memory network and activates all of the components. It bypasses the cognitive censor and activates the so-mato-sensory experience. If they are comfortable, clients can keep their eyes closed as the questions are asked and the components are activated. While they name the emotions, body sensations, and NC, they go deeper into the memory and are primed to begin the desensitization. By asking for the NC after the emotions and body sensations, the belief comes from the body experience and bypasses the thinking mind. In this way it comes quickly and spontaneously, without discussion that can divert attention from the processing and deactivate the network. (See Appendix 1 pages 328–329 for the Modified EMDR Procedural Steps Checklist and the Sample Vignette.)

MODIFYING THE PROCEDURAL STEPS FOR CLIENTS WITH COMPLEX TRAUMA

For many clients with multiple childhood traumas, their memories of abuse are stored in fragmented form, with the thoughts, feelings, pictures, and body sensations in separate compartments. This compartmentalization of the memories often makes it difficult for them to come up with all of the usual components for the target. The modified procedural steps work well for these clients (Parnell, 1999). In addition to the streamlining and order change, there are some additional modifications I recommend.

SAFE PLACE AND RESOURCE INVOCATION

It can be helpful to invoke the safe place and resources before starting the processing. When clients are going to process what they know to be something highly charged, it can be best to guide them to their safe place after identifying the issue or memory to be worked on. In the safe place clients can call on the resources developed in prior sessions as they process the memory. Some clients may want a large contingent of protectors. These resources can be their adult self with the child self, protectors, and nurturing figures.

SOME HELPFUL INSTRUCTIONS FOR CLIENTS

The instructions given to clients in their safe place are meant to increase their sense of safety and control. For clients who tend to chain one memory to another, it can be helpful to tell them that they will process one memory and that it will have a beginning, a middle, and an end. They can also be reminded that they can stop at any time and return to the safe place. They are in control.

For some clients who need reinforcement of distancing the memories as they process, they can be told, "When you are ready you can bring up the incident and see it projected on a movie screen. As you watch the movie you can remind yourself that it is just a movie." Another similar suggestion is that they can imagine that they are watching the memory on a VCR. They can imagine themselves safe at home with family or friends as they watch the old memory. This instruction gives them a sense of distance from the memories and also a sense of control. They can be told that they hold the remote control to the video player in their hands and they can fast-forward, stop, rewind, or edit it whenever they wish. They can make it a still photograph, make it black and white, or take the sound out of it. "Remember, you are safe in the present, processing old memories from the past." The desired instructions can be established ahead of time with clients, who can tell therapists which instructions work best. Remember, the idea is to help clients feel safe in the present as they process the past. Clients do not have to reexperience the trauma in the way they did before.

PART II

USING EMDR WITH CLIENTS

3

EVALUATION AND PREPARATION
FOR EMDR

IT IS IMPORTANT IN the beginning phase of treatment to lay the ground-work and prepare clients for the EMDR trauma processing. If clients have complex trauma, the result of prolonged repetitive trauma in childhood and adulthood, this can take anywhere from a few weeks to several years. For clients without significant trauma and with good ego strength, it can be accomplished in a session or two.

In the beginning phase of treatment the therapeutic relationship develops and a strong therapeutic container evolves within which the reprocessing of traumatic material can take place. Therapists take *thorough* histories and assess clients' ego strengths and coping skills. EMDR resource installation can be used during this phase primarily to strengthen ego resources. It is important to remember that EMDR is *integrated* into a comprehensive treatment plan that includes many other essential parts and adjunctive tools.

TAKE A HISTORY OF THE PRESENTING PROBLEMS

When clients come in to see me, I want to know what specifically is trou-bling them. What are the presenting problems? Why are the clients seeking treatment at this time? It is helpful in the first session to ask about clients' *current symptoms*. Getting a clear picture of the presenting problems and symp-toms helps guide you in your treatment planning. Write this information down in your notes. It will help to keep you informed about progress in treatment and help focus the work.

If clients have PTSD from known incidents, the work is straightforward. Find out what happened and the aftermath of the traumatic events. For ex-ample, if the client had been raped, what happened after the rape? Did she tell anyone? If she did, what was the response? Did she get help? What kind of medical treatment did she need as a result of the assault? How was she treated by the police, by medical personnel? Did she experience any lasting physical effects from the incident? What symptoms is the client experiencing as a result of the trauma? What beliefs does the client have about herself? Are there any somatic complaints? All of these parts are important.

Clients who have issues, anxiety, and problematic behavior and those presenting with complex trauma require a more thorough evaluation of their complaints and symptoms. Examples of issues clients may bring to EMDR therapy are difficulty in relationships, work problems, feeling blocked in life, phobias and fears, somatic complaints, depression, anxiety, among others. I want to know specifically what their symptoms are. What are the negative self-beliefs? Later, when I take their developmental history, I listen for where those beliefs may have set in. For example, a client came in with the complaint, "I feel stuck in my life. I can never seem to move forward." He then described a lifetime of powerlessness in which he felt thwarted. When I took his history, beginning at birth, he told me his mother was in labor a long time. She was given a powerful anesthetic and they had to use forceps to get him out. "I was stuck, I couldn't get out." From his description I developed a hypothesis that his problems may have begun at birth, a potential target for our EMDR work.

Clients often come in with their own ideas about the origins of their symptoms. Some have had previous therapies where their therapists have helped them come to certain conclusions. I try to regard each new client with fresh eyes, taking into consideration past theories, but keeping my mind open to other possibilities. I have discovered that very often therapists are caught in their theories and do not see the true linkages. Very often symptoms are not linked by content, but through cognitions, body sensations, and emotions. For example, the fear of flying may have nothing to do with flying. It may be linked to a childhood in which the client's parents drank heavily and fought with each other. The client grew up feeling he had no control. When he gets in a plane he has to let go of control and trust someone with his life.

When taking a history of the presenting problem, ask clients: When did the problem begin? Was there an initial cause or incident that they know of? What was the earliest and the worst experience of this? How long have the clients been suffering from these symptoms? If it is an issue, what in the past is contributing to this problem? What are the current triggers? What, when, where, and how often do the clients feel triggered and experience symptoms of distress? What have the clients done in the past to try to remedy the problems? What has been helpful and what has not? How are the clients' current lives being affected by the symptoms and emotional difficulties? You want to know what the clients' goals for treatment are. What are the preferred behavioral states? Are there other issues or problems the clients would like to work on?

I find it very useful to get specific information on the symptoms. If clients are afraid of speaking in groups, is it any size group, or only large groups? Is it in social situations or in work situations? What happens when they are anxious? What do they do? What do they think about themselves? Typically, after EMDR sessions, clients' symptoms will change. Often they cannot remember what they were. Writing them down in the beginning will help you keep track of your progress.

Korn, Rozelle, and Weir (2004) reported that a symptom-focused approach to treatment planning and targeting was most effective in treating clients with PTSD. This has been my experience as well with clients with a range of presenting problems. With a symptom-focused approach therapists try to ascertain what in the clients' past are causing the symptoms in the present. After clients are sufficiently stabilized, the early contributors are targeted and reprocessed with EMDR. I also focus on the clients' goals for treatment. How will we know when clients have accomplished their goals? Goals can be reevaluated and changed along the way, but it is helpful to have an informal therapeutic contract, in which the goals are agreed upon and a treatment plan outlined. This focused, efficient way of working also keeps clients motivated. Clients can see that you are working for them and that you do not have your own agenda.

What is the presenting problem?
What are the symptoms?
What negative self-beliefs are associated with the problem?
What experiences in the past are linked to the symptoms?

As you take clients' histories you begin to develop hypotheses about the genesis of their symptoms and also evaluate whether the clients are appropriate for EMDR therapy. You need to know who you are working with, your clients' strengths and weaknesses, and how they relate to you. Are the clients suspicious and distrustful? Is there evidence of strong transference from the beginning? Do the clients have a personality disorder? Do the clients have an attachment disorder? With clients who are testy and distrustful from the beginning, I wait until the relationship is secure before beginning EMDR. During the course of information gathering, you prepare clients for EMDR trauma processing by answering questions and educating them about the effects of trauma and how EMDR works. As clients talk about their histories, sharing personal information, they begin to trust you and the therapeutic relationship develops.

DEVELOPMENTAL HISTORY

It is essential for EMDR therapists to take a developmental history with all of their clients. Many people open up early trauma memories during EMDR sessions that can trigger abreactions and dissociation. *One never knows what might come out during the processing sessions* and it is better to be prepared. I let potential clients know on the telephone before seeing me that we will not begin EMDR until I have taken a history and we have developed a relationship. Believing they should begin EMDR immediately, some people are not happy with this. They may choose not to work with me. Getting to know clients and establishing a good therapeutic relationship are fundamental to creating a safe container within the EMDR processing work.

It is best to view the gathering of historical information as part of the rapport-building process so that clients do not feel like they are being interrogated and objectified (a potential trigger for sexual abuse survivors who were treated as objects by the perpetrators). Therapists attempt to know the clients. At the same time, clients get to know their therapists. Although I realize it can be helpful, I do not use history forms in my practice. I find it is important for me to hear clients tell their story. Images and anecdotes will stand out that will make useful targets. Many of these might not have been thought to be significant outside of the narrative. Forms can feel impersonal and alienate clients from the beginning. If you do use forms, I think it would be better for you to fill them out as the client speaks rather than have the client fill them out.

Pacing is important. Clients with significant trauma histories may feel overexposed if they reveal too much about themselves too quickly. Therapists should be sensitive to this and refrain from asking questions that may be too evocative. You might go back and forth between inquiring about trauma history that can be emotionally upsetting and about experiences that were positive and resourceful. For example, the therapist might ask about any early losses and, after hearing about a number of them, ask about where the client felt loved and nurtured. Who is present and supports her in her life now? Remember, talking about traumas can be overwhelming, stirring up the past without processing it.

History taking can be as simple as a conversation during which clients tell the therapists what they think is most important about their childhood and how that may be affecting them now. The therapists fill out this narrative by asking questions that help to develop hypotheses about the etiology of the presenting problems. As clients tell their stories, the therapists listen for events, themes, limiting self-beliefs, and negative beliefs about the world—any of these may be good targets for EMDR processing.

Birth and Early Infancy

It is helpful to ask for information about the clients' birth, early infancy, and a narrative account of their childhood, asking questions about their relationship with their parents or other caregivers. You want to evaluate the *nature of their early attachments*. Was it consistent or chaotic? Was their mother borderline or simply anxious? Clients who had chaotic, borderline early attachment figures are more prone to PTSD and will require more time to develop a secure relationship with therapists (Schore, 1994). They may require more work to develop resources prior to EMDR processing of traumatic memories, resources that can aid in interweaves and session closure. Clients who were neglected in early childhood may have a more difficult time developing a trusting relationship with therapists. Also, they may have large gaps in their childhood memories that may not be the result of abuse, but rather of neglect (Schore, 1994). Who were the primary caregivers? What was their relationship with their mother like? What was their relationship with their father? Sometimes the parents are not the primary caregivers. There may have been a nanny, grandparent, foster parent, or older sibling who parented them. It is important to know about these figures who can be installed as resources.

What was their relationship like with their siblings? Siblings can be the source of torment for younger children, affecting their self-esteem and security. They can also be a source of comfort and support. Were there disruptions of attachment due to death, divorce, substance abuse, hospitalizations, or other causes?

Was there substance abuse in the family? Who in the family used, what, how much, and what were the consequences of the use?

Latency and Adolescence: Social and Sexual Development

It is important to inquire about their *social and sexual development*. After learning about their early life, ask about the latency years. How did the clients do in school? Oftentimes children who have been traumatized have a difficult time concentrating in school. Some have learning difficulties that contribute to low self-esteem. What was school like for the clients? Sometimes children are secure at home but have difficulty with learning, which affects how they feel about themselves. Cruel or insensitive teachers can damage children, affecting their ability to learn as well as their creativity. These experiences in school can create the template for how clients view themselves as workers.

How did the clients do socially growing up? Did they have close friends growing up, or were they isolated and alone? Did their families move frequently, causing disruptions in the development of lasting friendships? Experiences on the playground and fitting in or not with other children can also be significant. These small "t" traumas can affect how people view themselves throughout one's life.

What was their adolescence like? How did they feel about their own sexual development? How did they feel about their bodies? What was their experience with dating? What was the quality of their romantic relationships? What is their history of intimate relationships? Are there any traumatic experiences that have led to limiting beliefs and behaviors?

Adulthood

What were the significant events in their adult life: education, employment, relationships, marriages, divorces, births, illnesses, deaths? Were there traumas in their adult life?

TRAUMA HISTORY

You want information about significant traumas clients experienced. How old were they when they experienced them? What happened? What was their response at the time? What was the system's response? Were they soothed and taken care of, or were they neglected? Did the clients experience any significant losses? The losses can be due to death, divorce, or moving. Sometimes children are raised by nannies or other caretakers who leave for one reason or another. Children who move frequently experience the loss of friends and neighborhoods. Did they lose a beloved pet?

ABUSE HISTORY

If you are working with clients who were abused as children, you will want to gather information about their abuse history. Who were the perpetrators?

When did the abuse begin? How old were the clients at the time? When did it end? Was the abuse a one-time occurrence or did it occur over a period of time? What was the frequency? Did your clients tell anyone about the abuse? Did others know about the abuse? If it was reported, what was the response from the adults and/or system? Were the clients ignored? Punished? Rescued? Blamed? Disbelieved? What kind of abuse took place? What was the severity? Were there threats involved? Was there physical violence involved? Did your clients always remember the abuse or did memories of the abuse emerge at some time later in their lives? What beliefs about themselves and the world did your clients develop as a result of the abuse? Do your clients see themselves as bad because they enjoyed the attention of the abuser or experienced sexual arousal? Do they feel ashamed or worthless for their failure to protect themselves or others? Did they as children or teens perpetrate abuse on others? Have your clients engaged in abusive behaviors as adults?

This information may be gathered over time in a way that is comfortable for clients. It is important that they not feel like they are being interrogated and that they feel safe enough to reveal the information to the therapists. Information about triggers, dreams, body memories, and flashback images should be noted for use as potential EMDR targets. Many adults who have been sexually abused don't have clear visual memories of abuse but have symptoms indicating that abuse may have occurred.

Clients who have been physically or sexually abused as children run the gamut from highly disturbed individuals with severe character pathology with few coping skills to people with intact ego structures who have some life-limiting symptoms and good coping skills. In general, the severity of symptomatology depends on the severity, frequency, and duration of abuse; the age of the victims at the time of the abuse; the victims' relationships to the perpetrators; the victimizer's treatment of the victim; the family's and/ or system's response to the abuse; and, "host" factors such as temperament, quality of early attachment, family history of mental illness, ego strength, and general resiliency.

History of Mental Health Treatment

You also want to know about any history of mental health treatment. What worked and what didn't—and, why? Clients who report a long history of unsuccessful therapy may have dissociative identity disorder (DID). Are they currently seeing another therapist? See page 77 for a discussion of working adjunctively with EMDR. You may want to get signed releases to contact former or current mental health professionals.

During the history-taking, note how the clients relate to you. Do they seem comfortable and able to talk easily to you? Or, do they seem detached, anxious, or hostile? Do the clients have a character disorder? Many people who were sexually abused as children have borderline personality disorders (Herman, 1992), a factor that affects the treatment and the use of EMDR in the treatment. How good are their ego functionings? How do the clients handle anxiety? What are their primary defenses? Do they dissociate when talking about disturbing memories? Do a basic mental status examination. Are the clients oriented to place and time? Do they have a thought disorder? Are they delusional? You do not want to do EMDR with someone who is actively psychotic.

HISTORY OF MEDICAL PROBLEMS, PROCEDURES, AND MEDICATIONS

It is important to know about clients' histories of medical problems and procedures including physical illnesses, accidents, hospitalizations, and past medical procedures. These experiences can significantly impact a person's life. Young children who are hospitalized or who have medical procedures do not have the cognitive structure in place to make sense out of what is happening to them. Children will interpret hospitalization as abandonment, as if they are being punished because they must be bad. They feel powerless. Their symptoms can appear the same as those in adults abused as children, with the same negative self-beliefs ("I'm bad," "I'm powerless") body sensations, and emotions (fear, anger, shame). Many clients I have worked with developed phobias as a result of anesthesia, particularly ether administered to them as children. Having a mask placed over their faces and being told to breathe in a noxious gas terrified them. A generation of parents was advised to give their children enemas. Overzealous parents harmed their children, creating symptoms of victimization. Even dental work can cause lasting traumatic effects (Parnell, 1997a).

Hospitalization can disrupt attachment in early childhood and can affect a child's development. School-age children who have been hospitalized for several weeks or months may have difficulty adjusting socially when they return to school. This may affect how they view themselves and their ability to form relationships. How did the families respond to their children's illness or condition?

I want to know if clients are taking any medications or supplements. Have they taken any in the past? Did the medications or supplements help? Benzodiazepines have been reported to reduce treatment effects (Shapiro, 2001). If the client is taking these medications you may want to ask them to refrain from taking them before sessions. If they cannot do that, process with EMDR and then redo your work when they are no longer taking the medication. Clients taking narcotics for pain may also find that EMDR will not be as effective. Remember, there must be emotional charge for processing to occur. So if the medication they are on flattens their affect or cuts all of their anxiety, they will not process. Clients taking antidepressants generally are able to process with EMDR. However, if their affect has become too flattened and they have lost all anxiety with the medications, the processing may not work. It can be helpful to consult with their psychiatrist to adjust the medication.

In my experience clients with some kinds of clinical depression do not process with EMDR. For example, when beginning resource installation they might be able to see a safe place, but not feel it. Their affect is flat and they are disconnected from themselves. When processing with EMDR, instead of moving to an adaptive resolution of the trauma, they spiral downward, associating to more negative experiences. I have found that when these clients become stabilized with antidepressant medication, or nutritional supplements such as EMPowerplus,* used to balance the central nervous system, they are able to process normally and resolve the traumatic memories (Kaplan, Fisher, Crawford, Field, & Kolb, 2004; Kaplan, Simpson, Ferre, Gorman, McMullen, & Crawford, 2001; Popper, 2001).

IDENTIFICATION OF CLIENT RESOURCES

The identification of resources from clients' earlier and current life is very important in this work. These resources, which may include *positive memories*, can be used throughout the EMDR therapy to add ego strength, a sense of integration, wholeness, and empowerment to clients. They can be memories of safety, comfort, support, nurturance, trust, achievement, and pride. They may include memories of being mentored, images of positive role models, and experiences of social recognition.

As part of the history taking, therapists also help clients to identify those people in the clients' life who were important loving, nurturing figures, or protectors for them such as relatives, friends, friends' parents, teachers, counselors, coaches, librarians, clergy people, and so on. Some clients cannot

---

*Information on EMPowerplus can be found from the Truehope Institute, Ltd., www. truehope.com.

name anyone from their immediate family who was kind but, when questioned, might be able to find a teacher who "saw" them, "recognized" their specialness, and cared about them.

Along with the important support people in clients' early lives, you want to find out what they did to survive. What did they do to cope then, and what do they do now to cope with difficult circumstances? Did they go for walks in nature, or go to a special place? For some children summer camp helped them cope with the rest of the year. Others spent as much time as they could at friends' houses. Some clients excelled at school, sports, or outdoor activities. Did they have an imaginary friend they talked to or an angelic presence? One client would go to the library as a child where she would feel safe. The image of this place became her safe place during our EMDR work.

SPIRITUALITY

It is helpful to know what spiritual resources clients have. Some people connect to something larger than themselves when they are in nature. What images evoke spiritual feelings for them? Have they had what they would consider spiritual experiences? These experiences might have come from dreams, childhood, or near-death experiences. Sometimes clients have never told anyone about these experiences, yet they have had a powerful impact on their lives. Experiences of awe and beauty can be summoned to bring inspiration and a broader perspective. What religion did they practice as children? What are their spiritual beliefs now? Some people don't feel a connection to the religion of their childhoods but have found comfort in other expressions that do not fall within the Judeo-Christian rubric. What brings them a sense of peace and well-being? Are there religious figures who bring them comfort? Many people feel a connection with angelic beings. Do they believe in God? If so, is there an image that represents the Divine Being to them?

Meditation and prayer can also be helpful supports for clients. Do the clients have a meditation practice? Have they ever learned to meditate? Has prayer been helpful during times of stress?

DIET AND EXERCISE

It can be helpful to ask clients about their diet. Do they eat regularly and have a balanced healthy diet? Too much sugar can also create imbalances. How much caffeine are they taking in on a daily basis? People who drink a lot of coffee and caffeinated soft drinks may have problems with anxiety and sleep. Do your clients get regular exercise? Sometimes working on basic health can help clients cope better with stress.

ASSESSING READINESS FOR EMDR

An important part of the preparation phase of treatment is assessing readiness for EMDR. There are a number of factors to consider before using EMDR with clients (see Figure 3.1).

THE THERAPEUTIC RELATIONSHIP

The foundation for this container is the therapeutic relationship. The relationship should be stable, rapport comfortable, and trust established. A sense

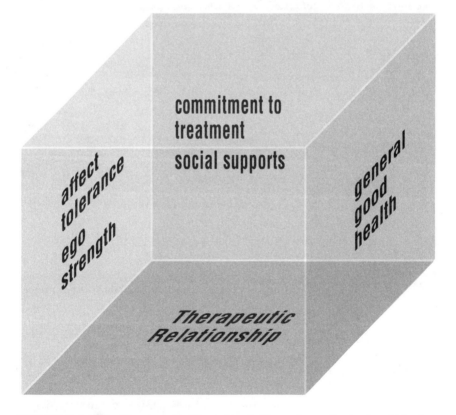

FIGURE 3.1 "The Therapeutic Container": These ingredients should be in place before beginning EMDR treatment.

of safety is important, especially for clients who were abused as children and have complex trauma. Because their trust was violated, it is essential before any trauma reprocessing begins that they feel secure in their relationship with the therapist. This development can take weeks, months, or years, depending on the needs of the client. Yet for some high-functioning clients, a rapport can be established in a session or two. Clients must feel safe enough to trust therapists to tell them *truthfully* what they are experiencing during the reprocessing of a traumatic incident. They don't have to tell you all of the details, but they do need to tell you enough to let you know that the traumatic material is moving through the system and is not stuck.

The clients' ability to trust you is also important during the reprocessing of the traumatic memories because when clients access their child self during the reprocessing of traumas that occurred during childhood, they may lose all contact with their adult self. The therapeutic relationship is like a lifeline connecting the client to you and present-day reality.

The therapist and therapeutic relationship are also important ego resources for clients. Clients incorporate the therapist as a positive self-object, who then becomes a source of caring and support during times of difficulty. Some clients report hearing my voice giving them advice or consolation during difficult times.

The therapist and therapeutic relationship can be used as resources when the client is stuck during EMDR processing sessions. For example, the therapist can come in and rescue and comfort the client's child self, if necessary, when the client is looping in distress. Eventually, the client's internal voice replaces that of the therapist. I believe that during EMDR processing and resolution of trauma, the therapist's kind presence is installed along with the positive cognition and new image. If clients choose to install me as a resource, I like to have additional resources installed so that I am part of a team. But I want to stress again the importance of the therapeutic relationship as an essential resource for the client prior to processing work.

For some higher-functioning clients, the therapeutic relationship does not take long to establish. In some cases, as the therapist takes the history, there is an ease and rapport. After one or two sessions both the therapist and client feel ready to proceed. For clients with histories of disrupted attachment, it may take longer to establish a bond, and the bond may become broken from time to time, requiring repair. When that happens, the EMDR processing work stops until both therapist and client feel comfortable resuming EMDR. Until clients feel that they can trust the therapist, EMDR trauma processing should not be started. Clients must be able and willing to be open to the possibility of feeling vulnerable, a lack of control, and the reexperiencing of some of the physical sensations from the incident that they will target with EMDR (Shapiro, 2001).

The therapist must also be able to trust the client. You need to trust that clients are telling you the truth about their substance abuse, self-harming behaviors, suicidality, and current symptoms. Trust is a two-way street. If clients are not trustworthy, there is no solid foundation for the work. Therefore I do not recommend using EMDR until trust is well established.

COMMITMENT TO SAFETY AND TREATMENT

Along with the development of a strong therapeutic relationship, it is important that there be a commitment to safety and treatment. Issues and behaviors that interfere with treatment should be addressed. These include alcohol and substance abuse problems, suicidal behavior and parasuicidal behavior such as self-mutilation, and serious relationship difficulties such as sexual acting out and abusive relationships. Is the client committed to safety and treatment, and if so is he or she willing to address these problematic behaviors? Motivation and commitment are very important. Some clients may begin EMDR trauma processing with some of these behaviors, but with a willingness to work on controlling them. For example, if clients cut themselves, are they willing to work toward ceasing the behavior? Are they willing to work on it with EMDR? Clients may need adjunctive treatments for such issues as drug and alcohol abuse, compulsive behaviors, and eating disorders.

Don't do EMDR with someone who is actively suicidal or homicidal. This may seem obvious to you, but not everyone understands this. I heard of a case of a therapist doing EMDR with an unstable Vietnam veteran who was suicidal, was abusing his spouse, and had a loaded gun at home. He ended up taking his life after an EMDR session. The therapist knew his history and had done no stabilization work.

It is important that your clients be committed to not hurting themselves. If they have suicidal thoughts, will they make a non-self-harming contract? If you don't feel secure enough with your client, don't proceed with EMDR. In one case, the client had severe PTSD and had thoughts of harming himself. His thoughts scared him. Though he had no plan, he was afraid he might act impulsively. I referred him to a psychiatrist for a medication evaluation, after which he was prescribed an antidepressant. We decided that we would wait to do EMDR until he felt more stable with regard to the suicidal thoughts and feelings. When he was feeling better, more contained, we began EMDR and he proceeded quite safely with his healing work.

Do clients have secondary gain issues that might impede their willingness to heal? The vet who is concerned about getting better and losing his disability check, the abuse victim who fears losing her support group and victim identity, and the client with fictitious disorder who craves your attention are all examples of clients who might have resistance to getting better. If you should have concerns about secondary gains with your clients, talk to them about it. Make sure you are working together toward a mutually agreed upon goal.

AFFECT TOLERANCE

Can your clients tolerate high levels of affect? Do they have good ego strength? If they have PTSD, or are going to be processing a highly charged memory, can the clients handle intense abreactions? Can they ride the emotional waves without panicking, shutting down the session, and running out the door? Can clients handle disturbance in between sessions that might arise without decompensating, requiring hospitalization, harming themselves or others? Will the clients call their therapists to let them know if help is needed?

Shapiro (2001) advised using what she calls self-control techniques with clients to assess whether they are good candidates for EMDR. These techniques include guided imagery like safe place, the light stream visualization (Shapiro, 2001), and other hypnotic techniques. If the client cannot do these, do not proceed with EMDR. For example, if clients suffering from PTSD cannot imagine a safe place or variant to calm themselves down, then spend time helping them develop the capacity to do this before attempting EMDR. In some cases the inability to respond to relaxing imagery is a sign that the client needs psychopharmalogical support. RDI can be used for both assessment of the client's readiness for EMDR and ego strengthening. In Chapter 4 I will provide a number of these techniques.

There is a window of arousal between hyperarousal and hypoarousal within which clients can successfully process with EMDR. Clients must be willing to feel their feelings but that doesn't mean that they have to reexperience the trauma. Distancing techniques can be used (putting up a glass wall, imaging it like a movie, etc.) so that they do not become overwhelmed. These tools will be described in more detail in Chapter 4.

Between sessions can your clients utilize healthy techniques to regulate their level of arousal? If they are upset, can they call their sponsor, go for a walk, talk to their pastor, imagine going to their safe place? Or do they take drugs and binge and purge? What are their coping skills, and do they use them when flooded with feelings? If clients are not able to use coping skills, wait to use EMDR until they can. Clients who have suicidal ideation, dissociation, or substance abuse may be treated with EMDR if they can tolerate the affect and use coping skills.

CURRENT FUNCTIONING AND SOCIAL SUPPORTS

It is important to find out about clients' current functioning, social supports, and employment status. Are they currently employed? Do they have a stable home environment? Do they have close friends and family, or are they alone and alienated? Do they have adult children they are close to? How do they get along with others? Are they part of a support group like AA, ALANON, NA, or a survivor group? If clients have little social support and are not functioning well, I generally do not recommend beginning EMDR in an outpatient setting until more of those things are in place. EMDR can be done in a residential setting that provides containment and safety. However, if clients are able to connect with inner resources and install them successfully, I might cautiously begin EMDR with small "t" traumas. You want to make sure that their lives are sufficiently stable insofar as their having a good support system and not undergoing any major crises such as impending loss of home or employment.

CURRENT HEALTH

How is their current health? When was their last physical? Do they have a history of seizures, migraines, or eye problems? If you have concerns, refer them to a physician, or consult their physician. Many people who have suffered from early trauma develop somatic problems. Are they taking any medications? If they haven't had a physical examination in a while, you might suggest that they schedule one. Because adults who have been sexually abused as children were betrayed by adults who were in positions of power and authority, they tend to avoid doctors and dentists because of the anxiety it arouses in them. This avoidance can jeopardize their health if this issue isn't addressed.

Sometimes physical problems can create symptoms that appear to be psychological in origin. Hormone fluctuations can cause changes in mood, loss of sexual interest, and sleep disturbances. Mitrovalve prolapse, a non-life-threatening abnormality in the heart, can cause symptoms that look like panic attacks. When a client tells me she wakes out of a deep sleep with panic, I wonder if it might have to do with her heart, or even sleep apnea.

As a rule, avoid eye movements with clients with histories of seizures and eye problems. Alternate forms of BLS can be used effectively. Clients with neurological impairment can be treated with EMDR (Shapiro, 2001), but if you have any concerns, consult a neurologist. In some cases, EMDR may not be as effective because the adaptive information processing is not working fully because of the organic impairment. In a few cases, I have worked with motivated clients who were not able to process due to organic brain disorders. The accelerated information processing system did not activate as it does with most of my clients. After consulting with their physicians, I have worked successfully with several clients with traumatic brain injuries and seizure disorders. I would not rule out working with clients with neurological impairment, but I would do so cautiously, with consultation. I would also understand if the processing did not seem to work.

If you are working with clients who have PTSD or have had significant traumas, you want to be sure that they are physically capable of handling high levels of affect. If your clients are elderly, physically fragile, have a heart condition, high blood pressure, or other medical conditions, discuss your concerns with them. When in doubt, have the clients consult a physician.

DRUG AND ALCOHOL ABUSE

Do the clients have a history of drug or alcohol abuse? According to Shapiro, "Clients with a substance abuse history should have in place appropriate supports, such as a 12-step program, before initiating EMDR treatment" (2001, p. 98). Are the clients currently using substances? Are they in recovery? Many people self-medicate with substances in order to manage affect arising from traumas. After processing the traumas with EMDR, some of them will experience a decrease in the desire to use. This was the case with my client Melanie whom I describe in *Transforming Trauma: EMDR* (Parnell, 1997). In the beginning of treatment she told me she had been either drunk or hungover for years. Before beginning EMDR I told her she would have to stop drinking and go to AA. When she stopped drinking she immediately began to experience flashbacks and nightmares. After targeting and reprocessing the traumas, she reported that her desire to drink went away. Other clients, however, may experience an increase in urge because of the emotions that have been stirred up and not fully resolved. It is helpful to educate your clients about both possibilities and set up safeguards. For some clients it would be safest and most effective for them to have EMDR treatment in a residential setting where they can receive support and containment.

In addition, caution should be taken with clients who have a history of crack cocaine addiction or amphetamine abuse (Shapiro, 2001).

OTHER SELF-DESTRUCTIVE BEHAVIOR

Do clients engage in self-destructive behavior such as sexual acting out, self-mutilation, gambling, or eating disorders? You want to know the history of these behaviors and their current status. You may want to wait until clients have more self-control before beginning EMDR, especially if the behavior is dangerous.

DISSOCIATIVE DISORDERS

You may want to screen your clients for *dissociative disorder* by using evaluative tools. The dissociative experiences scale (DES) developed by Bernstein and Putnam (1986) is the most popular of such instruments. The structured clinical interview for DSM-IV Dissociative Disorders-Revised (SCID-D-R) developed by Steinberg (1994) is a widely used diagnostic interview that allows the therapist to assess the severity of five dissociative symptoms and diagnose the DSM dissociative disorders and acute stress disorder. According to Shapiro (2001), using EMDR with DID is strongly discouraged without supervision and training in dissociative disorders and knowledge of the appropriate EMDR protocols. Clients with this disorder can become overwhelmed with affect. EMDR can also dissolve the dissociative barriers that have enabled clients to function. With the integration of information, clients may become overwhelmed and destabilized. A therapist experienced with DID and EMDR can be successful in treating these clients. EMDR is one tool among many such therapists would use. EMDR, however, is a power tool and should be used with caution. (See Appendix 1, page 332 for Clinical Signs of Dissociative Disorders.)

MEDICATION NEEDS

Do clients need medication or something to balance the central nervous system? The adaptive information processing system does not seem to work when the central nervous system is out of balance. Some depressed clients cannot access positive resources. EMDR is contraindicated for clients who are actively psychotic or in the throes of bipolar disorder. They should be stabilized before EMDR is used. I have worked with several clients who have done well with EMDR while on antidepressants and mood stabilizers. It is interesting to note that when medication stops working, EMDR processing no longer works either. However, when the clients' medications are changed or the dose increased, they were able to process again with EMDR.

LEGAL REQUIREMENTS

Clients who are involved in any kind of legal action where they may need to testify should be given informed consent. This would apply to a crime victim, a witness to a crime, a police officer being treated for a critical incident, or someone who is suing for emotional distress. The EMDR therapist should advise them and, if appropriate, their attorney, that the vividness of the picture can change, there can be a loss of extreme emotion, and the memory may dim. A woman came to see me because she wanted to clear the traumas associated with a date rape. She let me know in the first session that she planned to sue the perpetrator. I informed her that she might lose the emotional charge and intensity of the memory, affecting her case for damages. It was up to her to decide whether she wanted to proceed with EMDR. After discussing this, she decided to go ahead with the treatment.

How do you know if your clients are ready to do EMDR? Generally, if the therapeutic relationship is sufficient, the clients have coping skills and are committed to safety and treatment, have a support system, are stabilized, are not in crisis, and have sufficient ego strength (they can access inner and outer resources and have affect tolerance), then they can do EMDR. Diagram 3.1 shows a container that holds the trauma processing work. This container must be strong enough. Korn, Rozelle, and Weir (2004) made the following points in assessing readiness to use EMDR. Instability due to PTSD symtomotology is not a contraindication to using EMDR. EMDR was developed specifically to treat these kinds of clients. Lipke (2005) gave the same advice when working with combat veterans returning from Iraq. After basic assessment and resource installation, they can have EMDR trauma-processing sessions. In his experience, though destabilized in the beginning with regard to PTSD symptomatology, veterans become stabilized after processing their traumas. Korn et al. (2004) reported that neither diagnosis nor trauma history determines readiness for trauma processing or response to treatment. Clients can have very traumatic histories but have access to inner and outer resources that allow them to process through traumas rapidly. "If someone has PTSD, they may be highly aroused and symptomatic. But this is not a reason, in and of itself, to slow down or avoid trauma processing. Instead, this picture of distress is often *the* reason to introduce EMDR" (Korn et al., 2004).

Many clients don't require a great deal of preparation. They have good ego strength, affect tolerance, are functioning well, have good relationships and supports, have stable work, but have experienced some specific traumas. The therapist can begin to use EMDR soon with them. In the early days of EMDR, therapists did not prepare clients enough for the trauma work, whereas today many therapists overprepare clients (see Appendix 1, page 332 for Quick Assessment for EMDR Readiness in an Outpatient Setting.)

INTEGRATING EMDR INTO CLINICAL TREATMENT: HOW TO INTRODUCE EMDR TO CLIENTS

Key to clients' receptivity to EMDR is in how therapists first introduce it to them. For most therapists it is easier to introduce EMDR to new clients than it is to clients who have been in treatment for a while. Introducing it later to clients changes the therapeutic frame and can activate transference issues.

NEW CLIENTS

If new clients call presenting with a problem linked to a trauma, therapists can introduce the clients to EMDR on the phone. The therapists can explain that it is a well-researched method for treating trauma, and can direct the clients to some of the books on EMDR written for the general public (Parnell, 1997a; Shapiro & Silk-Forrest, 1997) and to the Internet to do research. In any case, I tell my clients that for the initial session or sessions we will meet, get to know each other, and that I will need to take a good history. Rarely will I begin EMDR processing in the first session. When I meet with them and listen to their presenting problem, I explain that EMDR may be a treatment that can be used along with talk therapy to help them with areas of difficulty. I explain that experiences from the past become frozen in time and that EMDR can help process these experiences so that they will no longer be disturbed by them. Therapists whose orientation is primarily psychodynamic can tell clients that EMDR can be helpful with clearing early experiences from childhood that are impacting their lives in the present. EMDR can be woven into the treatment, combining it with talk therapy.

OLD CLIENTS

When introducing EMDR to ongoing clients, it can be helpful to let them know that you have learned something new that you believe will be helpful to them. If it is in an area where clients have a specific trauma, you can tell them that this is a well-researched treatment that has been shown to be effective for treating trauma. Many therapists working with long-term clients find that they are at an impasse in their treatment. There are places where clients are stuck. Perhaps the clients have insight, but the emotions and behaviors have not changed, and the therapists and clients realize this. It can be helpful to bring this up with clients and then tell them that you have learned something new that you believe will help with these stuck places. Often clients are pleased that you thought about their treatment and cared enough to bring in something new that can help them. *Clients will be more likely to accept the change in the therapeutic frame if the therapists are enthusiastic and confident about EMDR.* If the therapists introduce it reluctantly, with doubts, the clients will be less open to it.

It can be more difficult to bring EMDR into a psychodynamic or psychoanalytic therapy than to a cognitive-behavioral one. In a cognitive-behavioral therapy clients are accustomed to a structured approach to treatment. In analytic treatment, the work is not structured in the same way. Changes in the therapeutic frame can feel disruptive. One man I worked with who had been in psychoanalytic psychotherapy could not tolerate the structure of EMDR. As soon as I began the protocol, even adapting it for him without the scales, it stimulated negative mother transference. He felt intruded upon, his boundaries threatened, and he put up a wall that kept him from allowing the processing to occur. This is not to say that EMDR cannot be introduced later into a psychodynamic psychotherapy. It has been done in many cases with good results. Be aware of the transference issues that may arise. These should be explored and addressed with clients. Transference issues also can make excellent EMDR targets. For example, if clients feel fear that you will abandon them, the fear can be explored and an associated childhood memory targeted and reprocessed. Transference issues that arise can be grist for the EMDR mill.

EXPLANATION OF THEORIES

In preparing clients for EMDR, you need to explain the theories about how trauma affects the mind and body, as well as theories about EMDR. Describe the structure of an EMDR session, answer questions, and address your clients' fears. I will not begin EMDR until the clients feel secure enough with me and the process. I will often suggest that clients read about EMDR before we begin treatment. I let clients know that they may experience strong emotions. I also warn them that because they might feel exhausted afterward, not to plan anything later that day. I inform them that the processing can bring up new memories or stir up feelings that might be disturbing to them. For that reason, it is best not to begin EMDR processing immediately before the therapist or client will have to miss sessions due to a vacation or other break. For clients processing large traumas, I might suggest that they have someone drive them to and pick them up from the session. Some clients might want to be sure to have their supports available.

It is important to let clients know that there are no guarantees. EMDR does not work for everyone, and not all clients are good candidates for EMDR. Clients often want to know how many sessions it will take to treat their presenting problems. They come in believing it is a brief therapy that should only require a few sessions. Unfortunately, this misconception must derive from the research on EMDR that has mostly been done on single-incident PTSD. In these studies, treatment effects have been shown after three sessions of EMDR. In my experience in private practice, very rarely have clients come in with only a single-incident trauma. Most of them have complex problems that require more time in treatment. One traumatic memory can be cleared in a session, but to alleviate clients' symptoms, many sessions may be needed targeting multiple contributors. I generally tell clients that I cannot give them a time frame before I take a thorough history, get to know them, and have a first session to see if they will be able to process. Oftentimes problems that seem simple initially are linked to earlier incidents that take much more time to clear.

During this time of preparing and informing the client about trauma and EMDR, some clients will decide they don't want to work with me, and I will assess that some clients are not ready for EMDR. It is important to address any fears clients might have. I do not push clients to begin EMDR until they feel safe. A question I ask clients throughout the course of treatment is "What do you need to feel safe?" For example, the client might say, "I need to know that I won't lose control." In that case I can help clients to set up some techniques for having more control. We can use distancing techniques, containment visualizations, and the installment of resources that might help them. I would reassure them that I will do my best to address their needs as we go along.

INFORMED CONSENT FOR EMDR

It is important to explain to clients that distressing memories may come up, they may have strong emotions, some people have dreams or nightmares after sessions, and other new memories can arise. They may feel quite tired after sessions. Following the processing of a significant traumatic incident, it can be best not to plan to do anything that requires concentration or their full attention.

SET UP SIGNALS FOR "STOP" AND "KEEP GOING"

Before beginning EMDR it is helpful to set up a signal for "stop." Clients can tell you "stop," open their eyes if they are working with eyes closed, or raise their hand. The stop signal gives clients a sense of control. I have found that some clients will signal stop when they are feeling stuck or overwhelmed. But most use the signal when they are at the end of a channel, have completed a wave of processing, and want to take a break and talk. Therapists can also set up a signal for "keep going" so that if therapists stop the BLS before the clients are ready, clients can signal to keep going without being disrupted.

TYPES OF BLS

There are many types of BLS that can be used with EMDR. The types of BLS used depend on the needs and preferences of the client. Therapists can be creative as well as flexible in their use of BLS.

EYE MOVEMENTS

When Shapiro developed EMDR she used eye movements as the BLS to drive the processing. Most of the research on EMDR has been done with eye movements. When therapists direct the eye movements, they can use their fingers (two together palm facing clients 12 to 14 inches from the clients' face) or an object such as a pen, toy, or other object to direct clients' attention. The therapists direct clients to move their eyes across their field of vision to the far right and far left. They find a comfortable speed and rhythm for the clients. Eye movements can be directed horizontally or at a diagonal. It is most important that clients be comfortable with the eye movements and that they not have any physical discomfort. If they wear contact lenses, ask that they remove them before beginning the eye movements. See Shapiro (1995, 2001) for instructions on how to direct eye movements manually. There are machines that have been developed to direct eye movements that allow therapists freedom to sit where it is most comfortable for the clients, so therapists can take notes and do long sets without physical strain.

There are, however, many limitations to using eye movements. Clients with eye problems should not use eye movements, nor should clients with a history of seizures or migraines. I avoid using eye movements with clients who have head injuries. Many people do not like eye movements and resist doing EMDR because it strains their eyes, is perceived as work, or they have a difficult time focusing on their inner experience and moving their eyes back and forth. It is difficult to cry and do eye movements. Because therapists in many cases sit close to the clients as they move their eyes back and forth, many clients become embarrassed and self-conscious, causing them to censor their processing. I have found from my trainings that people have more difficulty with eye movements than with other types of BLS that allow them to close their eyes and focus inside. Another problem with eye movements is that some clients become hypnotized. Clinician-directed eye movements can be very fatiguing for therapists who cannot sustain an even pace for long periods of time. Therapists have injured themselves with repetitive stress from this work. It is difficult for therapists to keep a steady pace and to keep their hands steady as they pass their fingers before their clients' eyes. The drooping fingers can be a distraction for their clients. Some therapists avoid using EMDR with their clients because of their physical limitations. Some clients have difficulty moving their eyes back and forth while attending to their inner experience. Others feel self-conscious about crying or expressing intense feelings in front of therapists who are sitting directly in front of them. When they change to another form of BLS with which clients can close their eyes and perhaps sit further from the therapists, clients can express themselves more freely.

The advantage of therapists directing eye movements manually is that they can alter the speed and direction of the BLS according to the needs of the clients. When clients are stuck or when moving through an abreaction, changing the speed or directions can be helpful (Shapiro, 1995, 2001). Eye movements provide more distance from the memory for clients, enhancing the dual focus of awareness necessary for successful processing. Some clients prefer eye movements to other forms of BLS.

OTHER FORMS OF BLS

For many years therapists have been using alternate forms of BLS effectively with their clients (Shapiro, 1994). Companies have developed devices to create BLS. There are small devices that have headphones and paddles that make tones and vibrations bilaterally. Clients can hold the paddles and hear the tones simultaneously, or use one form of BLS alone. There is even a light bar that has auditory and tactile components. Tapes and CDs have been created for EMDR that produce sounds bilaterally using headphones. Therapists can forgo machines and tap on clients' hands or knees. There are pros and cons to each form of BLS. For some clients, closing their eyes as they listen to bilateral tones or passively having their hands or knees tapped makes it easier for them to process.

Many clients prefer tapping on the knees or hands. I do not suggest this type of BLS to most clients who have sexual abuse histories because it can be too triggering. Male therapists should especially be careful when offering this type of BLS. Tapping on the knees leaves the clients' hands free to move. Knee tapping can be very comforting to clients. It feels soothing and they can feel that their therapist is there with them. I have had clients with early abandonment and neglect who could not tolerate any other form of BLS. One woman who had been abused as a child and had a very sensitive nervous system asked me to tap on her knees very slowly and softly. I have found that with tapping, the attunement to clients is the closest. Clients can go deep into their process and feel their therapists there with them. Clients can close their eyes or open them as they wish. Closed eyes help them to go deeper into the memory and feelings, but can be a problem for clients who go too deep and lose their present awareness. If that happens, the therapists can ask clients to open their eyes.

The machines that clients hold in their hands or tones they can listen to also work well. The machines create more distance, which might be more appropriate, and they offer options of type of sound, speed, and volume. Clients can stand up and move while attached to the devices. This offers a great deal of freedom that can be very useful in sessions.

In my practice I introduce clients to the machines first and let them try them out. I believe this is a way to desensitize them to EMDR and it gives them the idea from the beginning that they are in control, that they have choices. I don't believe any one type of BLS is better than any other. I want clients to choose what is most comfortable for them. I also let them know they can change it at any time: they can adjust the speed and volume. I instruct them with, "Just let me know what works best for you." If clients do not like the machines, I will introduce tapping.

ESTABLISHING A METAPHOR TO USE

One of the important concepts in EMDR is the dual focus of attention. There are times when clients who are processing very emotionally charged traumatic memories lose the dual attention and feel like they are reexperiencing the event. It is helpful to be able to remind them that they are safe in the present. One way to do that is to establish, prior to beginning EMDR, a metaphor that can be used to create distance. Examples of metaphors clients have used are: imagining that they are on a train and they are watching the scenery passing by; imagining that they are on the banks of a river and watching the river flow by; imagining that they are watching clouds pass by in the sky; and imagining that they are safely watching a movie. If in the middle of EMDR sessions clients are abreacting, therapists can remind them of the metaphor: "Remember it's only a movie," or "It's just the river flowing by." These words can be comforting and help create the necessary distance to keep the processing moving along.

TREATMENT ISSUES

A number of treatment issues—from patient and therapist resistance, pacing, session duration, and the use of EMDR as adjunctive therapy—may arise. It is helpful to be aware of these issues to know how to work with them.

RESISTANCE

Resistance to treatment can arise for EMDR therapists as well as clients.

Therapist Resistance and Countertransference

It can be difficult for therapists to integrate EMDR into their practices. After the training, enthusiasm for using EMDR quickly diminishes without the support of other EMDR practitioners and ongoing consultation. Even therapists who have support will put off doing EMDR with clients who could benefit, rationalizing that their clients need more preparation. They fall back into their comfortable ways of working with clients, even if their ways are not the most effective. Many therapists overprepare their clients, using time that could be better spent helping the clients clear traumas. After completing EMDR training I encourage therapists to use it as soon as possible with their clients. Do the necessary preparation, but most clients do not need a lot of resourcing. I can't emphasize enough the importance of ongoing support for using EMDR in your practice. Study groups, consultation groups, workshops, and trainings help therapists to advance their knowledge and skills. Do not do EMDR in isolation. If you live in an area with few other EMDR therapists, do phone consultation with an EMDRIA-approved consultant. With more confidence, clients will feel safer too.

Do your own personal work. Therapists should experience EMDR for themselves and work on their own issues. How will you know what it is like to clear something if you haven't done it yourself? How will you know that EMDR is effective? When you have done your own work, you will trust the EMDR process in an embodied way. You will understand why interpretations by therapists are annoying, interfering with the clients' own innate wisdom that unfolds naturally. You will understand what it means to ride the waves of an abreaction and arrive at an adaptive resolution. If you can do it, then you know your clients can too. Doing your own work also helps with countertransference issues that can arise. If your clients are triggering you in some way, you can use that as a target for your own work.

When therapists have not done their own personal work, they limit their clients. How can you help clients with something if you have the same issue and haven't resolved it? Therapists may envy their clients who are healing things they have not been able to heal in themselves. Doing your own work keeps you from holding your clients back from their healing potential. Therapists have many limiting beliefs about what is possible to heal. In my work as an EMDR trainer and consultant, I often see therapists holding their clients back from full resolution of a trauma because of their own limiting beliefs. When you do your own work, you see for yourself what is possible and go beyond your previous beliefs.

Sometimes therapists resist EMDR by falling back into talk therapy. EMDR sessions can be emotionally exhausting for therapists as well as clients. Therapists may not want to work so hard. Some therapists are afraid of the strong affect some clients express during sessions. The therapists may try to control the expression by shutting down the session too soon, directing the clients to a safe place, or getting into a discussion with the clients. The therapists may feel like perpetrators, causing innocent victims to experience pain and suffering. Remember that when clients feel their feelings during EMDR, they move through them quickly and the feelings are cleared from their system. EMDR is helping, not hurting them. It is like the pain one must endure when an abscess is cleaned, a process that is painful but necessary for healing. After the wound is cleaned, the body feels better and is no longer focused on the pain it went through. In the same way, after an EMDR session clients are more interested in their feelings of wholeness, and not the pain they went through to get there. Unfortunately, many therapists avoid doing EMDR completely because they feel overwhelmed and are afraid of the intensity of the clients' emotions; they don't trust that *they* or their clients can ride the waves to that adaptive resolution. Talking can be easier for therapists, but not as helpful to clients.

It can be difficult for some therapists to *let go of control and trust the process*. Being open to the unknown and not having to understand or interpret the clients' experiences can be difficult. In EMDR processing sessions we take a leap of faith with our clients as they process unbearable trauma memories. Fear of letting go of control is a serious countertransference issue for many therapists. It is vital that therapists manage their own anxieties and counter-transferences in order to adhere to the protocol and not interfere with the clients' processing. *It is essential to successful EMDR that therapists stay out of the way and trust the process*. Therapists should trust their clients' inherent capacity for healing. Along with consultation and getting one's own EMDR therapy, mindfulness meditation is helpful practice for learning to be in the moment and trusting the unfolding of mind-body experience without interference.

Therapists can also experience projective identification, another counter-transference issue common with trauma survivors (Korn, Rozelle, & Weir, 2004; Parnell, 1999). When this arises in the treatment, the therapist may experience the burdens, feelings, and negative self-beliefs of the client (Korn et al., 2004). Sometimes therapists may feel the hopeless, helpless, incompe-tent, or fearful feelings the clients are not processing. It can be helpful for therapists to guide the clients in feeling their own feelings and then targeting the associated memories.

When clients loop during processing, therapists can feel overwhelmed and at a loss to find interweaves. The therapists' anxiety and feelings of incompetence can interfere with their access to interweave solutions that can get clients back on track. Instead of trying different interweave strategies until one works, therapists take the clients to a safe place and essentially stop the session, thereby leaving the clients with a trauma that has been put on hold and not resolved.

Do not do EMDR trauma treatment in isolation. The work is incredibly challenging. Individual and group consultations are important. Go to train-ings, workshops, and conferences. Start or join a study group.

Client Resistance

In addition to therapist resistance, there may also be client resistance to doing EMDR. Many clients are ambivalent about EMDR; they know it's good for them, but it's painful, so they avoid it. Some clients will come into a session in which EMDR was planned and stall by talking, diverting the therapists from focusing them for their session. Other clients will come in late so there isn't enough time to do EMDR, or they cancel the session. I have had clients fill much of the time talking, and then be angry with me when I tell them that our time is almost over and we will not have time to do EMDR.

I have learned that many clients expect me to interrupt them when they are talking and ask them directly if they want to do EMDR. With many clients who are talking a great deal, I will gently interrupt them and ask them if they would like to do EMDR this session. We will then begin to focus on developing a target for the day's session. With some clients I will begin the session by handing them the headphones and pulsers so that they are set up to begin the session.

Being direct with clients can be difficult for psychodynamically oriented psychotherapists, and easier for therapists with a cognitive-behavioral orientation. It is important to manage the sessions by helping clients stick to the agreed-upon therapeutic contract and goals for treatment. It can be helpful to explore the resistance with clients. What is the resistance about? Is there a way the therapists can help the clients feel safer? What do they need from the therapists? What do they want from treatment? The resistances may even be targeted. What are the blocking beliefs? Secondary gains?

Sometimes clients and therapists collude to avoid doing EMDR. Clients are afraid of opening things up and therapists are unsure of their own skills, afraid of the intensity, or have other countertransference issues. Consultation can be helpful in looking at these issues and working them through.

There can be secondary gain issues for both therapists and clients for resisting doing EMDR. Some clients will avoid doing EMDR because they are afraid of getting better too fast. Who will I be without these symptoms? Some therapists may also be concerned that their clients will get better too fast and they will lose their practice.

PACING OF TREATMENT

Depending on the needs of the client, EMDR can be used every session or it can be interspersed among integrative talk sessions or with other methods. I have seen clients on many different schedules according to their needs. There are some clients who do well with 90-minute or longer sessions on a weekly basis. They spend the first part of the session talking and checking in, reevaluating the work from the week before, and then are ready to focus and reprocess a new memory. For some clients this pace would be too intense for them; they need a single 50-minute session to talk and integrate the information from the EMDR processing session. Some clients with good ego strength can tolerate several EMDR sessions in a week, working intensively in a short period of time on an area of difficulty.

The pacing of treatment should be flexible, adapting to the changing needs of the clients as much as possible. Since the majority of the change for clients with PTSD occurs within the first few sessions, it can be helpful to work consistently with them for the first few weeks to help them over the hump. After that, though symptoms may remain, they usually are not as debilitating and the pacing of treatment can slacken. For example, a client I was working with had severe delayed-onset PTSD after an incident triggered symptoms associated with the memory of her sister's murder. We worked intensively over several weeks with EMDR double sessions targeting the early trauma. During this time she experienced relief from her worst symptoms, but because there were also childhood traumas, she needed further sessions to fully treat the PTSD. She did not require weekly sessions for this work the way she did in the beginning of treatment. A more relaxed pace was sufficient.

Some clients cannot tolerate EMDR processing on a weekly basis. They need more time to integrate the information between sessions. For some they like to come in every other week for EMDR, while others prefer to intersperse talk-therapy sessions with their EMDR sessions. One woman who had an extensive abuse history, I saw twice a week for 2 years—one 90-minute EMDR session followed 3 days later with a 50-minute integrative session. She later decreased the frequency of her sessions to a weekly 90-minute session and then weekly, 50-minute sessions with occasional 90-minute EMDR sessions. Finally, she decreased to one 50-minute session every other week until she ended treatment. Some people have worked every session with 90-minute EMDR sessions, whereas others will do intensive EMDR work for several weeks and then wish several shorter integrative sessions.

In EMDR clients have to learn to process their memories at a pace they can tolerate so they will not feel overwhelmed and revictimized. Therapists need to check to see how the clients are functioning between sessions. This can be a problem for some sexual abuse clients who have difficulty asking for what they want or are not in touch with themselves enough to recognize their needs. Therapists should pay attention to the pacing since some clients, believing EMDR will immediately erase years of abuse, may try to push their therapists into doing EMDR processing every session. They may come into treatment wanting an EMDR session every week or twice a week. For many sexual abuse clients, this is contraindicated.

After intensive EMDR processing of an abuse memory, clients may want to spend several sessions talking about and integrating the information that came up during the EMDR work. It is helpful at the end of an EMDR session to discuss with the clients what they feel they need in scheduling the following session. For some clients, even if they think they want to do another

90-minute EMDR session the following week, they may change their minds when they return and assess how they feel, with the therapists' guidance. Postponement of EMDR processing should not necessarily be interpreted as a resistance. The work can be *so* intensive that some clients need to spread the EMDR sessions out more so that they can better integrate the information that came up and feel grounded and stabilized enough before further processing.

Art, sand tray work, somatic experiencing, guided imagery, and EMDR resource work can be a useful ways to help with the pacing of treatment. Art and sand tray work can facilitate the integration of the information that has come up and give clients more of a sense of control of their process. EMDR resource work can help the clients connect to adaptive memory networks that can provide a stabilizing effect.

SINGLE OR DOUBLE SESSIONS

In my practice I usually schedule 90 or 100 minutes for the first EMDR session to determine how much time clients need. After that first session clients and I decide how much time we should schedule for future sessions. Shapiro (1995, 2001) recommends that therapists schedule 90 minutes for EMDR processing sessions, but some clients process very quickly and do not need 90 minutes. Some with small "t" traumas are able to reprocess a memory in 50 minutes without difficulty. Even clients with major traumas don't always need or want 90 minutes because it is too much time for them. There are clients who cannot afford double sessions, or their insurance does not cover it, or their HMO does not allow it. If you are limited to 50 minutes, I recommend the following: Do your preliminary resource installation in a separate session from the processing session. Identify the memory that you plan to work on. Then, in the EMDR processing session, make good use of your time. Focus quickly on the target and begin reprocessing soon. Don't spend too much time talking. A lot can be done in 50 minutes if you focus quickly on the target and begin to reprocess. You may need to use interweaves more proactively than you would if you had more time. Also you will need to focus the work, returning to the target more frequently. Watch the time. Toward the end of the session use interweaves to help close. If you focus, you can complete a piece of work in 50 minutes. Many clients do very well with 50-minute sessions. These tend to be clients with small "t" traumas that are linked to symptoms and behaviors.

Some therapists will do the assessment phase of EMDR in one session, setting up the target memory, then do the EMDR processing in the next session. I don't usually recommend doing this unless you will be seeing the client soon, because this can activate the clients' memory network, causin̖ them to feel distressed until you do EMDR.

Some clients need 90 minutes for sessions in the first part of treatment, but as their major traumas have been resolved, they can suffice with 50 minutes. Sometimes a session and a half, or 75 minutes, works well. All of this depends on the flexibility of the therapists' schedules. For some clients with major traumas, I will insist on double sessions because I do not believe they can safely process the traumas without sufficient time. If their budget is an issue, a double session every other week may be a compromise, with the understanding that they will call if they need help between sessions.

ADJUNCTIVE EMDR

There are situations when the EMDR therapist is asked to work adjunctively along with clients' primary therapists. It may be that the clients have sought out EMDR, or the referral may come from primary therapists. I have a number of recommendations for adjunctive work.

I recommend first of all that the primary therapists get trained in EMDR and do the work themselves. It is always more complicated when more than one therapist is involved in clients' treatments. Because splitting is often a problem for clients with complex trauma, clients may idealize one therapist and find fault with others. In some cases it is better if clients are transferred to EMDR therapists. Sometimes clients take a break from working with their primary therapists and do EMDR for a period of time with other therapists. They can return to the original therapists later.

In my experience adjunctive EMDR works best when the trauma is specific and the boundaries of the relationships are clear. For example, a client who is in long-term therapy has had a car accident and needs EMDR to get over the fear of driving. The EMDR therapist works specifically on the accident.

There needs to be clear communication between primary therapists and the EMDR therapists. A treatment plan should be agreed upon by all involved. A clear understanding should be established about what role each therapist will play in the clients' treatment. It is important to make clear from the beginning that the EMDR therapists are not the primary therapists. Because EMDR is so effective, clients often shift their loyalty and attachment to the EMDR therapists. It can be helpful to set up a specific number of sessions and to reevaluate after they have been completed.

Even though the primary therapists have taken a history, it is still important for the EMDR therapists to do so, and to evaluate clients for appropriateness for EMDR. Confer with the primary therapists before accepting clients if at all possible. Otherwise, meet with the clients and explain that you will need to consult with their primary therapists before proceeding further. You want to rule out borderline personality disorder with the therapists. You also want to assess what the primary therapists' expectations are. You may need to educate the therapists about what EMDR is and how it works, and answer any questions. The primary therapists may be trying to get rid of difficult clients. In addition to evaluating whether you can work with the clients, you want to ask yourself whether you can you work with their primary therapists. It is helpful if you already know the primary therapists. If you don't, you may want to interview the therapists to see whether you are compatible. There are therapists who may not share your theoretical orientation and may not have adequate ethical standards. You have to be able to work as a team.

I have found it helpful in some cases to meet with the primary therapists and the clients together. I have even done some EMDR sessions with the primary therapists in the room. Though expensive for the clients, this can reduce the possibility of splitting, provide education for the primary therapists about EMDR, and provide good support for the clients.

Adjunctive EMDR works best if:

- the work is time limited, focused on a specific trauma or symptom;
- the primary therapist and EMDR therapist know each other and work well together;
- the client has good ego strength;
- the client is not borderline or attachment disordered.

Do not do adjunctive work if:

- the client is unstable, borderline, in crisis, or has complex PTSD;
- the client requires long-term EMDR work;
- you don't have a good working relationship with the primary therapist;
- you don't have a clear therapeutic contract with the client and therapist.

4

TOOLS AND TECHNIQUES FOR EGO STRENGTHENING

IT IS IMPORTANT to sufficiently prepare clients for EMDR trauma processing. You should not begin EMDR trauma processing until the clients are sufficiently stabilized and have affect management skills. The preparation time required varies widely between clients. Many clients don't require a great deal of preparation. They have good ego strength, are functioning well, have good relationships and supports, have stable work, but have experienced some specific traumas. Even clients who are exhibiting strong symptoms of PTSD, such as flashbacks, nightmares, anxiety, avoidance, and intrusive thoughts and images, can begin EMDR after basic resource installation if the symptoms from which they are suffering are a result of the trauma itself (Korn, Rozelle, & Weir, 2004; Lipke, 2005). However, for clients with fragile egos, especially those with early attachment disorders and traumatic childhood histories, more preparation is needed. If the symptoms are a result of an underlying personality disorder, use more caution.

Many clients require help with ego strengthening and affect regulation in the beginning phase of EMDR, as well as during the middle phase of treatment, when EMDR processing of traumatic memories is occurring. Ego strengthening can be likened to the development of a container that will be strong enough to hold the emotional turmoil. It is also like increasing the capacity of a conduit to carry a strong electric current; if the conduit is not strong enough, there will be resistance that will impede the flow of energy. Because of the intensity of abreactions that EMDR frequently evokes during the processing of traumatic memories, particularly childhood abuse memories, it is essential that clients develop sufficient ego resources prior to EMDR processing. Clients who have been abused require ego strengthening so that op a greater capacity for self-soothing, clarity of thinking, ...u the ability to experience and process strong emotions.

Resource development refers to strategies therapists employ to support the clients' development of positive resources. Hypnotherapists have worked with resource development for years and have developed many effective techniques (Phillips & Frederick, 1995). Milton Erickson believed that the unconscious minds of individuals contained all the resources needed to resolve their problems and that it was the therapists' task to help the patients activate their own natural inner resources (Erickson & Rossi, 1976).

The development of client resources can take weeks, months, or years, depending upon the needs of the clients. For some chronically depressed clients who were severely neglected as children, resource development and ego strengthening can be the focus of their therapy and the trauma processing a less important aspect (Wildwind, 1993).

IDENTIFICATION, DEVELOPMENT, AND INSTALLATION OF INNER AND OUTER RESOURCES

Some clients lack the necessary internal resources for successful EMDR processing of traumatic memories. This is especially true for those with histories of abuse or neglect or both. Some have difficulty connecting with positive inner resources. For others, the positive resolution of the image at the end of a session does not hold and they experience distress later during the week, with their SUDS elevating. Their stored negative life experiences overwhelm their internal reservoir of positive experiences, self-esteem, and resilience. They have difficulty with emotional self-regulation. Oftentimes these clients, instead of processing their memories to an adaptive resolution, get caught in a gigantic negative memory network from which they cannot extricate themselves. Unable to connect to positive internal resources, these clients become stuck. In particular, clients who were neglected in early childhood do not naturally access nurturing or protective ego states or memories. Because of these difficulties, I spend quite a long time developing and installing positive internal resources in the preparation phase of EMDR with clients with severe early childhood histories of abuse and neglect. Spending more time in the development and installation of inner resources increases the success rate with traumatized clients and decreases the chances of retraumatizing them.

EMDR can be used to strengthen positive internal resources. We have found that eye movements or other bilateral stimulation increases or further develops positive feelings or experiences (Leeds & Shapiro, 2000; Parnell,

1999; Shapiro, 1995, 2001). As mentioned earlier, people who subjected to early trauma or neglect experience what Schore (1   ͜) calls synaptic pruning, which makes them more vulnerable to PTSD, overly attentive to adverse stimuli, and hypersensitive to their environments. They tend to interpret experiences negatively. These people also don't notice benign everyday experiences; rather, they scan the environment for what might be dangerous (McFarlane, Weber, & Clark, 1993).

It may be that by developing and installing positive resources with EMDR, we are helping to make changes in the brain's circuitry. It is as if the adult who was traumatized as a child has a brain where the circuitry is "lit up" around negative life experiences; positive, or benign, life experiences are stored in the dark. What we may be doing with the development and installation of positive resources is lighting the dark part of the brain and adding new pathways between memory networks that heretofore were separate.

I have collected a number of suggestions for resource development and installation (RDI) from colleagues and from the literature, many of which have been borrowed from guided imagery. Use your clinical judgment and attunement with your clients to determine which ones might be most helpful. The second edition of *Eye Movement Desensitization and Reprocessing* (Shapiro, 2001) includes guidelines and procedures for EMDR RDI.

I suggest that therapists spend time in the beginning phase of treatment identifying the needed resources with the clients. These resources can then be installed during the sessions. By "installation" of resources I mean the use of BLS paired with the positive resource to increase and strengthen it. In theory, EMDR clears what is dysfunctional from the system, allowing what is adaptive to come to the foreground in awareness. We have also found that when BLS is used with memories or experiences that were positive, neutral, or adaptive, they get stronger. Therefore, if you want to increase your clients' positive resources, you have them bring up memories that were positive or adaptive, evoke the image, body sensations, emotions, sounds, and other sensory associations, and then add the BLS for a *short* set. Shapiro (2001) recommends 6 to 12 passes of right-left alternating BLS. It is important to use short sets because oftentimes clients will flip to the polar opposite and associate to negative memories. Don't get hung up on the number of passes. Watch your clients. If they want to go longer, that is fine. If it was too long, do shorter sets. Remember to ask the clients what is working for them. It is best to use a slower speed of BLS for installation. After one set of BLS you ask, "What do you get now?" If it is strengthened, do another short set. You may continue with a few sets if it remains positive. Some clients prefer longer sets of BLS to install resources. This is fine as long as the resource remains positive. If the resource should flip to the negative or become contaminated in some way (e.g., a menacing figure appears in the safe place), you may ask the clients to choose other resources to install, or do other ego-strengthening work. Clients can do their own BLS to install resources. They can move their eyes back and forth, tap on their own knees, or do the butterfly hug (Artigas, Jarero, Mauer, Lopez-Cano, & Alcal, 2000; Boel, 1999). For the butterfly hug clients place their hands on opposite shoulders or crossed on the chest, tapping alternately. The butterfly hug is often used in groups to install resources or for self-soothing outside of sessions. Shapiro (2001) advises screening clients for DID prior to using RDI because it can be destabilizing for them.

The following are suggestions for the development and installation of resources. I remind you that it is my view that the use of EMDR is an art—not a science or a technique—and it is important that therapists attune to clients and the needs of the moment. I offer a number of suggestions that may stir your imagination and creativity and help you to find a way of working with clients who are complex. Please feel free to improvise on the theme.

ESTABLISHING A SAFE PLACE

Part of the client preparation before beginning the reprocessing work is to help clients establish a place wherein the clients can go in their imagination and feel totally safe and protected. Therapists may begin sessions with the safe place, use it as a place the clients can go to during difficult processing to take a break and regain a sense of control, and use it to close down incomplete sessions. For clients who need to develop more of a sense of self-constancy, each EMDR session can begin and end with the safe place. This increases the sense that they are the same person in different situations and can hold on to the safe place at home between sessions. Clients can also practice going to their safe place between sessions as a means of self-soothing, and can even use it before going to sleep at night. The safe place can also be a place where the clients' allies gather to add extra safety and support. (This will be described in more detail later in this chapter.)

The clients' ability to establish a safe place is an important part of the assessment of the clients' readiness to begin EMDR processing. I generally will not proceed with EMDR if clients cannot find a safe place or other calming imagery. Some clients, for unknown reasons, do not process like other people (I suspect some of them have neurological differences). The accelerated information processing system does not activate with BLS. As I mentioned earlier, sometimes when clients cannot establish a safe place it is a sign of a central nervous system imbalance that requires medication or some other means such as EMPowerplus—a nutritional protocol used for the treatment of bipolar disorder and other mental illnesses—to create a balance before EMDR can be effective.

For example, two clients came to see me around the same time, both presenting with signs of depression. One woman was very distraught, crying through most of the first two sessions. She felt stuck in every area of her life. Through the history taking, I could find no large traumas or serious problems that explained her distress. The other woman was also depressed, but her depression was linked to the end of a romantic relationship. Unlike the first woman, this woman had some serious traumas in her background. When I attempted to install a safe place with the first client, she could imagine her art studio where she had loved to paint, but could feel no safety or calm. It was as if there were a glass wall between the image and her feelings. I tried to enhance the sensory experience and positive memory network associated with it and also tried other images, to no avail. The second woman, however, was a different story. Though more traumatized than the first woman, she was able to imagine a place she loved at the beach and feel a sense of calm and peace with the imagery.

As a result of the safe place exercise, I was hesitant to begin EMDR with the first woman, and comfortable with the second. After informing the first woman that I did not believe EMDR would work for her, we tried it on a small trauma. Just as I had thought, she was unable to process at all. Because of the depression, she could not connect to affect, either positive or negative. We closed the session and debriefed. I encouraged her to see a psychiatrist and try antidepressants. When she returned a few weeks later, she told me she was feeling much better. She was able to install the safe place successfully and to process with EMDR. The second client, who was also depressed but was able to install safe place, processed her traumas effectively with EMDR.

For clients who cannot establish a safe place or who need extra resources, there are other guided visualizations, which I will describe in this chapter.

In order to develop the safe place the therapists and clients work together. The therapists adapt the safe place instructions for each client's unique needs. What is important to achieve? Do you want to create a place of peace and calm where the clients can turn off the outside world and the triggers to emotional upset? Do you want this to be a place where clients can access their inner resources? The safe place can be a known place or it can be an imaginary place. Many people choose a place in nature such as a beautiful beach or mountain lake. It can also be symbolic, such as in the arms of a large mother bear. Art can be used to create or enhance the safe place. Clients can draw the safe place and then install it with BLS. For clients who have a difficult time finding a safe place, they can draw a "safe island" on a large piece of butcher paper. Standing in the center of the paper, they draw a large circle around themselves. They are instructed that they can put anything and anyone they want on the island. The island they create can then be installed with short sets of BLS. In developing the safe place the therapists and clients together create a place of self-nourishment, safety, and comfort where the clients can be creative; this is especially useful for depressed clients. For very fearful and traumatized clients, I suggest that they make the safe place extra safe by putting up a protective barrier around it made of anything they wish. Some have chosen to put up a force field as in *Star Trek*, while others have brought in fierce protectors to guard it.

It is best to avoid a place from childhood that might be associated with pain from the past. The therapeutic relationship and therapist's office can also be used as the safe place, if no other place can be found. For those clients who find the word *safe* too triggering, substitute the words *comfortable or peaceful* instead.

By elaborating the safe place with drawings or sculpture, clients form a more stable connection with it. They can also write about it in their journals. One client had a difficult time finding a safe place because the perpetrator of her trauma was a very powerful man. Together we explored what she needed to feel safe, and she came up with the image of a circle of giant redwood trees with deep roots and branches that went high into the sky. To make this place even more secure, she imagined a powerful force field around the circle of trees with fierce protector deities outside.

Before beginning the safe place experience, therapists can help clients enter a state of general relaxation by using a variety of known relaxation exercises. Or clients may have their own ways to relax. Some people can contact an image and feeling of a safe place easily, requiring little preparation. This is individual and the time necessary for relaxation depends on the emotional state and body state of the clients.

It is helpful for the therapists to activate the senses associated with the safe place imagery. What do you see? What do you smell? What do you hear? What do you feel? I'll ask the clients, "Do you have a good sense of it now?" Or "Let me know when you can really feel your safe place." When the clients signal me yes, I begin a short sequence of BLS, maybe 6 to 12, to install it. I might ask, "Is it getting stronger?" If it is I might go a little longer with the BLS. I watch my clients for signs of deepening relaxation or increased agitation. If I see their breathing increase, I will stop immediately and ask them what is happening. Though for many clients the BLS works quite well to install the feeling and imagery more securely, for some clients the BLS opens up processing of traumatic material. Clients who have had many experiences of being unsafe may begin to associate to those experiences when the word *safe* is used. If this happens, stop the BLS and explore with the clients what they are experiencing. The therapists and clients may need to develop another safe place using imagery only. They may also want to use the word *comfortable* or *peaceful* instead. I have had some clients who flip to the negative so quickly, I can never use BLS to install the safe place. With them, I use imagery only. As with everything in EMDR therapy, stay closely attuned to your clients and accommodate what you do according to their needs.

Shapiro (2001) recommends the use of a cue word with the installation of the safe place. For example if the clients' safe place is a beach, they can imagine the beach and say the word *beach* as they receive the BLS to install it. Then between sessions they can practice using the safe place imagery and cue word during times of anxiety or distress. For instance, if they have to make a speech and are anxious, they can say the word *beach* and imagine their safe place.

The following is a method of guiding clients into a relaxed state.

GUIDED RELAXATION TO SAFE PLACE

Have clients sit in a comfortable relaxed manner with the legs uncrossed and the hands gently resting on their knees. Let them know that you will be doing a guided imagery and that when the image and feeling are strong, you will do some BLS to make them even stronger. Ask them to close their eyes and take a deep breath. Tell them that they are going to go down a flight of 10 steps, and at the bottom they will find a place where they feel totally safe and protected. With each step they take down, they will feel more and more relaxed, letting go of all tension. The therapist counts down one step at a time, with suggestions about the clients getting more relaxed, tension melting away, and so on. When the clients get to the bottom of the stairway, you instruct them to go and find their safe place, a place where they feel totally safe and protected. It can be a real or imagined place. You can help them to increase the intensity of the experience, making it more vivid for them by asking them to notice what they see, hear, feel, smell, and taste. You want to be sure that they are feeling totally relaxed, safe, and comfortable in this place. For some clients, you might suggest that they secure this place even more by imagining a protective circle or shield around them that keeps out anything that is harmful.

Safe Place Script

This is a script for helping clients develop a safe place after becoming relaxed:

With your eyes closed, imagine yourself now in a beautiful, peaceful place. . . . This might be somewhere you've visited before or somewhere you just make up in your imagination. . . . Just let the image of the place come to you. . . . It really doesn't matter what kind of place you imagine as long as it's beautiful, quiet, peaceful, and serene. . . . Let this be a special inner place for you . . . somewhere where you feel particularly at ease . . . a place where you feel safe and secure . . . at one with your surroundings. . . . Maybe you've had a place like this in your life . . . somewhere to go to be quiet and reflective . . . somewhere special and healing for you . . . or it could be a place you've seen in a movie . . . read about . . . or just dreamed of. . . . It could be a real place . . . a place you know . . . or an imaginary place. . . .

Let yourself explore and experience whatever quiet imaginary place you go to as if you were there now. . . . Notice what you see there . . . what sounds you hear . . . even the smells and aroma you sense there. . . . Notice especially what it feels like to be there, and immerse yourself in the beauty, the feelings of peacefulness . . . of being secure and at ease. . . .

As you explore this special inner place, find a spot that feels particularly good to be in . . . a spot where you feel especially calm . . . centered . . . safe and at ease. . . . Let yourself become comfortable in this spot. . . . Let this be your safe place. . . . Let this be your power spot . . . a place in which you draw from the deep sense of peacefulness and safety you feel here. . . . Now just let yourself experience what it is like to be in this place. . . . (Wait a few moments before beginning again. Continue to keep your voice lower than usual because the client is in a deeper relaxed state.)

Keeping your eyes closed . . . how would you describe this place?

At this point begin BLS. Depending on the response, ask a few questions to help strengthen the imagery. The therapist can use short sets of BLS after the client responds to questions.

What season of the year is it? . . . What time of day is it? . . . What aromas do you smell? . . . What sounds do you hear? . . . How are you dressed? . . . How are you experiencing your safe place? . . .

As you relax and are aware of how it feels to be here . . . tell yourself you can return anytime you wish. . . . This is your special place . . . a place where safety, rest, and peace are always available at your own choosing. . . . If you like you can choose a cue word that will help you to remember your safe place. *(Therapist adds more BLS as client says cue word to him- or herself.)* In the future you can say this word to bring back the feelings of your special place.

When you are ready, slowly open your eyes and come back to the room. . . .*

Suggestions For Clients Who Cannot Develop A Safe Place

Some clients who have been severely traumatized cannot seem to be able to develop a safe place. Attempts are met with negative or scary imagery and more feelings of unsafety. The main purpose of the safe place is to help clients find a means of calming the nervous system, a self-control technique. There are many other ways to accomplish this same purpose.

In cases where clients cannot develop a safe place, I offer suggestions.

• Because the word *safe* can be triggering for clients who have been severely traumatized, eliciting memories of not being safe, the words *comfortable, peaceful,* or *relaxing* can be substituted for the word *safe.*

• Have clients bring in a quality that will make the safe place safe. In some cases the safe place is not strong enough for the clients to feel safe. Therapists can ask the clients, "What do you need for this place to be safe?" In some cases the clients may need to bring in a resource quality to make it safer. The therapists can ask, "What quality would you need to make this place safe for you?"

Client: I would need to feel strong and powerful.

Therapist: Can you think of a time when you felt strong and powerful?

Client: Yes. When I was running regularly.

Therapist: Can you bring up a memory of running when you felt strong and powerful?

Client: Yes.

---

*Adapted from Bresler (1986) and Rossman (1987).

Therapist: Focus on that. >>>>>> (6–12 saccades)

Therapist: What's happening now?

Client: I feel strong, I feel good.

Therapist: Can you bring that feeling into your safe place?

Client: Yes.

Therapist: Go with that. >>>>> (6–12 saccades)

Therapist: How is it now when you think of your safe place?

Client: It feels good, much better.

• Suggest to clients that they bring a safe object or person into the session. This object can be something like a teddy bear, blanket, or an object associated with a safe person in their lives. One young girl I worked with brought her dog to the session. The dog's presence helped her feel much safer. When she wanted to take a break from the processing she would put her arms around the dog. I have had other clients bring their partners, parents, or friends to sessions. Some couples therapists work with one partner supporting or witnessing the other work in session.

• Clients can bring up an image or metaphor of stability, resilience, and triumph (Korn, 1997). For example, clients who have been feeling weak might bring up an image of a large, powerful mountain. Ask the clients to notice what they feel in their body when they bring up that image. "I feel strong, powerful, grounded." The therapists reinforce the image and feeling by adding BLS. If the feeling of stability, resilience, and triumph increases, add the positive cognition "I am strong" with the feeling and image. The image can be anchored by asking the clients to press their palm with their fingers and with BLS to further install it. At a future time the clients can invoke this feeling of strength by pressing on the palm and bringing to mind the image of the mountain.

• Install positive memories or conflict-free images. Clients can bring up memories of doing something that they find comforting or relaxing that bring them pleasure. Images can include things like memories of baking bread, eating lunch with a friend, cuddling with their children or grandchildren, or playing a musical instrument. The idea is to find images of doing things that will help clients relax their nervous systems. Many people who have experienced early traumatization develop nervous systems that are attuned only to potentially dangerous stimuli, thus totally missing, or not registering in their memories, ordinary, nontraumatic daily life experiences that would counter their perception of the world as an entirely dangerous place (McFarlane, Weber, & Clark, 1993). For that reason, the development of positive images and mindfulness practices serve to develop new neuropathways in the brain and serve as important ego-strengthening methods.

Phillips (1997a, 1997b) suggests that clients install positive, conflict-free images (see Appendix 1, page 334 for the Protocol for Development of the Positive, Conflict-Free Image). Positive conflict-free images derive from experiences in the clients' everyday lives when they felt present and whole. They can be real experiences from the clients' daily lives, like gardening, stroking a cat, or walking in a park. The image is strengthened by asking for sensory details and then installed by using BLS. It is important to emphasize the somatic component of the imagery. You want clients to feel free of anxiety and fear. The conflict-free images help to create a sense of wholeness and increased feeling for the clients that their lives are not *all* terrible. It helps with self-soothing and affect regulation.

Case Example of Using Positive-Memories Images and Conflict-Free Images

Ruben came to see me because he was suffering from chronic PTSD. As he told me his history, one of the worst cases of noncombat adult PTSD I had ever heard emerged. Ruben had been a successful businessman with a wife and three young children when a string of terrible traumatic events unfolded. The first took place on a business trip to South America. While flying in a small jet, the plane began to go out of control, spinning as it sped toward the ground. Everyone in the plane screamed, certain they were going to die. Miraculously, the pilot managed to regain control before crashing, pulling up and regaining altitude. Because he did not speak the language of any of the other passengers, Ruben was not able to debrief the experience. He pushed it out of his mind and went on with his trip. Not long after he got home, another disaster struck. An enormous fire burned his house, and all the houses in his neighborhood, to the ground. Not long after that, there was a major earthquake that destroyed his business. By the time I saw Ruben, his nervous system was so shot he could no longer work. He was easily triggered, exhausted, numb, and fearful. He had lost the sense of pleasure in life. Before these events, he had had no significant traumas. Despite the PTSD, he had good ego strength. He had an uneventful childhood, close relationships with his parents and friends, success at school and work. He had been physically active and loved to play the piano. From the beginning an easy rapport developed between us.

When we tried to find a safe place I soon recognized that it was impossible. There was simply no place he could imagine that felt safe. I began to inquire about activities he enjoyed, things that helped him feel calm, whole, and good. It was a struggle. So many things we came up with reminded him of the traumas, or were things he could no longer do or enjoy since the traumas, or he just could not *feel* anything anymore. Finally, we came up with three positive images that we installed. I wanted to have several because I was concerned that sometimes one or the other might not work or be appropriate. I wanted him to have as much control as possible before beginning EMDR. There were also distancing techniques I used to enhance his sense of control. (I will describe these later.)

The first image we found was of hitting golf balls on a driving range. It was an activity he could imagine himself doing that helped him feel at ease. It was also something he could still find some enjoyment doing. As he imagined hitting balls, I asked him what he felt in his body and to notice the smells, sounds, and sensations. I asked him to let me know when he had it activated, and then I tapped on his knees.

The next image we installed was playing the piano. When he imagined himself playing the piano he felt calm and relaxed. We had difficulty finding a third image. Because it is difficult to feel both love and fear, I asked him what he felt when he thought about his children. He told me that he felt the love for them in his heart. I asked him to bring his attention into the region of his heart and to think about his children in a way that made him happy and at ease. He immediately began to smile, and he seemed to relax. I then tapped on his knees to install the image and feeling.

During the months of work together we would begin and end sessions with one of the images he had installed. Whenever he felt overwhelmed and wanted to take a break, he would bring up one of the images so that he could rest and regain a sense of control. He was also able to use them between sessions when he felt triggered.

The following are examples of images clients have used: the memory of baking bread, hiking in the mountains, sitting at a sushi bar, riding a horse, having a meal with a friend, playing with a kitten or puppy, watching baby ducks on a lake, walking among spring flowers, playing a musical instrument. Installing positive memories and images can be helpful for clients who are chronically depressed or have histories of serious abuse or neglect. As I mentioned earlier, many of these clients do not attend to positive or neutral stimuli. They have developed a kind of tunnel vision. Installing conflict-free images can help these clients begin to broaden their perceptual field, adding in new neuronetworks.

I have found that installing safe places (or other images), plus nurturing and protector figures, in the beginning of treatment helps to create a stronger container for the trauma-processing work. I believe that because we have stimulated the memory networks where these resources reside, clients have easier access to them, and can even sense them in the background when they begin the trauma-processing work. For some clients we only spend a few minutes identifying and installing these resources during one session. If they are able to easily locate and install them, we may only need to do this one time. That way I know they have the ego strength and resources readily available if an interweave is necessary. It's my safety net for doing trauma work. For many clients we may never refer to their resources again because the processing moves along without the use of interweaves. For other clients, because these resources have been installed, they come up in their processing linking up as interweaves the clients do themselves. For example, a client might pull in his older brother to protect his child self. For more fragile clients, I will install safe places and nurturers and protectors before we begin each EMDR trauma-processing session. They need the reminder of the resources each time to strengthen the safety net and to make the resources more available to them.

NURTURING FIGURES

I have found it to be helpful for clients to identify nurturing figures to use as inner resources before beginning EMDR processing. As with the safe place or conflict-free image, the clients' ability to find and install a nurturing figure or figures is an important part of the assessment for EMDR readiness. These inner allies can include real or imaginary figures from the present or past, inner guides, and animals. As you may recall, during the history taking, therapists look for those people from the clients' past who were loving, safe, nurturing figures for them. There may be a parent or stepparent, sibling, grandparent, nanny, aunt or uncle, teacher, coach, doctor, counselor, friend's parent, or clergy person who was an important source of caring for the clients. Occasionally the clients will want to install the therapists as nurturer. In those cases I try to have additional resources as backups to reduce the dependency on me. There may be people from clients' current life who are important resources for them, such as a current spouse, friends, or lover. They can even be figures from movies, TV, books, historical figures, or people from popular culture. Spiritual figures can also be used as nurturers, for example, Quan Yin, Tara, Mary, Jesus, a Native American elder, or an angel. The same figure can be used as a nurturing figure, protector figure, and wise figure.

The adult self can be used as a nurturer too. Schmidt (2002) recommended installing a nurturing adult self for clients who have unmet developmental needs. She has created a protocol for enhancing this ego state in which clients connect with their innate qualities such as empathy, compassion, confidence, courage, and strength. Schmidt asks them if they have a mental picture of that part of themselves.

For clients who have always taken care of themselves, and have never had anyone take care of them, I try to find another nurturing figure in addition to their adult self. It can be anyone or anything that has nurturing qualities.

For some clients animals can be valuable resources. These can be pets from the clients' present or past (e.g., a protective dog) or animals for which the clients have a special affinity. Many clients have used their past or present dogs or cats as nurturers. Sometimes an affectionate dog was the only nurturer the client had as a child. One woman chose a cow as her nurturer. She remembered putting her arms around this gentle animal during times of loneliness she felt as a child growing up on a farm. This animal had provided comfort to her that she could still feel when she thought about it.

Sometimes people have a special connection with an animal (for example, wolf, bear, lion, panther, coyote, eagle) that may carry the numen of a power animal (Harner, 1980). Some have used mythological creatures such as dragons as resources. An example of how these animal resources used in EMDR can overlap with Native American traditions was in the case of a young man I worked with on a traumatic memory from childhood. During the preparation phase he told me he had always felt a spiritual connection with hawks. He said that he saw them all the time and that they felt both nurturing and protective to him. Though he was of European descent, he had always felt an affinity with Native American spirituality. In our first session as he closed his eyes to bring up the image of the hawk to install, I saw a hawk fly in front of the window. During the session as he processed the childhood trauma, he told me he felt the presence of the hawk. To my astonishment, when we ended the session, a hawk again flew by the window.

For clients with histories of abuse or neglect, I will try to get more than one figure. For clients working on memories from childhood I will ask them to find a nurturing figure or figures who can nurture the child self.

After finding the figure, I ask clients to close their eyes and bring up the image as strongly as they can. "See your grandmother in her nurturing aspect. When you can feel her nurturing you, let me know." At that point I will begin the BLS. I might ask the clients to tell me when it feels complete, when they feel it more deeply. If there is more than one resource I will usually install one at a time. You might suggest that the clients imagine themselves being held by their nurturing figure. As they hold that image and feel themselves being held, add BLS.

I have had several clients with histories of neglect and meager nurturing who have had difficulty finding nurturing figures. Before beginning the trauma work targeting the early memories, we searched hard for nurturing figures. I helped the clients by offering suggestions. In one case a female client came up with the actress Meryl Streep as her nurturing figure. She could imagine her as a loving mother who could provide her infant self with the love and attention she needed to develop in a healthy way. Another woman struggled to find anyone at all. We searched through her history, current relationships, and even figures from movies. Finally we came up with a figure from *The Secret Life of Bees* by Sue Monk Kidd, a book that has as one of its primary characters a strong, powerful nurturing African American woman named August. This woman had the capacity to nurture her child self. When we found this figure, it was as if a light had come on inside of her. She became essential to our EMDR work. Not only did the sense of her presence create a stronger container, but she was used in interweaves to nurture the child self.

I have seen clients come up with nurturers I would not have thought of. For instance, several clients have chosen their adult children as nurturing figures. They told me they could imagine calling on their sons or daughters to nurture their child selves. In another case the client chose as nurturers her parents when they were older adults. When she was a child and they were young adults, they did not do such a good job nurturing her. But over time they matured and developed into wise, kind people she could imagine caring for her child self. In another case, the client's mother was dysfunctional when the client was growing up, but got therapy and became a close confidante and support in her life. She was able to install her mother in her present aspect as a nurturing figure.

With some clients who could think of no one to be a nurturer, I asked them if they could remember times when they were able to love and nurture another person or even a pet. What I was attempting to do was find the nurturing quality within the clients and then install that so that they could bring that in for themselves if necessary.

Therapist: Can you remember a time when you held or comforted your daughter?

Client: Yes.

Therapist: Bring up a memory of doing that. What do you see?

Client: I see my daughter around three years old cuddled on my lap and I'm rocking her in the rocking chair and singing her a song.

Therapist: Can you feel the feelings of love and nurturing toward her?

Client: Yes.

Therapist: Focus on that while I tap on your knees.

In this case the adult self could be used as a nurturing figure.

PROTECTOR FIGURES

Protector figures can be people or animals real or imagined from the clients' early life or current life that the clients feel can protect them. The therapists and the clients' spouses or partners can also be protector figures for the clients. For instance, one client had no one in her childhood who protected or defended her but was currently in a loving marriage with a man who would defend her fiercely if needed. She installed him as a resource and was able to bring him up in imagery when her child self felt threatened by the perpetrator during EMDR processing. Memories of positive interactions with these protector figures can be installed with BLS. Clients can use the same figures for nurturers and protectors.

Clients' adult selves can be protector figures for their child self. Schmidt (2002) recommends installing a protective adult self for clients who have unmet developmental needs, particularly those who have been neglected and have had disruptions in early attachment. As with the nurturing adult self, she asks clients to get in touch with a number of skills and traits that she tells clients they already have and then names them as the clients feel them inside. They include things like the ability to be protective, courageous, strong, logical, confident, and grounded. After the clients feel all of these qualities within themselves, she asks them to bring all of them together into a single sense of self and installs them with BLS. If the clients have an image that represents the protective adult self, that is installed. It is important that the clients have a body sense of the resource. As I said with regard to using the adult self as nurturing figure, I believe for some clients it is important to install other figures as backups.

CHILD SELF AND ADULT SELF RELATIONSHIP
ASSESSMENT AND DEVELOPMENT

Very often during EMDR processing with an adult traumatized as a child, clients suddenly access the child self in its separate memory compartment and begin to process the past from the child's perspective (Parnell, 1999).

Commonly clients become caught in looping or stuck processing and need help from the therapist in the way of interweaves. I have found it useful in the preparation phase of treatment to have the clients access the child self before EMDR processing begins in order to evaluate the state of the child self and adult self relationship. Sometimes one will find that the child does not like or trust the adult or that the adult does not like or trust the child. This is important information because during the processing of a traumatic event with EMDR the therapist may find that the adult has turned on the child self or that the child cannot depend on the adult self to act as a protector resource. It is better to know this ahead of time. Having a good, strong, loving relationship between the clients' adult and child selves is useful for interweaves and aids tremendously in the healing process.

The following is a description of how the adult self–child self relationship can be accessed and evaluated:

The therapists begin by guiding the clients in finding their safe place. After the safe place has been established you can ask the clients to invite their child self into a protective circle that they imagine surrounds themselves. You can then begin a dialogue between the adult and child selves to evaluate the nature of their relationship. Generally the clients keep their eyes closed and the therapists ask the clients questions directed either to the adult selves or to the child selves. For example, the therapists might ask the child selves how old they are and how they are feeling. Then the therapists can ask them what they need? How do they feel about the adult selves? What is happening in their lives? A client might respond, "I am 3 years old. I feel scared. I know my daddy's in the house somewhere and my mommy's not home." The answer to any of the questions can lead to more questions as the therapists gather information. At some point the attention can shift to the adult selves to get their opinions and impressions of the child selves. "How do you feel about her? Do you think you can meet her needs?" are possible questions. The therapists are attempting to find out what the child selves are like, their current emotional state, and the quality of the relationship between the adult and the child selves. If there are problems between the two (for instance, the child may feel betrayed by the adult), the therapists must seek a way to remedy the problem. It is like doing inner family therapy. A whole session or sessions may be taken up with trying to heal hurts from the past and developing a caring bond between the adult and child selves.

When a caring relationship has been established, you can ask the clients to imagine holding their child selves on their laps, play with them, or engage the child selves in some positive nurturing way. These feelings can also be installed with BLS. Once the relationship has been established, the adult selves can serve as resources for the child selves during times of blocked processing and as aids in creating an increased sense of safety for closing sessions.

An Example of Using Guided Imagery to Assess the Client's Adult-Self–Child-Self Relationship and to Develop Nurturing and Protective Resources in the Client's Safe Place

Joe had been severely physically and sexually abused by both of his parents for several years, beginning when he was around 2 years old. When he came in to see me he was quite fragile and extremely distraught over the betrayal by his girlfriend and their subsequent breakup. I felt that before I could start EMDR I needed to develop his inner and outer resources, beginning with an assessment of his child-self to adult-self relationship. The following is a transcript of a dialogue I had with Joe's inner child after I had guided him to his safe place and had him imagine a protective circle around the adult Joe and another one around the child Joe.

Therapist: How old are you?

Joe: I'm 4—or maybe 2.

Therapist: What does little Joe need?

Joe: He needs love . . . he needs people around him to love him and appreciate him. . . . He needs to be fed—he was hungry sometimes.

Therapist: How does he feel?

Joe: He doesn't feel too good. (*Joe switches to first person from the child's perspective and the emotional charge increases.*) I'm tired of them hitting and yelling at me. Leave me alone in the genitals. Someone has been touching me there. I have been overstimulated, messed with.

Therapist: Who are you close to? (*I am inquiring about other resources.*)

Joe: My grandmother. She lets me eat when I want to eat and doesn't put me on a schedule or program my head. I feel safe with her. She wouldn't let anything happen to me—she'd be absolutely fierce.

Therapist: How do you like big Joe? (*I'm gathering information about the adult-self–child-self relationship to find out if big Joe can be a resource for little Joe.*)

Joe: I like big Joe.

Therapist: What do you like about him?

Joe: He's big and strong and protective of me and his friends, he knows how to do things . . . he's generally nice and gracious to people, he's basically honest. He's more of a poet and lover than a warrior, inside he's happy-go-lucky. He's got a big heart, he could love the world, he's adventurous . . . he tries new things.

It is obvious from little Joe's response that he can connect with his adult self, but now I need to find out if the adult Joe can connect with the child Joe.

Therapist: How does big Joe feel about little Joe?

Joe: Big Joe likes little Joe. He's a sweet happy bubbly boy that rattles around, tries to talk and understand things. He's very caring and affectionate, nice little being to be around. He tries to be independent. He has a calm nature. He wants to live. He's hoping things will change. His parents call him a hopeless case, mouth almighty, tongue everlasting.

At this time after seeing that there was a good adult-self–child-self connection, I wanted to further reinforce this sense of safety and the feeling that Joe's adult self could be a protector figure for his child self. I begin by talking to little Joe who is in a protective circle separate from big Joe's.

Therapist: Go inside big Joe's circle and sit on his lap. Feel his arms around you giving you a feeling of protection and safety.

Joe: (*After a few minutes Joe reported the following.*) Surrounding our circle are big huge cats like cheetahs and leopards—about 6 feet tall at their haunches. They won't let anything hurt us. They are like my real family. The circle is composed of giant cats and inside nothing can happen to me. They are fiercely protective. Also inside the circle is my grandma who is nurturing and protective of me. There is love and protection in the circle. The cats are outside protecting us.

From this inner dialogue I was able to determine that there was a strong positive adult-self–child-self relationship. I also found out that Joe had his grandmother as a nurturing and protective ally, in addition to a fierce circle of giant cats. I felt very encouraged by Joe's feeling a strong connection to all of his allies. Despite the years of abuse, Joe was able to love and nurture himself through the imagery and was able to summon other resources for help when needed; Joe and I used these resources throughout our work together. We used the resources to begin sessions, as interweaves, to reinforce his safe place when the processing became too intense and he wanted a break, and for closing sessions. He was comfortable using imagery that would evoke in him the desired feelings of safety and nurturing.

IMAGE OF A WISE BEING

The image or feeling (if no image arises) of a man or woman of wisdom can be used as a resource. This image represents an integrated whole being that is wise and powerful. An image of a Greek goddess or an Indian medicine man are examples. These images can come from client dreams, active imagination, guided imagery, or EMDR processing.

SPIRITUAL RESOURCES

Clients may also identify important spiritual resources. These may include figures such as Jesus, Mary, Kwan Yin, the Buddha, angelic beings, spirit guides, and images from nature. These figures are imbued with a power that feels numinous and suprahuman. After clients identify the spiritual figure, the therapists can ask the clients for more sensory detail to more fully evoke the experience. As the clients hold in their mind the image and feeling of the figure, the therapists employ BLS to install the resources.

If spiritual figures had appeared in a dream or had been called on in the past for support, memories of these times can be targeted and the positive image and feeling further strengthened with BLS.

Schmidt (2002) installed spiritual resources in her developmental needs meeting strategy. She has five different meditations for guiding clients to what she calls a *spiritual core self*. According to Schmidt, the spiritual core self is the essence of who the person is, a core of goodness that has been there since the moment of conception. In her guided meditations she helps clients connect to this core self and then adds BLS. It is interesting to note that often as a result of a complete EMDR session, clients will naturally come to this experience of an essential self that is untouched by trauma. I recommend these meditations and resource installations for use in preparing highly traumatized clients for EMDR.

An example of installing a spiritual resource was in the case of a client named Molly who felt a strong affinity with Kwan Yin, the female Buddha of compassion. She brought up the image of Kwan Yin that felt strong and compassionate. As she held the image and feeling in her mind, I tapped on her knees. She felt the image strengthen and experienced a more intimate relationship with Kwan Yin. Afterward, when Molly felt overwhelmed by the terrible abuse memories she was processing and the excruciating physical pain she felt in her child's body, she would take a break and imagine being held in Kwan Yin's loving arms. I would tap on Molly's knees to install this feeling of warmth and safety from a power that felt infinitely compassionate. After feeling renewed energy from the experience, she would return again to the disturbing memory and process it to the end. Her ability to shift from being in the midst of a traumatic memory to the experience of love and safety gave her a sense of increased control and confidence in the therapeutic process.

Another client contacted a figure she referred to as her childhood "spirit guide." We spent time bringing up memories of help she had gotten from her inner guide. I knew that her spirit guide could be a resource if and when she needed it.

Clients can also process and strengthen spiritual experiences. These might be experiences they had in nature, a peak experience during an athletic feat, or an experience during meditation or prayer. After installing, these experiences can be recalled to bring strength and comfort.

After clients have installed safe place, nurturing and protector figures, and spiritual figures, they feel like they have a team supporting them. Schmidt (2002) recommends bringing the nurturing adult self, protective adult self, and spiritual core self together into a circle and installing them together. In this way they form a resource team. In any event, after the installation of resources, traumatized clients feel more support; they are not alone, as they were when they experienced the trauma.

INNER ADVISER

The inner adviser is another resource that can be installed prior to beginning trauma processing work. The inner adviser or wise self is an aspect of the ego that represents wisdom and offers a balanced perspective (Rossman, 1987). It can be a valuable ally during EMDR processing and between sessions. The adviser can be called on in times of difficulty or if the processing becomes stuck. When they develop the inner adviser, clients can derive a greater sense of connection to their own inner resources. Many clients light up with surprise and awe at the wisdom that comes out of their own mouths. The development and installation of the inner adviser provides clients with another tool and assures therapists that clients can access their own source of wisdom and creativity. If I have concerns that the safe place and nurturing and protector figures may not be sufficient resources, I will guide clients to find an adviser and install it.

After clients are in their safe place, therapists can tell them that they are going to meet their inner adviser, an aspect of themselves that is wise and can offer guidance when they ask for it. When the inner adviser appears, the therapists ask the clients what the adviser looks like and if he or she has any advice to give at this time. Therapists may choose to install the feeling of the inner adviser with BLS. Therapists tell the clients that the inner adviser is available when they need him or her and can call on him or her when they feel a need to. Inner advisers appear spontaneously to clients during the guided imagery and take a variety of forms, such as fairies, wise women, grandfathers, trees, waterfalls, elves, wizards, Jesus, hawks, snakes, Native American elders, goddesses, and older version of the client. It is important that clients not judge what comes up for them and that they accept the advice that is given as long as it is compassionate.

Inner Adviser Script

The most critical and important aspect of the inner adviser is to *empower* clients. The adviser can also be present as a source of support and comfort. When finding the inner adviser, have clients frequent the safe place first. Let them know that when they find the adviser, you will do short sets of BLS.

As you relax in your safe place, invite your inner adviser to join you in this special place . . . just allow an image to form that represents your inner adviser, a wise, kind, loving figure who knows you well. . . . Let it appear in any way that comes and accept it as it is. . . . It may come in many forms—man, woman, animal, friend, someone you know, or a character from a movie or book.

Accept your adviser as it appears, as long as it seems wise, kind, loving, and compassionate . . . you will be able to sense its caring for you and its wisdom. . . . Invite it to be comfortable there with you, and ask it its name. . . . Accept what comes. . . .

Keeping your eyes closed . . . describe your inner adviser and tell me its name. *At this point begin the BLS. Do short sets and check-ins to see how the client is doing. If it continues positive, do longer sets.*

When you are ready tell it about your problem . . . ask any questions you have concerning this situation . . . now listen carefully to the response of (*name of adviser/advisers*). . . . You may imagine (*name of adviser/advisers*) talking with you or you may simply have a direct sense of its message in some other way. . . . Allow it to communicate in whatever way seems natural. . . . If you are uncertain about the meaning of the advice or if there are other questions you want to ask, continue the conversation until you feel you have learned all you can at this time. . . .

After a long pause ask the client what is happening. After he or she tells you, begin BLS again.

As you consider what your adviser told you, imagine what your life would be like if you took the advice you have received. . . . If you have more questions continue the conversation. *If the client continues the conversation with the adviser again, pause, then ask what is happening. Resume BLS.*

When it seems right, thank your adviser for meeting with you, and ask it to tell you the easiest, surest method for getting back in touch with it. . . . Realize that you can call another meeting whenever you feel the need for some advice or support. . . . Say good-bye for now in whatever way seems appropriate, and allow yourself to come back to the room. . . .

*At the end spend time debriefing the experience. Take care that the client is fully back in the room before ending the session.**

FIGURES FROM BOOKS, STORIES, MOVIES, TV, HISTORY, OR CARTOON CHARACTERS

Figures from books, stories, movies, TV, history, or cartoon characters can also be used as positive resources. If the client has been inspired by a particular figure and finds it strengthening, it can be used as a resource—even if the figure is fictional.

One of my African-American clients used Frederick Douglass as a resource. Douglass was born a slave and was severely abused but had the internal strength to escape slavery and become a great abolitionist and leader. One chapter in Douglass's autobiography, *The Life and Times of Frederick Douglass* (1941), was particularly important to my client. It was titled "Resisting the Slave Breaker" and was Douglass's account of his inner conviction that he could never be beaten again by the slave breaker. Douglass struggles for hours with the man who is trying to break his spirit, and finally Douglass succeeds in defeating him. Together, we often referred to Frederick Douglass and used him as a role model and resource for inner strength.

Some clients may want to draw on imaginary superheros like Superwoman or Superman for inner strength, power, and courage. Others use historical figures like Eleanor Roosevelt, Martin Luther King, and Mahatma Gandhi.

INNER STRENGTH

Inner strength is the ego capacity that enables our clients to make it to our office and engage in the difficult and painful healing work. Somehow, they

---

*Adapted from the Interactive Guided Imagery™ techniques developed by Martin L. Rossman, M.D. and David Bresler, Ph.D., from the Academy for Guided Imagery, 30765 Pacific Coast Highway, 369 Malibu, CA 90265.

are able to cope with unbearable circumstances and keep going. Phillips and Frederick (1995) focused specifically on the development of inner strength as a powerful ego-strengthening strategy. The following is a script for the development of inner strength by Phillips and Frederick that I adapted to use with EMDR and resource installation.

Script for Meeting Inner Strength

I would like to invite you to take a journey within yourself to a place that feels like the very center of your being, that place where it is very quiet . . . and peaceful . . . and still. And when you're in that place . . . it's possible for you to have a sense of finding a part of yourself . . . a part that I will refer to as your *inner strength.*

This is a part of yourself that has always been there since the moment of birth . . . even though at times it may be difficult for you to feel . . . and it is with you now. It's that part of yourself that has allowed you to survive . . . and to overcome obstacles wherever you face them. Maybe you'd like to take a few moments of time to get in touch with that part of yourself . . . and you can notice what images . . . or feelings . . . what thoughts . . . what bodily sensations are associated with being in touch with your inner strength. And when those images or thoughts or feelings or bodily sensations or however it is coming to your are clear to you in your inner mind, and when you have a sense that the experience is completed for you . . . then let me know. (*When the client indicates "yes" begin BLS—tapping or auditory stimulation. They can be instructed to tap on their own knees if touch from the therapist is not okay. Continuing tapping.*)

In the future, when you wish to get in touch with inner strength, . . . you will find that you can do so be calling forth these images, thoughts, feelings, bodily sensations, and that by so doing you will be in touch with inner strength again. (*Continue tapping.*)

And when you're in touch with this part of yourself, you will be able to feel more confident . . . confident with the knowledge that you have, within yourself, all the resources you really need to take steps in the direction that you wish to go . . . to be able to set goals and to be able to achieve them . . . and this part of yourself, it's possible to feel more calm, more optimistic, to look forward to the future. (*At this point particular goals that the client has shared with the therapist may be stated.*)

And in the next days and weeks to come, you may find yourself becoming calmer and more optimistic about your life . . . and you will find that at any time during the day it will be possible for you to get in touch with your own inner strength by simply closing your eyes for a moment, bringing your hand to your forehead, evoking the image of your inner strength, and reminding yourself that you have within you . . . all the resources you really need. The more you can use these methods to be in touch with your inner strength, the more you will be able to trust your inner self, your intuition, your feelings, and the more you will be able to use them as your guide.*

You can make a tape of your voice guiding your clients in this exercise, which they can play between sessions to take an active role in the development of inner strength.

POSITIVE MEMORIES

It can be helpful to go through clients' histories and focus sessions on the memories when they felt loved, nurtured, powerful, in control, and *safe*. These can include memories of receiving support, nurturance, or guidance from parents, siblings, grandparents, aunts and uncles, other relatives, teachers, clergy people, friends, and lovers or partners. For example, if the client had been listened to and cared for by a certain teacher in grade school, have the client bring up the memory, with the emotions, body sensations, and other senses if possible. Then add the BLS. This processing of positive memories breaks up the old stories clients have of never being listened to or cared for, and new associations may arise of other times clients were listened to. Suddenly, they may see that they had created an erroneous assumption about themselves and their lives. EMDR processing of the positive life experiences can dissolve the solidity of the negative self-concept as EMDR strengthens what is positive and adaptive.

Sally, a client with an early history of physical and sexual abuse and the traumatic loss of her mother as a young child, struggled with chronic depression. We focused several EMDR sessions on fragments of memories of being loved by her mother. Part of Sally's trauma was the loss of the memories of her mother; this loss resulted in Sally's difficulty in providing nurturing and comforting to herself. We began the bilateral knee tapping while she focused on body memories (she had no visual memories) of her mother holding her in her lap, and she could feel the comforting of her mother's embrace as I tapped on her knees. Visual memories emerged during the sets of tapping that strengthened the feeling. Prior to the resource installation, she believed she had not been loved and was unlovable. After the strengthening of the

---

*Adapted with permission from Phillips, M. & Frederick, C. (1995).

positive memory of her mother's loving her, she felt that her mother did love her and she could assert that she was lovable. Later, we used the memory of her mother during the processing of traumatic memories to help with interweaves and session closure.

Memories of positive or neutral experiences and adaptive coping efforts can also be targeted. One man I worked with had a terrible history of emotional neglect. He suffered from a chronic low-grade depression and diminished self-esteem. His early childhood was quite bleak and included sexual abuse. We began our EMDR work in the beginning phase of treatment by focusing on any positive memories he had of his childhood. We targeted these positive memories and processed them. As his depression and the global feeling that his whole life was miserable lifted, he felt lighter and more hopeful.

Memories of being healthy, strong, and without the current problem can also be installed. For example, memories of how a client felt when she was sober can be focused on with BLS. A client with an eating disorder can bring up a memory when she was a normal weight and was eating in a healthy way. Can she remember what her body felt like? Can she bring up a memory when she was eating in a healthy way in a body that felt strong? These memories can be installed with short sets of BLS.

MUSIC

Some music evokes a sense of strength, courage, peace, beauty, and joy. Music that strengthens positive feelings and has meaning to the client can be installed with BLS. Clients can bring in pieces that they deem particularly inspiring. As they listen to it, add BLS to strengthen the positive feelings. Therapists may also choose music with lyrics that they feel would be beneficial to clients. Another variation would be having clients sing a soothing lullaby to their child self while you do the installation.

MOVEMENT

Movement is another valuable resource. Clients can be asked to remember a time when they physically did something empowering. "Remember when you were running and you felt strong in your body!" "Remember doing Tai Chi!" "Remember how it felt during your Model Mugging course to be able to protect yourself!" A colleague of mine who is also a yoga therapist installs yoga poses like Mountain or Warrior with clients who are needing to embody more of the qualities of strength or power.

Clients can also move their bodies during the session and install the movement with BLS. One man I worked with felt empowered when he stood up. As he stood up and felt himself large and physically grounded, I tapped on his back to install the feeling. Other clients may want to move their hands and arms.

IMAGES FROM NATURE

For many clients nature has provided a refuge and can be a source for positive resource images. The image of a clear mountain lake can bring a feeling of peace and calm. A towering mountain can evoke a sense of enduring strength and power. The vastness of the ocean in which one's problems are seen as mere waves is another resource image from nature. One client used the image of the weeping willow tree providing shelter, refuge from summer heat, and a swing from its supple branches as a positive resource.

IMAGE OF A POSITIVE GOAL STATE

Clients can be asked to imagine a positive goal state or future self (Popky, 1997). When clients can bring up the image, BLS is employed to strengthen it. Clients can imagine what their life would be like if they left their job, stopped drinking, or left a relationship. As they imagine their future, they may begin to loosen the threads of the knot that has kept them stuck in their current situation. They may begin to see the possibility of a way out.

INSTALLING SKILL DEVELOPMENT AND A SENSE OF MASTERY

Positive experiences the client brings into session from their week can be installed. These can include their success at handling triggers, tolerating distress, and being assertive. As clients think about these positive incidents, ask them to attend to how they feel in their body. What positive belief do they have about themselves when they think about that? Have them hold the positive image, body sensation, emotion, and positive cognition together and do some sets of BLS. Entire sessions can be spent installing successes so that clients can more fully integrate them.

Clients can practice contacting their chosen resources between sessions. They can tap on their knees or do butterfly hugs as they imagine their safe place, nurturing figures, protector figures, and inner guides. I have heard reports of police officers sitting in their patrol cars discretely tapping on their knees. Imagining their resources before going to sleep at night can help with sleep difficulties. Clients can also practice putting disturbing emotions, thoughts, and memories in a container. Therapists can do RDI throughout the course of treatment, using it to reinforce therapeutic gains and to focus on what is working for the clients. Having sessions of RDI woven through treatment is a good way to aid the pacing of treatment and helps clients integrate more fully their progress.

RESOURCE INSTALLATION FOCUSING ON A CHALLENGING CURRENT LIFE SITUATION, BLOCKING BELIEF, OR MALADAPTIVE SCHEMA

Leeds and Korn (1998) presented a protocol for the identification and installation of resources that focuses on helping clients come up with the resources needed for current life difficulties, blocking beliefs, and maladaptive schemas. This protocol is helpful for clients who do not have the ego strength to do EMDR and cannot handle the emotions and distress EMDR might stir up for them in their current life. It is also used for performance enhancement in clients with good ego strength. The following is a modification of Leeds and Korn's protocol that I have found helpful.

1. Therapists can begin the identification of the needed resource by asking clients to focus on a current life situation that is difficult for them, a blocking belief, or a life issue.

2. Next the therapists ask the clients what quality or qualities they would need to better deal with the situation, belief, or issue.

Explore with the clients times when they had that quality or qualities. If they cannot think of one, they can think of someone else dealing effectively with this type of situation. The person could be someone they know personally, someone from a movie, TV, book, history, or religious figure, or anyone else. It could even be a symbolic representation of this resource.

3. Next ask the clients to describe the images or memories they have chosen in more detail. Have the clients provide sensory detail: What do they see, hear, feel, smell, or taste? What emotions do they feel and what do they feel in their body?

4. The therapists can ask the clients to say a cue word or phrase with the resource they want to amplify.

The installation of the positive resource may or may not be done, depending on the client. Some clients will flip to the polar opposite when BLS is used or may begin processing traumatic memories. For others, the addition of BLS will enhance the client's felt sense of the resource.

5. The installation of the positive resource is done much like with the standard protocol for traumatic memories: the clients are asked to focus on the image, feelings, the cue word or phrase (if one is used), and the therapists add the BLS. A short set of BLS is used (6 to 10 passes or taps are used initially). Watch the clients for changes. If they look distressed, stop immediately. Otherwise, after the set ask them what comes up for them. If they report that the positive feelings have gotten stronger, continue for 2 to 3 sets of BLS. Stop the BLS when you feel that the resource has been strengthened. If the processing has become negative, stop immediately and consider choosing another resource.

6. You can repeat this process for many different qualities the clients want to develop and strengthen. A future template can be added having the clients imagine using the resource in different situations.

For example, a client comes in to treatment because she is having difficulty at work. She feels intimidated by her boss and she does not know why. Whenever he comes up to her desk she becomes speechless, feels stupid and small, and can hardly think. She is puzzled by her reaction because he is a nice man and has done nothing to cause her current feelings. This is a pattern she has experienced in her relationship to many men. When you take her history you learn that she was physically and sexually abused by her father, a tyrant who controlled everyone in the family. Because her symptoms are troubling her in the present and interfering with her ability to do her job, you want to give her relief as soon as possible. Because of the number of abuse incidents, she is afraid that opening them up will make it harder for her to function. She is not ready for the intensity of EMDR trauma work. The issue she identifies is having difficulty feeling her own power and standing up for herself with men.

Therapist: When you think of the situation with your boss at work, what picture is most disturbing to you?

Client: It's when he is standing next to my desk looking down at me.

Therapist: When you bring up that picture, what emotions do you feel?

Client: Fear.

Therapist: What quality or qualities would you need to handle the situation the way you would like?

Client: I would need strength and power.

Therapist: Can you think of a time when you had strength and power?

Client: Yes. A couple of weeks ago my daughter came home from school and told me that her teacher had humiliated her in front of the class. I immediately called the principal and teacher and arranged to meet with them. I told them that this was wrong and that it could not happen again. The teacher apologized to my daughter and me.

Therapist: When you think of that situation, what picture comes to mind that represents the moment when you felt the most strength and power?

Client: I see myself facing the teacher and principal in the classroom. I feel strong.

Therapist: Good. Now I want you to close your eyes for a moment and really feel what that feels like in your body, the strength and power. When you have a good sense of it, let me know and I will tap on your knees. (Client takes a moment, nods her head. Therapist begins to tap on her knees, right, left. Therapist notices a relaxation in the client's face.)

Therapist: What do you notice now?

Client: I feel strength in my legs and arms.

Therapist: Focus on that. >>>>>> (6–12 saccades)

Therapist: What's happening now?

Client: I'm remembering another time when I was strong and stood up for myself.

Therapist: Go with that. >>>>>>>

The therapist continues following the client's positive associations until they finish. Then returns to the picture with the boss.

Therapist: When you bring up the picture with your boss, what comes up for you now?

Client: I feel bigger, more in my adult self.

Therapist: Are there any other quality or qualities you might need?

Client: Yes. Self-confidence.

Therapist: Can you think of a time when you were self-confident?

Client: No, I can't think of any times.

Therapist: Can you think of someone you know, or even someone from a movie or book?

Client: Oprah. She has self-confidence.

Therapist: Close your eyes and go inside. Bring up an image of Oprah displaying self-confidence. As you see that image, what do you feel in your body?

Client: I feel energy in my legs. My back feels straighter.

Therapist: Focus on the image and feeling in your body. >>>>>

Therapist: What's happening now?

Client: I feel better. It feels good.

Therapist: Let's return to the picture with your boss we started with. What comes up for you now?

Client: It feels okay. I feel more like an adult now.

Therapist: Go with that. >>>>>>

Client: It feels better. He's a nice man. I really like my job.

Therapist: Can you imagine yourself at work in the future?

Client: Yes.

Therapist: Imagine that. >>>>>>

They then close and debrief. The therapist can also install the cue word *Oprah* and anchor it as the client puts her thumb and middle finger together along with the image and sensations of self-confidence. Then during the week if the client is in need of self-confidence, she can say the word *Oprah* and put her thumb and finger together to elicit the feeling.

This protocol can be used for performance enhancement. A client who has to make a speech and is afraid can use resources. The therapist can ask the client what image he has that is disturbing him about making a speech. He then describes a future scene standing in front of a large audience, and he forgets what he is supposed to say. The therapist asks him what resource or quality he needs.

Client: I need to be a confident speaker.

Therapist: Can you think of a time when you were a confident speaker?

Client: No.

Therapist: Can you think of someone who is?

Client: Yes, Nelson Mandela.

Therapist: Close your eyes and go inside. Bring up an image of Nelson Mandela speaking. What do you notice in your body? What are you feeling? When you have a good sense of him let me know. >>>>>>

Therapist: What comes up for you?

Client: I can really feel it. I can do it.

Therapist: Bring up the image of Nelson Mandela, say his name to yourself, and put your middle finger and thumb together. In this way you can bring this feeling up when you want it. >>>>>> Now when you imagine giving the speech, what comes up for you?

Client: I feel more self-confident.

Therapist: Go with that. >>>>>>

Resource work can be used with clients struggling with addictions and eating disorders. "When you desire to use, what resource do you need to help you stay sober?" Clients can install their sponsors or friends as supports. Memories of health and strength can be installed. "Can you remember times when you were eating in a healthy way?" "Can you remember a time when you were sober?" "What did that feel like in your body?"

OTHER COPING SKILLS

There are a number of coping skills that therapists can assist clients in developing during this beginning phase of EMDR preparation and ego strengthening.

Relaxation/stress reduction skills are very important for clients who are highly traumatized. For many of them life is full of stressful triggers. These relaxation techniques can also be very useful between EMDR sessions to calm clients. There are many forms of stress reduction, including systematic relaxation to different guided imagery. The light stream visualization technique (Shapiro, 1995) is useful, and there are many commercial tapes available (e.g., Miller, 1996). Also, therapists can make relaxation tapes for their clients in the office that they can use between sessions. As clients learn to relax, they gain a sense of control over their bodies that have heretofore seemed so out of control.

Grounding skills are also important to teach clients who have been traumatized and tend to dissociate. These clients commonly go "out of their bodies" when stressed or triggered. Teaching clients to feel their bodies, be aware of sensation, and to be present during sessions is helpful. Engaging in regular physical exercise helps clients to become more embodied, and walking outdoors in a beautiful setting can be physically and spiritually rewarding. Yoga practice, especially slow-moving, mindful yoga, which stresses presence rather than physical prowess, is preferable. Mindfulness training is also a useful grounding practice.

The following is a guided visualization and breathing exercise for teaching grounding.

GROUNDED BREATHING SCRIPT

Find a comfortable way to sit so that your back is straight but relaxed and your feet are uncrossed and resting on the floor. You may also sit cross-legged if you wish. Close your eyes and be aware of how your body feels. Notice the places of contact . . . your bottom on the seat and your feet on the floor. Be aware of your breathing. Where do you feel it? What is its rhythm? Now imagine that as you inhale a deep full breath, you are taking the air from deep within the earth. This breath comes up through your legs and fills your belly . . . then your chest . . . and now your throat. When you feel the breath in your throat, hold it a moment, then exhale, letting the air leave the throat . . . then the chest . . . and now the belly . . . releasing the air back down into the earth. When the need arises to take another breath, again breathe in from the earth, filling the belly, chest, and throat . . . pause, and then slowly exhaling, throat, chest, belly, back down into earth. Let the air fill your body. Let the inhalation and exhalation be gentle and smooth. Be aware of the sensations in the body. If your mind wanders away, gently bring it back to the breathing. Smooth and gentle. Be present. The goal is attained moment to moment.

MINDFULNESS PRACTICES

Mindfulness practices have their origins in ancient Buddhist meditative traditions. These practices have been taught in the West for many years. Detailed descriptions of the practices have been presented by several authors, including psychologists who have integrated the practices into their clinical work and the understanding of the mind (Goldstein, 1976; Kabat-Zinn, 1990; Kornfield, 1993; Linehan, 1993a, 1993b; Parnell, 1997a, 1997b). Several meditation teachers have taken these practices out of the meditation hall and brought them to people's everyday lives. Jon Kabat-Zinn, a longtime meditation practitioner, developed a pain reduction program at University of Massachusetts Medical Center that was featured on Bill Moyer's program *Healing and the Mind* and is now being taught in hospital settings across the country for pain and stress reduction (Kabat-Zinn, 1990). Linehan saw that this practice could help her borderline clients become more present in their daily lives and be better able to cope and so made mindfulness skill development central to her dialectical behavior therapy (Linehan, 1993a, 1993b).

Mindfulness practice helps people develop the ability to be more present for whatever arises. When practiced over time, it can decrease dissociation and enable people to be more fully "grounded" and "embodied." Mindfulness practice develops a witness awareness or observing ego that helps people observe and describe their experience without judgment. Clients learn that they can be with whatever arises with less personal identification and reactivity. This practice cultivates the ability to be "mindful," a continuity of presence and awareness in daily life. The ability to notice and be with ordinary life experiences is undeveloped in many people who have been traumatized as children (McFarlane, Weber, & Clark, 1993). Thus mindfulness training is very important for developing new neuropathways in the plastic brain. Mindfulness training also develops "bare attention"—the ability to be present, curious, and open to the body and mind in a balanced, nonjudgmental way. Mindfulness practitioners develop a compassionate attitude toward themselves, as the body and mind are no longer experienced as enemies. People also report an increased experience of equanimity—a more balanced experience of life, an understanding that phenomena arise and pass away in a more open field of awareness, with attachment to pleasant and unpleasant states of mind and body lessening.

Both Vipassana meditation and EMDR use dual attention or awareness. For Vipassana meditators, the attention is on the breath or other predominant objects of awareness. The EMDR clients focus both on therapists' fingers or other stimuli and an inner object like an image or body sensation. In each case, a detached impartial witness awareness is cultivated and developed. An important part of the instructions given to EMDR clients is to "just let whatever happens happen, without discarding anything as unimportant" (Shapiro, 1995, p. 142). Clients are asked to notice any changes in thoughts, feelings, and body sensations and to simply report to the therapists what they are experiencing. Therapists ask clients after a set of eye movements, "What do you get now?" or "What's happening now?" (Shapiro, 1995, p. 143). A simple objective report is given of the latest phenomena to arise. This simple reporting without interpretation or discussion seems to aid clients in disidentifying with the psychological material and, as with Vipassana meditation, to develop a witness awareness. Clients experiencing strong abreactions are told in a calm, compassionate, reassuring manner that what they are experiencing is in the past, it is old stuff, it is like the scenery and they are safely in the present on a passing train (Shapiro, 1995).

Vipassana meditation enhances the development of "bare attention." According to Goldstein, "bare attention means observing things as they are, without choosing, without comparing, without evaluating, without laying our projections and expectations onto what is happening; cultivating instead a choiceless and non-interfering awareness" (1976, p. 20.) The quality of bare attention allows one to be more fully grounded in the present; it allows one to be open to the here and now without adding anything else to it.

The practice of mindfulness cultivates a continuity of presence and awareness throughout one's daily life experience. This practice overlaps and complements EMDR treatment (Parnell, 1997a) and can be helpful in several ways to clients who have been traumatized and are in EMDR therapy. The formal practice as taught in a retreat setting is divided into three parts, which will be briefly described: sitting meditation (Vipassana meditation), walking meditation, and eating meditation.

Vipassana or Insight Meditation

One begins sitting meditation by finding a quiet, undisturbed place to meditate. The ringer should be turned off the phone, and the person should let others know that he or she is not to be interrupted for the time of the meditation. It is helpful to meditate at the same time each day for a set period of time. First thing in the morning or last thing before going to sleep is a good time. For people who have been sexually abused and have quite a lot of trauma in the mind and body, short periods of meditation to begin with are recommended—5 to 10 minutes—and then increasing the time with more comfort. One should sit in a comfortable, upright position, on a cushion, on the floor, or on a chair with one's feet firmly planted on the floor. Vipassana meditators are instructed to simply observe the breath, thoughts, feelings, and body sensations without clinging, condemning, or identifying with them (Goldstein, 1976). Phenomena that arise are observed by a detached witness awareness.

The meditation begins with a focus on the sensation of the breath either at the nostrils or in the belly. The meditator notices the sensation of the in and out of the breath or the rising and falling of the belly. When the mind wanders from the breath, they are to notice it and then gently return the attention to the breath. Mental notes are used, such as "in and out" or "rising and falling," to help keep the mind focused. This focus on the breath is the first instruction given in the practice. This gentle returning to the present moment over and over again trains the mind to be more present.

After meditators have learned how to be somewhat present with the breath, they are taught to notice when thoughts arise that take their attention from the breath and to make the mental note "thinking, thinking," and then return to the breath. They are not to analyze the content of the thoughts, just to notice that thinking is occurring. Later instructions add the noticing of other mental and physical phenomena, such as emotions, body sensations, and judgments. These are noted, and then the meditator returns to the breath. For example, if a strong emotion like fear arises, the meditator feels it, notes "fear, fear," stays with the sensation until it no longer pulls his or her attention, and then returns to the breath. If the thought arises, "I'm never going to be able to concentrate," he or she notices that, and notes "judging, judging," and returns to the breath. An entire meditation session can be spent finding the mind has wandered away and bringing it back, over and over again. With practice, meditators increase their ability to be present with whatever should arise in their field of experience.

Walking Meditation

Walking meditation involves discrete periods of time from 10 minutes to 45 minutes or longer of slow walking, during which the meditator is instructed to pay attention to the sensation of the movement of the lifting, moving, and placing of the foot. The meditator chooses an unobstructed path of several feet to walk and focuses on the sensation of the movement in a moment-to-moment unfolding process. Upon reaching the end of the path, the meditator turns around and begins again. The goal is attained in each moment—there is nowhere to go except here. During the walking meditation, like the sitting meditation, one notices when the mind wanders off, and gently returns to the walking after making a mental note, for instance, of "thinking, thinking." The walking can be extremely slow, almost microscopic in noticing every subtle sensation, or faster, focusing on grosser sensations like the large muscle groups of the foot and leg or the feeling of the foot's contact with the ground. What is most important is the development of a continuity of presence, "being here now." This can be a very useful practice for abuse survivors to help them to be more aware of their bodies in movement. It can feel very painful and difficult, but beginning with short periods of the meditation and increasing it can help them to become more grounded and present in their bodies.

Eating Meditation

Many people lose awareness when eating, finishing their food without even tasting it. The practice of mindful eating can begin with the experience of eating a raisin. Meditators are given a handful of raisins and instructed to notice and to be present as fully as they can be for the experience of eating one raisin at a time. They are told to notice the sensation of lifting the arm, the feeling of the raisin in the fingers, the feeling of the raisin in the mouth, and the sensation and taste of the raisin as they bite down on it. Attention is paid to chewing, to swallowing, and then to the desire to repeat the process. Again, the aim is to be present to the full experience of eating. For many people, this is a remarkable experience because such an ordinary experience is experienced as something quite new. After several minutes of experiencing a fresh relationship to raisins, meditators are instructed to bring this same attention to their regular meals, eating slowly and mindfully, noticing when the mind wanders away and bringing it back to the experience of eating.

One can see how this practice can potentially help clients who have been sexually abused to become more conscious when they are eating. Many of our clients have eating disorders as a result of the abuse and their disconnection from their bodies. Bringing more awareness to the process of eating can also bring awareness of the triggers for overeating, bingeing, and purging, and insights to the connections. If clients tend to dissociate during eating, that can be noted and worked on during sessions. Triggers for problematic eating behavior can also be targeted with EMDR.

TECHNIQUES FROM SOMATIC PSYCHOTHERAPY AND ENERGY PSYCHOLOGY FOR EGO STRENGTHENING

Somatic methods can be used for ego strengthening and affect tolerance. Clients can be asked to find a *body safe place*. "Can you find a place in your body where you can feel a sense of safety? This can be a part of your body that feels uncontaminated by trauma or pain. Would you be willing to find a place in your body that is slightly more comfortable than the rest of you?" (Phillips, 2000). When clients identify the place, ask them to bring their attention there and then add a short set of BLS to install it. If clients are especially fragile, you might just use the attention without adding BLS. Levine (1997, 1999) uses a technique from somatic experiencing called pendulation in which clients bridge with their awareness back and forth between areas of discomfort and places of relative expansion in the body.

It can be helpful to teach clients to tune in to their bodies. "Scan your body. What do you notice?" Teach them to listen to their bodies. Can they locate places of pleasure as well as discomfort? Hakomi and sensorimotor therapy (Ogden, Minton, & Pain, 2006) and focusing (Gendlin, 1981) are other body-based therapies that can be used for trauma treatment.

Thought field therapy, a psychological technology that activates meridian points to manipulate body-mind energies, has also been used in conjunction with EMDR for affect regulation (Hartung, Galvin, & Gallo, 2003; Phillips, 2000).

TECHNIQUES FOR CREATING DISTANCE
AND/OR CONTAINMENT

Sometimes clients and therapists are concerned that the memories to be processed with EMDR are too charged. Clients might be hesitant to begin EMDR. It is a key concept in EMDR that there needs to be charge in order for successful processing. Yet too much charge can cause clients to dissociate and stop the processing.

DISTANCING TECHNIQUES

Therapists can help to modulate the intensity of target memories by employing distancing and containment techniques. There are several distancing techniques that are drawn from hypnotherapy that can be used prior to beginning EMDR processing of a traumatic memory. These same techniques can also be used in the middle of a processing session to help clients gain distance if they are overwhelmed, dissociating, or request more distance from the memory.

• "Imagine you are watching it as a movie." Ask clients to imagine they are in a safe place, perhaps in their home, and that they are going to watch a movie of the traumatic event. They can have whomever they want with them as they watch. Their protectors and nurturing figures can be there. They can put the movie in a DVD player or VCR and watch it on their TV. They can hold the remote control in their hands. They have control. They can start or stop the movie whenever they wish. They can put it on pause and go to their safe place or take a break if they want to. They can fast-forward it. They can make it a still picture, make it black and white, and can take the sound out of it. What is important to emphasize is that they are in control.
• "Imagine that there is a glass wall between you and the image." Clients can imagine watching the scene with a wall separating them from it.
• "Imagine your resource figures there with you." Clients can imagine their nurturing and protector figures there with them as they go through the event.
• Clients can have real support people there with them. They can have

their partner, parent, or friend next to them or holding their hand. They are not alone and can feel the support in the present as they process the past.

The indication to me that I will need to use distancing techniques are clients' trepidations about beginning EMDR processing. My typical question to clients is, "What do you need to feel safe?" If clients say, "I'm afraid of being overwhelmed, that it will be too much for me," I offer distancing techniques and see what appeals to them.

For example, Ruben from the earlier example, who had experienced a series of traumas that left him with chronic PTSD, was very concerned about being retraumatized by EMDR. He decided that what would help him was the image of watching the movie. He imagined sitting comfortably at home on a couch holding a remote control. He could control the image and remove the sound if he wished. He imagined support people sitting next to him who helped him feel safe. Then, when he was processing a traumatic memory and he became overwhelmed, I could remind him that he was safe in the present, it was just a movie. Did he want to take the sound out of it? Make it a still photograph, or fast-forward through it?

In another case, I spent several sessions preparing an adolescent girl for EMDR processing of a gang rape she had experienced several years before. In this case I worked with her, her mother, and her father, explaining the effects of traumas on the mind and body as well as how EMDR worked. She chose animals and humans as protectors and nurturers, which we installed one at a time. Then she drew a picture of herself in her safe place with her nurturers and protectors, which we installed with BLS. She loved the feeling of control the resource work provided her. Then, when she and her parents and I believed she was ready for EMDR processing, she brought her mother, father, and dog to the session as supports. She also brought the picture of her safe place with nurturer and protector figures, which we installed again. She liked the idea of imagining the memory as a movie she could put in the VCR while she held the controls. As this was an overwhelming trauma, I wanted to provide her with as much distance and control over it as possible, at the same time leaving enough charge to process. Before beginning EMDR she was instructed that she was in control and could stop whenever she wanted to. The preparation we did helped her to process the memory.

CREATING AN IMAGINAL CONTAINER FOR AFFECT MANAGEMENT

Omaha (2004) recommends creating an imaginal container. This container serves to limit pressures and feelings and helps clients to not become overwhelmed. It is used to contain distress, emotions, and problems in and out of sessions and provides clients with control over emotions that feel too great for them. It can help minimize disruption to clients' daily life. It can hold material that emerges during EMDR sessions that are not directly related to the target and are affecting the clients' ability to process. The container can also be used to close incomplete sessions.

Clients can be instructed: "Bring up an image of a container that is large enough to hold every disturbing thing, but do not focus on any particular thing or image. Be sure it has a lid that is secure. You can label the container. Imagine a valve on it that allows you to take out what you want and to put in what you want a little at a time. It can be opened only when it will serve your healing. If you want, you can arrange for a place to store the container. Make sure no part of you is in the container. Then imagine these things passing into the container. Now seal the container." The imagery can be installed with short sets of BLS or not.*

Some therapists ask their clients to imagine a book with all the clients' issues in it. They can open or close the book when they want. They can put it on the shelf. Clients can create a container for sounds. They can be asked to imagine putting disturbing sounds or words on a tape or CD and putting them in a case that is stored until they are ready to open it.

For clients who are afraid of being overwhelmed by a memory, I have suggested that they work on only one part of it. The rest can be put aside in a container. In this way they can have a sense of control. I have also used a container for clients who want to preserve the good memories or good parts of a perpetrator who was also an attachment figure. "Would you like to put the good memories of your father in a container where we can keep them safe so that you can work on the disturbing part?" In this way clients can focus on reprocessing disturbing memories without censoring themselves (see Appendix 1, page 335 for a Summary of Resources, Coping Skills, and Techniques for Creating Distance and/or Containment).

---

*See Omaha (2004) for more information.

5

CASE FORMULATION

IT IS IMPORTANT in EMDR therapy to develop a good working case formulation that will guide your treatment. Although EMDR was developed for treating PTSD, clients seek EMDR to treat a range of presenting problems. These include difficulties with relationships, employment, anxiety about performance, self-esteem problems, depression, anxiety, phobias, substance abuse, eating disorders, grief, or an overriding malaise. EMDR is effective in treating complex trauma from childhood physical and sexual abuse. For detailed information on how to work with this population, see my book *EMDR in the Treatment of Adults Abused as Children* (Parnell, 1999).

The following are some guidelines for case formulation, many of which build upon information provided in the previous chapters.

1. Gather information on the client's presenting problems, symptoms, and goals for treatment.

2. Take a thorough developmental history up to the present time.

3. Get information on the client's current functioning, supports, and coping skills.

4. Develop hypotheses about the etiology of the client's symptoms. Listen for key events that may link to the symptoms. Listen for patterns of limiting beliefs that link to the current symptoms.

5. Assess ego strength, affect tolerance, and rapport. Can the client install safe place, nurturing figures, and protector figures? Do you feel a rapport with the client? Do you believe the client will be able to handle high levels of affect? Is the client willing to go there with you?

If you believe that the client can handle high levels of affect and manage between sessions, begin to prepare the client for EMDR. Explain the theories about the effects of trauma, theories about how EMDR works, and what to expect from an EMDR session. Set up a stop signal and signal for keep going, as well as a metaphor for creating distance. If the client responds well to this preparation, you may begin to develop with the client a target map based on the history provided you. With some higher-functioning clients, this can be done in a session or two. Then I usually schedule 90 minutes or longer for the first EMDR session in order to give us sufficient time to process whatever should come up. After that, I will be able to determine how much time the client needs for future EMDR sessions. In some cases 50 minutes is enough.

6. Develop a target map with the client. What key memories are linked to the current symptoms? Arrange these targets chronologically, like beads on a string. Target and reprocess the earliest or strongest memories first. Work your way up the strand. Remember to process the past before trying to solve the problems in the present.

If the client is not yet ready for trauma processing, continue with stabilization work, which can include resource development and installation and medication evaluation.

Case Example: Client with Delayed Onset PTSD

Josette sought treatment because she was suffering from severe PTSD. Although neatly and fashionably dressed, she felt as if her life were falling apart. She was so disturbed she could not even put words together in a sentence to tell me what had happened to her. By the end of the first session I ascertained that 25 years before her sister had been murdered in a gang shooting. Josette had come upon the scene after it had occurred and was horrified and shocked by what she saw. Instead of dealing with the emotional repercussions, she filed this terrible experience away in her mind, went to college in another state, and continued with her life. She didn't speak of it to anyone, not even her husband. Then, a month before she came to see me she happened upon a similar crime scene that opened the old wound and sent her into a tailspin.

An affable woman with bright blue eyes, an easy rapport quickly developed between us. Prior to being triggered and developing PTSD, she had been functioning well. She had been married fifteen years and had three children and many friends. She had a job she enjoyed. Her PTSD symptoms included insomnia, anxiety, depression, hypervigilence, suicidal ideation, difficulty concentrating, and bouts of uncontrollable weeping. Because of her problem focusing, it took several sessions to take her history. She cried easily and her thinking was tangential and loose. Because I was concerned about the severity of her symptoms, I did not want to begin EMDR until she was more stabilized. I referred her to a psychiatrist for a medication evaluation, after which she was prescribed an antidepressant. Over the weeks it took for the antidepressant to take effect we continued to meet, talk about her past, and do some resource installation. She was able to install safe place, nurturing, protector, and wise/spiritual figures. When she was feeling stronger, the medication helping, we began to prepare to do EMDR.

We spent several EMDR sessions focusing on the original traumatic incident, the murder of her sister. We followed the standard protocol for trauma beginning with targeting the most disturbing scene. There were many parts to this incident, including scenes in the hospital, involvement with law enforcement, and a trial. After clearing each of these scenes, we targeted the recent scene that had triggered her. We continued to target and reprocess any present-day triggers. Over time her symptoms improved. She was able to talk about what happened without distress, her mood and concentration improved, and she was sleeping better.

Although overall there was significant improvement, some symptoms remained. We recognized that there were earlier contributors from her childhood that needed to be reprocessed as well. She had grown up in an unsafe neighborhood and had a verbally and physically abusive stepfather. Her feelings of anxiety had deeper roots that would take more time to alleviate. When this became apparent, we decided to change the focus of treatment and began to target the significant childhood traumas that were linked to her remaining symptoms. We developed a target map that included the earliest, most significant childhood traumas. We began to reprocess these incidents, adding new targets according to what new information arose between sessions.

USING THE STANDARD PROTOCOL
FOR CURRENT ANXIETY AND BEHAVIOR

For many problems Shapiro's standard protocol for current anxiety and behavior can be used. This is known as the three-part protocol. Shapiro (1995, 2001) recommended that the initial or earliest memory be processed first, followed by the most recent or most representative example of a present situation that causes the anxiety, including present-day triggers. Finally, a future projection of a desired emotional and behavioral response is targeted.

In my experience, and that of others (Korn, Rozelle, & Weir, 2004), it is most important to find a target that is linked to the current symptom or problem. I can't emphasize enough the importance of doing symptom-focused work. Too often therapists open clients up to a survey of their childhood traumas without focusing on the client's goals. I recommend obtaining a history that includes the earliest, most charged, and recent examples of the problem. For example, if the client has difficulty speaking in groups, you can ask for the first time he had that experience, the worst, any other times that stand out, and a recent example. When clients don't know the origins of their symptoms, the bridging or floatback technique (see Chapter 7, page 154) can be used. I have found that often the symptoms are not linked to the content. For example, fear of flying may not be linked to a traumatic experience on a plane. It may instead be linked to the *feeling* the person has when he is trapped in a small space and can't get out, along with the belief, "I'm powerless." This might be associated to a birth experience or an experience under anesthesia. Therapists often mistake the content for the roots of the problem.

It is generally best to work chronologically. Target the earliest memories first. You want to get at the roots of the problem. For example, if the client presents with difficulty speaking in groups, you can ask her if she can remember the first time she felt this way? If you can find the earliest, most charged memory that is most associated to the current symptom, you will get the greatest treatment effect. It is essential, however, that the memory that is targeted have emotional charge. Therefore, if a later memory is more linked to the symptom and has greater charge, you will want to use it for your target. For example, a client with a dog phobia may describe her first fear of a dog when she was 3 years old and a big dog barked at her, but a memory at 6 years old in which she was bitten has the most charge. You will want to target the experience at 6 even though it came later. The idea in EMDR is to go for the largest generalization effect. The memories with the greater charge will give you the greatest effect. Remember, you need to have charge in order to get processing.

If the problem in the present is amplified by experiences from the past, target those experiences first. A common error I see with EMDR therapists at my trainings and in my consultation groups is targeting a recent situation and not looking for the root experiences. When this happens what will frequently occur is that the client will process superficially, opening up many networks without completion. It is as if all the memory networks light up without completing any one of them. Clients who are activated without resolution can feel very distressed and lose confidence in EMDR and their therapists. I think of it as taking off the top of a weed without getting the roots. The weed will just grow back. But if you get the roots, you have gotten rid of the problem.

Sometimes the client cannot bridge back initially, so the therapist starts with a current situation. I recommend, however, that when this is done, and an earlier memory emerges, you make the earlier memory the target, returning to check its progress, SUDS, and installing the positive cognition there. It is inherently comforting to complete an early memory with EMDR. The past is wrapped up in a package, stored as the past, and a generalization effect emanates out through the associated memory networks. Even if you get one small piece of work done and complete, it can have a powerful generalization effect. In targeting and reprocessing the roots of the problem, you will require fewer sessions.

There are times when the charge *is* in the present situation and it is appropriate to target it. For example, a client was in a distressing work situation and didn't know what to do. After exploring the situation and any past links, it became apparent that it was about the present, not the past. In this case the standard EMDR protocol was used, targeting the worst part of the current situation, reprocessing it, and then doing a future pace.

HOW TO DETERMINE A TARGET FROM
A CURRENT ISSUE OR PROBLEM

When clients present with a current issue or problem, begin by exploring and gathering information about it. What are the symptoms? How are the clients currently impacted? How long have they had the problem? What have they done in the past to try to alleviate the problem? What are the different aspects? Is this about the current situation or is it a problem linked to something from the past? If the reaction to the current situation is bigger than it should be given the situation, find out what in the past it is linked to. This can be done by exploring the clients' associations, asking what they think it is connected to, or bridging back. Think, *What in the past is connected to the problem in the present?*

Oftentimes clients know what is connected to the current problem. There are key memories that are obviously linked. Sometimes clearing one significant experience is all that is needed to alleviate symptoms, whereas in other cases several sessions are required with several target memories. During the preparation phase therapists and clients collaborate to create a map that will guide them in selecting targets for reprocessing. What were the important memories? Target and reprocess them chronologically like beads on a string, working your way up. Many times when you start with the earliest or strongest memory, it will generalize up the network so well that you will not need many sessions. Some of the key memories you planned to target may already be cleared. When you reevaluate your work from the previous session, check the significant memories from your map to see if they still have charge. It can happen also that you begin with a map of targets to process, and you find that you need to add new ones or adjust the map.

TIPS FOR FINDING TARGETS

1. What are the clients' symptoms? What brought them into therapy? Get specific, including negative cognitions, emotions, and body sensations.
2. Are there any precipitating incidents? What memories are linked to the symptoms?
3. List the memories chronologically. Note the level of distress.
4. Develop a target map.

For example, a client comes in to see you because she is having problems at work. You ask her what specifically is the problem? She tells you she knows it is irrational, but she gets upset whenever her boss walks up to her desk to ask her a question. When you ask her what happens, she tells you that she chokes up, feels stupid, and can't think straight. In the process of taking her history and looking for key memories that link to her symptoms, you learn that she had a critical, overbearing father, a mean teacher in sixth grade who intimidated her, a high school basketball coach who demeaned her, and more recently an abusive boyfriend. In developing your target map, you look for charged incidents associated with each of these important figures. There may be several key incidents with some of these figures. Note them and organize them chronologically. Determine which to target first, according to its activation or emotional significance. Begin by targeting the earliest or most charged experience with her father. After the processing of that memory is complete, check the other memories from her map. Are they still charged? Sometimes reprocessing the earliest, most charged memory can have such a strong generalization effect that it clears the rest of the memories up the chain, alleviating the presenting problem and symptoms. Then, in subsequent sessions, continue to check her symptoms and reprocess the early memories. After those memories are clear, do a future pace. Ask her to imagine a situation in the future where her boss walks up to her chair. What happens now? If she says she feels fine, add BLS to install the positive feelings and beliefs (see Figure 5.1).

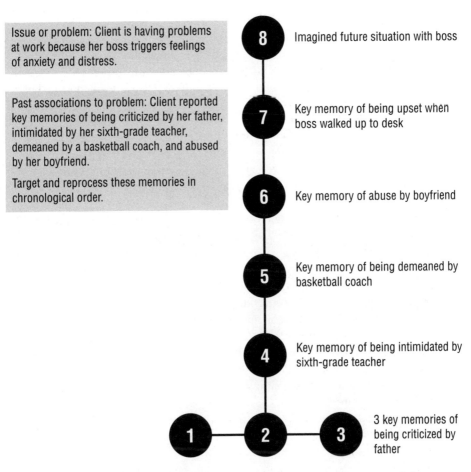

FIGURE 5.1 A schematic diagram illustrating target memories and the order in which they should be processed in treatment. Target memories are connected by associated images, emotions, body sensations, and cognitions. Note: Circles represent the target memories; numbers represent the order of their processing.

Case Example: Silvia's Fear of Dying

Silvia sought EMDR treatment because she was terrified of dying. A healthy woman in her late 50s, she wanted to get her affairs in order and write a will, but the anxiety that even thinking about her death evoked kept her from moving forward. As we explored the origins of her fear, she told me she believed it was connected to her Catholic upbringing. Growing up she was immersed in Catholic culture that stressed hell as punishment for any sin. Her mother, priest, and nuns at school were constantly painting a vivid picture of what would happen to her if she died with mortal sins. A conscientious child, she lived in terror that one of her thoughts or actions would send her into eternal damnation. Her mother in particular used the threat of hell to control her behavior. Even though as an adult she no longer held the same beliefs she did as a child, the frightening images she had taken in from that time were locked in their own time capsule. Her goal in treatment was to be able to write a will and not be terrified of dying. When she could do that we would know that the therapy had been successful.

During the history taking, she identified key scenes that were linked to her fear of death. There were memories of fearful stories from her mother, a priest, and a nun from parochial school. Together we developed a target map for processing these memories (see Figure 5.2). We decided to begin with the earliest memory first and work our way up chronologically. Each week we would reprocess a memory related to hell. The following week we would check the memory from the week before to see if the work had stuck. If there was still charge we would continue with the scene until it was complete. Also, each session I would ask her about how she felt about writing her will and how she felt about death. In this way I was able to monitor her progress. At one point she wanted to modify our plan and work on things she had done in her life that she felt badly about and considered mortal sins. Although her fear of hell had decreased significantly, she still was not 100% certain it wouldn't be her fate. There were two incidents from her 20s for which she had deep regret. On two separate sessions we targeted these memories. Upon the completion of her processing she was able to forgive herself and experience freedom from the fear of hell.

At this point she experienced a significant decrease in fear of death and hell, but she still was not ready to write her will. "What prevents you?" I asked. When she explored this question, she said it had to do with her current relationship with her partner and her issues with money. In the next two sessions we talked about these issues without doing EMDR. We then did an EMDR session targeting a small-*t* trauma experience with her partner

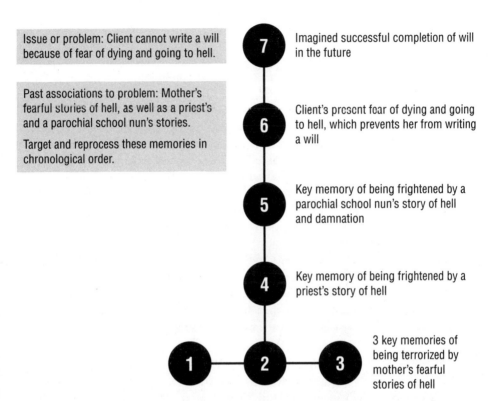

Issue or problem: Client cannot write a will because of fear of dying and going to hell.

Past associations to problem: Mother's fearful stories of hell, as well as a priest's and a parochial school nun's stories.

Target and reprocess these memories in chronological order.

7 Imagined successful completion of will in the future

6 Client's present fear of dying and going to hell, which prevents her from writing a will

5 Key memory of being frightened by a parochial school nun's story of hell and damnation

4 Key memory of being frightened by a priest's story of hell

1 2 3 3 key memories of being terrorized by mother's fearful stories of hell

FIGURE 5.2 A schematic diagram illustrating Silvia's target memories and the order in which they should be processed in treatment. Target memories are connected by associated images, emotions, body sensations, and cognitions. Note: Circles represent the target memories; numbers represent the order of their processing.

related to money. Finally, she came in and told me that she was ready to write her will. We did an EMDR session with her imagining what she needed to do to write the will. She then imagined actually doing it.

Case Example: Client Who Was Distressed About Moving

Betty came to see me because she was upset about a planned move. Emotionally she was having a large reaction that was disturbing to her. She wanted relief from her anxiety and distress. Divorced 4 years earlier, she was planning to move to a new town with her 10-year-old daughter because she was beginning a new job. She told me that when she thought about moving, she would immediately begin to cry. When I asked her what her fears were, she said, "I am afraid I can't manage all I have to do. I can't take care of my daughter. She will have a lot of pain and I can't help her." I asked her how her daughter felt about moving and to my surprise she told me that she was looking forward to it because she was unhappy with her current school. When I heard this, I concluded that her fear for her daughter was a projection. I asked her how she felt about the move. Was it something that she wanted? She told me that she wanted it. It was a good job and she liked the town. She even had a friend in the town. All of this information indicated to me that there was something from the past that was affecting how she felt about the move in the present.

I asked her if she had any thoughts about what was making her so upset about this move. She told me that she had moved a lot as a child, 12 times to nine different schools. It was very hard on her. "I felt strange and lonely. My mom was never there for me. I never had any roots." When I asked her what the worst time was, a time that felt similar to what she was feeling now, she remembered a time when her parents had divorced and she had moved from the countryside to a town.

Therapist: What picture represents the worst part of the memory?

Client: I was with a group of children. They asked me if I had seen a movie on TV. I said I had seen it, even though I hadn't. My mother didn't let us see TV. The kids elaborated on the movie and I went along with them, telling them that I had also seen those parts. Then they laughed at me and said that they had made it up. I felt so ashamed and sad. *(She begins to cry. I decide to do a modified protocol because the memory is activated and ready to process.)*

Therapist: What do you feel in your body?

Client: I have tears in my eyes. My chest is tight. So is my throat.

Therapist: What do you believe about yourself?

Client: I'm worthless.

Therapist: How disturbing does it feel to you on a scale from 0 to 10 with 0 being not disturbing or neutral and 10 the highest you can imagine?

Client: A 10.

At that point I began to tap on her knees.

As she reprocessed the memory with the children, she also linked to many other times she had moved and felt alienated. She realized that her mother had done the best she could at the time. She also realized that she had developed power and strength as a result of her experiences. During the sets of BLS she would link up to her current situation with her daughter, connecting past, present, and future. At one point she said she was stuck. She couldn't find a way to help her daughter in the future deal with the move. I asked her to go back to the original picture and tell me what came up. I felt that she was trying to solve the future before she had completed processing the past. Sure enough, when we went back to the original picture she had a new memory. She remembered that she had loved to play active games with boys in the outdoors and that when she moved the girls were more sedentary and passive in their playing. When she did a set of BLS focusing on that, she had a realization. "I can bring new things to them. I could teach them to play new games." This brought her relief. She then was able to see that it would be true for her daughter as well. Her daughter would have something new to offer the children in the town they were moving to. When we returned to the original picture her SUDS was a 1.

Therapist: What keeps it from being a 0?

Client: There's something with my little child. She feels a little lonely.

Therapist: Go with that. >>>>>>>>>

Client: I feel much better. I comforted her. Now it is a 0.

We installed the positive cognitions, "I can adapt and I have things to offer others." I then asked her to go to the current move. How did she feel?

Client: It feels okay. It's a good thing.

Therapist: Imagine the move. (*Future pace.*) >>>>>>>>>

Client: It feels fine.

We did a body scan. She said her chest felt open and clear. We then debriefed. She was smiling, beaming, and feeling very positive about her future.

Case Example: EMDR to Help Prepare for an Examination

Felix came into treatment because he was very anxious about taking an upcoming professional examination. He was concerned his anxiety would prevent him from doing his best. The exam had essay and oral components. He was most anxious about the essay part. I asked him what fears he had and he said, "Not knowing enough, blanking out. I don't have enough in me to answer the questions deeply enough." I then began to take a history of the presenting problem and to gather specific information about his symptoms. I asked him if he had been studying. Sometimes people are too anxious to study.

Felix: Yes, but a month ago I couldn't study. Now, it feels like I don't know the information.

Therapist: Do you have a history of test anxiety?

Felix: I've always gotten by but never aced essays. That's where I've felt helpless. There are no clues like in a multiple-choice test.

Therapist: What can you tell me about your experiences with essay tests?

Felix: Six years ago I was in seminary and there were lots of essay exams. They were rough. I always had the feeling that I wasn't prepared enough.

Therapist: Do you have any earlier memories?

Felix: As a kid I believed I wouldn't know enough. Somehow I was always getting by.

At this point I did not have a clear idea of where the test anxiety had come from. The information he was giving me was vague. There was no obvious precipitant. For that reason I decided to use the bridging technique to try to find a clearer target from the past. I began by asking him to give me an example of a time when he felt anxious taking an exam. I bridged back from that charged experience.

Therapist: Can you think of a time when you were taking an essay exam and you felt anxious?

Felix: Yes. It was when I was taking an Old Testament exam 6 years ago.

Therapist: Close your eyes and go inside. Let yourself go back to that time when you were taking that test. What picture represents the worst part of that?

Felix: It's the empty page. It's the empty page of the blue book. That's what bothers me.

Therapist: As you see the empty page of the blue book, what emotions do you feel?

Felix: Terror.

Therapist: What do you notice in your body?

Felix: My heart is beating fast. I'm biting my nails. My mouth is dry, and so is my throat. I'm sweating.

Therapist: What do you believe about yourself?

Felix: I get by because I'm lucky.

Therapist: Trace it back in time. Let whatever comes up come up without censoring it. Go back as far as you can. (*He's silent for a few minutes.*)

Felix: I'm in grammar school.

Therapist: What picture do you have?

Felix: I see a classroom. The desks are nailed to the floor.

Therapist: What's happening?

Felix: It's all empty. I don't see any classmates. I am very alone.

Therapist: How old are you? (*I'm trying to place this scene in time.*)

Felix: Around 8 or 9.

He said that the negative cognition was "I'm alone." (I omitted the PC and VoC because I was concerned it would take him out of his experience and into his head for analysis.) He said he felt lost, helpless, and frightened. Panic. His SUDS was an 8. In his body he felt a shortness of breath and an impulse to move his head from side to side very quickly. I began to tap on his knees. >>>>>>>>>

Felix: (*He speaks during the tapping.*) I can't believe no one else is here. I wonder what I am doing here. I don't feel like I belong. What kind of a place is this? I don't think anyone knows who I am. I'm just going to have to sit here and wait. I would like to get out of here. But I'm not allowed to. . . . How come I'm the only one here? . . . Now I'm flashing on experiences my mother had as a kid . . . experiences she had in the Holocaust. She was very alone. . . . Now there are other kids in the room. The classroom is now filled up with typical chattering. I see a globe, an aquarium, the room is taking on life. The teachers keep switching. (*I stop tapping.*)

Therapist: What's happening now?

Felix: There are two energies. One mean nasty teacher and the other a loving, kind teacher. It's like a flipbook, coming up from different sides and competing for attention, pulling me in. Which way am I going to go?

Therapist: Go with that. >>>>>>>>>> What's happening now?

Felix: It feels flat.

Therapist: Let's go back to the image of the empty classroom. What comes up now?

Felix: It's empty.

Therapist: How disturbing does it feel to you on a scale from 0 to 10?

Felix: A 7. I feel older, more objectified. >>>>>>>> *(Again he talks as I tap.)* The aquarium is empty again. The desk next to me that was empty on the inside. The desk is nailed down. This image is more salient than the blue book. Someone is meant to be there . . . a companion, guide. Someone who's not there. . . . I was told my mother miscarried after I was born . . . I'm just looking at that empty desk. *(I stop tapping and pause.)*

Therapist: What's happening now?

Felix: I'm thinking that that miscarriage was bigger than I ever imagined. It was treated matter of factly. My mother said, "I had a miscarriage and didn't want a kid anyway." Whether it's the missing person in the empty desk I don't know. >>>>>>>>> Everything is popping around in me. I feel like I need to wait a little. I need to let things settle down. *(I pause and wait while he is silent.)* There seems to be a pain right here. (He indicates his right arm.)

Therapist: What's it like?

Felix: Trying to find something.

Therapist: *(At this point I feel the processing getting diffused. I want to see if the target is being processed and where he is now.)* Let's go back to the scene in the classroom. What comes up for you now?

Felix: Isolation. Extreme isolation. >>>>>>>>>> *(At this point he has a memory from childhood of his father trying to teach him math. I tap as he narrates.)* It is a very bad day of my dad trying to help me with division. His European snobbery is lashing out at the American way of doing math. Any idiot would understand this is the wrong way. He's so mad. I'm not getting anything but anger and frustration compounding my frustration at not knowing the math. It's not a good way to have him explain this. I would love to get away, out of the kitchen right now. I want to calm him down. He's supposed to be my helper. Now I've got two problems. An angry father and math problems I can't solve. . . . I'm stuck at school and stuck here. I feel suffocated, not death, but torture. There's no way out. *(At this point I thought that he might be stuck in the processing so I asked him.)*

Therapist: Does the processing feel stuck or is it moving?

Felix: It feels slow. *(I believe he needs an interweave to get it back on track.)*

Therapist: What would have helped you?

Felix: Slower step by step how to get from 2 to 4 . . . slowing down the learning.

Therapist: How about a patient adult to help you learn step by step?

Felix: I know just the person. (*He brightens as he thinks of the person. I begin tapping and he narrates.*) >>>>>>>>>>> He was a very close friend of my dad's, very patient, methodical, always checking in with me to see where I am. He's validating also.

Therapist: What's happening now?

Felix: I feel warmer, lighter, healthier, more in tune with how I think things should be. >>>>>>>>>> When working with stress I can see how I get frustrated. (*At this point it feels like he is at the end of a channel. I want to see where he is in regard to the original picture.*)

Therapist: When you go back to the scene in the classroom with the desk, what do you get now?

Felix: It feels much better. (*I asked for the SUDS and he rated it a 2 or 3*).

Therapist: What keeps it from being a 0?

Felix: Habitual anxiety. >>>>>>>>>> (*He narrates his experience while I tap.*) The anxiety feels like it reaches to the center of the earth. Usually I feel it has me and I also feel responsible for holding on to it. I don't want to let go of it. . . . Now I'm pissed off at the desk. Your emptiness I could do without. If it were a mouth I would like to shove my fist into it . . . fill it with food. . . . A red apple, put books into it and let some life in it . . . (*He is filling the empty desk with the resources he needs, food and information. His voice is increasingly confident.*) I see a chair that folds up and down. I would like to invite my dad's friend to sit in that chair. . . . If he were sitting there he would help me figure it out in a very loving way. (*He's bringing in his own resources, doing his own interweaves.*) I can't even close the lid of the desk right now. It's a very stubborn open desk.

Therapist: What's happening now?

Felix: It feels good. (*I ask him for the SUDS and he reports a 0.*)

Therapist: What do you believe about yourself now?

Felix: I believe I can keep that desk open. . . . A new understanding. This imagination is as real as the empty desk. I can call on my imagination resource and my understanding.

Therapist: Hold the picture with that belief together. (*Installing PC.*) >>>>>>>> (*After installing the PC with the early picture, I wanted to go up to the scene from graduate school from which we bridged to see if that had changed.*) Let's go back to the scene from graduate school in which you are taking an essay exam and see the empty blue book. What comes up now?

Felix: That's still scary. (*I'm surprised that it hasn't changed, given that he processed the earlier memory so thoroughly. I want to know why.*)

Therapist: What makes that scary?

Felix: I don't have the open desk. (*Meaning the desk with all his resources.*)

Therapist: (*I do an interweave to link the resource of the open desk with the blue book experience.*) Can you imagine having the open desk with the blue book experience?

Felix: Oh yes! >>>>>>>>>>> I see stuff flying out of the desk onto the pages of the blue book.

Therapist: How disturbing does it feel now, 0 to 10?

Felix: Not at all.

Therapist: What do you believe about yourself?

Felix: I can access the open desk whenever I need to.

Therapist: Hold the picture of the blue book with the belief together. >>>>>>>>>

(*After installing the PC I wanted to bring him to the test he would be taking in the future and see if he could bring this positive feeling there.*)

Therapist: What comes up now when you imagine taking the test in 3 weeks?

Felix: It feels good. (I tap as he talks.) >>>>>>>>>> I see an energy flow from me to the open desk to the blue book and now to the computer. I need the medium of that desk, whatever that is.

Therapist: What do you believe about yourself now?

Felix: If I need to, I can access my resources. There's enough, I've got enough. (*I installed these beliefs with the image of taking the test. After that I ask him to scan his body. He reports a feeling of lightness.*)

Therapist: How do you feel now?

Felix: Very grateful.

In the next session I checked in with him to see how he felt about taking the examination. He said that he felt very good, confident. He had the strong feeling that he had access to his resources. He could imagine the desk full of what he needed, that he could open up and locate whatever he would need when he took the test. A generalization effect continued for him, with an increased sense of well-being and self-assurance.

LONGER-TERM THERAPY WITH MULTIPLE COMPLEX ISSUES

Sometimes clients come into treatment with a number of issues they want to work on that will require long-term psychotherapy. Some clients come in believing they have something simple to work on and it ends up being much more complex. Unlike traditional psychodynamic psychotherapy, I try to keep the work focused on the goals the clients and I set up from the beginning. In this way we make the best use of the time and clients know I am taking their needs seriously. As the therapy progresses, the goals can be changed. Rather than assume that they share the understanding, I find it is helpful to address the goal change directly with clients. You are in a sense renegotiating your therapeutic contract. For example, the client may seek treatment for a relationship issue focusing EMDR on that for several sessions, then change topics and begin to talk about work issues. In this case I might check in with her about the relationship issue, see if there was more to do on that and whether she had accomplished her goals. Then I make explicit a new focus for the therapy with new treatment goals. I have found that by focusing my clients on their goals and accomplishments, they feel more encouraged and successful with the work they have done and feel more hopeful for future work. It also empowers them, providing them with more of a sense of control and self-efficacy. They feel like they are getting their time and money's worth. Therapy doesn't drag on indefinitely.

When clients come into treatment to work on core issues originating from childhood, I let them know from the beginning that it will probably be longer-term therapy. It is important to keep in mind that problems that have multiple contributors generally take longer to clear. Deeply entrenched self-constructs that have been reinforced by multiple experiences throughout a lifetime require targeting many associated memories before change may be experienced. EMDR in my experience can be very effective for these clients, but it takes patience, working with transference, and understanding and being comfortable with psychodynamic constructs. Don't be discouraged. Keep going. What I have found is that there may be a sudden shift of the system after working diligently on a pattern or the shift may be subtle and gradual. This is where it is important to continue to reevaluate your work. Go back and check the symptoms the clients came in with. You and your clients may be surprised at what has changed that they have not noticed. Focusing on what *is* working and what *has* improved is essential in the work.

Expectations for EMDR can be too high, especially for changing entire core schemas in a short period of time.

Case Example: Client Who Felt Stuck and Unhappy in Her Life

Fran sought treatment because she felt stuck in her life. A creative person who loved to paint and write she was unable to find work that fulfilled her passions. She was miserable. Her goals in therapy were to find work she loved, write, and paint more. During the history taking I learned that she grew up in a very creative household where everyone was an artist, but her mother was narcissistic and very competitive with her. The unspoken understanding was that if she were better than her mother, she would risk losing her mother's love.

Much of the first months of our EMDR work focused on her relationship with her mother. Along with the EMDR we did talk therapy. Our work included a behavioral component. We had an agreement that every week she would write a certain number of pages and bring them in to our session to show me. This enabled her to be accountable to me and to herself. I could also be supportive of her in a way that her mother had not been. When she did not do the agreed-upon writing I would ask her what got in the way? Sometimes we targeted the limiting beliefs and their origins with EMDR. At other times she discovered that the assignment was more than she could do and we decreased the amount of writing according to her needs. We targeted and reprocessed many memories, all small-*t* traumas involving her mother. The first weeks of therapy she would come in complaining about her life and feeling hopeless. Her core beliefs that she was powerlessness, unlovable, and not creative enough were very ingrained. It was important that I did not believe her negative self-constructs and that I continued to target the roots of her belief system. The work was slow going. I had to be aware of my own countertransference from her projective identification: feelings that I was powerless to help her and that I wasn't good enough. Instead of believing these projections, I focused her on their origins and found the targets to reprocess.

Through consistent work on the early memories, she became more hopeful, productive, and happy. She was writing regularly. At one point she shifted the focus of the work to her relationship with her husband. We did some EMDR sessions on their conflicts and I referred them to a couples therapist. The work with Fran lasted about a year. By the time she left she had met her goals and had even found a job she liked.

Case Example: Client With A Driving Phobia that Linked to Early Traumas and Core Self-Beliefs

In another case, which began as something seemingly simple but ended up long-term and complex, the client came to see me because she had a driving phobia. Wanda and her husband had been in a serious car accident 2 years before in which a speeding teen had T-boned their car at an intersection, striking the passenger side where she was sitting and causing her extensive life-threatening injuries. In our initial interview she told me that her chronic back pain caused her to be unable to return to work. She was also too afraid to drive and she was terrified of being a passenger in a car. When she described the accident she used a sentence to describe it that stood out in my mind. She said, "The car came out of nowhere and struck us." Her words conveyed the feeling that this had been a random, senseless, violent attack from which they were unprepared and helpless to defend against.

In the initial interview Wanda told me that she was happily married and had close relationships with her two sisters. Her mother, whom she had loved dearly, had died of cancer 10 years earlier. It was when she told me about her father that I realized that her symptoms were about more than the car accident. She described her father as a doctor who had extreme, unpredictable bouts of rage during which he would beat her mother or her sisters and her. Wanda was the mediator, who did her best to take the temperature of the situation and try to calm her father before he hurt someone. She lived in terror with a feeling of helplessness. As she recounted her story, she told me that many times she feared for her life and for the lives of her mother and sisters. What seemed to stand out for her especially was the randomness of the attacks; they came out of the blue, much like the car that hit her. As she spoke about her past, tears sprang to her eyes and she began to cry. It was especially painful for her to recall the violence toward her mother.

Over the next few sessions I learned more about Wanda's history, the accident, her painful recovery, and her resilient spirit. She had a lot of support in her life from close friends and family. Though her father lived in a nearby city, she rarely saw him. She didn't like or trust him. Wanda was able to install safe place and nurturing and protector figures without difficulty. She had good ego strength and there was a comfortable rapport between us.

Because her father's violence seemed to connect to her accident, I thought that we should begin our work by clearing some of the most charged incidents with her father first and then work on the accident. My feeling was that if we began with the accident, it would either link back to the earlier incidents, or she would not get relief from her symptoms until we did the earlier work. This was a judgment call on my part. It is possible that if we just focused on the accident, her symptoms would have improved. I discussed all of my thoughts about this with her and together we decided to work on the childhood incidents first and work our way up chronologically.

We met every week for double EMDR sessions (100 minutes, two 50-minute sessions). This gave us enough time to talk about how her week went, check for dreams, triggers, and new memories, and check the work from the week before. Wanda became actively engaged in the work, reporting major insights about her life and functioning every week. She processed the early traumas well, feeling the feelings, riding the waves, and coming through with new understanding and relief. We worked on the early traumas over a few months. When we had cleared the most disturbing ones, I asked her if she was ready to do the accident. Together we decided to focus on the accident and the aftermath in the following sessions.

Over the next few weeks we used the standard trauma protocol to work on the accident. We began with the most charged part, when they were struck by the car, and processed that scene to a SUDS 0. We then worked on each of the different frames that were associated with the accident: what led up to it, the ride in the ambulance, the emergency room, the surgeries, and the physical therapy she had undergone. When she reported she felt done with all of those scenes we scanned through the entire incident looking for any charge. We focused on the hot spots with more BLS. After several sweeps through, she reported it was a SUDS of 1. She installed "I survived" as she played through the entire incident in her mind. I then asked her if she could imagine driving in the future, perhaps just a small distance, like in a parking lot? She said she felt she could. She imagined this future scene in her mind with BLS. After a clear body scan we debriefed. She was smiling, glowing, confident. She said she felt great and that she would try driving. I told her to do what she felt comfortable doing and that we would continue to work on this the next session.

To my astonishment, when she came in the following week she told me that she had driven. She and her husband went to a parking lot to practice and she felt so confident she just kept driving. She was so proud of herself and her accomplishment! We worked some more that session on areas from the accident and recovery that were still charged. In sessions that followed we targeted her fear of being a passenger in a car. After about 4 months her goals for treatment had been accomplished. However, she did not want to

stop therapy. The work she had done had opened her eyes to her psychological structure, core beliefs, and behaviors that impacted her self-esteem,
work, and relationships. Many of these patterns stemmed from the childhood traumas and coping strategies she had adopted in order to survive in
a threatening environment. At this point we began a longer-term therapy,
targeting both large- and small-t traumas that linked to her beliefs and
behaviors.

Typical of EMDR work, the major shift in PTSD symptoms occurred
in the first few sessions, but for the subtler, more entrenched core beliefs
and behaviors, it took much longer. Many EMDR therapists and clients
become discouraged with the latter. You have to remember that it takes
longer to shift deeply entrenched self-constructs because there are multiple
contributors.

6

REEVALUATING THE THERAPY

REEVALUATION, SHAPIRO'S (1995, 2001) eighth phase of EMDR treatment, takes place at the beginning of each session prior to beginning reprocessing. When the client comes in for the session, the therapist inquires about anything of importance that has come up related to the issue that was worked on in the previous session. The client may have had dreams, insights, memories, thoughts, or flashbacks, or noticed some new physical sensations. Clients who keep journals, write poetry, or do artwork as part of their between-session work may bring that in and talk about it. The therapist asks the client to refer back to the target that was worked on in the previous session to check to see if anything new arises. Has it lost its charge? For example, the client may have another memory associated with the one that was cleared that now feels upsetting. The therapist and client then decide what the next target for EMDR processing will be, depending on what has come up during the week. Reevaluation lets you and your client know how the therapy is progressing. Is this working? Checking your work from the previous session and from time to time checking in with the symptoms the client came in with helps direct the treatment and provides a sense of hope and accomplishment. If you can return to the list of symptoms from your history taking at the beginning of treatment and ask about it, clients can let you know what has changed and what still remains to be targeted. Often clients will experience a reduction in their symptoms and not be aware of it. It is like the experience for someone who has been in pain: When the pain is gone, they do not continue to think about the pain or how they used to be in pain. They just live normally. With EMDR, after there has been a shift, and clients are free from past emotional pain and symptoms, they forget that they used to be in so much pain. They are just living fully.

A common question I am asked by my EMDR consultees is how I know if EMDR is working. The best way to find out is to check the target. When

you return to the original picture or incident, what comes up? If it is changing, losing its charge, then it is working. Check the clients' symptoms. If
their symptoms are improving, it is likely that EMDR is helping. How do
clients view themselves? Have their negative beliefs changed? Have their
behaviors changed? Is there a reduction in flashbacks, nightmares, phobias?

For example, a woman came into treatment to work on several phobias
that were limiting her life. She was afraid of crossing bridges, feared flying,
and was terrified of bugs and spiders. She suffered from constant anxiety
that pervaded her everyday life. Nightmares haunted her of being chased
by bad guys and she was easily triggered into bouts of panic. A successful
businesswoman, she worked hard to compensate for her limitations. After
taking her history, it became apparent that the anxiety and phobias were
linked to severe physical and sexual abuse in her childhood that had continued for years. The therapy focused on targeting and reprocessing the
childhood abuse incidents. In the sessions following EMDR she would report
how her week had gone and then her symptoms would be checked. Could
she cross the bridge? How was her level of anxiety? Were there things she
was able to do now that she was not able to do before? Was she still having nightmares? Although the work was long-term and painful, when we
checked her symptoms and behaviors we could see that she was improving.
She felt happier, lighter, and more hopeful. Some of her phobias had van-
ished. Checking her symptoms gave her hope and encouragement to keep
going.

In another case, the client sought EMDR treatment because of a relationship problem. She was upset that her partner had decided to move out of
their apartment into another apartment in the same complex. He had no
intention of breaking up with her; he just wanted more time and space to
himself. Though she understood this, she was deeply shaken, overwhelmed
by fears of abandonment. She wanted to work on clearing the fears that
she believed came from early childhood experiences so that she could be
comfortable with the new living arrangement. Over the next several months
we worked on childhood memories that were linked to her difficulty with
her partner. She began to branch out and wanted to work on other issues.
I sensed from her a feeling of minor dissatisfaction with the work. When I
asked her how she felt about her living arrangement, she told me she loved
it. "I like having more time to myself." The problem she had come in with
had been resolved without her being aware of it. She had already moved on
to wanting to work on other things. I was able to tell her that it appeared
the EMDR had been working. That realization encouraged her to continue
to work on other issues.

As I said in Chapter 3, I believe it is important to take a thorough history of the presenting problems and also good developmental history. Then, begin to focus the therapy on the problem that is most important to the client. Don't be rigid about this, but it can be helpful to complete one thing before beginning another. For example, a client came to see me because she believed it was time to marry her partner of 15 years, but she felt resistant to going ahead with it. Her goal in therapy was to remove the psychological obstacles to getting married. In our work together we targeted and reprocessed experiences from the past that caused her to be afraid of marrying. We reprocessed a past marriage that had difficulties, fights she had had with her partner, and memories from childhood. In couples therapy she addressed current issues in the relationship. When we began each session I would ask her, "Have you set the date for your wedding yet?" Each time she would answer, "No, but I'm getting closer." Then, I would ask, "What gets in the way of your setting the date?" We would then target and reprocess the block. Finally one day she came in and said that she wanted to work on a different issue. I asked her, "Have you set the date for your wedding?" She told me she hadn't but felt very close to doing so. I could sense her resistance. I gently pressed her to tell me what was in the way. She closed her eyes for a moment and checked inside. She said it had to do with money. Was it about her partner or with something from her past? It turned out to be linked to memories of her parents fighting about money. We targeted and reprocessed a memory of observing one of her parents' fights. When that was complete, I asked if she could imagine getting married. She said she felt good about it. The next session she came in wearing an engagement ring. She was married a few months later.

In another case I was working with a young woman who felt blocked creatively. She was in despair about her life and her inability to find meaningful work. Each session we worked on memories from the past linked to her current blocks. Her agreed-upon assignment each week was for her to do some kind of creative work. She said she wanted to write, so we made the contract that she would write a few pages each week that she would bring in for me to see. If she did not keep her agreement, we would explore what got in the way. She felt my support and that I was taking her problem seriously.

This way of working, focusing on symptoms, is different from what is done in traditional psychodynamic psychotherapy, in which the therapist follows whatever the client brings up during the session. I have found that in doing symptom-focused work, clients feel held and cared for by the therapist. Their needs are being taken into consideration. Therapy doesn't drift along for years without completing anything. When the symptoms are checked, clients have more control over the therapy and can decide when they have accomplished what they came in for.

From time to time I like to do a review of the therapy. I will review my notes and the clients will review their journals or logs. We can look at which symptoms and behaviors have changed and which remain to be worked on. This is especially helpful for clients with complex, early-childhood traumas. They can feel like they are making little progress because of the quantity of symptoms. When you review the work, it can provide a sense of hope. When a memory is cleared, it usually does not come back unless there are aspects of it that had not been revealed. Clients often don't realize symptoms have been reduced until they check back.

The following are areas to ask your client about.

FUNCTIONING

How are your clients functioning since your EMDR session? I usually begin sessions by asking my clients, "How did your week go?" or "How did you do after our EMDR session?" Were they able to manage their affect after the session? Did they have a flood of material coming up? Did the work destabilize them, or did it help settle them down? Some highly traumatized clients do very well after EMDR, whereas others feel overly activated. The feedback from clients lets you know how to pace your treatment. For example, for some clients with multiple abuse memories, it may be best to see them twice a week or more. Some clients with multiple childhood traumas do best with a double EMDR session (90- to 100-minute session) followed by a single integrative session in which they talk about what came up for them during EMDR. Some clients prefer EMDR sessions every other week because they need more time to integrate the material on their own. The feedback from your clients help you adjust the therapy according to their needs. Do they want to take a break from EMDR for a while until their job is less stressful? Perhaps it is better to do more resource installation to shore up their ego strength.

CHECK THE LOG OR JOURNAL

I ask most of my clients to keep a journal or log of their experiences during the week. Many authors have written about the use of journals (Bass & Davis, 1988; Davis, 1990; Myers, 2003; Taylor, 1991). I recommend that clients find a quiet, undisturbed time to write in a journal or notebook that is kept strictly confidential. In these journals clients can write their thoughts, feelings, insights, and dreams that occur between sessions. Because the writing is for them, they should be instructed to write whatever comes to mind without censoring it and without worrying about proper grammar and sentence structure. For many, the writing helps them to process material between sessions. For some people, just jotting their observations down on Post-its can be helpful, or even speaking into a little tape recorder when something occurs to them. They can note insights, triggers, new memories, flashbacks, and dreams. Keeping a journal or log helps clients become observers of their own experience.

For example, one client created a nightly ritual wherein she would light candles, sit in a quiet private space, silence her mind, tune in to her inner experience, and begin to write. By doing so, she contacted an inner wisdom that helped her understand her irrational thoughts and feelings. From her pen would flow an understanding she did not know she had of her inner process. She could ask her inner child questions and answer through the writing. She also began to write poetry for the first time. Journal writing continued to be a valuable resource for her after therapy ended.

Often clients who have been traumatized experience symptoms related to the traumas, but may not understand the connections between the symptoms and the traumatic experiences. Flashbacks, nightmares, anxiety, and fear triggered by TV or movies can be experienced like assaults that are seemingly disconnected and unrelated to their present-day life. These experiences can make them feel like their lives are out of control. Encouraging clients to note these experiences helps them to target them and work on them systematically with EMDR. EMDR processing helps to give the symptoms meaning by revealing the connection between the triggers and the early experiences.

Clients often begin to feel like detectives collecting clues. Thoughts, feelings, and dreams are collected and brought in to sessions for processing. Distressing symptoms become meaningful and are keys to opening the doors to the past and aiding in the healing process. All of their experiences become grist for the EMDR mill.

Some clients may choose to use art between sessions. They may draw, paint, or make collages. Art can be used to continue the processing begun in the EMDR session. If clients are feeling something they don't understand, they can draw or paint it. Clients can also draw or paint their safe place and resource figures as a way of reinforcing them. Mandalas can be drawn to help in the containment of psychic material (Cohn, 2005). Therapists can ask their clients to show them their artwork. The art produced can be used as targets for EMDR sessions.

As well as giving clients a sense that they have some control, the journal and artwork also serve as permanent records of the clients' healing process. Because EMDR is typically intense and many changes can happen so rapidly, it can be very helpful to have this record for review. It can be quite encouraging to review the many changes that have taken place from time to time. Because of the length and intensity of the therapy, clients may forget how they were when they first came into treatment as they focus on the suffering they wish to alleviate in the future. One client inventoried all of her problems in many different areas of her life a few times a year. When she reviewed what she had written in the previous months, she felt renewed encouragement despite being in a current difficult place in her treatment. For her and many other clients, once one disturbing memory was cleared with EMDR, it did not return. Things that were problems in the past were no longer problems and sometimes were forgotten as having been problematic, unless recorded.

For many clients, journal writing is a tool that they continue to use after therapy is over. It is a means for them to maintain an ongoing relationship with their deeper selves.

SYMPTOMS

Check the clients' symptoms. Are they still having panic attacks? Did they have nightmares this week? Could they drive across the bridge? How are they sleeping? Are there still suicidal thoughts? Refer to your notes and ask the clients if the things you have noted have changed. Triggers should also be reported, as well as any areas of reactivity or difficulty. As clients are talking, the therapists take notes and listen for possible targets. Are the clients still being triggered by the same things, or are they less reactive? Are there themes emerging that should be explored more fully? A client with severe PTSD reported no panic attacks during the week, was sleeping better, was able to think more clearly, and was less anxious, but he was still being triggered by his ex-wife. I could see from his report that he was improving, but that we needed to focus on the current triggers.

BEHAVIORAL SHIFTS

What behavioral shifts do the clients notice? Are they more comfortable in social situations? Are they less reactive with their partners and children? What do they notice has changed? What hasn't changed? Is the client with the driving phobia able to drive? Can she do short distances in the car, or is she still unable to drive at all?

DREAMS

Ask clients if they have had any dreams. Many people develop an active and very vivid dream life that is a continuation of the EMDR processing. Encourage clients to write or draw their dreams and bring them to sessions. They make very good targets for EMDR. I will discuss ways of working with dreams in Chapter 7.

INSIGHTS

Did your clients have any insights since your last session? Sometimes a new understanding will flash into their mind. Encourage them to write these down. Insights are an indication that the processing is continuing. One client would never reach a 0 SUDS during the session. But as soon as she was in her car driving home, she would have an insight that would complete things.

NEW MEMORIES

Sometimes new memories will come up following EMDR sessions. Clients may notice flashback images or new body sensations arising. Ask clients to take note of them and bring them to the sessions. Adults with multiple childhood traumas often do not attain a 0 SUDS at the end of the session. The processing of a target can bring up associated memories that arise more intensively during the week. For instance, a woman working on the memory of being sexually abused by her neighbor may get the SUDS down to a 2 or 3 but feel something else connected to it—just a *feeling*. During the week fragments of the associated memory may come up for her, fleeting images appearing and disappearing in the corner of her eyes and leave her feeling sick in the pit of her stomach. She may feel that these image fragments relate to the work that was done the previous week. These memory fragments can be used as EMDR targets.

SYSTEM CHANGES

Because EMDR clients can make rapid progress, it can cause changes to the systems they are a part of. These changes may need to be addressed. For example, a woman I worked with was fearful and dependent because she was raped as a college student. As a result of the EMDR work, she became more self-assured and independent, a very different woman from the woman her husband had married. Her change destabilized the marriage. She needed to take a break from EMDR and begin marriage counseling with her husband.

It is always important to find out how clients are functioning, how they are integrating their EMDR work.

THE TARGET

The target from the previous EMDR session should be checked to see if it has changed. The therapists ask the clients to "bring up the image we worked on last week and tell me what comes up for you." As the clients refer back to the image or incident, they report what is perceived. By checking the target, therapists have more feedback about how the EMDR therapy is progressing (is the target image at a higher, lower, or unchanged SUDS from the previous session?) and gives them additional information for target formulation. The checking of the target can reveal a new associated memory that was not apparent the previous session. If the target still has charge, the therapists may choose to continue to reprocess it. However, in some cases the clients may feel that something else feels stronger and more compelling, and needs to be targeted for the session. For example, the SUDS on target from the week before may be at a 3, but a dream the client had may feel like a 10. The client may want to focus on the dream (which may be associated with the target) instead of the target image. In general I prefer to finish reprocessing the target to completion, but will not insist if it doesn't feel right to the client.

7

TARGET DEVELOPMENT

THE DEVELOPMENT OF targets is a very important step in EMDR and causes many therapists difficulty. Targets are like doorways or entryways into the memory complex. If you do not find the doorway, you will not be able to enter into the processing.

TARGETING SINGLE-INCIDENT TRAUMAS

When treating a single-incident trauma, begin by targeting the memory of the incident (Shapiro, 1995, 2001). Ask the client for the picture that represents the most charged part and build your target from there. It is important to activate the memory network sufficiently in order for processing to occur. Targets that are too vague or not emotionally charged will often lead to surface processing that does not feel engaged or productive.

Using the standard EMDR procedural steps, process the memory to completion. After targeting and reprocessing the traumatic incident, target any flashback scenes, nightmare images, current triggers, and, if appropriate, a template to address avoidance behavior. If time allows, this can be done in the same session, or it can be done over several sessions. When clients return after working on the trauma, check in and see how they are doing. Are their symptoms improving? What happens when they bring up the scene they worked on from the previous session? If there is still some charge, retarget it and continue to process it. Places where they are still experiencing distress can also be targeted.

For some clients' traumas, beginning with the most charged part of the memory does not generalize throughout the incident. Make sure to reprocess all the pieces of the incident, from beginning to end (e.g., what led up to the rape, the rape itself, the aftermath, the family's response, trial, etc., as well as a future pace). (See Chapter 11 for the protocol for working with recent traumas and critical incidents.)

TARGETING FOR CLIENTS WITH MULTIPLE TRAUMAS

Many clients seek treatment for problems that have multiple contributing factors. Treatment is most effective when target memories are carefully selected and reprocessed. This treatment can take longer, especially if a problem has deep roots and is caused by many incidents.

THE STANDARD THREE-PRONGED EMDR PROTOCOL

Shapiro (1995, 2001) describes the standard EMDR protocol as having three parts that guide the overall treatment of clients. Within each part, therapists apply the standard procedural steps to selected targets. In EMDR treatment therapists reprocess the following targets:

- Past experiences linked to the presenting problem or symptomology;
- Present situations or triggers that currently activate the symptoms;
- Future situations.

Shapiro (1995, 2001) recommends clustering the traumatic incidents into groups of similar events and then targeting a representative incident for each group. In targeting in this way, clients can experience a generalization effect through the memory network and not have to reprocess each traumatic memory individually. Shapiro also recommends asking clients for their 10 most disturbing memories from childhood, assessing the level of disturbance of every event and arranging them in order of disturbance for reprocessing. From my clinical experience I have found that rather than organize target selection in this way, it is more effective to develop targets that are most directly linked to the presenting symptoms. It should be remembered that not all traumatic experiences create symptoms of PTSD. Our interest as therapists is to treat the clients' symptoms, not memories. The more directly linked the memories are to the current symptoms, the stronger the treatment effect. It is essential, too, that the target memories and the associated networks be activated in order for EMDR to be the most successful.

Korn, Rozelle, and Weir (2004) also found this to be true. On September 12, 2004, in Plenary Session 301 titled, "Treatment Outcome Research of EMDR" at the EMDRIA Conference in Montreal, Canada, Bessel van der Kolk presented historic data from a major National Institute of Mental Health–funded study with important implications for the biological impact of EMDR treatment of PTSD and for its further clinical acceptance as the standard of care for PTSD. Following the summary of the study data, Deborah Korn chaired a panel presentation, "Looking Beyond the Data: Clinical Lessons Learned From an EMDR Treatment Outcome Study." This panel highlighted clinical lessons important to EMDR-trained therapists. Dr. Korn, who had served as the clinical consultant for the van der Kolk study, was joined in this panel with additional presentations by Jeff Weir and Deborah Rozelle who had served as treating clinicians in the study. Some of their lessons learned confirmed long-standing practices, such as the importance of taking a structured history and developing a focused treatment plan linking specific presenting complaints with specific ("activated") etiological, traumatic memories. Rozelle described the team's definition of activated memories: "A traumatic memory is considered an activated memory when the client reports cognitive, sensory, and affective arousal and distress related to an identified incident or incidents." For the vast majority of study subjects with complex early childhood trauma, instead of needing extended stabilization, the clinical team found that target selection and sequencing was critical to achieving effective outcomes within the eight sessions available within the research design.

When working with clients with PTSD from multiple traumas, take a structured history (as described in Chapter 3) and organize a map of potential targets. Only use activated memories that have an elevated SUDS and appear linked to the current symptoms. Work chronologically, beginning with the earliest traumas. However, if there is a memory that is more charged than the earliest, begin there. More activated memories take priority over earlier ones. What in the past is linked to the symptoms in the present? Specific, well-elaborated memories are better than vague memories. Work collaboratively with your clients. Discuss your thoughts with them. When discussing the memories, for the map, Korn, Rozelle, and Weir (2004) recommended using headlines with minimal elaboration rather than details. In this way clients are less likely to activate the trauma memories and feel overwhelmed. The targeting map is used to organize, focus, and help the treatment stay on track. Sometimes, during reevaluation, new memories will come up that will require adjustments to the map. Be flexible. After checking the previous session's target, and reprocessing any remaining charge, the new memory can be targeted if it is activated and linked to the symptoms.

Many clients suffer from PTSD from traumas but don't have specific memories to organize and map. For these clients, using the bridging technique that I describe later in this chapter can be used effectively. It is most important to find the early charged links to the current symptoms and behaviors.

TIPS FOR TARGET DEVELOPMENT

1. *Light up the memory network as clearly and completely as possible*, engaging the different components (image, NC, emotion, and body sensations) so the processing can best move unimpeded to completion.

2. *Get some kind of image if possible.* Even if the image is vague, it stimulates the visual memory track. The image can be abstract, such as a red blob that represents the client's anger or a drawing that represents what the client is experiencing. The image can be metaphorical, symbolic, or dreamlike. For example, with a person who has no visual memory but has strong body sensations, you can ask, "What image goes with the feelings in your body?" The client might say, "I get the image of someone stepping on me." That image can then be used as the target image. If clients have difficulty visualizing, it is not a problem. Clients can go with a vague sense of a scene. However, make the image as clear as possible. Bring in details. Have clients *see* as fully as possible what is around them.

3. *Don't worry about the order of the setup.* Allow clients to provide you with the necessary information as it unfolds for them. If clients tell you about their emotions and body sensations before the NC, don't worry. Note them and move on.

4. *Skip the SUDS, PC, and VoC if you don't have the time or it interferes with the flow of the clients' process.*

5. *Have clients who have difficulty finding and eliciting a memory stay in the memory as strongly as possible while the different target components are identified and stimulated.* For many clients, coming in and out of a memory disrupts the flow and causes them to leave the experience to intellectualize. Therefore, get the image, NC, emotion, and body sensations while the client is in the memory experience. Having clients close their eyes as they bring up the memory can help them to stay with it without interruption. The whole setup can move smoothly and rapidly this way.

Some clients provide you with all or most of the target components as they are describing the memory they want to work on. The setup process can flow smoothly without needless breaks if you don't attempt to get the target information in a specific order. You can ask clients for the information that wasn't provided in the narration they gave of the memory and then begin the BLS when you feel you have the memory network well stimulated.

6. *Use the NC that best stimulates a strong emotional response.* The NC is an irrational belief that was developed *in the past* that clients still feel *now* when they bring up the memory. To develop the NC, ask clients to bring up the

memory fully and feel themselves small. Elicit the memory as strongly as you can. Bring in other senses if necessary. What was the child thinking at the time? When the child state is activated, ask what they believe about themselves now. You can help clients find the best NC, offering suggestions if they are having difficulty coming up with something. Use simple language and short sentences that the child in the memory would use. If clients still can't get a NC, you can tell them that beliefs are often formed unconsciously at the time of the trauma. And then ask them what negative belief the adult imagines the child might have formed unconsciously.

I can tell we have found the right NC when, as I repeat it to clients, they respond with a reflexive "ouch" that is clearly noticeable and recognizable, as when touching a wound. You are looking for a negative emotional resonance that more fully activates the memory network. The therapist or client may repeat the NC aloud to help facilitate the activation.

7. *Emotions should also be emphasized.* There can be several different emotions felt, including seemingly contradictory feelings like love and rage. Some clients won't be able to identify an emotion. Don't worry about it! It may be in a compartment that is not as yet accessible. Sometimes clients can be aware of an emotion that is not yet felt. They have a "sense" that terror is there but cannot feel it. The SUDS may be low, but they have a "feeling" that the memory is very charged.

If they cannot identify emotions, focus on the body sensations. Often clients feel something but don't know what to call it. Don't push for a label. Ask them to pay attention to the feeling itself in the body. Again, what is important is that the emotional/somatic component is stimulated by the client's awareness.

8. *As clients focus on the memory, have them scan their body for any sensations.* "What do you feel in your body when you bring up the image?" For many clients, attention to their bodies makes them aware of the location of emotions and sensations that may be body memories. These sensations that arise when the memory is evoked can be important pieces of the memory that is being stimulated. Clients are often surprised by them.

Many people who have been sexually abused as children have difficulty sensing their bodies. They left their bodies as a defense against the feelings and they believe their bodies are not safe places. It is necessary to teach or guide many clients to experience the sensations in their bodies. They may dismiss or not attend to certain body sensations that are subtle but very significant. Attending to a constriction in the throat or a tingling in the hands during the setup may yield important information during the processing. If clients respond to the question about body sensations with "nothing," ask them to look more closely. Tell them that even subtle sensation is important information. The process of locating the body sensations is helpful training for these clients.

An area of sensation may be amplified by asking clients to use their hands to press on that area as the BLS begins. This is helpful for clients who have a difficult time feeling their bodies; it stimulates the sensation channel during the processing.

TARGETING TRIGGERS AND FLASHBACKS

Many clients become triggered by experiences in their daily lives, and these triggers make good EMDR targets. What triggered them? What image represents that? For example, a vet was triggered when his wife walked up behind him and he didn't hear her. The scene that triggered him becomes the target.

Therapist: When you bring up the picture of your wife behind you, what do you believe about yourself?

Client: I'm not safe. (*Skip the positive cognition because you don't know what "I'm not safe" refers to.*)

Therapist: What emotions come up for you when you bring up the picture?

Client: Fear, anger.

Therapist: How disturbing to you is that to you on a scale from 0 to 10 with 0 being no disturbance or neutral and 10 being the most disturbing you can imagine?

Client: A 10.

Therapist: Where do you feel that in your body?

Client: In my chest and arms.

You can also explore with the client what he thinks the trigger is connected to in the past, or bridge back to an earlier memory. Many clients experience visual flashbacks that can also be targeted with EMDR. Often, clients do not know what these flashbacks refer to and have very intense emotional responses. Reassure clients that they don't have to know what the flashback is about and tell them that the information that is needed will unfold during the EMDR processing. The following case illustrates using a flashback as an EMDR target.

During reevaluation of her previous session, Zena (described in *EMDR in the Treatment of Adults Abused as Children* [Parnell, 1999]) reported that during the week she had flashbacks. "I'm around 5 years old and I'm at someone else's house. I feel scared and it feels like someone is in the bedroom." That was all the information she had. She had no idea what the flashback was referring to, and it was very disturbing to her. She told me that it seemed to have been precipitated by an overnight stay at a friend's house when her friend's husband came home while Zena was sleeping and thus triggered her anxiety.

We began the EMDR processing with the flashback image of the 5-year-old on top of a bed at someone's house. The feeling was fear. The belief was "I'm not safe." >>>>>.

Zena: I can see all the houses on the block. I feel scared. >>>>> I'm outside in front of the house. (*A memory is beginning to materialize.*) It's right next door to Johnny's house. >>>> I'm still outside the house, there's a girl who lived there and I don't like her—she said she had better clothes than me. She had three brothers.

Therapist: What are you feeling?

Zena: I'm feeling more scared and anxious. >>>> I'm inside the house now.

Therapist: Do you recognize where you are? (*I am asking her because if she recognizes it, more of the pieces will come together faster for her. It will then leave the dreamlike quality. I thought she had recognized where she was already.*)

Zena: I don't know where this is.

Therapist: Go with that. >>>>>

Zena: I see the bedroom. There are posters and stuff on the walls . . . boy's stuff. >>>> I'm still in the bedroom . . . and somebody else is too. >>>> I can see who's there . . . it's her big brother. He's bigger than me but I like him and the way that he looks. (*She has now recognized who the people are and where she is. The pieces are coming together.*) >>>> We're laying down on his bed and watching TV. He used to rub my back while we watched TV. . . . I liked that, it felt good. >>>>> We did stuff. (*She becomes quiet. She is now into the disturbing part of the memory, which we continue to process to completion.*)

THE BRIDGING TECHNIQUE FOR TARGET DEVELOPMENT

This technique, which I described in my book *EMDR in the Treatment of Adults Abused as Children* (Parnell, 1999) and was adapted from the hypnotherapeutic technique called affect bridging (Watkins, 1971, 1990), can be used for clients who are stabilized and have the ego strength to handle traumatic memories or scenes that can emerge as surprises with the bridging.

The idea with the bridging technique is to activate as many of the memory components as possible (picture, emotions, body sensations, and self beliefs) and then trace the whole complex back in time to get an early scene that can be reprocessed. EMDR is most effective if we can get to the earliest root memories of the clients' current symptoms and process them to completion. Processing these early memories creates a more thorough generalization effect through the clients' memory network. Remember, we want to find the earliest experience linked with the symptom, or one that has the most emotional charge. We want to employ the three-pronged protocol, targeting and reprocessing the past, then targeting and reprocessing present referents, and then doing a future pace.

Frequently clients think that what has arisen is *not* associated with the sensations, but I trust that the unconscious mind has its own logic and I nearly always explore the scene or image that has arisen with the clients. Then, I use this image as the target image, even if it seems irrational. In nearly every case in my experience, the image that arose was a significant target that led to important new insights and information.

BRIDGING FROM A SYMPTOM, ISSUE, OR CURRENT PROBLEM

Often clients come in to treatment because they have symptoms, issues, or a current situation they are overreacting to because something in the past is affecting them and they don't know why. When therapists explore the past, they cannot find clear memories that are linked to the current symptoms. Sometimes clients have theories about their symptoms from past therapies but have no evidence to support them. I have found that often these theories are incorrect, the clients' symptoms caused by experiences they would never have thought to be significant. I have found the bridging technique to be helpful in working with phobias when there is no clear precipitant for the phobias. I have also found the bridging technique helpful for clients who do not have clear memories that link to their symptoms, for instance, clients who want to work on low self-esteem but can't remember any particular incident that caused them to feel that way. I have used the bridging technique for a range of symptoms and problems including fear of flying, fear of driving, insomnia, procrastination, aversion to sex, anxiety, low self-esteem, work problems, relationship issues, intimacy problems, and many phobias. You can also find targets by bridging back from triggers and transference.

Steps for Bridging From a Symptom, Issue, or Current Problem

1. Ask the client for an example of the problem. "Can you think of a time recently when you had this experience?" "Can you think of a time when this came up for you?" You want a time that has emotional charge. (Case of a woman triggered by lovemaking with her husband. A recent charged experience was the night before.)

2. Ask the client for the worst part of the recent situation. "Close your eyes and go inside. What picture represents the worst part?" ("It's when he's on top of me. His face is so close to mine that I can't breathe.")

3. Ask the client for the emotions that go with the picture. "As you see that picture, what emotions do you feel?" ("Fear, anger.")

4. Ask for the body sensations that go with the picture and emotions. "What do you notice in your body?" ("My heart is racing. I am having trouble breathing.")

5. Ask for the negative cognitions. "What do you believe about yourself now?" ("I'm going to die.")

6. When all of the elements are activated, bridge back in time. It is essential that the memory network be well activated. It is important that the client stay in the experience. Don't let clients intellectualize or try to figure things out. Stress the importance of not censoring their experience. Whatever scenes come up are probably significant. Encourage clients to go back as far as they can, but remember that it must have charge. Images that come up may not be memories. They can include composite scenes, confabulations, symbolic images, and metaphors, created scenes from stories they heard, or images from vicarious traumatization. For that reason I don't ask them to go back to a memory. These images that are linked to their symptoms are usually very significant. "Trace it back in time, let whatever comes up come up without censoring it."

(A memory of her brother putting a pillow over her face comes up. She was about 4, her brother 8, when they were roughhousing on the bed.)

7. Target and reprocess the scene to completion. Modify the standard EMDR procedural steps by omitting the PC, VoC, and SUDS if you believe including them will deactivate the memory network, making it difficult for the client to reprocess the scene. However, you should install a PC that emerges from the processing at the end.

8. Return to the recent picture or situation and check for any changes. "When you go back to that scene with your husband, what do you get now?"

9. If cleared and close to positive resolution, add BLS. ("I feel comfortable and safe with him now.")

10. Do a future pace. "Can you imagine making love with your husband in the future?" (Client: "Yes." Therapist: "Go with that.")

11. If the recent situation is not cleared, explore what else there is. You can bridge back to another scene if time allows, or plan to check in the next session.

See Figures 7.1 and 7.2 on the following pages for an illustration of processing target memories using the bridging technique.

Case Example: Presenting Issue Client Resisted Reading

Kelly was a psychotherapist in her 40s who wanted to work on her resistance to reading. I began by taking a history of this issue. She wanted to read more but didn't like to. She did like reading novels and newspapers, but not professional literature. She believed it was unethical that she wasn't reading more. She currently had Margaret Mahler's *Psychological Birth of the Human Infant* and had only read a few pages. I asked her if she ever listened to lectures or books on tape and she said that it was "cheating" and wasn't good enough. Even taking continuing-education classes was not sufficient.

She told me that as a child she had some learning disabilities. She was pulled from her regular classroom to be taken to a special reading class. One memory that stood out was being taken by her mother to have a brain test as a child. She had already worked on that memory with EMDR and it didn't feel charged to her. She also had an older sister who told her that she took too long to be born and so was "overcooked."

After talking with her, I believed there were two issues that affected her reading. Because of childhood learning difficulties she had low self-esteem with regard to her reading even though she no longer had problems reading. The second was the erroneous belief that she had to read in order to be adequate professionally. Clearly there are many ways to keep up professionally other than by reading.

We began by establishing the type of BLS she wanted to use. She chose tapping on her knees. We then installed a safe place, which was a place by a river with friends where she had camped. We then identified nurturing figures—a female friend and her former therapist—which we installed. I decided to use the bridging technique to find the target.

We began by using the image of Margaret Mahler's book, which she was having difficulty reading.

Therapist: Close your eyes and go inside. Bring up the picture of Margaret Mahler's book. Now open the book and begin to read it. What emotions do you feel?

Bridging steps:

1. Find an example of the problem.
2. Ask the client for the worst part of the situation. What is the picture?
3. What emotions come up?
4. What do they notice in their body?
5. What do they believe about themselves?
6. Trace it back in time, let whatever comes up come up without censoring it. Find an associated image or memory.
7. Target and reprocess the scene to completion.

Recent example of the presenting problem: Client is triggered by lovemaking with her husband.

Picture: "His mouth over mine so I can't breathe"

Emotions: Fear, terror

Body sensations: Heart pounding, difficuty breathing

Negative cognition: "I'm going to die"

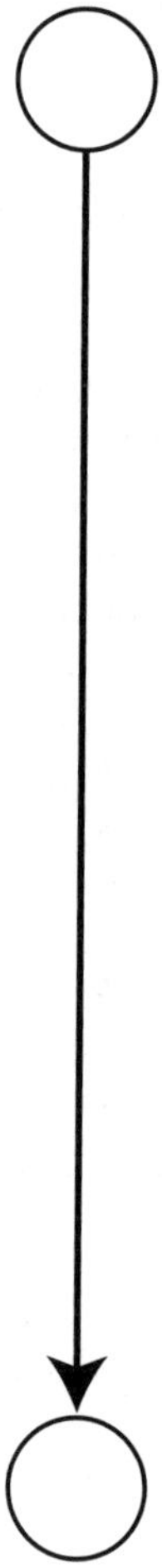

Key memory of brother putting a pillow over client's face

Emotions: Terror

Body sensations: Struggling for breath, sensation in arms, hands, and face

Negative cognition: "I'm powerless"

FIGURE 7.1 A schematic diagram illustrating how to bridge to target memories from a symptom or current problem. Target memories are connected by associated images, emotions, body sensations, and cognitions. Note: Circles represent the target memories.

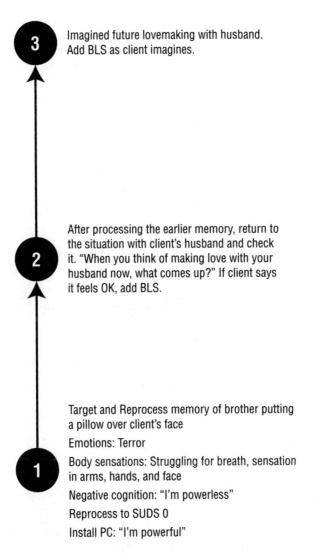

FIGURE 7.2 Targeting and reprocessing past, present, and future memories, beginning with the earliest memory found from bridging. Note: Circles represent the target memories; numbers represent the order of their processing.

Kelly: I feel inadequate. It will be hard for me. It feels stressful. I feel anxiety.

Therapist: What do you notice in your body?

Kelly: I feel tension in my chest and neck. And my shoulders are tight.

Therapist: What do you believe about yourself?

Kelly: I'm stupid.

Therapist: Trace it back in time. Let whatever comes up without censoring it. (Kelly is silent for a few moments; there are signs of emotion in her face.)

Kelly: I have a few pictures. The first is of taking some kind of test and being told I have poor comprehension. The second is in second or third grade. We had a special reading group. I would be taken out of class. I remember hearing someone call me a retard. The last one is of the time my mother took me to get an EEG.

Therapist: Go through the pictures that came up and choose the one with the most negative charge. *(I want to use the most charged memory because I want the strongest generalization effect.)*

Kelly: The strongest one is the one in the classroom where the kid calls me retard.

Therapist: What picture represents the worst part?

Kelly: I'm standing up like I'm the only one standing up and I hear *retard.*

Therapist: What emotions do you feel?

Kelly: Angry.

Therapist: What do you notice in your body?

Kelly: Tension in my chest. I want to scream. I feel dizzy. *(She reported a SUDS of 7–8.)*

Therapist: What do you believe about yourself?

Kelly: I'm a retard. *(I omitted the PC and VoC because she was already in the memory, the issues were performance, and I didn't want to deactivate the memory network by measuring it.)*

Therapist: Bring up the picture, emotion, and body sensations, and say to yourself, "I'm a retard." Let whatever happens happen without censoring it. *(Begin tapping.)*

Kelly processed memories from school and adulthood having to do with reading. We would return to the picture of her second-grade class from time to time. When her SUDS was a 0, I asked her what she believed about herself now?

Kelly: I can read and I have choices about what I read.

We installed those PCs, which interestingly enough covered the two issues I had seen at the beginning: how she felt about her ability to read and her choice of what to read. Then I brought her to the present situation with the Margaret Mahler book.

Therapist: When you imagine opening the Margaret Mahler book, what comes up for you now?

Kelly: I close the book and return it. I don't have to read it. I can listen to it on tape. I can read what I want to. I have choices.

Therapist: Go with that. >>>>>>> (*Kelly smiles and laughs. Of course she has choices, she realizes now.*) Can you imagine yourself in the future reading?

Kelly: Yes.

Therapist: Okay, imagine that. (*Add BLS.*)

We ended with a body scan and debriefing.

Case Example: Presenting Problem Discomfort in New Groups of People

Ronnie, a bright, sturdy woman in her 50s wanted to work on her feelings of discomfort in groups. She said that it was something she had felt all her life. "I never feel like I fit in. I become quiet, in the background. I keep to myself." When we explored this, she said it applied to small as well as large groups of people. She thought that maybe it was because her family moved so frequently during her childhood and she was constantly having to fit into new groups of people. I asked her if any examples stood out for her. She told me it was really hard for her to move when she was 15. She had a boyfriend and was happy at school. The memory held a lot of grief for her, but it didn't seem related enough to the presenting issue to me to use it as a target. I felt better bridging back to see what came up. If this image was the right one, then I trusted she would bridge back to it.

I began by asking her if she had a memory that she could bring up of a time recently when she felt uncomfortable with a group of people.

Ronnie: I was at a silent meditation retreat rooming with a group of five women I didn't know. For some reason they all left the room together at the same time. I felt completely left out.

Therapist: Close your eyes and go inside. What picture represents the worst part of that?

Ronnie: I'm left in the room by myself while the group is all together outside.

Therapist: As you see that picture, what emotions do you feel?

Ronnie: Sad, alone.

Therapist: What do you notice in your body?

Ronnie: My throat is tight, my stomach fluttery.

Therapist: What do you believe about yourself?

Ronnie: I'm unworthy of their regard. I'm alone.

Therapist: Trace it back in time. Let whatever comes up come up without censoring it. (*Ronnie closes her eyes for a few minutes.*)

Ronnie: I'm 15 in the South. We've just moved here. A girl in my class tells me that I don't belong. But there's something earlier. (*She is silent for a while, and then speaks again.*) I'm about 8 years old and I'm sitting in a car reading a book about Mexican children. I'm realizing for the first time that the world is a much bigger place than I had imagined.

(*I don't believe she has gone back as far as she can related to this issue, so I encourage her to go back even farther. She still has her eyes closed.*)

Therapist: Can you go back even farther?

Ronnie: (*Silent for a few minutes, rapt in her inner exploration.*) I am very little. I'm playing at my mom's feet. She's ironing, not paying any attention to me. I can't get her attention.

Therapist: How old are you?

Ronnie: Around 3. I'm looking up at her. I'm on the floor. I can see her legs and the underside of the ironing board. I feel so lost and alone. (*This memory is earlier than the others she mentioned before and has a lot of charge to it. I decided to use it as our target.*)

Therapist: What do you believe about yourself?

Ronnie: I'm unlovable.

Therapist: What would you like to believe about yourself?

Ronnie: I am lovable and worthy of love.

She rated her VoC a 2.

Therapist: What emotions do you feel?

Ronnie: Really upset.

She rated it a SUDS of 8.

Therapist: What do you notice in your body?

Ronnie: I feel clenched up. Tightened up, caving in. *(At this point I began to tap on her knees. She goes deeply into the process.)* >>>>>>>

Ronnie: My adult self knows that my mother was deeply depressed. But my child is bewildered. She believes it is her fault.

Therapist: Go with what your adult self knows. *(I say this because I want to encourage the link between the child and adult memory networks.)* >>>>>>>>>

Ronnie: I'm angry. Not at her, but at the whole situation. The moving was very hard on my mother. She was depressed and so was my father. >>>>>>>>>

Therapist: What's happening now?

Ronnie: I'm around 15. I'm acting out sexually, sneaking around. I felt horrible. The whole family broke down. >>>>>>>>>>

Therapist: What's happening now?

Ronnie: There is a wall behind my eyes. A Niagara Falls of tears unable to come.

Therapist: Go with that. >>>>>>>>

Ronnie: I can feel it. >>>>>>>>> It subsided back. *(She blows out a big breath.)* I'm seeing light.

Therapist: Let's go back to the original picture, with your mother. What comes up now?

Ronnie: It's not very vivid.

Therapist: On a scale from 0 to 10 where 0 is no disturbance or neutral and 10 is the highest disturbance, how would you rate it now?

Ronnie: A 3.

Therapist: What keeps it from being a 0?

Ronnie: Anger and compassion all mixed up.

Therapist: Go with all those feelings. >>>>>>>>

Ronnie: I see a lineage of women suffering alienation from depression. This is going to stop with me. >>>>>>>>

Therapist: What's coming up now?

Ronnie: I feel peaceful.

Therapist: Let's go back to the 3-year-old with your mother. What comes up now?

Ronnie: I feel quiet inside. I see a line of women. I turn around toward my mother. I made that contact. I feel us both being held. >>>>>>>>>>

Therapist: What's coming up now?

Ronnie: I feel love going into Mom. We healed so much together over the years. I am loved and completely worthy. >>>>>>>>> I feel love. I am overflowing with compassion for my younger self. It's okay now. >>>>>>>

Therapist: When you bring up the image of the 3-year-old, what comes up now?

Ronnie: I feel loving and compassionate.

She reported her SUDS was 0. Her PC, which we installed, was "I am loved and loving." Her VoC was a 7+. I then asked her to check in with the other memories she had mentioned in the beginning of our session and see what came up for her.

Ronnie: I feel compassion for myself. I feel a quiet watching but knowing that I'm loved and loving.

Therapist: Can you now imagine bringing yourself into another group situation? Can you imagine how that would be? (*She seems to have cleared the past, so I'm doing a future pace with her.*)

Ronnie: Yes. >>>>>>>>>

Therapist: How's that?

Ronnie: I feel like a participant, and more of a leader.

Therapist: How does your body feel?

Ronnie: I feel light yet grounded.

We then debriefed the session. I advised her to pay attention to her dreams, associations, and new memories and insights and to see what came up for her the next time she was in a new group situation.

Case Example Issue: Client Has an Aversion to Being Touched

Anica wanted to work on a long-standing issue. She said she had an aversion to being touched. "I can't stand to be touched." If she doesn't initiate it, she said she doesn't like to be hugged. She also had problems with sexual intimacy. "It's hard for me to be open and let go." She saw a therapist who wanted her to imagine being touched, but she couldn't tolerate it. Though she had no memories of sexual abuse, she suspected there might be repressed memories. Her older brother was mean to her. I think it is important to note here that it is essential that therapists not assume sexual abuse when clients report symptoms like hers. So often we are wrong.

Anica was functioning well in her life and had many friends and supports. She was able to readily install a safe place, and nurturer and protector figures. I decided to bridge back from an example of her aversion to see if we could find what in the past was linked to the symptom.

Therapist: Think of a time recently when you felt aversion to touch.

Anica: In intimate situations with my husband.

Therapist: What bothers you the most?

Anica: It's the feeling of someone coming toward me expecting something of me.

Therapist: Okay, close your eyes and go inside. Bring up the image of someone coming toward you. What emotions do you feel?

Anica: Shame, fear.

Therapist: What do you notice in your body?

Anica: My mouth and private areas.

Therapist: What do you believe about yourself?

Anica: I'm ugly, ashamed, I feel fear.

Therapist: Trace it back in time. Let whatever comes up come up without censoring it.

Anica: I get two pictures. The first is a picture of the nuns in school giving religious instruction and humiliating me. The second is an image of my dad reaching for my mom and her pulling away from him.

Therapist: Which one of the two has more charge?

Anica: The one with my mom pulling away from my dad.

Therapist: When you bring up the picture, what do you believe about yourself?

Anica: Affection is unacceptable. I'm not wanted.

Therapist: What emotions do you feel?

Anica: Sad, alone, no one cares.

Therapist: Bring up the picture, emotions, and body sensations, say to yourself, "Affection is unacceptable," and let whatever happens happen. >>>>>>> What's happening now?

Anica: I saw a sequence of pictures. None with my brother. I was taken care of but not talked to. No one was affectionate with me. >>>>>>> Pictures of the nuns laughing at me. Pictures of the nuns being cruel. They never helped my self esteem. >>>>>> School reinforced what was going on at home. My mother was very controlling. >>>>>>> I never learned how to allow people to love me.

Therapist: Go with that. >>>>>>>>

Anica: I moved to college. I made mistakes with sex that reinforced my belief that sex is bad. >>>>>> I married at 31. I had to do it all by myself. I never had a caring man. >>>>>> I took care of my husband. He was not a loving person. >>>>>> This doesn't really have to do with sex. I never had a chance to learn to be close to people.

Therapist: Go back to the picture with your mom. What comes up now?

Anica: That's your problem (*She's talking to her mother.*). >>>>>> I don't have to feel worthless. >>>>> I'm thinking about my mom. I am wiping out the negative and remembering the positive. (*She seems calmer now, brighter, happier.*)

Therapist: When you bring up the picture, how disturbing does it feel to you now on a scale of 0 to 10?

Anica: A 0.

Therapist: What do you believe about yourself now?

Anica: I'm free of that.

She told me that the VoC was a 7. We then installed the PC with the picture.

Therapist: Let's check the other two pictures you started with. When you bring up the picture of the nun giving religious instruction, what comes up for you now?

Anica: It's more humorous. It's not a part of myself.

Therapist: Think of that. >>>>>>> Is there any charge to that picture now?

Anica: No.

Therapist: What do you believe about yourself now?

Anica: I'm okay.

We installed that PC.

Therapist: Let's check the second picture, your mother being angry. What comes up now?

Anica: That was her problem. I can let people in.

Therapist: Go with that. >>>>>>> Can you imagine someone coming up to you to hug you? (*I am doing a future pace.*)

Anica: Yes. It's not a problem.

Therapist: Imagine that. >>>>>>>

Anica: It feels fine.

At the end of the session she gave me a hug. When she came in the next session, she told me that the day after our session she spontaneously let a friend massage her feet, something she had never been able to do before.

BRIDGING FROM THE SYMPTOM OF INSOMNIA

I have worked successfully with several clients suffering from insomnia, bridging back to find the source of the problem.

First, explore what specifically is their difficulty. Is it falling asleep, staying asleep, early waking? How long have they had the problem? What have they done to try to remedy it? Rule out medical contributors. What do they think it is linked to? If they don't know and you have ruled out medical issues, try to find the target by bridging back.

In one case the client, a 45-year-old woman, had been suffering from insomnia as long as she could remember. She had tried a lot of different things to help her, none successfully. She told me she would start to fall asleep, but wake up with a start, her heart racing. She couldn't let herself fall asleep.

Therapist: Can you think of a time recently when you had this experience?

Client: Yes, last night.

Therapist: Close your eyes and go inside. Bring up the moment from last night when you had difficulty sleeping. What picture do you see?

Client: I'm lying there in bed, just drifting to sleep, when I jolt awake.

Therapist: What emotions do you feel?

Client: Fear, anxiety.

Therapist: What do you notice in your body?

Client: My heart is racing. I feel something in my urethra. *(I think maybe this is sexual abuse. I don't tell her about my hypothesis.)*

Therapist: What do you believe about yourself?

Client: It's not safe to fall asleep.

Therapist: Trace it back in time, let whatever comes up come up without censoring it. *(She is silent for a few minutes.)*

Client: I'm about 7 years old. I have just wet the bed. I'm trying to change the sheets before my mother walks in and yells at me. I had a terrible problem with bed-wetting throughout my childhood. I used to get into a lot of trouble. I was humiliated. *(It makes sense; she cannot allow herself to fall asleep because if she lets go into sleep, she may wet her bed.)*

We targeted and reprocessed the scene with the bed-wetting. Then we returned to the scene from the night before.

Therapist: What do you get now when you think of that?

Client: I don't wet my bed now. I can control myself. I can let go and go to sleep.

Therapist: Imagine that. >>>>>>>>>>

After that we did a future pace. "Imagine yourself sleeping in the future."

In another case, the client, who was a cancer patient, traced her fear of falling asleep to a memory linked to her grandfather's death when she was a little girl. She remembered her mother telling her that death was like sleeping. Instead of comforting her, it terrified her, linking sleep with death. After reprocessing this memory, she was able to fall asleep.

BRIDGING BACK FROM TRANSFERENCE

You can bridge back from the transference as you would from a symptom. If the client is feeling something about the therapist in the moment that is linked to earlier material, the therapist should first repair anything in the relationship that has triggered the reaction. For example, if the client is feeling like she can't trust the therapist because the therapist was late for the session, the therapist can apologize and listen to how the client feels about this. When there has been sufficient repair and the client feels safe, bridging can be done from the trigger to an earlier memory.

"When you bring up the moment when you noticed I was late, what emotions do you feel? What do you feel in your body? What do you believe about yourself? Now trace it back in time. Let whatever comes up come up without censoring it. Go back as far as you can."

Case Example: Bridging From the Transference

Martin, a 55-year-old client, told me that he felt upset by my reaction to something he told me in our previous session. When I asked him what it was that upset him, he said that it was the puzzled look I had on my face. He told me that it made him feel like he shouldn't be talking. He didn't really count. I talked with him about it some more; I couldn't recall when it had happened. He told me that it was a feeling that came up for him a lot in his relationships. I asked him if he would like to explore it, to see if we could find out where this came from in the past.

Therapist: Close your eyes and go inside. What picture do you have of what triggered you?

Martin: It was your face, looking quizzical and not getting what I was saying.

Therapist: What emotions do you feel?

Martin: I feel really nervous. I feel like I need to do it better. I want to tuck in tight across my shoulders. (*He bends forward, putting his shoulders together.*)

Therapist: What do you believe about yourself?

Martin: I shouldn't talk.

Therapist: Trace it back in time. Let whatever comes up come up without censoring it.

Martin: This came up with my mother all the time. If I start a sentence, my mother will make it be about her.

Therapist: What picture do you have of this?

Martin: I have a sense of trying to talk to my mother. I'll be talking to her on the phone. It is more hearing her voice. (*Even though it isn't very clear, this will be his target image, along with the sound of his mother's voice.*)

Therapist: As you imagine talking to her on the phone, what emotions do you feel?

Martin: Frustration, anxiety.

Therapist: What do you notice in your body?

Martin: I feel tight all over, especially in my chest.

Therapist: What do you believe about yourself?

Martin: There's no room for me to be me.

Therapist: Go with that. >>>>>>>

At this point he reprocessed several memories with his mother. He realized that it was her problem, not his. He was not responsible for her. He could express himself. He installed the PC, "I can be myself," and then returned to the triggering incident with me. He said he felt fine. He felt he could talk, he could express himself. He felt more separate from his mother. We would continue to work on this issue in future sessions.

BRIDGING FROM PROBLEMATIC BEHAVIORS

I have also had success working with problematic behaviors such as procrastination, overeating, bingeing, cutting, and drinking. Bridging back and finding the roots of the problem and reprocessing them can help to change the behaviors, sometimes quite quickly. The trick here is to activate the memory network of the moment *before* they did the behavior. What was their internal state—emotions, body sensations, and cognitions—right before they acted? For example, loneliness might be a trigger for eating. Light this up, and then trace it back. If the early contributors to the behavior can be targeted and reprocessed, the behaviors can shift.

1. Ask clients for an example of when they did the behavior. ("Can you give me an example of when you found yourself bingeing recently?")
2. Ask clients to focus on the scene, to bring themselves to the moment *right before they began to do the problem behavior*. ("Can you bring yourself to the moment right before you opened the refrigerator?")
3. Ask for the picture they see. ("What picture do you see?")
4. Ask for the emotions. ("What emotions do you feel?")
5. Ask for body sensations. ("What do you notice in your body?")
6. Ask for beliefs. ("What do you believe about yourself?")
7. Bridge back. ("Trace it back in time. Let whatever comes up come up without censoring it.")

Case Example: Procrastination on Dissertation Writing

Mona came to see me because she couldn't write her dissertation. She was stuck and afraid she would never be able to finish it. She didn't know what was blocking her. I asked her what would typically happen. She told me that she would set aside the entire day to write, fully intending to do so. "But when I was ready to go into my office and sit down to work, I would get this thought in my head that I wanted to make a cup of tea. I would then find myself in the kitchen making tea. Then, I would think that I would like to make lunch. I love to cook. So I would begin to make a big meal. I'd then eat it, and then clean up. By that time the day would be gone and I wouldn't have enough time to get anything done." I decided to try to focus on the moment when she changed direction and went into the kitchen instead of her office.

Therapist: Can you think of a time recently when this happened?

Client: Yes, yesterday. I was on my way to work on my dissertation when I went to make a cup of tea.

Therapist: Good. Close your eyes and go inside. Bring up the moment when you turned and changed direction. Can you do that?

Client: Yes.

Therapist: What emotions do you feel?

Client: Fear, anxiety.

Therapist: What do you notice in your body.

Client: My heart is racing. My throat is tight.

Therapist: What do you believe about yourself?

Client: I'm stupid.

Therapist: Trace it back in time. Let whatever comes up come up without censoring it. (*She is silent for a while, then speaks.*)

Client: I have an image of myself as a child. I have just brought my report card home. I have all A's but one B+. My father is angry about the B+. I feel terrible about myself. (*We target and reprocess this memory, until she has a 0 SUDS and install the PC, "I'm competent, I can do it."*)

Therapist: Let's go back to the scene we started with, when you are going toward your office to work on your dissertation. What comes up now?

Client: I'm walking right into my office, sitting down at the computer, and writing. I can do it!

Therapist: Go with that. >>>>>>>>

Client: It feels great.

Therapist: Can you imagine writing your dissertation now, doing what you need to do to complete it?

Client: Yes.

Therapist: Imagine that. >>>>>>>>>

After this session she was able to work on her dissertation without difficulty. She then moved on to focus on other issues.

Case Example: Developing a Target from a Symptom of Compulsive Eating

Linda wanted to work on a problem that she had developed recently that was troubling her. "I'm compulsively eating peanut butter. Shoveling spoonfuls into my mouth. I don't know why. I'm gaining weight. I never used to do this. I make a peanut butter sandwich and pile the peanut butter on. I feel out of control."

She told me that it was a new behavior, that she didn't know why she was doing it. There were no known triggers or precipitants that she was aware of. I decided to bridge back in time to see if we could find what this behavior was connected to.

Therapist: Close your eyes and go inside. Bring up a time recently when you were eating peanut butter by the spoonful. What emotions are you feeling?

Linda: Guilt, out of control, craving.

Therapist: What do you notice in your body?

Linda: Tension all over. There's something about my mouth.

Therapist: What do you believe about yourself?

Linda: I can't have it.

Therapist: Trace it back in time. Let whatever comes up come up without censoring it. (*She is silent for a few minutes, then speaks.*)

Linda: I'm small, around 7 years old. I'm in the kitchen eating peanut butter. I just want to eat it. Then my mother comes in.

Therapist: What emotions do you feel?

Linda: Guilt, craving.

Therapist: What do you feel in your body?

Linda: Tension.

Therapist: What do you believe about yourself?

Linda: I did it wrong.

Therapist: Okay, I'm going to begin tapping on your knees now. Just let whatever comes up come up. *(I don't check the SUDS because I could see from her description that it was charged, and didn't want to bring her out of her experience by measuring it.)* >>>>>>>>>> *(She is silent for a few minutes, emotion shows on her face, and then she opens her eyes and begins to speak.)*

Linda: My family was poor. There wasn't enough food. My mother is trying to control everything. >>>>>>>>> My parents immigrated to the United States and made a choice to be poor. It was their choice, not mine. I can choose to have things. I have choices now. >>>>>>>> That feels true.

Therapist: Let's return to the original picture. What do you get now?

Linda: I feel sorry for the girl. My mother had five kids, too many. I craved attention from her. I loved going to the store with her because I got time alone with her. >>>>>>>>> Now I'm using a knife to spread the peanut butter, not a spoon.

We continued to process until her SUDS was 0.

Therapist: What do you believe about yourself now?

Linda: I can have good things. I have choices.

We installed this PC. Then I asked her to return to the scene we began with, when she was recently eating peanut butter.

Therapist: What do you notice now?

Linda: The craving is gone. I can eat it if I want. I have choices.

After installing this PC, I asked her to imagine herself in the future with peanut butter. She said she could have it in moderation. It felt fine. We then debriefed the session. She told me that she realized the peanut butter craving was connected to a larger issue for her. It had to do with having things. "I want to be able to have things without feeling guilty." She said that although there was more to do on it, she felt complete with the peanut butter. We planned to continue to work on the issue in future sessions.

BRIDGING FROM EMOTIONS

There are times when clients experience emotions that feel irrational and confusing. They don't know why they are feeling the way they are. You can bridge back from the emotions, too.

1. Ask clients to close their eyes and bring their attention to the emotion.
2. As they feel the emotion, where do they feel it in their body?
3. What do they believe about themselves?
4. Say, "Trace it back in time. Let whatever comes up come up without censoring it." Ask the clients to go back as early as they can. What we are looking for is a felt sense connection to the current emotion. I try to get clients to trace the feeling and belief back to the *earliest or strongest memory*.
5. The picture or scene that comes up is what is then used for the target. Do the standard EMDR setup on that scene and process to completion. Modify, omitting the PC and scales if they deactivate the memory network.

Case Example: Bridging From Overwhelming and Confusing Feelings

David described symptoms that had been bothering him for a long time. He felt an upwelling of love energy that felt overwhelming and confusing. He said it hurt his body. There was also a "glitch" in his upper back that radiated to his head. "My chest will hurt like a pressure that is constant and is related to emotional stuff." When we explored it, he could not identify where the symptoms came from. After installing a safe place and nurturing and protector figures, we bridged back to find the origin of his symptoms.

Therapist: Close your eyes and go inside. Get in touch with the feelings you were telling me about. What do you notice in your body?

David: My belly is tight. (*He begins to tear up.*)

Therapist: What do you believe about yourself?

David: If all this comes through, I can't handle it.

Therapist: Trace it back in time. Let whatever comes up come up without censoring it. (*He's silent for a while.*)

David: In high school I was shut down. And in junior high school I was fairly shut down. In sixth grade I dropped out of baseball.

Therapist: Do you have a picture?

David: Yes. I see myself in sixth grade smoking a cigarette in a wooded area.

Therapist: What do you believe about yourself?

David: I don't fit. I can't belong.

Therapist: What would you like to believe about yourself?

David: I know how to fit and belong.

His VoC was 1. He reported feeling numb. His SUDS was 5. He felt it in his head.

As soon as he began to process, his level of distress increased and he began to cry. During the session he realized that he was a sensitive child who felt what other people felt and was overwhelmed by the information. By the end of the session he understood how he functioned and his adult self could explain it to his child self. He was able to open to his feelings and accept them. He reported that the pain in his shoulders and chest was much improved. He believed he was fine as he was.

Another way to develop a target from an emotion is to ask clients for an example of when they felt it, and then use that situation to bridge back.

1. Can you think of a time when you felt _____ (the emotion)? Can you think of a time when you were triggered?
2. Close your eyes and go inside. As you think of that time, what picture represents the worst part of that? Can you find the moment when you were triggered into feeling _____?
3. What do you notice in your body?
4. What do you believe about yourself?
5. Trace it back in time. Let whatever comes up come up without censoring it. Go back as far as you can.

Case Example: Client With Outbursts of Anger

Mary Ann wanted to work on what she described as her "anger problem." She said she would have uncontrollable outbursts of anger. "The rage comes up and out. I just spew out the most horrible feelings and words. I dump them on my 12-year-old daughter. She ignites me." Mary Ann believed her rage attacks were linked to her ex-husband who assaulted her when she was pregnant. She also told me that her mother had physically abused her.

Mary Ann easily installed a safe place, and nurturing and protector figures. I then asked her if she could remember a time when she felt the rage. She said that just the night before she had blown up at her daughter. About an hour before her outburst, she had informed her daughter that she was not going to go to an informational meeting that evening. Then her daughter "acted like a parent" to her and asked her again if she was going to go to the meeting. "She said the meeting was only 45 minutes long and that I should go. That is what set me off, her telling me what to do. When people don't take what I say and trust that I mean it, and trust my words, I get triggered. I feel like I'm not being taken seriously."

I asked her to close her eyes and go inside.

Therapist: See if you can find the moment that you were triggered into rage.

Mary Ann very quickly pinpointed the moment. She saw the two of them walking down a path and heard the words that set her off. She felt the rage ignited in her.

Therapist: What do you feel in your body?

Mary Ann: I feel this energy go up from the back of my head like flames.

Therapist: What do you believe about yourself?

Mary Ann: No one believes me.

Therapist: Trace it back in time. Let whatever comes up come up without censoring it.

Mary Ann came up first with a memory of violence from her ex-husband, followed by memories of her mother abusing her. I encouraged her to go back as far as she could. She came up with a memory from adolescence that she felt was significant.

Mary Ann: I'm 15 and she is beating the crap out of me. I was out past curfew and had come home and she caught me in the hallway.

She said she was feeling pain, confusion, and anger. She described a swell of emotion in her body. Her NC was "I'm helpless." I began to tap on her knees. She spoke aloud as she processed long sets.

During the session she processed the years of abuse she received at her mother's hands. No one in the family believed that her mother was hurting her. She brought up a memory from the year before when her mother was dying. MaryAnn told her mother she loved her, hoping that on her deathbed her mother would show some affection. Instead, her mother replied, "Whatever." Returning to the original picture, she remembered that her older brother had come home and saw what their mother was doing. He intervened, telling his mother that she had to stop immediately. He warned her that if she ever beat his sister again, he would to the same thing to her. It was the first time anyone had witnessed the abuse or believed her. Her mother never beat her again. Mary Ann realized that there was a chain of abuse from mother to daughter stretching back generations. She wanted to put an end to it. When we returned again to the scene of her mother beating her, she saw that she was no longer stuck in the hallway. She had moved to the kitchen and the whole scene had faded. The emotional charge was gone, now a 0 SUDS. Her PC was "I am strong and powerful," which we installed.

Then I asked her to return to the scene with her daughter that had triggered her originally. She reported that she no longer felt the rage, or anything at all. "I can just tell her I don't want to go to the meeting."

For the final step, I asked her if she could imagine times in the future when her daughter might tell her what to do in a parental way. "What comes up for you now when you imagine that." She told me that she felt fine about it. It didn't feel like a problem. I told her to imagine it, as I tapped on her knees. After that she scanned her body, reporting that she felt clear and good. I advised her to notice what came up with her daughter during the week and to see if there were any more triggers to anger. We would work on anything that came up in future sessions.

BRIDGING FROM PHYSICAL SENSATIONS

Sometimes clients present with physical symptoms that appear to be body memories or have a psychological origin. When clients have somatic experiences that are distressing to them in some way, you can use the body's experience as the entryway into the processing. You can ask the clients to focus directly on the physical sensations, then ask for the emotions, body sensations, and NCs, and then process. But, in my experience, it is preferable to bridge back and find specific memories associated with the symptoms. It is also easier on the clients as it produces fewer surprises that can be upsetting. In addition, it is much easier to contain a specific memory than an entire network of associations that can be activated if you go in on body sensations that have multiple contributors.

1. Ask clients to close their eyes and bring their attention to the body sensation.
2. As they feel the sensation, what emotions come up for them?
3. What do they believe about themselves now?
4. "Trace it back in time. Let whatever comes up for you come up without censoring it."
5. Target and reprocess the pictures or scenes that come up.

Case Example: Bridging From Body Sensations*

Claire suffered from the emotional and physical aftereffects of having been raped when she was between the ages of 2 and 3 years old by the family maintenance man who was like a grandfather to her. The abuse involved oral sex on him and vaginal rape. The pain she experienced during the rape was so intensive that she fainted, and she remembered that after he raped her she had diarrhea, vomiting, and bleeding. When she told her mother that, "Mr. Smith made me sick," her mother responded, "Oh people don't make you sick! You have the flu." The abuse only stopped when her family moved away.

As a result of this horrific physical and sexual abuse, Claire suffered considerable damage to her reproductive system and urinary tract. In her 20s, she had three surgeries related to the forgotten abuse, including urinary tract surgery, a prolapsed uterus with torn ligaments, and a hernia in her groin area. At the time of one surgery, the doctor told her that it looked like she had been gang-raped. Also, she had had frequent yeast and bladder infections since her 20s and a problem with chronic muscle contraction in the area of her urethra.

Claire had locked the abuse memories away in some far part of her mind until she was 31 years old and ended an abusive relationship. The ending of the relationship stimulated the old memories and caused her intense anxiety and somatic symptoms.

Claire was referred to me by her physician because of her pelvic pain caused by the chronic contraction of the muscles in her pelvic floor. The physician believed that the muscle contraction was related to the abuse she

---

* From EMDR in the Treatment of Adults Abused as Children (Parnell, 1999).

had suffered as a child and thought EMDR might help her heal. Because she had no specific memories of the abuse, I decided to bridge back from the physical symptoms.

We began our first EMDR session by focusing on the muscle contraction in her urethra area. She closed her eyes and brought her attention to that area, and I asked her what emotions she felt. She said she felt terrified. Then I asked her what belief went with that feeling.

After a few moments she replied, "If I let go, my insides will fall out." Then I asked her to trace it back in time. She was silent for a while, and then replied, "I see myself as a little girl with her toes turned in, holding on to the wall. I have the sensation that things feel loose and that fear. I tensed all the muscles to keep that from happening. I feel complete turmoil and distress . . . and everyone else is acting like things are normal. It's crazy making."

From her narration we had all of the target components necessary to begin the processing: the body sensation (muscle contraction around the urethra), the NC ("If I let go my insides will fall out"), the emotion (fear), and the image (the little girl trying to hold everything inside).

Before beginning the processing, she chose a place of power she knew with nurturing and protector figures in the four directions as her safe place. She placed her grandmother in the north, her husband in the south, a wise old woman in the west, and herself as a nurturing maternal figure in the east.

Claire began by contracting her urethra muscles tightly to amplify the physical sensation and focused her attention in that area. She focused on the image of the little girl holding her insides in and the belief that she had to contract the muscles or her insides would fall out. Her SUDS was a 10.

The session was very intense, with a great deal of somatic processing. She cried and breathed rapidly. She remembered Mr. Smith's kindness and she remembered his threatening to kill her and her dog if she ever told. She remembered this "kind" man cutting her little finger to show her he was serious. This piece of the memory was particularly terrifying to her. She struggled with seeing that the same man was both good and evil. This was difficult for her, but her adult self came in and explained to her child self how this was so.

During the processing Claire experienced letting go of the contractions in her genital and abdominal areas. Later in the session she felt pain in her neck and shoulders. This was revealed to be associated with a memory of forced oral copulation. At one point she felt sick, dissociative, and terrified. It was too much for her child self. When I asked her if she would like to go to her safe place for a break, she said yes and went there, wherein the maternal figure held Claire in her lap and comforted her. When Claire felt strong enough to continue, she asked to resume the processing.

Claire continued to process the old memories in her mind and body and experienced many energy shifts. As the contractions in her body released, she experienced powerful energy running through her. By the end of the session she felt herself to be powerful and saw Mr. Smith as weak and small. She believed that she no longer needed to hold herself in by contracting her muscles.

The next week, she reported that she felt good after the session. When we checked the image of the little girl trying to hold her insides in, she had difficulty getting the picture at all and the emotions were not there, so we targeted another memory that had arisen associated with the abuse.

Case Example: Client With Chronic Pain in His Shoulders and Neck

Kevin was a psychotherapist with a thriving practice. He had had chronic pain in his shoulders and neck that he believed had a psychological etiology, which he didn't know. In this session we bridged back from his symptoms.

Therapist: Close your eyes and bring your attention to your shoulders and neck. What emotions do you feel?

Kevin: I feel overwhelmed. I'm afraid.

Therapist: What do you believe about yourself?

Kevin: It's my responsibility. I can't do it.

Therapist: (*Begins bridging.*) Now trace it back in time. Let whatever comes up come up without censoring it. Go back as far as you can. (*Client pauses for a while and then begins to speak.*)

Kevin: I'm young, I think around 8. I'm in bed asleep and my mother comes in and wakes me up. She's afraid that someone is in the house. My father is away. She leaves to check the doors. I feel I'm supposed to protect my mother and myself. I feel overwhelmed. I can't protect my mother and myself.

We targeted and reprocessed this scene until his SUDS was 0. His PC was "I am capable, but it was not my responsibility," which we installed. We then returned to the present.

Therapist: When you come back to the present, what comes up for you?

Kevin: I can balance out my clients and my life. I feel capable. It is not for me to put on my shoulders. I feel a huge relief in my shoulders and neck. They don't hurt anymore.

Therapist: Can you imagine taking that into the future?

Kevin: Yes. >>>>>>

We then closed and debriefed the session with him reporting relief from neck and shoulder pain. In our next session he reported that his neck and shoulders were no longer hurting.

Kevin: The weight is gone. The muscles aren't strained.

Case Example: Client With Puzzling Somatic Symptom

Whenever Jenna felt emotional she would have difficulty breathing. This was a problem she experienced all through her life. She had no idea why this would happen. When I asked her when she had recently felt this, she said "As soon as I spoke about it I felt it in the moment." I decided to bridge back from the feeling that was activated right then and there in the session.

Therapist: Close your eyes and go inside. Bring your attention to your breathing. What emotions do you feel now?

Jenna: Terror, fear.

Therapist: What do you believe about yourself?

Jenna: I can't breathe. I'm going to die.

Therapist: Trace it back in time. Let whatever comes up come up without censoring it. Go back as far as you can. (She's silent for a few moments.)

Jenna: There's a scene with my brother. I'm terrified. (Her anxiety has increased considerably. She's frantic.) He's preventing my breathing. It's like a near-death experience.

Therapist: How old are you?

Jenna: 10.

Therapist: What's happening?

Jenna: We're roughhousing. He was aggressive and I was playful. And there was a time in the water. He was trying to kill me.

At this point we targeted the experience where her brother nearly drowned her. She processed that memory as well as one at 10. As she cleared the memory she began to take deep full breaths.

Jenna: I'm reclaiming my breath. I can live. I'm going to put my breath back in.

She installed these PCs. When she returned to the present, she felt herself able to breathe fully. She then imagined breathing in the future.

BRIDGING FROM A NC

Many clients have core negative beliefs or schemas that form the foundation for their negative self-concept. Experiences throughout a lifetime contribute to these schemas. NCs can be used to develop targets for EMDR processing when clients do not have images or memories they can readily identify as root causes for their current problems. Many clients seek treatment because of the negative self-concepts; they no longer want to believe that they are inherently bad, powerless victims and are not valuable. The bridging technique can be used to find memories from the past that link to the beliefs. It can take many sessions working consistently on this structure to shift the beliefs. These structures are often created from many small-*t* traumas. Bridging helps to find key examples from which you can work.

1. Ask clients to close their eyes and repeat the negative belief to themselves, e.g. "I'm not safe."
2. "As you say those words to yourself, what emotions come up for you?"
3. "Where do you feel that in your body?"
4. "Trace it back in time. Let whatever comes up for you come up without censoring it."
5. Target and reprocess the scene.

For example, imagine you have a client who believes she is powerless and has no clear idea where this belief came from. Her difficulty manifests in standing up for herself in her intimate relationships and at work.

I would ask her to close her eyes and repeat, "I am powerless" to herself and to notice what emotions she feels as she says those words, and then what she feels in her body. She might say, "I feel sad and alone," "There is a tightness in my chest and a sick feeling in my stomach." I next ask her to trace it back in time. "Let whatever comes up come up without censoring it." I try to get the client to trace the feelings and beliefs back to the earliest or strongest memory possible. "Notice whatever images pop into your mind; don't censor anything." Usually I find that an image comes into the client's mind that has a charge. In this example, it might be an image of being a small child being humiliated on the playground by a bully. The image might also be a fragment of a scene. The image that emerges becomes the target image.

If the client is unable to come up with anything by bridging, you can have the client repeat the NC, feel the feelings in her body, and then begin the BLS. This method has a higher likelihood of producing more diffuse processing but can be useful for locating a more defined target such as a memory. If a memory or an image does come up early on in the processing, that memory can be referred back to during the processing and SUDS check. I have found that the bridging technique for developing a target from a negative belief creates a more direct route to the primary material to be processed for symptom resolution than beginning with the NC alone. The former produces a more specific target that is more likely to produce more complete and thorough processing of a memory.

Case Example: Client With Low Self-Esteem

Eileen wanted to work on her low self-esteem. "I can't do it" was a belief that pervaded her life and limited her sense of self-efficacy. When we explored the origins of the belief, she told me that she didn't know where it came from. Because I could not find an incident from her history to target, I decided to bridge back from the belief.

Therapist: Close your eyes and go inside. Repeat to yourself, "I can't do it." What emotions do you feel?

Eileen: Sad, helpless.

Therapist: What do you notice in your body?

Eileen: Tension in my chest and throat.

Therapist: Trace it back in time. Let whatever comes up come up without censoring it. (*She is quiet for a few moments, then speaks.*)

Eileen: I have an image of myself at around 7 years old. I'm trying to learn to ride a bicycle. I can't do it. No one is helping me.

This is the picture we worked on. We developed the target and then processed it to completion. Her PC at the end was "I can do it!"

You can also bridge back from a NC by asking clients for an example of a time when that negative belief about themselves came up. For example, a client with the belief, "I am unacceptable," was asked for a time when he felt like that. He said it was when he was in the grocery store and the clerk didn't help him right away. Using that picture with the emotions, body sensations, and belief, "I'm unacceptable," he bridged back to a memory from childhood in which his family shunned him. The early memory was targeted and reprocessed.

USING ART FOR TARGETS

Art can be a helpful tool for aiding in the development of EMDR targets (Cohn, 1993a, 1993b). The client can "draw the issue of why you are here," "draw what you are feeling," or "draw the disturbing scene." The drawing is a projection of the client's inner experience. Feelings, ideas, and images are externalized in the picture. The drawing helps clients to gain distance from overwhelming feelings and helps to clarify the feelings and incidents. Sometimes clients produce artwork between sessions that is loaded with meaningful symbolism, and this art makes excellent targets.

In one picture, the therapist and client can learn a wealth of information about the client's inner experience at once (i.e., closeness, distance, bonds, divisions, similarities, differences, energy investment, and context of family relationships). Unlike verbal processing, which tends to be linear, drawings provide a spatial matrix. For example, if the client draws a picture of his family, where is he in relation to his parents? Does he draw himself as very small or very large? Is he separate from the rest of them, or included close to them? Who is not included in the picture? What colors does he use? Does he draw with more force when he draws his father? Because "a picture is worth 1,000 words," a multitude of EMDR cognitions can come from one such picture. In my office I have crayons, craypas, markers, paper of different sizes, and a large drawing board that can be held on the client's lap. Allow at least 15 minutes for drawing.

One can use drawing when the client has strong emotions and does not know why. I might say, "Draw your feelings." The client might scribble on the page forcefully with black, red, orange, and purple markers. This visual representation can be referred back to during the processing. One client was very upset, feeling a kind of inner chaos, and didn't know why. I asked her to draw what she was experiencing and she drew dark red swirls in a tight ball. "Anger and fear" went with that image. I asked her what she felt in her body, and she said, "A swirling energy in the front of my body." Finally, I asked her what she believed about herself and she said, "I'm out of control." She then began the BLS. By the end of the session her SUDS was down to 0 and she felt in control and calm. She drew another picture that represented the new feeling that we installed with BLS.

You can also use drawing when the client is having difficulty coming up with a target memory. For example, one woman remembered being beaten by her father but was having difficulty focusing on any scene. I asked her if she would like to draw a picture of the problem, one that represented it. She drew a picture of her father very large and dark hitting a small child with a belt, her mother depicted small on the edge of the page.

When the client has completed the picture, you can put it up on the wall or set it at a distance so that you can view it with the client. As you look at the picture together, ask the client to tell you about it. Ask any questions you have about it. "What is that red mark over there?" Do not interpret what the client has drawn. After viewing the drawing, turn it over. Have the client focus on the inner picture with the emotions, body sensations, and NC and begin BLS. If the client is emoting after viewing the picture, begin immediately with the BLS. After a set ask, "What's happening now?" At the end of a channel return to the image. Don't turn the picture over again unless the client requests that you do because, as in all EMDR sessions, the picture changes. "When you bring up the picture what do you get now?" Sometimes the client will want to make a new drawing, or make changes to the old one. For example, one woman drew a picture of herself very large, surrounded by helper people. When she finished drawing it and viewed it, she realized that she didn't believe others could really help her. As she processed the picture, she began to make changes on it, drawing more connections among herself and the helpers. Finally, when the processing was complete, she drew an entirely new picture, one that showed her the same size as her helpers, giving and receiving nurturing in a fluid, integrated whole.

As part of the debriefing it is valuable for the therapists and clients to view the before and after pictures at the close of the sessions. It can be astonishing to see the progress made in the sessions. It gives clients something tangible and undeniable that they can take from the sessions. It is typical for EMDR clients to forget the distress they came in with. The drawings can be kept in a large folder in the therapists' offices. Having a concrete record of their progress provides a valuable support to clients. Over time, the therapists and clients can go back and review past sessions. It can be deeply gratifying seeing the dramatic transformation that has unfolded as recorded through the drawings.

Christa Diegelmann, a German psychotherapist, developed a protocol that uses art and BLS called CIPBS (conflict imagination, painting, and bilateral stimulation), which she uses with cancer patients as well as others suffering from PTSD (see Appendix 2, page 339). Her preliminary research has shown this treatment to be effective (Diegelmann, 2006; Diegelmann & Isermann, 2003).

Diegelmann uses a large piece of drawing paper that the clients fold into quadrants, instructing clients to draw in the squares, starting in the upper left field, then upper right field, then lower left, and ending with the lower right. More than one sheet of paper can be used. The safe place is drawn on a separate piece of paper. First clients draw the safe place, which is installed with BLS. Then the clients are instructed to draw the conflict or problem. Next the therapist asks for the SUDS. The NC, PC, emotions, and body sensations are omitted. For clients who are too distressed, or when it does not seem appropriate therapeutically to get a SUDS, the BLS is begun without taking it. Clients can tap bilaterally on their knees or cross their arms in front of their chest and tap their shoulders in the "butterfly hug." Clients are instructed to "tap until something new appears," meaning a change of their image, a new image, a new idea, emotion, color, or whatever, and then to draw it without censoring it. For example, one client began by drawing black on the page. After the BLS the therapist instructed her to draw the change. She drew red across the next page. When the therapist asked her about what she drew she said, "All I see is red." Then the therapist said, "Go with that, and tap again until it changes."

Clients draw, and tap again until it changes, draw and tap until they come to a resolution and the SUDS are reduced. At the end the clients look back from the perspective of the last picture to the first picture and tap again. During this "test," usually the impact of the new solution or perspective is intensified. If a new disturbing aspect of the original target occurs, this can be processed in the same way.

At the end of the session the clients and therapists can view the progression of the work contained on the pages. During the process some clients give short reports but the single pictures are not discussed or commented on by the therapists. Diegelmann believes that the structure of the four relatively small fields give clients more a sense of a process. The single picture is not that important (except the last one). It also serves as a distancing technique, making the pictures small. If after the comparison of the last and first pictures a still stronger positive image arises, this can be drawn on a separate piece of paper.

This protocol has been very helpful with clients suffering from life-threatening diseases like cancer. It can help alleviate the acuity of the distress and provide support for coping. CIPBS helps clients get in touch with their individual resources. Often what is experienced is a feeling of something greater than oneself that arises through the creative process itself. This gives a sense of hope and new perspectives, which might help to achieve a new, well-balanced self-perception. The drawing taps this creative force and also helps to contain what can feel overwhelming when one is facing a life-threatening illness. Putting one's feelings on a page creates a "built-in" distancing effect. CIPBS is a more gentle form of trauma exposure.

DREAMS AS TARGETS

Dreams make excellent targets for EMDR processing because they are door-ways into the unconscious and provide a wealth of material. Oftentimes, clear and vivid dreams arise between EMDR sessions as a continuation of the work that was done in session.

There are a number of different ways to work with dreams. The following are two suggested protocols.

PROTOCOL FOR USING DREAMS AS TARGETS

1. The client tells the therapist the dream. It can be helpful to have the client close his eyes and bring the dream as vividly to mind as possible.

2. Ask the client to scan the dream and identify the most disturbing parts of the dream. "What image represents the most disturbing part of the dream?"

3. After the images are chosen, ask for the NC. "What do you believe about yourself in this image?" If the client cannot come up with anything, or the question does not make sense given the dream, skip the NC. Omit the PC because it does not make sense here.

4. Identify the emotions and body sensations that go with the images—these should be more readily available.

5. Then, as with the standard protocol, bring up the image, NC, emotions, and body sensations and begin the BLS.

6. Process until the dream is no longer charged—a SUDS of 1 or 0.

7. Ask the client what he believes about himself when the dream images are brought up and install the PC.

Some clients prefer to start at the beginning of the dream because *all* of it feels very significant to them and it does not make sense to them to begin in the middle.

Targeting the Beginning of a Dream

1. Begin with the first image in the dream and get as many of the target components as possible associated with that image (i.e., NC, emotions, body sensations).

2. The dream may unfold like a lucid dream remaining in symbolic form, it may immediately link to a memory, or it may go in and out of memory and dream symbolism.

3. From time to time go back and check the beginning of the dream for charge.

4. If there is no longer charge in the beginning of the dream, scan the rest of the dream for charge.

5. Target any charged places and process them.

6. Target and reprocess any "hot spots" until the client scans the entire dream from beginning to end without any charge.

7. When the client rates the dream a SUDS of 1 or 0, ask the client for a PC that goes with the dream.

8. Install the PC with the dream.

For many clients, the dream immediately links into a memory. This memory then becomes the target that you refer back to during the processing. At the end of the session you can install a PC that fits with the memory and then check the dream if time allows. If it seems useful, install a PC that goes with the dream.

Some dreams have many different parts. Note them as the client recounts the dream. You can break the dream into the different parts, starting with the beginning of the dream. After completing the processing of that part, move on and check the next part. If charged, you can process that part. In this way continue processing each part to completion until the entire dream has been processed and is no longer disturbing.

EMDR Session Using a Nightmare as a Target*

A session with Marge began with her reporting disturbing dreams of being chased, night after night. She felt "freaked out," anxious, and very depressed. She was also having difficulty concentrating. She believed the dreams had to do with the memories emerging around molestation by an elderly male neighbor, John, when she was about 10. We began with her image of being chased and feelings of fear and anxiety. Her NC was "I'm not safe." Her body became quite agitated as she thought about the dream, and she wrung her hands and squeezed a tissue. >>>>>

Marge: Nothing yet.

Therapist: What do you feel? (*I ask this because I want to know what nothing means.*)

Marge: Afraid. (*"Nothing" meant the image had not changed.*) >>>>> I can see his house . . . the back of the house. (*She is referring to John's house. A memory related to John is emerging.*) >>>> (*She is increasingly agitated as she processes, squirming in the chair, wringing her hands. Her breathing is rapid and shallow.*) I can still see the house.

Therapist: What are you feeling?

Marge: Still freaked out. >>>> I can see him. . . . He doesn't have a mean face . . . he looks nice at his house. >>>>> I can see the inside of the house . . . it's dark. . . . I don't like being in his house. . . . I feel strange. >>>> He's gone . . . it feels like an elephant is sitting on my chest. >>>>

We continued to process this memory of molestation by John until completion. When she came up with a PC that went with the memory, we installed it. By the end of the session she felt safe in the present and relieved that the reason for her nightmares had been identified and processed.

---

* From *EMDR in the Treatment of Adults Abused as Children* (Parnell, 1999).

PART III

THE EMDR SESSION

8

THE PROCEDURAL STEPS

AFTER THE HISTORY taking and evaluation have been done, the clients assessed for appropriateness of EMDR, prepared for trauma processing, and the therapeutic relationship established, the clients are ready to proceed with an EMDR session (see Appendix 1, page 325).

INSTALLING OR EVOKING RESOURCES

For many highly traumatized clients, it is helpful to have them revisit their safe place or conflict-free image prior to beginning their EMDR processing session. They can also evoke their resource figures for added support if they wish, adding BLS to install them. For some clients it is sufficient to recall the resources before they begin their session, without BLS. Many clients don't need to bring up resources at all prior to beginning sessions.

IDENTIFYING THE PRESENTING ISSUE OR MEMORY

"What issue or memory would you like to work on today?" The clients and therapists work together to come up with the best target for the session. Let's say a client wants to work on the memory of being raped when she was a student in college. This was a trauma that has affected her entire life, making her fearful and dependent.

CREATING AN IMAGE

After the clients have described the memory they want to work on, the therapists ask them for the image of the most disturbing part of the memory. Some clients who have several memories of assaults might want to begin with the first one, the most distressing one, or an incident that best represents the other ones. Clients who do not have a very clear memory can begin with a vague memory that they do have. The image may get clearer with the processing. What is important for reference is that there is a visual representation of the incident. Therapists ask, "What picture represents the worst part of the incident?" You want the picture that has the most charge for the clients because it will create the largest generalization effect through the memory network. You can ask the clients to close their eyes and scan the scene and then tell you where they feel the most charge. You want the moment when there was the shock to their system. In the example of the woman who was raped, the most disturbing image was the look on the man's face. If clients have difficulty, you can ask them if they were to take a snapshot of the scene, what would they see? If they can, have them make the image as clear as possible. The point is to stimulate the visual part of the memory network.

For clients who have trouble visualizing you can:

• use the word *imagine* rather than *visualize*. Even if the image is vague, it stimulates the visual memory track.

• ask them to draw the conflict or problem. The image can be abstract, such as red scribbles that represents the clients' anger or a drawing that represents what they are experiencing.

• ask questions to help locate the clients in place and time. "How old are you?" "Where are you?" "What room in the house?" "Who's there with you?" "What is happening?" They might respond, "I'm 5 years old. I'm in the house I grew up in. I'm at the dinner table. I'm with my family. My father is yelling at my brother." Clients can begin with a vague sense of a scene.

The images can be metaphorical, symbolic, or dreamlike. For example, with a person who has no visual memory but has strong body sensations, you can ask, "What image goes with the feelings in your body?" The client might say, "I get the image of someone stepping on me." That image then can be used as the target image. The client might say, "I don't have a specific memory of being put down by my father, but I can imagine the look on his face." You can target the father's face. However, it may bring up many memories without being able to clear them all.

A composite of several different incidents can be used as the target image. For example, a client might develop a composite image that represents all of the incidents that took place at the dinner table. In this way he can process many incidents at one time without having to process them one by one. Some clients have blurred many incidents in their minds and can't clearly distinguish one from the other. It is fine just to have them bring up the composite image that represents the incidents. It is important to remember that we are not looking for accuracy of the memory. We are trying to stimulate the memory network with what the client can access now.

A *memory fragment* can be used as the target image. Some clients have memory fragments rather than full memories. For example, the image of a client's childhood bedroom may elicit a feeling of fear and stimulation in the genital area. In such a case, the therapist can target the image of the bedroom with the client's associated emotions and body sensations.

Triggers can be used as target images. Many clients become triggered by things in their daily lives, and these triggers make good EMDR targets. What triggered them? What image represents that? If, for example, in exploring the trigger you find that it was a man's hairy chest that triggered your client, target the image of the hairy chest.

Visual flashbacks can be target images. Often, clients do not know what these flashbacks refer to but they have very intense emotional responses. Reassure clients that they don't have to know what the flashbacks are about and tell them that the information that is needed will unfold during the EMDR processing.

You can also target images of *what the client imagined happened*. These are images clients have created in their minds that are linked to their problems or symptoms. These visual representations can be reprocessed just like other memories. For example, one man I worked with had had serious medical traumas as an infant. Born with hydrocephalus, he was one of the first infants to receive a shunt. When we targeted his first brain surgery I asked him, "When you think of the brain surgery when you were an infant, what image do you have?" He immediately had an image of a baby on an operating table surrounded by surgeons. As he told me this, he began to shake with terror. The picture opened up the memory network allowing us to process the memory that had been stored all of his life. For clients who believe they had traumatic births, I have asked them, "When you think of your birth, what picture do you have?" For a client who had a near-death experience, I asked him, "When you think of nearly dying as a child, what picture do you have?" For a client who had been born prematurely and put in an incubator and believed her fears of being alone stemmed from that experience, I asked, "When you think of yourself in the incubator, what image do you have?" In all of these cases the clients were able to tap into memory networks that had affect, body sensations, and NCs. After stimulating the networks, they processed the memories to conclusions. All later reported reduction in symptoms.

Images that have been created from *vicarious traumatization* can also be used. For example, a woman I saw was suffering from PTSD and grief after a close friend was killed when the plane he was on crashed into one of the towers of the World Trade Center. I asked her, "When you imagine your friend's death in the plane crash, what picture do you have? What is the most disturbing part of that?" She immediately came up with a picture of him and the other passengers that was vivid and highly disturbing. It was this picture that was the epicenter of all of the traumatic components of the memory. For a woman who had lost a colleague in an office building mass shooting but did not actually see it, I asked her, "When you imagine the shooting, what image represents the worst part?" She saw a vivid image of her friend at the moment of death, terrified, blood everywhere. It was as if she had been there. We reprocessed this image to completion.

I have also targeted stories clients have in their minds that they might have heard from childhood. For example, children whose parents were concentration camp survivors may have vivid images from stories their parents or other relatives may have told them. These images can be targeted and reprocessed. Sometimes children hear stories or see something happen to another child and it is as if it happened to them. These images can also be targeted.

You may have clients imagine a *negative future*, one that they have already created in their minds and are reacting to. For example, one woman was feeling very depressed. After exploring her current life we found that she was concerned about turning 60. A vibrant, beautiful woman, when I asked her what image she had that went with turning 60, she immediately came up with an old withered crone, bent over and alone. As we targeted and reprocessed this image, many insights arose about the beliefs she had about herself and aging. By the end of the session the crone had dissolved and she saw herself as she was with a future full of possibilities.

I have even had clients bring up a picture of their fear of death. One man who worked in hospice was himself afraid of dying. I asked him to bring up the most disturbing picture he had of his death and tell me what it was. We then reprocessed this image. By the end of the session he had imagined his death and felt himself at peace. He saw it as a normal, natural process.

Images from books, movies, or TV, can be targeted and reprocessed. These images can trigger strong emotional responses in clients. For some it is the content of the show that is distressing, whereas for others the material is a trigger for earlier material. Clients may have no idea why they have been triggered—they just feel very upset. In any case, clients may experience anxiety, nightmares, intrusive images, and increased anxiety. The images that clients found most distressing in a movie can be used as an EMDR target. For example, for one man who was afraid of the water, it was the image of a man being eaten by a shark, a frightening scene from the movie *Jaws*. Ever since he saw the movie as a boy he had been afraid of swimming in the ocean.

The point in focusing on the image is to stimulate the memory network and to provide a place of reference to return to. The emotions, cognitions, and body sensations will all change, and though the picture will change in intensity and details, what remains is a reference place to return to in order to check the progress of the processing.

NC (NEGATIVE COGNITION)

The NC is a self-referencing belief that is erroneous. The therapist asks the client, "What do you believe about yourself now?" or "What negative belief do you have about yourself now?" or other words that serve to elicit the belief. The NC should have *affective resonance*, meaning that when clients say the words in the present, they can feel an emotional response that reverberates through their memory network. Even though clients know the statement to be untrue, it still has a feeling of truth to it. For example, when a client brings up the memory of a rape, her body responds with fear. The belief "I'm going to die" may arise, even though she knows herself to be safe at the moment in your office.

The NC is typically an "I" statement, but can also be a general statement about the world, e.g., "The world isn't safe."

The NC must be a belief, not a description or an emotion. "I feel afraid" is not an NC. It must also be self-referencing, not a statement about what others think or feel about the person. For example, "People don't like me" is not about how the person views him/herself. When you get a belief such as that, ask clients, "What does that say about you?" They might respond, "I'm not lovable."

The best NCs are short, concise statements that can be generalized. These beliefs form the foundation of a false self-structure that cause us to form a perceptual filter through which we view ourselves and our world. Experiences in childhood form the original building blocks of this structure, which are added on to throughout one's life. Because they have been reinforced over and over again, these beliefs feel true. When the early beliefs are targeted and reprocessed, they can begin to dissolve the false structure, freeing up energy so that clients can live more flexibly according to a situation instead of through rigid habits.

If a client gives you a long statement for her NC, you can summarize it for her. Simplifying it helps to find the kernel that has the most charge to it. If, for example, the client says, "I'm no good at baseball," and it is a true statement, you can ask the client, "What does that mean about you?" He might respond, "I'm incompetent," a good NC.

Use the NC that best stimulates a strong emotional response. The NC is an irrational belief that was developed in the past that clients still feel *now* when they bring up the memory. To develop the NC, have clients fully bring up the memory. Elicit the memory as strongly as you can. Bring in other senses if necessary. If you are working with a memory from childhood, you might ask clients, "What was the child thinking at the time?" When the child state is activated, ask what they believe about themselves now.

If clients are having difficulty coming up with something, you can help them find the best NC by offering suggestions. Use simple language and short sentences that the child in the memory would use. I can tell we have found the right NC when, as I repeat it to clients, they respond with a reflexive "ouch" that is clearly noticeable and recognizable, as when touching a wound. You are looking for a negative emotional resonance that more fully activates the memory network.

Another suggestion for clients having difficulty coming up with a NC is to change the order of the protocol: picture, emotions, body sensations, then NC. "Close your eyes and go inside. Bring up the picture as strongly as you can. What emotions do you feel? What do you feel in your body? What do you believe about yourself?" Usually by changing the order of the setup and activating the emotions and body sensations—essentially activating the right side of the brain—I elicit the NC from the body and bypass the left thinking brain. I have found this to be the quickest, easiest, and most effective way to find the NC. The belief that comes is concise, is in present tense, is immediate, and has affective resonance.

There are some clients for whom it is best not to ask for NCs and PCs. Lovett (1999) does not recommend asking children for NCs, as she believes it is detrimental to the therapeutic relationship. Diegelmann and Isermann (2003) do not recommend asking for NCs with cancer patients because it does not feel appropriate to ask a person with a life-threatening illness for such a statement, and Colelli (2002) also advises against it with firefighters. Shapiro stated, "When the thoughts, emotions, or situation appear to be too confusing or complex, it is appropriate to continue without the negative cognition" (2001, p. 134). In all of these cases the therapists determined that it was clinically inappropriate to use NCs, as it threatened a rupture in the therapeutic relationship.

It is helpful to take note of the NC and write it down.

PC (POSITIVE COGNITION)

The PC is usually a present desired, self-referencing belief that corresponds with the NC, but can also include statements like, "it's over." By *correspond* I mean it is parallel to the NC. An example would be if the NC is "I'm bad," the PC could be, "I'm good" or "I'm okay." A PC of "I'm smart" would not correspond to "I'm bad." In order to elicit the PC the therapist might ask, "When you bring up that picture or incident, what would you like to believe about yourself *now?*" In the example from above, the rape victim might say, "I'm safe now." If the PC that the client offers does not correspond with the NC, work with clients to adjust one or the other until they do. The PC must also be possible, not grandiose and impossible to attain. As with the NC, simple, concise statements that can be generalized are best. Therapists can assist clients in coming up with the best PC. Try to avoid using the word *not* in the PC. There are some exceptions, like the statement "It's not my fault," which cannot easily by stated without the word *not.*

Therapists can help clients come up with statements and see which one feels right. You can use process PCs, statements that are moving in the direction of change, such as "I can heal," "I can make better choices." In some cases in which fear is the predominant emotion, a positive self-statement is not possible. You can use a PC that is not self-referential, such as "It's over."

Don't spend too much time struggling over the cognitions. If it is not working smoothly, move on to the next part of the protocol. According to Shapiro (1995, 2001), identifying the PC helps set a direction for treatment and stimulates alternative neuronetworks. She also believes that it offers clients a sense of hope. If in your clinical judgment the PC is not helpful for the clients or the therapy, omit it at the beginning. As I explained in *EMDR in the Treatment of Adults Abused as Children* (Parnell, 1999) asking for the PC can create a break in empathy when working with adult survivors of abuse. When a break in empathy is deemed possible, it is best to omit the PC in the beginning. Later, at the end of the session, a PC will arise out of the processing that can be installed. (See Appendix 1, page 335 for a List of Negative and Positive Cognitions.)

It is helpful to take note of the PC and write it down.

THE NC (NEGATIVE COGNITION)

- is a negative self-referencing belief;
- is an erroneous belief;
- still feels true in the present;
- has affective resonance;
- is stated in the present tense;
- is not a feeling;
- is not a description;

- is not about how others view the client (e.g., "My father doesn't love me");
- is a general statement that is short and concise (e.g., instead of "I'm not a good dancer," "I'm incompetent");
- can be an essential core belief;
- uses language a child would use if processing a childhood memory;
- is a statement that can be simplified by the therapist for the client;
- is such that the order of the protocol can be rearranged so that the NC is found after the emotions and body sensations;
- can be omitted if the client is struggling or if it is not clinically useful.

The PC (Positive Cognition)

- is usually a positive self-referencing belief, but can include statements like "It's over";
- should correspond with the NC;
- must be possible;
- should not have the word *not* in it;
- can include process PCs such as "I can make better choices";
- is such that the therapist can assist the client in finding it;
- can create a feeling of hope for the future.

VOC (VALIDITY OF COGNITION) SCALE

The VoC scale was developed by Shapiro (1995) as part of her original EMDR research. The VoC is a measurement of how true the PC feels on a scale from 1 to 7. "When you think of that picture or incident, how true does (repeat the PC) feel to you now on a scale of 1 to 7, where 1 feels completely false and 7 feels completely true?" Typically, if the memory is charged, clients rate the VoC quite low. By the end of the session, when the charge has been dissipated, the VoC rating goes up.

The VoC can be tricky to explain to clients. We are asking them to rate how true a belief *feels* when they bring up the disturbing memory in the present. When clients have difficulty with this, I will ask them to close their eyes and go inside. "Bring up the picture of the rape as strongly as you can, focusing on the man's face. Now say to yourself, 'I'm safe now.' How true does that statement feel to you, on a scale from 1 to 7, with 1 completely false and 7 completely true?"

Many clients and therapists become thrown off by the word *now*. What we are asking is when clients elicit the memory in the present, what do they experience? The *now* is what they experience when they light up that memory network. We want to know how the memory is presently held in their network. In order to elicit the network, I will often ask clients to close their eyes and go inside, bringing up the memory as strongly as they can. When they do that, they are back in the memory again.

EMOTIONS/FEELINGS

Ask clients what emotions they feel. "When you bring up that incident and the belief (NC), what emotions do you feel now?" You want the emotions the clients feel in the present as they bring up the incident. For example, "When you bring up the image of the man's face and the belief 'I'm going to die,' what emotions do you feel now?" She might respond, "Shock, terror, and anger."

There can be several different emotions felt—including seemingly contradictory feelings like love and rage. Have clients note all of them, as they are all part of the memory network you are trying to activate. Some clients won't be able to identify an emotion. Don't worry about it. It may be in a compartment that is not yet accessible. Often clients don't have names for what they are feeling. They feel something but don't know what to call it. Don't push for a label. Ask them to pay attention to the feelings themselves in the body. It is most important that the emotional/somatic components are stimulated by the clients' awareness.

Sometimes clients can be aware of an emotion that is not yet felt. They have a "sense" that terror is there but cannot feel it. The SUDS may be low, but they have a "feeling" that the memory is very charged. If they cannot identify emotions, focus on the body sensations.

SUDS

After clients have told you what emotions they feel, ask them to rate them on the SUDS. This scale, developed by Wolpe (1991), rates the level of disturbance from 0 to 10, with 0 being no disturbance or neutral and 10 being the highest disturbance. "On a scale of 0 to 10, where 0 is no disturbance or neutral and 10 is the highest disturbance you can imagine, how disturbing does it feel to you now?" In our example we would ask the client, "When you bring up the image of the man's face and say to yourself 'I'm going to die,' how disturbing does this feel to you now, on a scale from 0 to 10 where 0 is no disturbance or neutral and 10 is the highest disturbance you can imagine?" She might rate it a 10. We want clients to rate how disturbing the memory feels to them when they think of it in the moment, not when they reflect back and think how disturbing it was at the time it occurred. Sometimes clients will rate the SUDS lower than it actually is at the beginning because the memory network is not fully activated. It is not uncommon for the SUDS to go up much higher when the processing begins.

Some people have difficulty with the number scale, and for children it may be too difficult for them to use numbers. In those cases, they can indicate with their hands, close together or far apart, to show how disturbing the memory feels to them. There are also pictures of faces on a card ranging from happy to sad that clients can point to. Clients can also draw how distressed they feel. Drawings can indicate progress in a session (Cohn, 1993a, 1993b). A SUDS reading is taken at different times during the processing to measure progress.

In clinical practice, if clients are visibly distressed and crying, skip the SUDS and, if it is all right with the clients, begin BLS. Stopping crying clients in order to get a SUDS rating can cause them to feel that the therapists do not care and can be harmful to the therapeutic rapport. Please remember that the therapeutic relationship is the foundation for all the work we do in EMDR. It is most important that clients feel cared about and attuned to. We don't want them to feel that a technique is being imposed on them.

LOCATION OF BODY SENSATIONS

Next we want to activate the somatic aspect of the memory network by asking clients for the location of body sensations. *"Where do you feel the disturbance in your body?"* You might even ask clients to scan their body for any sensations. In the above example the client might reply, "In my stomach, arms, and genital area." For many clients, attention to their bodies makes them aware of the location of emotions and sensations that may be body memories. These sensations that arise when the memory is evoked can be important pieces of the memory that is being stimulated.

Body memories can surprise clients. For example, a client processing the memory of an accident may feel his head hurt on the side where it was struck. Some clients who have had surgeries feel woozy with the memory of anesthesia and can even taste or smell it again. One woman who was targeting the memory of a near-disastrous plane flight during which the plane lost an engine and was plummeting to earth noticed that she felt a great deal of tension in her forearms. She realized that she had gripped the armrests as hard as she could during the rapid descent.

Many people who have been sexually abused as children have difficulty sensing their bodies. They left their bodies as a defense against the feelings and they believe their bodies are not safe places. It is necessary to teach or guide many clients to experience the sensations in their bodies. They may dismiss or not attend to certain body sensations because some sensations are subtle but significant. Attending to a constriction in the throat or a tingling in the hands during the setup may yield important information during the processing. If clients respond to the question about body sensations with "Nothing," ask them to look more closely. Tell them that even subtle sensation is important information. The process of locating the body sensations is helpful training for these clients.

An area of sensation may be amplified by asking clients to use their hands to press on that area as the BLS begins. This is helpful for clients who have a difficult time feeling their bodies and stimulates the sensation channel during the processing.

DESENSITIZATION

Desensitization begins after clients activate the components. "Bring up the image, emotions, body sensations, and repeat (the NC) to yourself. When you have it, let me know. Let whatever happens happen without censoring it." The goal is to stimulate the memory network in which the memory is locked so that its various components can be reprocessed. It is important to take them back into the emotional experience before starting the BLS. Remember, memories must be activated in order for processing to occur. If measuring the VoC and SUDS decreased the charge, you must help clients activate the memory again.

In the example of the rape memory, I would instruct her in the following way: "I'd like you to bring up the image of the man's face, the emotions of shock, fear, and anger, along with what you are feeling in your body and repeat to yourself, 'I'm going to die.' When you have it, let me know and I'll begin the bilateral stimulation." After she signals me that the memory is activated, I begin the BLS.

The therapeutic stance is one of grounded, spacious attunement. Therapists are grounded in the present, creating a feeling of stability. They are spacious, allowing whatever arises in the clients and in the therapists to be there without judgment. In this way the therapists communicate to the clients that whatever arises is okay, promoting acceptance, a welcoming of the content of the body-mind process. The therapists are also attuned to the clients. Connected, feeling with clients, the therapists nonverbally communicate that the clients are not alone in the trauma.

If you are using eye movements, begin slowly and increase the speed as fast as the clients can comfortably move their eyes. If you are using tapping or other BLS, go at the speed the clients have told you is most comfortable. After the first set you might ask how it is for them and if they would like any adjustments. During desensitization, clients go through a multidimensional free association of thoughts, feelings, and body sensations. Some clients have intense emotional releases, whereas others process more cognitively, their emotions more subtly released. Many experience fantasies and imagery that is dreamlike. Clients have their own processing styles and different memories are processed differently. For example, for clients who have been in car accidents, much of their processing may be somatosensory, feeling their body thrown forward, pain in their neck and back, stomach clenching, and sensation in their hands where they gripped the steering wheel. The emotions associated with the accident can be fleeting, and there may be little visual memory, especially if the incident happened at night in the dark. When processing other memories, perhaps a memory of childhood abuse, they may express intense emotion.

For many clients, you can tell when to stop the BLS by watching for the waves. Many clients process in waves. There is buildup of intensity followed by a decrease. Some clients will take a deep breath, others will swallow, and some will open their eyes to indicate they have completed a wave. It is not always obvious by looking at clients to tell when to stop. It is more difficult to tell where clients are when they have their eyes closed. I can often track clients by attuning to how I feel as they process. When I am attuned to my clients I can sense when they are in the processing and when it has been released. I can *feel* the release. There is a lightening up, a feeling of openness in my body. I follow the energy and listen to my body response. When clients are intensely processing, my attention is riveted. After a wave has passed, there is a sense of relaxation. When the therapists and clients are attuned in this way, there is synchronicity, and even a feeling of oneness that I believe is "installed" in their nervous system as a positive resource. It is helpful to have a clear mind and have worked on your own issues. Meditation practices such as Vipassana meditation are helpful in developing clarity and attunement.

At the end of the wave, stop the BLS and ask an open, nondirective question like, "What do you get now?" "What's happening now?" "What's coming up now?" or "What are you noticing now?" If they are doing eye movements, you might ask them to close their eyes, take a deep breath, and then after a pause ask, "What is coming up for you?" Don't ask what they are feeling. You don't want to guide the client. You want to know what their experience is.

All clients have their own processing styles. Some clients process in long sets of continuous waves, one after another. For these clients stopping the

BLS too soon derails their processing, causing them to lose their trains of thought and associations. It feels disruptive to them to stop. Some clients process in discrete waves with a noticeable beginning, middle, and end. Some process extremely rapidly, needing as few as 5 saccades to complete a channel. For one woman, a highly intellectualized client who spoke so rapidly she hardly stopped to breathe, she processed most of a highly charged molestation memory in 5 saccades. After a set of perhaps 20 passes I asked her what was happening. She told me she was thinking about what she was going to have for lunch. Because of her intellectualized style and lack of affect during the set, I assumed she hadn't processed anything. But when I asked her to bring up the memory again, the SUDS had been significantly reduced. She was able to process the entire molestation memory in just a few minutes and had a significant reduction in her symptoms in one session. There are clients who process memories like a flipbook, going through them in rapid succession. These clients are like super processors defying the therapist's beliefs about what is possible. One client processed dozens of abuse memories in one session. I never would have believed it possible given her trauma history.

It can be helpful to ask the client to let you know when to stop. After the first few sets of BLS they understand the meaning of the wave experience and can feel themselves when it is a good time to stop. This isn't "Stop, I'm overwhelmed"; instead, it's "Stop, it's time to check in, reflect, and talk about what just came up." The processing and talking help with the integration of the material the clients are processing. It also helps them to stay connected to the therapists and to remember that they are safe in the present as they process the past.

Some clients prefer to talk as they process. This helps them feel more connected to the material and to the therapists. This can be helpful as it lets the therapists know where clients are as they go along. For some clients, however, talking distances them too much from the memory and they don't process. In general I refrain from directing clients from talking or not talking in the beginning. I let them do whatever feels best to them. If, however, when they return to the original picture and it has not changed, I then ask them not to speak and to focus on the body sensations and emotions.

If clients go for a long set of BLS and do not speak, I might stop them and ask what is happening. This is especially true in the case of new clients. I want to know if they have dissociated or gone off on a tangent.

Help the client maintain a dual focus of awareness, safe in the present as they process the past. Use your voice if it is helpful to your clients. Your voice reminds them of your presence and serves to create distance from what they are processing. For some clients the therapist's voice may be a distraction from their processing and not help them. According to the needs of the clients, you might comment during a set of BLS, "That's it. Good. That's it." Do not interpret or comment on the content. It is essential that the therapists stay out of the clients' ways. It is most helpful to use your voice when clients are abreacting to remind them that they are safe in the present as they process the past. "That's it. It's old stuff. Just notice it." You might use the metaphor of the river, video, or train. "Remember, it's just a movie."

With clients who tend to dissociate, you might ask them to keep their eyes open, even if you are doing tapping or auditory stimulation. Having eyes open helps to maintain the present awareness and they will not go as deeply into the memory. It can also be helpful to have them talk as they process. This also helps maintain the dual focus of awareness. Ask clients if they would like to return to their safe place if they are completely overwhelmed and interweaves are not working, or they request it. It is always better to complete the processing than to go to a safe place. In Chapter 9 I will have more recommendations for working with dissociation and abreactions.

Clients do not have to show emotions when they process for the processing to be working well. Sometimes the processing is so rapid that the affect flicks by their awareness, barely registering. EMDR does not have to look a certain way for it to be successful. Don't push for affect. Don't push for anything. Follow the clients' process. Therapists are so conditioned to dig for emotions that they can cause clients to feel they aren't doing it right. Some clients just don't process with much affect, and still have a successful reduction in SUDS and symptoms. Some memories have more emotions than other memories. Often clients have many insights and not much happening in their bodies. This is fine.

The way to tell if the processing is working is to return to the original picture or incident. "Let's return to the original picture. What do you get now?" If it has not changed—the picture emotions, body sensations, and NC are the same as when you began desensitization—then focus on the body or emotions. But if it has changed and the client wasn't emoting, don't worry about it. It is my feeling that if therapists impose their views that it is essential to emote during EMDR, then they are communicating to the clients that the clients are wrong. Who they are and how they process is wrong. I feel very strongly that it is most important not to add to the EMDR process anything that is not needed. Stay out of the way as much as possible. Trust the clients and the process. Intervene only if the process is stuck or you are running out of time. By allowing the processing to unfold organically, you support clients' confidence in their own inner wisdom.

Some clients process primarily kinesthetically, with few images or stories, just sensation arising in different areas. Some have no imagery at all. This type of processing can go on for many sessions. You can tell that the processing is progressing by returning to the original picture or incident and checking it. If it has changed, then the processing is progressing. One man I worked with processed in this way. His body would jerk and shake, his arms would move spontaneously, and he would yawn. There was very little content, but the image he began with decreased significantly in disturbance.

I think of EMDR processing like a dance. The first session with clients is awkward because the clients and therapists have not yet found their style of working. Do they like long sets or short ones? Do they like to talk or remain silent? Do they indicate *stop* by opening their eyes? Don't worry about stepping on their toes. When in doubt ask the clients. Did I stop you too soon? Did I go too long? Would you like me to tap faster?

After the clients report their experience, say: "Go with that" or "Focus on that." (Don't repeat the clients' words or statements unless the clients are confused about what to go with. No reflective listening.) I don't like to say, "Stay with that," because clients think they are supposed to hold on to the image. The idea is to keep a flow of processing going. Nothing remains the same. Don't let clients talk for too long. You can tell that they have talked too long when there has been a loss of energy or focus in the work. The momentum has been lost from the processing. It can feel too analytical, less of a full body-mind process. You want to keep the processing moving along. Clients and therapists who are used to talk therapy may get caught up in analysis and discussion of content. This can derail the processing and waste time. Yet, you also don't want to cut your clients off if what they are saying feels important to them. There is an art to this. If you feel your clients are derailing the process by talking too long, gently encourage them to "go with that," and begin BLS. Also, if it feels as if the energy of the processing has been dissipated by talking, return to the original image or incident and check it. "Let's go back to the scene we started with. What comes up for you now?"

If clients ask you what they should go with, tell them to go with the most charged thing. *Follow the charge.* In general, we want to go with what is disturbing to the clients. Because what is positive and resourceful will increase on its own, we don't need to focus on the positive during the desensitization phase. As we focus on the dysfunctional information, it will decrease and the healthy part will grow and strengthen naturally. The exception to this would be in the case of clinically depressed clients or clients with histories of neglect. If positive feelings or cognitions should arise, I might focus on them for a set or two.

If clients report two things of equal charge, ask, "Which one feels the most charged to you?" If they can't decide, you can ask them to choose one and focus on it, and return to focus on the other later. I think of this like a fork in the road. Take one road now and then come back if you wish to take the other one. Often what happens is that the second one is resolved during the time they process the first, and there is then no reason to return to the other.

Clients tend to process down *channels of associations*. These channels radiate from the target and can be imagined like fingers on a hand. Channels can include associated thoughts, images, emotions, body sensations, and memories. Clients may have several sets processing one channel, or only one set may complete it. You can tell that clients are at the end of a channel when they report that nothing is happening. Sometimes they will say they are stuck or blocked. When this happens, ask them to return to the original picture or incident and tell you what comes up now.

If the processing becomes too diffuse, they seem to be associating to tangential memories, or they connect to memories they don't have time to process or don't want to go into, bring the clients back to original scene or incident. It is important during the processing to keep the clients from becoming too dispersed in the processing. Some clients can go down many different associated channels that get further and further away from the original issue or memory. In these cases it can be helpful to return to the target image and check in. For example, the therapist might ask, "When you bring up the image of your brother fondling you in bed, what comes up for you now?" This check-in gives therapists an indication of how much of the reprocessing has been done. If in this case the client responds, "I feel angry now when I see the picture," then the therapist knows that things are processing (note: the client began with feelings of fear). The therapist says, "Go with that," and directs the client to move her eyes again. If you have a short session, you may return to target more frequently to help manage the time. When in doubt, return to the target.

One of the most common fears for multiply traumatized clients is that they will open up too many memories and become flooded. You can make an agreement with the clients at the beginning of the session that you will work on one memory and if another should open up, they can signal you to stop. Then return to the original picture or incident.

Return to target if:

- the client says, "It's blank," "It's stuck," or "Nothing's happening";
- the client is opening up a memory he/she doesn't want to process;
- you want to contain the work and keep it more focused;

- you are running low on time;
- the processing is too diffuse;
- you want to check your work and see where you are;
- you are in doubt.

Don't:

- talk while the client processes unless it is to say encouraging words;
- interpret;
- repeat the client's words (no reflective listening);
- get into a discussion with the client between sets—keep the processing moving along;
- be afraid of abreactions—ride the waves;
- direct the client—it is always better to ask.

If a client starts to work on one memory and during the processing open
up an earlier, more charged memory, make the earlier, stronger memory the
target you return to. For example, the client targeted the memory of being
accosted by a policeman in a subway station. The experience frightened her.
Soon after beginning the BLS she found herself processing the image of being
a baby and being terrified of her father. The image of the baby became the
target that she was returned to. After processing down a channel, the therapist
asked her to return to the image of the baby. She continued to return to this
scene until she had a SUDS of 0 and a PC was installed. After that, she was
asked to bring up the image of the policeman. She said that it no longer
bothered her. BLS was added as she focused on that. This procedure follows
the three-pronged protocol that was described in detail in Chapter 7.

If clients describe new material or any disturbance, continue with BLS. If
they report no disturbance, take a SUDS reading. "When you bring up the
incident, on a scale of 0 to 10, where 0 is no disturbance or neutral, and 10
is the highest disturbance you can imagine, how disturbing does it feel to
you now?" If the SUDS is 0, proceed to the installation of the PC. If the
SUDS is greater than 0, ask, "What keeps it from being a 0?" When clients
tell you, say "Go with that," then do more BLS. Don't take the SUDS if the
clients are still in the middle of processing. Remember that every time you
take the SUDS, you take the clients out of their experience. This can derail
the processing. If they are reporting disturbance, you don't need to scale it;
just keep processing. It is most helpful to take the SUDS if you suspect the
processing is stuck and not progressing, or if you think the clients have
completed reprocessing the target.

Some clients will never give you a 0 SUDS; they don't believe in 0s.
Others will give you a 0 because they feel sorry for you and they want to

please you. If that is the case, encourage the clients to go a little longer. I have had many experiences of clients thinking they had gone as far as they could and, with my encouragement, continued on for another set, only to find that an important piece was yet to be processed.

When the clients return to the image and report that it doesn't disturb them anymore, the therapists take a SUDS reading. "Bring up the original incident. On a scale of 0 to 10, where 0 is no disturbance or neutral and 10 is the highest disturbance that you can imagine, how disturbing does it feel to you now?" When the clients feel free of the emotional charge, reporting a SUDS of 0 or 1, it is time to proceed to the installation of the PC. Reminder: If there is no movement, or clients are "looping," return to the target to check it. Also, if the clients seem to be linking up many networks and you are concerned that they are going too far afield, have them return to the original incident or image.

DESENSITIZATION SEQUENCE

1. Activate the memory network (image, emotion, body sensation, and NC).

2. Add BLS and process.

3. At the end of a wave or channel, stop BLS.

4. The therapist asks, "What do you get now?" "What is happening now?" or "What are you experiencing now?"

5. The client answers. The therapist listens. The therapist does not comment or interpret what the client says. The therapist says, "Go with that" and begins BLS.

6. The client processes. The therapist checks in and says "Go with that." They go back and forth until the client reaches the end of a channel.

7. The therapist stops BLS.

8. The therapist asks, "What do you get now?"

9. The client responds with "Not much is happening, I'm stuck, blank."

10. The therapist asks the client to go back to the original picture or incident. "What comes up for you now?"

11. The therapist waits to hear what the client says.

12. If the client reports something that has charge, the therapist says, "Go with that" and resumes BLS.

13. If the client says, "It doesn't feel very disturbing" or "It feels flat or neutral," the therapist takes a SUDS reading. (Do not take SUDS if the processing is moving along. It takes the client out of the flow of processing.)

14. If the SUDS is above a 0, the therapist asks the client, "What keeps it from being a 0?"

15. The therapist listens to the client's response and then says, "Go with that" and resumes BLS.

16. If the client reports the disturbance to be a 0 or 1, then the therapist is ready to install the PC.

INSTALLATION OF THE PC

When the client brings up the original picture or incident and reports the SUDS to be a 0 or 1, or you need to close an incomplete session, you can install a PC. Link the PC with the original memory, incident, or picture:

1. "When you bring up the original picture or incident, what do you believe about yourself now?" (This belief may be the same or different from the one the clients came up with at the beginning of the session.)

2. "Think about the original incident and the belief (repeat the PC, e.g., 'I'm powerful'). From 1, completely false, to 7, completely true, how true does it feel to you now?" If clients report a VoC of 6 or 7, install it. If they report a lower VoC, ask, "What keeps it from being a 6 or 7?" Sometimes clients are confused; they think the PC refers to their whole life. In those cases, clarify by saying, "With just this memory, how true does that belief feel to you now?" Sometimes it helps to make it a process PC, by adding the word *can*. For example, "I can be powerful." Instruct the clients to hold the picture and the belief together. For example, "Hold the picture and the belief 'I am powerful' together." As the clients hold them together, do a set of BLS. Keep going as long as you see processing occurring. Then ask, "What comes up now?" If the clients report continuing processing, resume BLS until it no longer strengthens. You might even ask, "Let me know when it feels complete."

BODY SCAN

If you have a complete session, with SUDS 0 or 1, do a body scan. Otherwise skip to closure and debriefing.

"Close your eyes. Bring up the incident and the belief (repeat PC), and mentally scan your entire body. Tell me where you feel anything." If any sensation is reported, do BLS. If a positive or comfortable sensation is reported, add BLS to strengthen the feeling. If a sensation of discomfort is reported, reprocess until the discomfort subsides.

Skip the body scan if you are low on time. Also, if you are near the end of the session, do not add BLS if you or your clients suspect that more processing might open up other associated memories. If they feel something in their body, then ask, "What is that related to?" You can ask your clients. "What do you think the sensation in your throat is about?" If they say it is something they would like to say to the perpetrator and you have enough time, encourage them to express themselves, either out loud or in their imagination with BLS. If the clients tell you they think the sensation is related to another memory, make a note of it and include it in your closure; perhaps put it in a container or use the light stream technique (Shapiro, 2001, p. 244). Be very careful not to open up new material with BLS at the end of a session. It can create problems for the client.

CLOSE AND DEBRIEF THE SESSION

Tell your clients: "The processing we have done today may continue after the session. You may or may not notice new insights, thoughts, memories, or dreams. If so, just notice what you are experiencing, and write it in a journal or log. We can work on this new material next time. If you feel it is necessary, call me. Please walk around before you drive. You might even want to put some water on your face."

You may choose to close by returning to the safe place. For clients with multiple childhood traumas, it may be helpful to begin and end sessions with the safe or comfortable place. Then do a good debriefing. Talking about their thoughts and feelings about the session helps bring them back and reorient themselves to the present. It also helps the clients and therapists to connect in support of the therapeutic relationship.

CLOSING INCOMPLETE SESSIONS AND SUGGESTIONS FOR HELPING CLIENTS MANAGE BETWEEN SESSIONS

Often clients have incomplete sessions, especially if there are feeder memories (untapped earlier memories, see page 242), you are working on an issue with multiple contributors, or you are dealing with a chronic situation. For clients with multiple childhood traumas one trauma memory links into another and then another, making it difficult for the level of distress to reduce down to a level of calm and peace. EMDR therapists need to take the time necessary to bring these clients to a sense of safety and containment, even if it means going overtime. Therapists need to know various techniques for lowering the level of distress so that clients can safely transition back into their lives. It is essential that clients feel safe and emotionally contained before they are allowed to leave the therapists' office.

An incomplete session is one in which the clients' material is still unresolved, that is, the clients are still obviously upset or the SUDS is above 1 and the VoC is less than 6. Be sure to leave sufficient time at the end of the session to close it down, for most people, 10 to 15 minutes. Spend the remaining time talking with the clients about the session, helping them to begin to digest and integrate the material that has arisen during the session. Make sure the clients are grounded and in their body before they leave your office. Clients may need to splash cold water on their faces and walk around before they get in their cars and drive. If the clients are still too upset to leave your office, go overtime until they are in a calm state. Set up an appointment for later in the day or the following day if necessary. Do not leave clients in a distressed state for a week. Make sure the clients know they can call you if feeling upset or out of control. EMDR processing causes many clients to regress. Adults regressed to a child state may feel very distressed and unable to function properly. It is important to help the clients contact the adult self and feel the adult self functioning and in control.

STEPS FOR CLOSING INCOMPLETE SESSIONS

1. *Ask the clients' permission to stop and explain the reason.* "We are almost out of time and we will need to stop soon. How comfortable are you about stopping now?" If the clients are not comfortable stopping, find out how much time they need, and then continue until they are at a better place to stop. Go overtime if it is in the clients' best interest.

2. *Give encouragement and support for the effort made.* "You have done some very good work and I appreciate the effort you have made. How are you feeling?"

3. *Help the clients clarify what was gained in the session, or identify a PC (even if the SUDS is not a 0, look for some kind of positive self-statement. It can be a process PC, e.g., "I am learning to love myself.")* "What do you want to take away from the hard work you've done today?" or "What was the most important thing you learned today?" "What do you believe about yourself now when you bring up the original picture?" Write down the clients' response.

4. *Install the response with a short set of BLS.* "Think about 'I'm learning to love myself.'"

5. *Eliminate the body scan.* The body scan is not done because the therapist

knows there is still more to process. Time is better spent closing the clients down.

6. *Do a relaxation exercise. At this time protector/nurturer resources can be brought in.* "I would like to suggest we do a relaxation exercise before we stop." (The therapist suggests a form of relaxation, e.g., safe place, light stream, visualization, slow vertical or infinity eye movements.) The safe place and positive imagery can be installed with a short set of BLS. Don't use BLS if you are concerned the clients will resume processing.

7. *Do a containment exercise.* Offer the clients the opportunity to leave the distressing material/feelings in an imaginary container until the next time you meet to do this work again. Offer that the clients worked hard in the session and can contain the difficult feelings between sessions. The image of the material in the container can also be installed with a short set of BLS. Write down the container image to be used in later sessions.

8. *Provide closure and debriefing.* "The processing we have done today may continue after the session. You may or may not notice new insights, thoughts, memories, or dreams. If so, just notice what you are experiencing—take a snapshot of it (what you are seeing, feeling, thinking, and the trigger), and keep a log. We can work on this new material next time. If you feel it is necessary, call me."

There are a number of ways therapists can help clients feel more contained when the session is incomplete. The following are closure techniques that you might find helpful.

Therapist-Suggested Interweave to Help With Closure

Interweaves can also be for closing down incomplete sessions (see pages 33 and 251). Sometimes time runs out before the session is complete and the therapists, by using a strategic interweave, can tie things together for the clients in a way that brings rapid closure. During this time the therapists can be more active and directive, helping the clients bring in resources and connect disparate memory networks and ego states.

These interweaves can include any of the types described in Chapter 9. Often interweaves that bring in the adult self or protector/nurturer figures to comfort or protect the child self are useful to help in calming down clients who are distressed when the time is running low.

Therapist: Can you imagine your adult self coming in and protecting your child self?

Client: Yes.

Therapist: Imagine that. (*Add BLS.*)

For clients who are fearful of the perpetrator who is known to be old and feeble, a question eliciting the adult's perspective on present safety can be used.

Therapist: Where is your uncle now?

Client: He is dead.

Therapist: Think about that. (*Add BLS to link memory networks.*)

For the sorrowful child self, bringing in the loving adult self, nurturer figures, or spiritual figures can be helpful for closing.

Therapist: Can you imagine your grandmother holding your child self on her lap and telling her that she loves her?

Client: Yes.

Therapist: Go with that.

For clients who lived in chronic abusive situations, it can be helpful to end sessions by having someone rescue the child selves and take them out of the situation to a place of safety. This is detailed in Chapter 9.

A Socratic interweave can be used for clients who are hovering outside of their bodies because they believe it is not safe to be in their bodies.

Therapist: It wasn't safe to be in your body then. Is it safe to be in your body *now*?

Client: Yes.

Therapist: Go with that. >>>>>>>>

INSTALLING A PC OR IMAGE

It is important to install something positive at the end of a session. This can include a PC, statement, or image. It is my experience that installing something positive at the end of the session helps clients feel contained and grounded. You can ask clients, "What do you believe about yourself now when you bring up the original image?" Install what they come up with. The clients may have a process-oriented PC (Wildwind, 1993), a PC that shows movement in the direction of positive change. "I am learning to love myself" or "I can heal this in a safe way" are such cognitions.

If the target issue is still quite unresolved at the end of the session and a PC cannot be found, the therapists can ask the clients, "What did you learn from today's session?" When the clients report to the therapists what they learned, the therapists apply the BLS to install it. You can also ask, "What do you understand now?" In answering this question, the clients begin to form a coherent narrative, putting the pieces of their life together in a meaningful way. Some clients may ask the therapists to help them review the session and the therapists' notes. The areas of insight or nuggets of wisdom that came from the clients can be repeated to them along with the BLS for installation.

The therapists may want to guide the clients to their safe place and install images and statements about safety. It is most important that something positive is installed and that the clients feel that they have gotten something from the session. This installation of something positive or constructive feels very good to clients. It helps them to feel contained, cared for, empowered, and that they are moving in the direction of healing.

IMAGERY AS A CLOSING TECHNIQUE

For clients with complex trauma, I spend more time with closure and may use imagery to begin and end sessions. Whether or not it is complete, I often ask clients to return to their safe place, imagine their adult holding their child self, and feel as strongly as possible the feelings of safety and security. I might also ask them to bring in the nurturer, protector, and spiritual resources. Either I, or their imagined resources, repeat PCs discovered during the EMDR processing, along with affirmations that are beneficial to them. Often the positive statements are related to the issues of safety, responsibility, and choice: "You are safe now," "You were a little girl who was hurt by a mean, angry grown-up, it wasn't your fault," "You didn't have a choice then as a little boy, but you do now as an adult." Process PCs, which express movement toward health, such as "I'm beginning to heal," "The hurt is beginning to lighten," and "I can change," are also used if appropriate. When clients report feeling calm, peaceful, and safe, I may install the image, cognitions, and feelings with a short set of BLS.

The following is an example of a therapist-directed closure using resources the client had developed earlier.

Therapist: Okay, now imagine going to your safe place, along with your child self. . . . Imagine putting up that protective shield. . . . Imagine bringing in Bear to protect and nurture both the adult and child. Feel his warm fur and his large presence. Imagine Jesus there with you too with his warmth and love. You are safe now. Imagine holding the child and telling her that she's safe with you now . . . that she's a good girl . . . that you love her. . . . Let me know when you feel calm and peaceful. . . . Good. Now follow my fingers with your eyes. ⋗⋗⋗⋗⋗ Good. How are you feeling now?

Sometimes I ask the adult self to soothe the child self with caring words. Sometimes it is the nurturer, protector, or spiritual figures who are called upon to do the comforting. It depends upon the clients and their needs at the time.

There are times when I feel it helpful to use healing imagery to increase the feeling of healing. After clients have processed an intensive memory of having been assaulted, their bodies reverberate with the aftermath of the remembered abuse. Clients often feel raw and wounded. The therapists can suggest to clients: "Imagine healing light flowing down through the top of your head and down into all of the places of pain . . . the light gently heals these places with warmth and love. . . . Slowly the wounds are beginning to heal. . . . Feel the warmth and healing. . . . The healing light moves to all of the places of pain, bringing new life and renewal to all of those places. . . . "

You use the words and images that you believe will work best for clients and give them permission to create the imagery that works best for them. It can be helpful to develop imagery with clients that can be used in this visualization. One woman chose to imagine herself under a beautiful water-fall with crystal clear water that cleansed her body of pain from past assaults. We installed the imagery and feeling with knee taps. She was later able to imagine the waterfall when she took showers to continue the feeling of healing and renewal.

Another important use of imagery in closing sessions is for *containing the unfinished material.* There are many different imagery techniques that can be used. It is helpful to work this out with the clients ahead of time. Some clients like to imagine leaving their unfinished material in a file folder in the therapist's office where it will be stored until they come in for their next session. Other clients like the image of putting the material in a locked vault or safe.

A colleague of mine asks many of her clients to leave whatever feels uncontainable in some place in her office. Many clients choose a basket. She then asks them to "imagine all of the unfinished images, feelings, body sensations, tastes, and smells and put them into the basket." As they imagine this, she asks her clients to do a short set of eye movements or other BLS.

After the image and feeling of containment have been installed, she tells her clients that if they choose, they can continue to work on the contained material when they come back the next week.

Another colleague uses the following imagery to close incomplete EMDR sessions. Clients are asked to imagine the traumatic scene as if they were viewing it on a movie screen. The therapist then asks them to imagine the scene becoming miniaturized. Next clients are asked to imagine putting the scene in a chest that is a very strong container. They then imagine dumping the chest out of a boat so it goes out of sight, yet they know they can retrieve it whenever they like. After the visualization clients are asked to go to their inner sanctuary or safe place and bring in whatever guides or resources they might need. The resultant sense of safety may be installed with a short set of eye movements or other BLS.

Another method of containment is to have clients imagine that the remaining traumatic material is on a video that they can edit, or eject and store until they want to replay it at a later time. This gives them a sense of control over the material.

Some clients feel the need to do something physically symbolic to increase the sense of safety and containment. One woman, upon completing an EMDR session processing an abuse incident, still felt a sense of contamination in her current life from the perpetrator. After exploring various solutions to this problem, we came up with the idea of her physically destroying all of the gifts the perpetrator had given her. She felt these gifts were contaminating her in the present because they represented ties to the perpetrator. This woman systematically sought and found in her home all of the gifts and then smashed them with a sledgehammer until they were broken into tiny pieces. She burned what could be burned in a liberating fire in her fireplace.

ART AS A CLOSING TECHNIQUE

Art can be a useful tool for closing EMDR sessions. The physical act of drawing or sculpting something is grounding, and the product is a concrete representation of the client's inner experience. Clients can draw the new image, belief, or feeling that they have at the end of the session. The drawing brings into form that which had been privately held inside, and it can be shared with the therapist. If the clients began the session with a drawing, the drawing at the end provides a comparison and a sense of movement. The drawings give a concrete sense that change has occurred during the session and also information about what other work is yet to be done.

Clients can also draw the containment image. For example, the client who has imagined his distressing material in a chest at the bottom of the ocean might be asked to draw the image. The drawing further reinforces the sense of containment.

One woman who had been sexually abused as a child by her grandfather was afraid that the good memories of her grandfather would be contaminated by the bad ones. Just imagining the separation of the memories was not sufficient for her. After exploring various potential solutions with her therapist, she found a large box with a lid and placed physical representations of the distressing images inside it. She left this box containing the disturbing material with the lid firmly closed in her therapist's office, where she felt it would remain sealed and not leak into her present life.

Clients can also reinforce the feeling of safety at the end of the session by drawing the safe place with their adult and child selves and nurturer and protector figures. After drawing the safe place image, clients can take it home if they wish, as a reminder of their safety in the present.

LOVING-KINDNESS MEDITATION

I first learned metta or loving-kindness meditation from Sharon Salzberg at a Vipassana meditation retreat she was co-teaching with Joseph Goldstein in 1976. Since then I have practiced and taught this meditation and have found it very helpful for developing self-compassion and compassion for others. Many clients who were traumatized and betrayed by those close to them remain bereft. The physical wounds may be long healed, but their hearts remain damaged. Loving-kindness meditation in conjunction with EMDR can be a helpful means of bringing healing to the heart. I have used this meditation as a closing technique for many clients. It allows them to focus on loving themselves, further reinforcing the healing of the shame and self-hate so many trauma survivors feel. I believe that the development of compassion for oneself is an essential aspect of healing from trauma, especially child sexual abuse. The more we as therapists can reinforce and bring in compassion through our nonjudgmental caring for our clients, the better for our clients' healing.

For two years I led a meditation group for women who had been sexually abused as children. In this group I taught grounded breathing, Vipassana meditation, and loving-kindness meditation. I adapted these practices to the needs of the women, making the meditations shorter with more guidance. In the loving-kindness meditation, we focused on sending compassion to their child selves whom they imagined in the safety of their loving hearts.

Many of the women could barely manage sending love to their child selves, but they insisted on doing the meditation each time and wanted to begin and end the sitting period with it. They added words and phrases they wanted me to say, like "May I have compassion for my closed heart," "May I be safe," and "May I be free from fear."

What follows is grounded breathing I learned from Jean Klein, whose yoga and meditation seminars I attended for several years, and loving-kindness meditation (Salzberg, 1996). These can be done together or separately. Sometimes you might want to go right into the loving-kindness meditation after the EMDR work. These practices can be done in 5 minutes to 30 minutes or longer. You might choose to teach clients these practices before using them at the end of a session. It can be useful for some clients to do these practices at home between sessions. You can record your voice leading your clients in the meditation so that they can do the meditation at home. They can also do it on their own, or there are commercial tapes available for their listening.

Grounding Breathing and Loving-kindness Meditation

Find a quiet, undisturbed place to sit. Disconnect the phone and make sure that you won't be interrupted during the time of your meditation. You can sit cross-legged on a cushion or in a chair with your feet on the floor. It is important that you be comfortable and are sitting in an upright position.

Close your eyes and feel yourself sitting. Be aware of the places of contact . . . your bottom on the cushion and your feet on the floor. Be aware of your breathing. In and out. Feel the breath in the body. Let yourself relax into the present moment.

Now take a deep breath, drawing the air up from the earth, filling your abdomen . . . then filling your chest . . . and filling your throat . . . and then slowly exhale back down deep into the earth, . . . from the throat . . . chest . . . and then abdomen. . . . Now again breathe up from the earth, slowly filling the abdomen . . . chest . . . and . . . throat . . . then slowly exhale back down into the earth . . . from the throat . . . chest . . . and abdomen. . . . Let the breath be deep, full, and smooth. Feel yourself present moment to moment, one with the breath.

The expansion of the breath should be as full as possible: deep full breaths, breathing in from the earth, and exhaling slowly back down into the earth. Repeat the breathing and instructions for a several minutes. This breathing helps to calm, center, and ground. It is useful preparation for the loving-kindness meditation. This breathing can be followed by a guided imagery to the safe place, putting a protective boundary around the person and bringing in nurturer or protector figures if needed. The loving-kindness meditation can then be done within the "safe place."

Inner Child Loving-kindness Meditation

Now bring your attention to the area of your heart. Breathe in and out from your heart. . . . Let the breath be gentle and natural. In and out. . . . In and out. . . . Feel your heart becoming soft and warm. Breathing in and out of your loving heart. Now imagine your inner child in your heart. Your loving heart is a safe place for your tender child. Begin to send loving-kindness to this child self. (In a soft gentle voice repeat with pauses between phrases) May you be peaceful. May you be happy. May you be filled with loving-kindness. May you be free from fear. May you be free from suffering. May you be joyful. May you feel free. May you love and be loved. Use the words that work for you. Repeat them silently to yourself as you send loving-kindness to your child self. May you be peaceful. May you be happy. May you be free from suffering. May you be free from fear. May you be safe.

Continue on in this way, repeating words of loving-kindness to the child self. Clients may want to imagine their adult self holding the child in their lap as they repeat the loving phrases, and other nurturer or protector resources may also be in the space sending them loving-kindness. The meditation can focus completely on the child self or it can expand to include others.

Imagine in front of you someone you love very much. Imagine sending loving-kindness to that person. Just as I want to be happy, may you be happy. Just as I want to be peaceful, may you be peaceful. Just as I want to be free from suffering, may you be free from suffering. Just as I want to be free from fear, may you be free from fear. (The person can continue to repeat words that work for him or her sending loving-kindness to the loved one.)

The meditation can be expanded to include others the person loves and then expanded again to include family members and friends. It can be expanded to include the person's community . . . town . . . state . . . country . . . continent . . . world . . . finally the whole universe. You can have them imagine sending loving-kindness to all of the plants and animals as well as people. At the end of the meditation the person can imagine sending loving-kindness to all sentient beings in the universe. *May all beings everywhere be happy, peaceful, and free from suffering.*

Instead of the child self, the person can begin the meditation by sending love to him- or herself. *May I be peaceful. May I be happy. May I be free from suffering.* The idea is to generate a feeling of warmth and tenderness toward oneself. This is very difficult for many people. You can add, "May I have compassion for my closed heart" for those who have difficulty feeling compassion for themselves. This meditation can be adapted as you feel fit. Loving-kindness can also be extended to people who have caused harm. Some people may do this spontaneously. Use discretion with this part because premature forgiveness can cover over the deeper layers of woundedness that should be processed for full healing.

SUGGESTIONS FOR HELPING CLIENTS
MANAGE BETWEEN SESSIONS

There are several things you can do to help clients manage between sessions. These suggestions are meant for clients who have difficulty with affect management and object constancy.

TRANSITIONAL OBJECTS

Many clients who have been abused as children have a difficult time with object constancy, especially if the abuse was by a parent or someone close to them. Because of that, it is hard for them to carry the therapist inside as a positive inner representation for any length of time. They have a hard time remembering that their therapist continues to exist and cares about them between sessions. For this reason it can be helpful for clients to have what Winnicott called transitional objects with them that represent the therapist and the nurturing/healing environment as physical reminders. These transitional objects can take a variety of different forms. Some clients take objects from the office as a reminder of the therapist and the office as a safe place. Of course, one must be aware of transference issues that can arise and be cautious that the clients do not become overdependent on the therapist.

Making tapes of relaxation exercises and safe place—inner and outer resources invocation can also be helpful between sessions. These guided imageries are designed for each individual client and have the therapist's voice speaking directly to the client. These tapes can be very comforting to clients. Clients can play the tapes to help them sleep at night or to relax. If they feel disconnected from the therapists, they can play the tapes as a reminder of the relationship. The tapes can be particularly helpful when therapists take vacations and clients need regular reminders of the reality of the therapeutic relationship.

Clients need to know that their therapists also continue to hold them in their hearts between sessions. For some clients it is important for them to leave objects that represent aspects of themselves with the therapists in the healing space. Artwork, poetry, special objects, and childhood photographs are given to therapists for safekeeping. Sometimes they are gifts, and sometimes they are "lent" to the therapist for a time. I realize that there are various opinions about this issue and different ways of working with it depending upon one's theoretical orientation. I do not interpret the gifts because I feel that it would create an empathic break. Usually, there is an unspoken understanding of their meaning. I feel honored to be trusted enough to be asked to hold these things for my clients and do so until they request their return.

HOMEWORK

There are many things clients can do between sessions to help with containment or to facilitate the continuation of the processing, depending on what is in the clients' best interest. Journal writing is very useful to help clients continue with the processing and integration of material. Many clients find poetry writing an important outlet for feelings that cannot easily be expressed in prose form.

Clients can also be encouraged to do artwork. Drawing, painting, collage work, and sculpting can all be done to express feelings and images that arise for clients. Artwork is integrative and empowering. The focus should be on the expression, not the product. Let whatever wants to be expressed come out in whatever form it takes. Creative expression can be spiritual and enlivening, helping clients experience themselves beyond the victim identity.

Clients can be encouraged to take walks in nature, meditate, do yoga, tai chi, or other things that will help them reduce their stress and connect more with themselves. Attention should be paid to a healthy diet, regular exercise, and getting enough restful sleep. Some clients may find group work helpful or a course in self-defense or Model Mugging. As clients experience stress with the EMDR processing of painful memories, they should be reminded not to drink alcohol or take drugs. If it appears that clients are in need of antianxiety or antidepressant medication, a referral to a psychiatrist for a medication evaluation should be made.

9

TOOLS AND TECHNIQUES
FOR PROCESSING DIFFICULTIES

MANY DIFFICULTIES CAN arise during EMDR sessions that impede the flow of processing. What follows is a description of these problems and suggestions for working with them.

WORKING WITH ABREACTIONS

Many clients have strong emotional responses while processing traumatic material from the past. This is especially common when working with clients who were sexually abused as children. I have a number of recommendations for working with abreactions, some from Shapiro (1995, 2001) and others from *EMDR in the Treatment of Adults Abused as Children* (Parnell, 1999).

Abreactions are a common experience, but not necessary for client healing. Some therapists and clients mistakenly think that the EMDR processing isn't going well if the clients aren't having a strong emotional release. There is no right or wrong way to process, and everyone processes differently. Some people process subtly, while others have intense, loud emotional releases. Therapists should be prepared for either experience. It is helpful for therapists to remember that EMDR is not causing the clients' distress but rather releasing it from the clients' system (Shapiro, 1995, 2001). Abreactions are usually occurring as information is being processed. When the clients have passed through the abreaction, they usually feel some relief and are clearing the past painful information from their body-mind.

Abreactions can continue for several minutes at a time and can appear like waves. There is a buildup—a crescendo—and then the intensity diminishes. Sometimes clients will experience one wave after another in close succession as associated memories link. In these cases the therapists can continue with the BLS until it appears that either there is a completion of the processing or the clients want a break. Clients may have several abreactions in a session. The therapists watch the clients' body signals to know when to stop the BLS. The clients may take a deep breath, stop crying, stop twisting their hands, or appear more relaxed.

Throughout the abreaction the therapists provide gentle encouragement to continue with the BLS. If the clients are using eye movements and having difficulty following the fingers (or lights), the therapists might suggest to the clients that they "push my fingers (or the lights) with your eyes." If the clients are crying hard and the therapists are using eye movements, the therapists may want to change to tapping on the clients' hands or knees, or use other methods after asking the clients' permission. It is important to have spoken with clients ahead of time to prepare them for this possibility and to get their permission.

You should prepare clients for abreactions ahead of time and teach them that it is important to continue with the BLS until the disturbance has subsided. The BLS has been likened to keeping one's foot on the accelerator of a car as one moves through a tunnel. You don't take your foot off until you are out of the tunnel. Taking your foot off of the accelerator can cause it to take longer to get out of the tunnel. The clients can also become stuck in the tunnel. Inform your clients at the beginning of EMDR processing that they can stop at any time if they so wish. Agree upon a stop signal. This gives clients a sense of control over the process. As clients process, gently encourage them to keep going, that it is "old stuff," it is like scenery they see passing from a train. Reinforce the clients' dual awareness that they are safe in the present as they are processing the past.

The therapists should be compassionately present for the clients. The therapists must provide emotional stability and a sense of safety during the abreactions. The therapeutic stance I recommend is one of spacious, grounded attunement. The clients feel the therapists' caring, sensing that whatever arises in their experience is accepted unconditionally. The therapists are able to be present with the clients without becoming overwhelmed by the clients' process. When the therapists are able to feel with the clients, without fear and interference, it provides the clients with a feeling of safety and confidence in the process. The therapeutic relationship can also be likened to a life rope that connects the two; the clients have gone deep below the water and depend on the therapists to guide them up to the surface if needed. The therapists' occasional gentle reminders of "It's in the past" and "I am with you now" reassure the clients that the therapists are with them as they are immersed in the early traumatic memories.

It is important that you not give your clients the message that you can't handle the intensity of the feelings expressed. Anxious therapists close down sessions prematurely and direct clients to go to their safe place. Clients can feel ashamed of their feelings and be less willing to express them in the future. It can also frighten or alarm the clients and give them the impression that something is wrong. You should not try to shut down the abreactions too soon or attempt interweaves before clients are allowed to fully feel their feelings and move through them on their own. Intervening prematurely is a common error many EMDR therapists make because they don't understand or trust the clients' ability to process trauma with the BLS. It is my strong recommendation that EMDR therapists experience EMDR as clients in their own therapy so that they know from the clients' position what it feels like to process an abreaction to the end. Clients in the throes of a strong emotional release may frighten the therapists; but it feels much worse to the clients to be stopped by the therapists in the middle of an abreaction when the therapists are afraid. Clients can feel the information moving and clearing, which may not be apparent to the therapists. The therapists' countertransferences can interfere with the clients' healing and trust in the EMDR therapy.

Some clients abreact so loudly that it can present a problem to therapists who don't have soundproof offices and are concerned about disturbing or alarming their neighbors. Some of the screams may sound like someone is being murdered. These strong responses can come unexpectedly and surprise the clients and therapists. If you have clients who regularly have strong abreactions, it might be best to schedule them at a time when the work will not disturb others in the building and to warn neighbors that this could occur.

There are a number of ways to prepare clients for abreactive work. It is important that clients feel safe in the present as they process trauma from the past. Some clients who are following the lights on the light bar or using the tactile or audio stimulation might feel safer having the therapists sitting next to them holding their hand as they process. Clients may wish to have their partners, a close friend, or a concurrent therapist with them as they process. These present-day caring figures can give clients support and encouragement. It is important that these support people be adequately prepared for the processing sessions and that the therapists feel comfortable that they won't interfere or themselves be traumatized by the experience. Some clients derive comfort from having an object with them that represents safety to them. It might be a stuffed animal, a blanket, or a photograph of a loved one.

As I mentioned earlier, it is necessary for there to be emotional charge in order for processing to occur. If the charge is too high, however, the clients will dissociate and the processing will stop. There is a window between overactivation and underactivation in which we want to do the work.

There are a number of techniques therapists can use to try to decrease the clients' level of disturbance by manipulating the disturbing imagery. These techniques, which include imagining the scene like a movie, putting a glass wall between the client and the disturbing scene, and taking the sound out of it were described in Chapter 4. These techniques can be set up ahead of time and can also be used in the middle of an abreaction if the clients tell you the intensity is too much for them. For example, the clients might tell you, "I can't handle it." The therapists might ask, "What do you need to keep going?" The clients might respond, "I need for it to be less real, less intense." In that case the therapists might say, "Would you like to imagine a glass wall between yourself and the scene?" If the clients say, "Yes," say, "Imagine that," and then continue with BLS.

Some clients have difficulty expressing strong emotions in front of the therapists and inhibit their emotional releasing. They might correlate the expression of emotion with losing control. They might believe that if they let go of emotional control, they would fall apart completely and go crazy. They might also have difficulty trusting the therapists as they become vulnerable and regressed in the session. It is important to work with the clients' beliefs about having feelings, expressing feelings, and letting their feelings be seen. Some of these beliefs may stem from childhood experiences of punishment for expressing feelings. "I'll give you something to cry about," one angry father said before severely whipping his son. On the other hand, some children control their emotional expression as a way to retain a sense of dignity and control. "I decided I would never give him the satisfaction of seeing me cry." These experiences and beliefs might be important targets for EMDR processing sessions.

It is important that the therapists help to reinforce the dual focus of attention during EMDR processing. The clients are simultaneously conscious of their safety in the present as they process the past. Therapists may need to remind the clients that "it is in the past" and "you are safe now" during the processing because sometimes clients lose their witness awareness and become completely identified with the abused child from the past.

The following is an example of such a client. Jane's abreaction was a 10+. The session with her began with a relatively innocuous memory that she rated a 5 on the SUDS. Soon into the processing, this memory linked to a disturbing memory from early childhood. Jane became so overwhelmed by the traumatic memory that she had difficulty breathing, lost the use of her arms, and was convinced that she was going to die. The following is a summary of some of the interventions used.

The therapist was sitting in front of Jane, whose eyes were closed, and the therapist was tapping on Jane's hands. The therapist had no idea of the content of what Jane was experiencing but could see that she was terribly upset. Jane kept repeating out loud, "I can't breathe, I can't move, I am going to die," over and over again. She looped for several minutes. Her level of distress was not decreasing with the tapping. In fact, her distress was escalating.

The therapist first needed to bring Jane back into her body because she had dissociated, help her regain a dual focus of attention, and find out what she was experiencing so that the therapist could develop an appropriate intervention to get the processing back on track.

Therapist: Please open your eyes. Good. Jane, squeeze my hands. Good, you're here in the office with me now. (*The therapist is holding the client's hands, gently but firmly squeezes them.*) Feel your feet on the floor and feel your legs. You are okay now. You are safe now. How old are you? (*The therapist is trying to ascertain what the client is experiencing so as to develop an intervention.*)

Jane: I'm 3 years old.

Therapist: What's happening?

Jane: I'm on the floor of a room. My mother is in the bed. I think I am dying.

Therapist: Tell me what is happening to the little girl. (*The therapist is working hard to reconnect with the adult witness and to bring a sense of present safety to her. The hand squeezing also is intended to bring her more into her body as she has dissociated, and to be more present focused. Jane began to calm down and was able to describe her experience to the therapist. Jane was telling the story rather than living it.*)

The ability to go in and out of the story can give clients a sense of control over what feels like a present-time reality to them. As they can go in and out of the story, it begins to *feel* more like a story. Disidentification begins to take place.

Jane began to tell the story of what was happening, and the therapist began to tap on her hands again. The therapist asked Jane to keep her eyes open so that she could better maintain the present-time awareness. The processing continued with strategic interweaves used when necessary and regular reminders that what Jane was processing was from the past and that she was safe in the present. Jane was able to successfully complete the session and ended with a 0 SUDS.

DISSOCIATION DURING EMDR PROCESSING

Highly traumatized clients will commonly dissociate during EMDR processing of their traumas. This is especially true for clients who have been sexually abused as children. This is a normal response to overwhelming trauma, which can take many different forms. Clients can feel disconnected from their body, they may report no emotion in the middle of processing a terribly traumatic experience, they may report feeling like they are floating above their body, they may feel spaced-out or dizzy, or they may become sleepy or go numb. They might also suddenly speak in a completely different voice and have no idea what they are doing in the therapist's office! The clients' experience of dissociating during the processing may be a memory of dissociating during the traumatic incident being processed, or it may be that the clients are actually dissociating in the session as a defense against the intensity of the affect. Possibly the clients have a dissociative disorder. Often the therapists will feel light-headed and spaced out as they attune to the clients' experience.

When dissociation is suspected, you should stop the BLS and talk about what is happening with the client. If the dissociation observed is a memory of dissociating in the past, this memory may continue to be processed with EMDR in the session. You want to help the clients to attend to their body sensations and maintain their dual awareness of being safe in the present as they process old memories. It may be that the clients are in need of an interweave. I will commonly ask, "What do you need to be safe?" If the client says, "I need a protector," I will ask, "Who can protect you?" and I bring in a figure to help him. In some cases the clients need more distance from the intensity of the image and we can use some of the distancing techniques such as imagining it is a movie or putting a glass wall in front of it.

You might want to make the clients aware of their body. They can be instructed to feel the sensation of their contact with the chair and their feet on the floor. Clients can be directed to pound on the arms of the chair in unison with the eye movements (Shapiro, 1995). If the clients have their eyes closed and the therapists are using tapping or using auditory stimulation, the therapists can ask the clients to open their eyes and "look at me directly." This brings them back to the present time and reminds them of their connection to the therapist. Clients can be asked to tap on the *therapists'* hands left right, left right, as a means of creating the BLS and keeping the clients present in their body. The therapists can gently squeeze the clients' hands left right to help bring them back to their body awareness as the therapists keep them moving through the processing. In one case the therapist began by tapping the client's palms, then moved to squeezing the client's hands as the client began to dissociate. Then at one point in the processing, as the client became more "embodied," she began to squeeze the therapist's hands, continuing the BLS. With some of my clients who tend to dissociate, I ask them to hold smooth stones and feel themselves grounded as they process. This works well to keep them embodied.

Clients should be encouraged to talk about what they are experiencing during the processing if they are dissociating. Talking during the processing can increase the feeling of safety and connection between the therapist and clients. It can decrease their sense of isolation so many abuse survivors felt both during the abuse and subsequent to the abuse. The information clients provide during their narrative can also be used to develop interweaves if the clients become stuck. Finally, talking during the processing can help clients be more aware of being in the present moment relating to their therapists. The therapists can also remind the clients that they are safely in the therapist's office and that it is a safe place.

Pay close attention to the clients so that you can notice when the clients begin to dissociate. You can then gently remind the clients to "keep your eyes moving, you are here with me now in my office, you are safe now, stay with me, feel your body, good . . . good." If the clients have had their eyes closed during processing, they can be instructed to "keep your eyes open while you process." Eyes open helps maintain the dual focus of attention and keeps clients from going too deeply into the memory. Other suggestions to break dissociative trance include asking clients to change posture, asking them to move, having them change their breathing pattern, and also changing their gaze. Clients can hold ice, count backward, or sit in a different chair.

Kate, a woman in her mid-30s, who I described in *EMDR in the Treatment of Adults Abused as Children* (Parnell, 1999), believed she had been sexually abused by her father as a child. During the middle part of one session she began to dissociate when she began to get images of her father molesting her.

Kate: I'm pushing a person off of my body. >>>>>>>>> I got a clear image of a person being drunk, they were lifeless . . . inebriated and I was pushing them off my body. >>>>>> I can't imagine my father doing that—

Therapist: What are you feeling? (*I am checking to see what else is going on and to help her attend to her body.*)

Kate: Rage! >>>> Part of me feels like I'm leaving my body. I'm leaving my body to be peaceful. It's not safe to be in my body. (*She is dissociating and so I want to help get her back into her body.*)

Therapist: Be aware that it's not safe to be in your body. >>>>>>>>

Kate: I'm feeling mad. I keep seeing a body with its face in the pillow next to me. (*She came back into her body and again has the emotions and images.*)

The therapist's voice can be used to keep the clients connected and present during the processing. It reassures the clients that they aren't lost in the ozone. "That's it," "Good," "It's in the past," and "I'm here with you now" are utterances that help to calm the clients and help them know that you are with them in the present.

If the clients are dissociating because the incident is very upsetting to them, the clients and therapists may decide to close down the session, return to the safe place for a break, or debrief for a while and then return to the EMDR processing with attention paid to the body, safety, and dual awareness. The therapists and clients may want to talk about what caused the dissociation, which can provide valuable information about triggers. If the clients decide to continue with the processing, the above-mentioned techniques can be used to help the clients remain in their body and aware of being present in your office during EMDR processing.

I have found that with clients who tend to dissociate, we work together to come up with a method for working with it. Maybe they will signal me that they have left their body. I stop the BLS and ask them what they need to be safe. With one woman I would offer her smooth stones to hold to keep her present as she processed. It is helpful to educate clients about dissociation and to normalize it for them.

If it is suspected that the clients have a previously undiagnosed dissociative disorder, it is recommended that the therapist close the session, debrief the clients, and seek appropriate consultation or referral for the clients. Working with clients with dissociative disorders requires special training and expertise and is beyond the scope of this book.

CLIENT SLEEPINESS

Many clients become sleepy during EMDR processing, which may mean many different things. The therapists should talk with the clients about it and determine what is causing it to occur. Perhaps the clients are tired because of lack of sleep and the processing work is relaxing them and making them sleepy. The clients' eyes may be tired. If this is the case, they may want to stop EMDR for the session or change to tapping or auditory stimulation.

Sleepiness may also be the clients' resistance to the processing of emotionally charged information. If that is the case, talk with the clients about what they are avoiding by falling asleep. The resistance itself can be targeted with EMDR and processed. "Where do you feel the resistance in your body?" "What belief about yourself is associated with the resistance?" "Is there a memory or image that goes with the resistance?"

As discussed earlier, sleepiness can also be a form of dissociation. Eve was a client who would immediately close her eyes and nod off when processing an abuse memory with her brother. As soon as she would begin to close her eyes I would remind her, "Stay awake, keep your eyes open, it's old stuff," and she would open her eyes and continue to process the memory to completion. During the processing, Eve remembered that throughout her life she used sleep as a means of escaping the unpleasantness of her life, and her bed became a safe place or refuge. She realized that in her relatively happy present life she no longer needed to do that. She saw that she hadn't been fully awake to her life and that she had been repeating the old pattern out of habit.

Sleepiness during EMDR processing can also be a stimulated memory of being in that state of consciousness. Many clients who were sexually abused as children were molested while they were asleep in their beds. During the EMDR processing they may never feel fully awake, and the abuse memory may have a dreamlike quality, which coincides with the state they were in at the time of the abuse. Some clients were also drugged or given alcohol as children before or after the abuse. One client felt very sleepy, nodded, and noticed the smell of alcohol during the EMDR processing of an abuse memory. As the memory unfolded, she remembered that the abusers would force her to drink alcohol before they abused her. Another client recalled being raped while she was stoned. In these cases the therapist should keep the clients awake and continue to process the memory to completion with EMDR. It is helpful to have the clients talk aloud, describing their experiences in order to keep their minds alert so they can complete the processing of the memory. Usually after the memory has been processed, the clients who a few minutes before could hardly keep their eyes open return to a state of normal wakeful state of consciousness.

Some clients become sleepy during EMDR because they have been hypnotized by the eye movements. One woman was processing a horrendous rape with eye movements without any affect. After the first set of eye movements she reported no disturbance at all, a 0 SUDS. When she was asked to bring to her mind the original image of the rape scene to check if anything had been processed, she reported a SUDS of 10. She told the therapist that she had been informed in the past by a hypnotherapist that she was highly hypnotizable. For the next set of eye movements, she was asked to give a narrative account of her experience. As she spoke, she became aware of her emotions, which she was able to process. At the end of the session when she returned to the original image, it had lowered to SUDS of 0.

CLIENT NUMBNESS

Sometimes clients report feeling numb during EMDR processing. This is not necessarily an indication that they are not processing or that they have dissociated. Like sleepiness, it may be a memory that has been stimulated by the EMDR processing. I recommend that therapists treat numbness just like any other body sensation or experience. The therapists can ask the clients, "Where do you feel the numbness in your body?" and take a SUDS reading. "On a scale from 0 to 10, how numb do you feel?" The therapists instruct the clients to pay attention to the numbness in the body and begin the BLS. In my experience, the numbness usually changes with the BLS, and memories or associations emerge. If the numbness does not change, the therapists can ask the clients what they believe about themselves. It could be that a belief such as "It's not safe to feel" is blocking the processing. Any beliefs can be explored with the clients and then targeted with EMDR. The therapists can also ask, "What image goes with the numbness?" For example, Gillian reported an image of an enormous wad of cotton that represented the numbness and targeted that along with the feeling of numbness. Clients can also *draw* the feeling using art supplies the therapists have in the office. With the image or drawing, the sensation of numbness, and any belief that goes with it, the therapists can then incorporate the BLS and process the target.

CLIENTS WITH BODY MEMORIES WITHOUT VISUAL MEMORIES

Many clients come into treatment with body memories that feel to them like they are related to some kind of early sexual abuse, but the clients lack visual or narrative memory of what might have occurred. For instance, a woman sexually abused as a child without a visual memory of the incident may not know why she is afraid of men, avoids intimacy, can't seem to trust anybody, is sexually inhibited, and wants to scream with rage and terror when her husband touches her in a loving, sexual way. Her body remembers, but the body memory is not consciously linked up with the visual memory of the abuse incident. To herself and others her reactions seem irrational. For some of these clients, the processing of the body memory opens the door to the separate visual memory and brings about an integration of the disparate information. In these cases, EMDR seems to dissolve the barriers to the information locked away in separate memory compartments and, as a result, clients experience an integration of the images, body sensations, and behaviors that didn't make sense before when experienced separately. These experiences are often described by clients as puzzle pieces falling into place.

Many clients process body memories, and the associated visual memories never arise during the sessions. They experience many different physical sensations but do not see anything. There are different reasons for this phenomenon. For some clients it may be that the body memory is in a separate compartment from the visual and narrative memory, which have been completely disassociated. Both whole memories and memory fragments often seem to be locked in separate compartments in the body-mind. The images may be stored in one compartment; in another, the body's memory. In some of these cases the visual memory never links with the body memory. For some reason the linkage might be broken, or the neural pathways linking the different compartments are not stimulated during the EMDR processing. In my experience, clients have still benefited from the EMDR treatment despite the lack of visual memories. The following is an example of such a case.

Anya, who I described in *EMDR in the Treatment of Adults Abused as Children* (Parnell, 1999), came into treatment because she was having difficulty in her relationship with her partner and she believed the difficulty was linked to something traumatic she felt had happened to her as a child. Despite many years of therapy, she had no visual or narrative memory of what she believed had been sexual abuse but continued to have symptoms of abuse and a feeling that something had happened. We targeted her body sensations and associated beliefs and very intensive somatic processing resulted. During one EMDR session her body jerked and she writhed in agony. Despite the intensity of her body's response, however, no visual memories arose. When I asked her what she believed was happening, she replied that she believed that she was reprocessing an experience of labor and childbirth. She could not recall this ever happening to her, and no clear images emerged—just vague dreamlike imagery. I kept her moving through the intensive body abreactions by continuing with the eye movements until she reached a plateau and seemed calm. She had several of these intense body abreactions, which lasted several minutes during the session, and she experienced a sense of relief after each one. At the end of the session she felt calm and cleared of the disturbance in her body. Following the sessions she reported an improvement in her symptoms and a change in the previously held negative beliefs about herself. Her sessions typically involved this intensive body processing without a clear sense of what the historical origins were. By the end of several months' work, her symptoms and relationship with her partner had improved significantly and she decided to end her treatment.

One woman began to cry in panic during EMDR processing and slipped off of the couch onto the floor. She was then overtaken by spasmodic jerking simulating an orgasm. In her case, the therapist got down on the floor near her and gently encouraged her to continue with the eye movements following the therapist's fingers until the body reaction had subsided. The therapist and client were exhausted by the experience. In the week that followed her symptoms improved and she was no longer traumatized by the experience.

Many clients do not have visual memories of trauma because they couldn't see for some reason during the incident. It could be that their eyes were closed or the incident occurred in the dark. Many children are molested at night in bed. In one case the client had no visual memory because the perpetrator put something over her head. Clients often worry that they aren't doing EMDR correctly or it isn't working for them because visual memories aren't appearing. Clients should be reassured that it isn't a problem. They should be encouraged to continue to process what is coming up for them.

MEMORY CHAINING

Clients who have multiple early traumas often have a difficult time completely reprocessing a single memory because the memory they begin with links into another memory, which then links into another one and another, with none of them resolved during a session. These associated memories are like links in a long chain. Clients can become overwhelmed by the memories unlocked during EMDR processing and can feel like multiple doors have been opened and all the horrible skeletons in the closet are emerging at once. There are a number of suggestions for preventing this from occurring.

In the beginning of the session, the therapists can use guided imagery to help the clients go to their safe place. When the clients are there, surrounded by their nurturing or protector figures, the therapists can suggest that they can bring up the memory they want to work on and imagine it on a movie or video screen. The therapists state that they will work on one memory only. It will have a beginning, middle, and an end. If the clients want to take a break, they can at any time and return to the safe place. A signal for stopping is agreed upon. When the clients are ready, the memory can be brought to mind and the EMDR processing begun. This technique has been very helpful for clients who have a tendency to chain. It comforts them to know that they have control and they will only work on one memory at a time. This process can be done with the clients in the safe place projecting the memory on a screen, or leaving the safe place, knowing they can return there as needed and bring up the memory to be worked on.

Another technique I use when clients seem to be chaining is to return frequently to the target image and to check it. In this way the therapists keep the clients on a short tether so that they don't go very far from the target memory. The motto is "When in doubt, return to the original picture and check it." Let's say the client has been working on a memory of having been abused at age 3 by her father in the bedroom and after several sets begins to process memories at age 5 and 6 at the family farm. Ask the client to "please return to mind the image we started with, the one of you and your father in the bedroom. What do you get *now* when you bring up the image?" The therapist is looking for change in the image, emotions, beliefs, or body sensations. If the client says, "I now feel angry, not afraid," the therapist instructs the client to "go with that" and again begins the BLS. Clients don't seem to mind returning to the target memory when they have chained on to other disturbing memories. It doesn't seem to interfere with their processing and in fact seems to increase their trust in the therapist, who is paying attention to their process and not allowing them to wander off too far and open too many of those memory closets. The therapist should take note of the memories that have been opened up and use them as potential future targets.

USING INTERWEAVES AND OTHER STRATEGIES
TO RELEASE BLOCKED PROCESSING

When clients become stuck, or the processing does not progress on the path toward an adaptive resolution, therapists need to intervene more actively with solutions to unblock the processing and help set it back on course.

Clients sometimes loop, recycling through the same emotions, sensations, images, and thoughts in successive sets. Emotional intensity may remain unchanged. Sometimes the content changes, and the clients appear to be processing, but when the clients return to the original scene, the cognitions or emotions have not changed. This looping is like a broken record, with the clients stuck in a groove going over and over the same material. EMDR clients who are processing traumas that occurred in childhood frequently have difficulty with blocked processing or looping during the processing of highly charged emotional material. In many cases the adult and child memory networks do not link up with the BLS and consequently more interaction with the therapists is needed. Processing can also be blocked without high emotional intensity. The clients may tell the therapists "I'm stuck," there is no change, and the disturbance is not being processed. There are a number of different techniques for unblocking the processing, including interweaves.

There are three main steps for intervention with blocked processing:

1. Recognizing that the processing is blocked or incomplete;
2. Identifying the cause;
3. Intervening using noninterweave or interweave strategies.

RECOGNIZING THAT THE PROCESSING IS BLOCKED OR INCOMPLETE

There are several different ways that clients may be blocked in processing. One of the most common is what is called *looping*. Clients are looping when they are cycling through the same emotions, sensations, images, and thoughts in successive sets without a change in SUDS level. Typically the clients are very distressed but the BLS is not able to link up the different memory networks to keep the processing moving along.

When clients are looping with the same affect, they might be crying and repeating, "I'm going to die," over and over. Clients who are looping with the same cognition may not exhibit high affect, which can be confusing for therapists who may not realize for a while that the processing is not progressing. I have seen clients move from one memory to another with a similar theme, such as times when they felt powerless, without an evolution or resolution emerging. When they return to the original scene, the SUDS and cognitions remain unchanged. Clients looping with the body sensation might repeat that the sensation is not changing after subsequent sets of BLS. For example, they might continue to report a feeling of tension in the chest.

Sometimes there is a resistance to or blocking of processing that is different from looping. This may take the form of clients saying that nothing is happening after several set of BLS. They simply do not seem to be processing.

At times the processing is continuing, but there is little time left in the session and the SUDS is 2 or above. In this case therapists might need to become more proactive in helping the clients to weave networks together. Adults abused as children frequently are not able to complete sessions, especially if there were several abuse incidents. In these cases, therapist-supplied interweaves are very useful for closing the sessions. It is important that therapists not leave their severely traumatized clients at SUDS levels above a 3.

I rarely leave clients at a SUDS above 1 or 2. I have found that becoming more active in the use of interweaves is essential to helping clients close sessions in the safest and most effective ways. In my experience as an EMDR consultant, I have found that EMDR therapists are weak in this area. Many do not understand that it is important to actively use interweaves to close sessions. It is far more effective than the use of safe place and containment imagery alone in closing sessions with SUDS above 2. This will be described later in this chapter.

IDENTIFY THE CAUSE

There are many possible causes for the blocked processing. When you find the clients stuck, you want to begin to explore what the causes could be. Open questions are helpful in this regard. "What's coming up for you?" "What are you noticing?" "What do you believe about yourself?" "What do you need?" are examples. The therapists look at the clients' patterns and core issues, the common issues, and suggest a hypothesis. If the clients reject it, try something else. Working together, the therapists and clients look for the cause of the blocked processing. Sometimes it is quite obvious, other times it is not. The following are potential areas of blockage to explore with clients (see Appendix 1, page 336 for a Summary of What to Do If the Processing Is Looping or Stuck).

RETURN TO THE TARGET

One of the most common suggestions I will offer clients is to return to the original picture or incident. Often the processing is not stuck at all; the clients have simply come to the end of a channel and believe they are stuck because nothing is happening. One of my general rules is: When in doubt, return to the target and check it. "When you return to the original picture, what comes up for you now?" The clients might notice a change in emotion, or a body sensation might be most apparent. Then simply say, "Go with that," and resume BLS. Sometimes the clients might go off on long sets that don't seem to be progressing. The therapists might wonder, Is anything happening? In that case, stop BLS and ask the clients to return to the original image or incident. If it is changing (e.g., it has gotten more distant, changed from color to black and white, there are new elements in it, a new memory has linked in), then the processing is occurring. If not, then you may need to intervene in some way.

When the clients bring up the picture again I will ask, "What is happening now in the picture?" I might ask the clients to scan the picture for visual clues. You might ask the clients questions to provide more detail about what they are seeing or experiencing. Look for any areas of emotional charge or reactivity and focus on them.

Therapist· Go back to the original picture. What do you get now?

Client: Not much has changed, but I feel older, stronger.

Therapist: Go with the feeling of being older and stronger. >>>>>>>

Returning to the target in my experience does not derail the processing and provides a sense of comfort to the clients that they are being closely tracked by their therapists.

LOOK FOR BLOCKING BELIEFS

If the clients seem to be looping, I will commonly look for blocking beliefs. Blocking beliefs are beliefs the clients experience as true on an unconscious level and block the processing. You can find the blocking belief by simply asking the clients, "What do you believe about yourself?" If they answer, "Boys don't cry," you might say, "Go with that," or do an interweave. Sometimes by just saying aloud the belief that has been blocking the processing and then adding BLS, the processing will get back on track. Often, the clients are reluctant to express the blocking belief if it evokes feelings of shame, a broken agreement (prohibition against telling, threats of harm), issues of trusting the therapists, or taboo subjects. The therapists can offer suggestions or hypotheses to the clients, who accept or reject them. For example, if I suspect the client is experiencing feelings of sexual stimulation in the genitals, a body memory associated with the abuse memory he is processing, I might say something about this being an experience common to people who had been abused, normalizing it without asking him directly if he were experiencing this.

Sometimes clients may appear to be stuck in the body, but it is a belief that is causing the body sensation to be blocked. For example, if the clients feel a blockage in the throat, the belief might be, "It's not safe to tell."

There are four main issues with corresponding beliefs that frequently cause clients to loop or become stuck: safety, responsibility, and choice/control (Parnell, 1997a, 1999; Shapiro, 1995), and also shame (Parnell,

1999). Though there are other beliefs that can block the processing as well, these four issues come up most frequently when working with adults who have been traumatized as children. It is important to listen for these beliefs when they arise and intervene appropriately. These issues arise throughout the course of treatment, affect the transference and therapeutic relationship, and are important themes in the EMDR processing sessions. Keep these issues in mind as you explore with the client what belief might be impeding the processing.

Safety

Clients will often loop with the belief, "I'm not safe." This belief is common for traumatized people, particularly for adults who were traumatized as children because of physical or sexual abuse, neglect, or medical procedures. Adult clients abused in childhood may still unconsciously believe that the perpetrator can still harm them, even if they know that the perpetrator is old, disabled, or dead.

Clients who experienced traumas in their adult life can also believe they are unsafe. A person who has survived a serious car accident may believe it is not safe to drive.

Responsibility

Children tend to believe that they are responsible for the behavior of the adults in their lives. Almost all children blame themselves for the abuse they received. "It's my fault I made him mad. If only I were a better son, my father wouldn't have beaten me." Many adult children of alcoholics believe they are responsible for taking care of their families. They take on an inordinate amount of responsibility for themselves, their siblings, and their parents. This is also true in families where a parent suffers from a mental or physical illness. Police officers and war veterans who were not able to save a comrade may believe it was their fault.

Choice/Control

For many traumatized people, the moment of loss of power or control gets locked in their nervous system along with the belief, "I'm powerless" or "I have no control." This can be true for clients who experienced traumas in childhood or adulthood. Children, who were small and defenseless when they were traumatized or abused, often develop a sense of being perpetually helpless, a victim forever. This victimization may get repeated throughout their lives. The perpetrator took away their power and they continue to feel disempowered in their current lives. They didn't have a choice about what happened to them then, and they continue unconsciously to believe that they have no choice in their adult life now. Client empowerment is important in this work, and attention should be paid to this issue throughout the therapy, helping clients to draw from their own inner wisdom, to connect with their bodies in the present, and to reinforce assertiveness in their lives.

Clients with histories of repeated medical or dental procedures in childhood can also present with similar beliefs. As helpless children in hospitals receiving repeated intrusive examinations and injections, they develop the belief that they have no choice or control over their bodies. They cannot say no. They feel powerless in much the same way victims of abuse do.

Shame

The feeling of shame, with the beliefs associated with it such as "I'm bad, I'm disgusting, there's something wrong with me," will often stop the processing. Shame is a deeply felt emotion that many survivors believe defines their core self. "I am this shameful piece of shit. . . . If he's mad, it is because I am bad," one woman said. This feeling of badness becomes a self-defining belief that affects their self-esteem and forms the foundation for their self-concept.

Seductive perpetrators often convince children that they wanted the abuse they received. These children are often lonely and vulnerable, craving the attention these predators provide them. When their bodies respond with pleasure, the perpetrators tell the children, "See, you like it," persuading them that they were complicit in the act. When the children return, lured by the attention they are receiving, the perpetrators further convince them of their guilt. Because of this guilt and shame, the clients processing these memories will frequently loop in the feelings that can be so strong and upsetting, they cannot tell the therapists what they are feeling. In these cases it can be helpful for the therapists to guess the issues and address them with the clients. I have found that naming and normalizing shame feelings can help to diffuse them, making it possible to use an intervention to help the processing to resume.

The intervention sequence when the clients are looping with a blocking belief can look like the following. The client is looping and stuck.

Therapist: What do you believe about yourself?

Client: (*Tells the therapist what the belief is, for example:* "I'm incompetent.")

Therapist: Go with that. (*And add BLS, or do an interweave.*)

For example, in one case the client was a police officer who was processing the memory of having failed to fire his gun at an assailant who could have killed him and his partner. He was looping with a high level of affect and self-hate. "I should have shot him, I should have shot him." After several sets of BLS, the SUDS was not going down. He was still angry with himself.

Therapist: What do you believe about yourself?

Client: I'm a bad cop. I'm weak.

At this point the therapist devised an interweave that addressed the erroneous belief.

CHECK FOR FEEDER MEMORIES

A feeder memory is an unprocessed earlier memory that is contributing to the current problem and blocking the processing of the targeted memory. Sometimes clients are able to report that there is another memory coming up that is blocking the processing, but often it is necessary to stop and explore with the clients if there is an earlier memory. In some cases it is required to shift from processing the target memory and reprocess the feeder memory before the target memory can be processed.

For example, a man was processing the death of family members in a tragic accident when the processing became stuck. I stopped the BLS and asked him what was happening. He told me that he couldn't allow himself to cry. Together we explored this belief's origins in his past. He recalled a childhood incident when he cried after his dog was hit by a car and his father had beaten him. As a result he vowed he would never cry again. We directed our attention to the memory of his father beating him, targeted, and reprocessed it. When it was completed, we returned again to the accident. This time he was able to feel his feelings fully and to cry, allowing the processing to continue to completion. Sometimes it may be necessary to spend an entire session on the feeder memories, returning to the original target memory at another session.

ADDRESS CLIENTS' FEARS

It is essential to address clients' fears when they arise. Do not push clients to continue if they don't feel safe. The question I will ask is "What do you need to be safe?" There are many reasons clients become fearful during EMDR sessions. In the beginning many clients are concerned that they are not doing it right. They stop processing because they are assessing their progress and cannot allow themselves to let go and trust the flow of associations. When this happens I tell them that I will let them know if it is working or not. I also assure them that there are no right or wrong ways of doing it; it is different for everyone. Some clients come in with an expectation that they will have strong emotional releases, and when that doesn't happen they believe it's not working. In those cases I tell them that one does not have to have strong feelings in order to process.

Some clients are afraid of going crazy with the perceived loss of control, the intensity of the images and emotions that are coming up with EMDR processing, and the fantastical, dreamlike imagery that may be emerging. Address these fears and reassure the clients if necessary. Again, I will ask, "What do you need to be safe." If they say, "I need to bring in a protector figure," the therapists can do an imaginal interweave bringing in the protector. If they say, "I need you to hold my hand," the therapists can hold their hand. If they say, "I need to stop," the therapists can guide them to their safe place and bring in nurturing and protector figures if necessary. In some cases distancing techniques are needed to help the clients gain more control.

Sometimes the fear that will come up has to do with the therapeutic relationship. Perhaps the clients do not feel safe with the therapists. In that case the therapists do what they can to repair the relationship. Spend time talking with the clients until they feel safe. Do not proceed with EMDR if the relationship is not secure.

Because some clients may require help with medication to enable them to better cope with the emotions and anxiety that arise between sessions, having adjunctive psychiatric backup and support can be very helpful.

Clients abused as children commonly fear that in processing the "bad" memories associated with a close family member, they will lose the "good memories." The therapists can suggest that the clients imagine putting the good memories in a safe place where they will be kept separate from the "bad" memories. This safe place can be a safe, a file box, or anything the client can imagine where they can protect the good memories. Protecting the good memories can be done by using art, with the clients drawing the container with the good memories inside. The therapists may keep the drawing in their office where it will be safe and available to the clients. The clients then process the abuse memories while keeping the good memories safe. Later, when the clients are ready, the good and bad memories can be integrated.

Some clients may block the processing because they are afraid of getting better. Secondary gain issues may be blocking the processing. "If I get through these old memories, who will I be? Who will my friends be? What will my life look like?" The current symptoms, though debilitating, are familiar. If identified, these resistances should be discussed with the clients. Perhaps the therapy is proceeding too quickly, and the clients need more time to integrate the changes in self-perception and relating to others.

Sometimes new images or scenes may arise during EMDR processing that may shock the clients. I have had several clients stop processing because images arose that were sexual and involved parents or caretakers. In these cases the clients demanded to know if they were true. They were frightened and overwhelmed by the implications. "Does this mean my father abused me?" When this happens I tell clients that I don't know if it is true or not, and urge them to suspend judgment, allowing the processing to continue without drawing conclusions. Sometimes fragments of memories, scenes, and things children were told, images from movies or books, and dreams get confabulated. The mind struggles to make sense of the information. I have found that if clients are able to suspend judgment, information gets sorted out and eventually makes sense.

Sometimes if the processing is too much, clients can focus on only the part of the memory that they feel they can process during the session. The other parts they can imagine putting in a container. In this way they can focus on what they can handle and put the rest away to work on later.

LOOK FOR BLOCKING IMAGES

Sometimes during EMDR processing an image begins to come into the clients' awareness that is extremely distressing. It could be information that is new to them and is so shocking and disruptive to their view of themselves and their past relationships that they try to push it back out of awareness, or they close the door on it. The clients may feel so distressed by the image—even though they haven't fully "seen" it—that the processing becomes blocked and the clients begin to loop.

If you suspect that there is a blocking image, ask the clients, "What in the picture might be causing the processing to be blocked?" Ask the clients to scan the scene for any significant details. If it turns out that there is a very disturbing image, the clients may want to stop the processing and talk about it before proceeding. In one case the client became stuck in the processing. When I explored with her what she was seeing she told me, "It's too terrible to see." I then asked her what she needed in order to see it? She told me she needed to be stronger and feel more protected. She brought in a protector figure, held her hand, and then was able to proceed and see what she was so terrified of.

In another case, the client was processing a scene when she was a small child feeling neglected by her mother. She was stuck, and the processing not moving. We returned to the original scene, and it had not changed significantly. I then asked her to scan the scene. "What do you see? Look at your mother's face. What do you notice?" She saw that her mother was very young and afraid. She was overwhelmed with the responsibility of caring for a young needy child when she herself was needy and unsure of herself. After this we were able to craft an interweave that got the processing moving along.

LOOK FOR BLOCKING BODY SENSATIONS

Sometimes it is a body sensation that is blocking the processing. This might manifest as tightness in the throat or jaw, constriction in the chest, tingling in the hands, or any number of other ways. For clients who have difficulty attending to their bodies, you can direct them to "press the area of the sensation" to amplify it and to make it easier to bring the attention there. Clients can focus on the most pronounced sensation if there are many of them and they can't decide where to focus. Sometimes clients avoid their bodies because they feel sexual arousal—body memories that are being activated by the processing of the old memories. If this is the case, you might need to talk about any blocking beliefs, such as "I am bad for feeling this," and possibly do an educative interweave.

Clients can also use movement to emphasize something they are feeling in order to amplify it. They can move their hands or arms or stand up to increase the feeling and to unblock any blocked energy they might be feeling, for instance, a client who is processing a memory of being abused and is very angry, but frustrated because she cannot express it. The therapist can suggest that she stand up and move her body, as she feels compelled to do in the present, confronting her abuser in her imagination. Clients may act out punching, hitting, or even protecting themselves from blows. Movement can effectively activate the somatic memory component, which, with the BLS, can increase the effective processing of the traumatic memory.

Often, clients feel a constriction in the jaw or throat. Something wants to be expressed; it may not even be words, but simply sound. Encourage clients to speak words or make sounds aloud during processing. Clients can talk to the perpetrator or scream their terror into a pillow with the BLS. Expressing themselves in conjunction with the BLS helps to remove the blockage. I have had clients stand up, punch, scream, and growl through an abreaction.

Many therapists are trained to look for somatic processing and emotional releases. These are not necessary for EMDR to be working. Different people process memories in different ways. Don't push for any particular way of processing. It gives clients the message that what they are doing isn't good enough. I only push for the somatic or emotional when the processing is stuck or looping. Again, go back to the original picture and check it. If it is changed, the SUDS is down, and cognitions changed, the processing is working. It may have moved so fast that the clients and you were not aware of the somatic component. It is not necessarily resistance. If the SUDS has changed, it is working. If clients' symptoms are improving, it is working, whether or not they reported body sensations. However, at the end of the session, if there is something left in the body, then focus on that with BLS. The processing is not complete until the body is clear.

ORIENT IN TIME AND PLACE, AND CHECK OTHER SENSES (SMELL, HEARING, TASTE)

There are times when clients find themselves in a memory network that they cannot identify. They may not know where they are and feel lost, upset, and disoriented. It may be that a fragment of the memory is activated. Sometimes the processing is blocked because there is a sound, taste, or smell that has come into the periphery of their awareness that is activating a strong emotional response.

If the processing is stuck, the therapists can try to help clients locate themselves in place and time. How old are they? Where are they? After this the therapists can ask clients to describe what is happening. Have them scan the scene. Ask for sensory information. What are they hearing? Is there any dialogue in the scene? Are there any sound effects? Do they smell or taste anything? What are they sensing? The sensory information can be very helpful in orienting the clients and helping in putting the puzzle pieces together.

A client with a history of sexual abuse by her father and physical and emotional abuse from her mother began to loop at a high level of distress. I stopped the BLS and asked her what was happening. She could barely speak. I asked her how old she was. She said she was very young.

Therapist: Where are you?

Client: I don't know.

Therapist: What do you see?

Client: It's very dark. I don't see anything.

Therapist: What do you hear?

Client: I hear my mother nearby.

Therapist: What do you feel?

Client: It's damp and cold.

Therapist: What do you smell?

After that she realized where she was. She said that she was under the sink in the kitchen. She was put there by her mother who told her she had to be still and couldn't make a sound. She had the sense she had been left there for hours. I then said, "Go with that," and we resumed BLS and processing.

In another case the client was working on the fear of public speaking. She began with a memory of humiliation by a teacher. The NC was "I can't survive." The processing moved along well. I thought she was completing it. But when she returned to the picture, though it felt complete to her, she reported extreme anxiety running through her body. She said that the anxiety did not feel associated with the original picture. Something else had been activated and she didn't know what it was. I asked her what she saw. She said she saw a kind of blue light, and that she didn't feel like she was in her body. After more questions, she told me that she had nearly died in a car accident 20 years earlier. I then asked her what picture came to mind when she thought of the accident. She said she saw herself lying in a cow pasture after she had been thrown from the car. We then focused on this memory and reprocessed it.

TALK TO THE CHILD SELF

If the processing is blocked and the client is in a "child state," you can talk to the child self in order to find out what might be blocking the processing. "What does the child need? What does the child want? What does the child feel? What does the child long for?" It is helpful to use simple language and a gentle tone. "If the child is frightened, what is scaring him or her? What is the child self seeing that is distressing? What is happening in the scene? What does the child self need in order to feel safe?" This open exploration can lead to a blocking belief or image. The therapists can then design an interweave or other intervention to address the problem.

If the child says, "I need someone to help me," the therapist can ask, "Who can help you?" When the client responds, "I want my dragon to help," the therapist can say, "Imagine that," and add BLS.

CONSULT THE INNER ADVISER OR WISE SELF

Sometimes when the clients are stuck and neither the therapists nor clients know what the problem or the solution is, the clients' inner adviser or higher self can be consulted. The clients may have already contacted the inner adviser in the preparation phase of treatment as a resource or some kind of wise self or inner guidance may have emerged spontaneously during EMDR processing sessions. Ask the clients to close their eyes and contact this inner adviser, and when they have contacted this part, have them dialogue with it in order to find the source of the problem and the solution. Sometimes the inner guidance will give the clients a wise lecture! When the clients tell you this advice, add the BLS or ask the clients to imagine doing what has been advised. I have called on clients' inner guidance when I have felt at an impasse and haven't known what to do next. I have found it very helpful and empowering for the clients.

IMPLEMENTING NONINTERWEAVE STRATEGIES

There are a number of noninterweave strategies that therapists can try before using interweaves (see Appendix 1, page 336). Some of these will unblock the processing and get it moving again, while others, such as a safe place, may simply help the clients calm down and feel comfortable. Most of these techniques are described in Shapiro's (1995, 2001) *Eye Movement Desensitization and Reprocessing*.

CHANGE THE EYE MOVEMENT

If you are using manually directed eye movements with clients, you might want to increase or decrease the speed of the saccades, or change the direction from horizontal to diagonal or to vertical movements. Circular movement can also be helpful for unblocking looping.

CHANGE THE TYPE OF BLS

Some clients have difficulty moving their eyes back and forth while attending to their inner experience. Others feel self-conscious about crying or expressing feelings in front of the therapist. For these clients, closing their eyes as they listen to bilateral tones or passively having their hands or knees tapped makes it easier for them to process. If I suspect the processing is blocked because of the type of BLS being used, I explore this with the clients and offer them other choices. Some clients who have been sexually abused may feel uncomfortable being touched by the therapist. Auditory processing may be a better choice for them. Others like the contact with the therapist that touch provides as they process frightening experiences. The tapping reassures them that they are not alone. Oftentimes, clients will have their eyes closed as they are being tapped and begin to loop. In this case, it may be necessary to change to eye movements or to ask them to keep their eyes open so that they can maintain a present awareness as they process the past.

Some clients will begin with eye movements, change to tapping in midsession, and then return to eye movements later in the session. I have found that the processing continues with the changes in forms of BLS.

ALTER THE TARGET

There are a number of alterations of the target that can be done to decrease the intensity, making it easier to process the image for some clients who become stuck.

Distancing Techniques

The target image can be manipulated visually to make it less distressing to the clients. The image can be made smaller, black and white, into a still photograph, and it can be placed at a greater distance from the clients. The image can be seen like a video on a TV monitor or as a movie projected on a screen. They can imagine putting a protective barrier between themselves and the incident, made of anything they would like.

Hierarchy

Another manipulative technique is taken from Wolpe's (1991) desensitization work. Clients can place the feared object (e.g., the perpetrator) at a distance from them during the processing and progressively bring him closer in their imagination. Clients could also begin by having the perpetrator behind a glass wall and, when they are ready, remove the wall and have him at a distance coming closer to them in their imagination as they feel less fearful.

Change the Sound

Some clients will become stuck because the sound in the scene is too distressing to them. For someone who witnessed a shooting, it may be the sound of the gun firing. They can't move on in the scene because of the sound. In these cases the therapists can suggest that they turn the sound off. "See the picture without the sound." Then add the BLS.

For other clients it can be helpful to change the sound. In the case of clients who are distressed by the sound of someone's voice, the therapists can ask the clients to change the voice to something comical like Donald Duck's voice. "When you hear your father's scary voice in your mind, can you imagine changing it to Donald Duck's voice?" If they say "Yes," have them "imagine that" with BLS. This technique also works well for clients who have very critical or punitive inner voices. Changing the voice helps to create distance and disidentification from the voice.

CREATE A CONTAINER

If clients are feeling overwhelmed by the amount of material that is coming up, they can imagine creating a container into which they put the information they do not want to process. They can then focus on the part they feel they *can* handle. In this way they can do a piece of work that can be completed in the session. For example, if the client is processing a kidnapping and rape that went on for days, she can focus on just one part, the part she feels she can handle, and imagine putting the rest in a container with a tight lid. She can take other parts out when she feels ready. Clients can also put sounds, emotions, and body sensations into the container.

INCREASE THE SENSE OF SAFETY IN THE PRESENT

If clients are looping or stuck because they do not feel safe, it is important to do what you can to increase their sense of safety in the present. You can ask them what would help them to feel safer. You can remind them repeatedly during the processing that they are in your office and that they are safe now.

RETURN TO A SAFE PLACE OR CONFLICT-FREE IMAGE

Clients can return to the safe place or their conflict-free image they identified and developed earlier if they feel overwhelmed and want to take a break from the processing. They can imagine going to the safe place and bringing in their nurturing or protective figures to help calm them down and to increase the sense of safety in the present. When they feel securely in the safe place, the therapists can determine whether or not to install the feeling of safety with BLS. The clients may choose to remain in the safe place until the end of the session or may decide to return to the processing if they feel ready.

IMPLEMENTING INTERWEAVE STRATEGIES

There are times when using BLS and following the clients' process are not sufficient to keep the information flowing to a positive resolution. Clients sometimes enter into cognitive or emotional loops, repeating the same thoughts or feelings (or both) over and over. At these times the therapists can use interweaves, a proactive EMDR strategy that serves to jump-start blocked processing, to introduce information rather than depend solely on what arises from the clients. The statements or images the therapists offer serve to weave together memory networks and associations that the clients were not able to connect. Interweaves introduce a new perspective and new information or information that the clients "know" but do not have access to in the state of mind that is activated. There are many interweave methods and the selection of the appropriate method is mandated by the specific situation. After the interweaves are introduced, the processing begins to flow again. Traumatic experiences often seem to be stored in one part of the body-mind without being affected by more current information. Interweaves create a bridge between the parts of the clients' minds that have been separated. Interweaves facilitate the processing, provide developmental repair, increase ego strength, and move the clients toward greater stability.

Therapists can also use interweaves to help close sessions when time is running out. Shapiro (1995, 2001) used the term *cognitive interweave*, but I prefer *interweave* because many of the strategies include imagery as well as cognitions.

REVIEW OF ADAPTIVE INFORMATION PROCESSING

Because interweaves are used to jump-start stalled processing to get it back on track, I believe it is important to review the results of adaptive information processing when it is working well (see also Appendix 1, page 337 for a review of Important Concepts for Adaptive Information Processing).

EMDR integrates memory networks. When the processing is moving to an adaptive resolution, clients experience spontaneous linking of appropriate neuronetworks. Information that is held in one network is shared with another. As memory networks are integrated, the clients experience a broader perspective on the past event. A common example of this phenomenon is the integration of ego states, most commonly adult self and child self. Another example of memory networks integrating is when a memory frozen in time, such as a moment of terror and helplessness, is linked with the memory of what happened next that involved action and safety. Clients also spontaneously integrate internal or external resources during processing. Protector, nurturer, or wise figures may enter their processing, helping to bring it to completion.

The integration of networks also allows the clients to form a coherent narrative. According to Siegel, "The connection of the past, present, and future is one of the central processes of the mind in the creation of an autobiographical form of self awareness" (2001, p. 79). Adults who have experienced severe traumas as children often do not have a cohesive sense of themselves over time. Their sense of self is fragmented; they feel ungrounded. As a result of EMDR and the integration of networks that include pictures, emotions, body sensations, and cognitions, these clients feel whole and can provide a coherent narrative of their lives.

EMDR separates or disassociates networks that don't go together. Clients who are traumatized develop a generalized conditioned response to stimuli that are associated with the trauma. A rape victim, for example, may fear all men and be unable to differentiate safe men from unsafe men. EMDR often helps to decondition this response, disassociating networks or associative strands. For example, at the end of a complete EMDR reprocessing session the rape victim can differentiate her husband from the rapist.

EMDR shifts psychological memory to objective memory. Psychological memory is memory that is self-referential, emotionally charged, and feels like it is happening in the present. Objective memory is memory that has a global perspective; all of the parts of a situation are seen as a whole. This memory is not emotionally charged or self-referential. Clients will often refer to the memory they processed with EMDR as if they are reading about it in the newspaper, or it feels like it happened a long time ago. Psychological memory is implicit memory, stored in fragmented form on the right side of the brain. It lacks a cohesive narrative. Objective memory is explicit, integrated memory, involving both brain hemispheres and the frontal lobes.

When clients move to objective memory and their perspective has broadened, they often express compassion toward themselves and even toward those who have harmed them.

EMDR helps clients come to what is true for them. They develop a felt sense of truth that is body-based. At the end of sessions clients clearly state their understanding of what happened to them and those involved. "I was only a child," "I did the best I could," and "My mother was not able to love me because she was never loved herself," are statements clients make at the end of sessions with complete conviction. They know them to be true. An important step in the healing process for clients who were abused or neglected is to accept the limitations of their parents or caretakers, let go of the fantasy family they created to survive, and grieve the loss. After that, they can open to healthy relationships.

IMPORTANT TIPS FOR CREATING INTERWEAVES

Use interweaves sparingly. As much as possible, allow the processing to proceed without intervening. It is best to time interweaves in such a way that they don't feel intrusive or disruptive. Interweaves are suggested to clients, who are invited to reject them if they don't fit. It is best to ask a question. Designing interweaves is often a collaborative effort between the therapist and client in which you work together to find the right key that will unlock the door. Many therapists think they have to have the right interweave before they can offer it to the client. Using what you know about the client and the issues being worked on, you can simply ask a question or offer a suggestion. If it works, great; if it doesn't, think of something else. Together, you try to come up with something that fits the current problem. The interweave that is offered also does not solve the client's problem. Rather, it simply gets the processing going again until the next stop.

The primary issues that come up for clients with complex trauma are safety, responsibility, choice/control, and shame. Therapists should listen for these issues and develop the most appropriate interweaves that address them. These issues come up over and over again in different forms throughout EMDR therapy because they are associated with different memories and incidents. Don't be discouraged if it seems like the same issue keeps recurring. It is not an indication that the EMDR is not working. Many different incidents create the same beliefs. With persistent EMDR work, it is my experience that clients eventually shift at a deeper level. Current life betrayals or traumas may activate the old beliefs, but they don't seem as completely true to the clients anymore.

GUIDELINES FOR USING INTERWEAVES

- Use only when the processing is stuck or to help in session closure.
- Offer the interweave, then move out of the way.
- Don't interpret; inquire.
- Use simple language, few words.
- When processing a childhood memory, use language and concepts a child would understand.

COMMON ERRORS THERAPISTS MAKE WITH INTERWEAVES

Intervening too quickly. It is important to allow the processing to go where it can before intervening. This is a problem with therapists' affect tolerance. Clients need to feel their feelings fully and experience moving through them. It is important for them to come to see things as they were, grieve them, and move on. Don't short-circuit the processing. It gives clients the message that their feelings are too much for you, or are not safe for them.

Talking too much. Don't interpret or discuss things with the clients unless you are trying to create an interweave. Otherwise it derails the processing.

Bringing in a resource too quickly. When clients are abreacting, don't assume they need to go to the safe place or bring in a resource.

Not using interweaves when they are needed. Many therapists forget that they can intervene with interweaves. Clients are left to loop in abreactions for too long.

Neglecting to use interweaves to close sessions. If you are running out of time, or cannot get the SUDS down below a 2, begin to use interweaves proactively to link networks together. Clients will do much better between sessions if you do this.

INTERWEAVE STEPS

1. The client is looping or stuck.
2. Stop BLS and ask the client what is happening.
3. The client responds.
4. You can do one or more of the following: (a) Return to target and check it, (b) look for blocking beliefs, (c) look for blocking images, (d) check for feeder memories, (e) look for client fears, (f) look for blocking body sensations, (g) get oriented in place and time, (h) check other senses, (i) talk to the child self (e.g., What does the child need?), (j) consult the inner adviser or wise self. For example, if the client said she was afraid of the perpetrator, the blocking belief is "I'm not safe."

5. The therapist constructs an interweave. In the above example the therapist might ask the client, "Where is the perpetrator now?"
6. The client responds to the therapist's inquiry. For example, "He's dead."
7. The therapist says, "Go with that," and adds BLS.

Interweaves mimic spontaneous EMDR processing. Therefore one of the guides to deciding what is needed to craft your interweave is thinking about what EMDR does naturally, where the processing is stuck, and what you might do to get it going again. Interweaves can be used to link memory networks, separate or sort, educate, bring in resources, aid in the expression of forbidden impulses, and creatively solve problems. They can also be used to help the clients see the bigger picture and to assemble the pieces of a coherent self-narrative.

INTERWEAVE CATEGORIES

There are several interweave strategies that you might consider when your client is looping or stuck. I have organized interweaves into four categories: inquiry, resources, imagination and education (see Figure 9.1; see also Appendix 1 page 337 for a Summary of Interweave Categories and Subcategories).

Inquiry

Inquiry interweaves are cognitive interweaves that involve asking clients short questions that cause them to bring forth information from other networks that are then connected using BLS. The inquiry interweave links or sorts two or more memory networks together. The clients have all of the needed information in their mind but may require help in "merging the two memory files." In many cases, the adult memory network has information that is not connecting with the child self's network. Questions can also serve to separate associative strands that don't go together. Issues of safety, responsibility, control, and shame commonly arise.

There are several interweave types that fall under this category.

INQUIRY INTERWEAVE SUBCATEGORIES

- Socratic
- "I'm confused."
- "What if your child/best friend/client/spouse, etc. did it?"

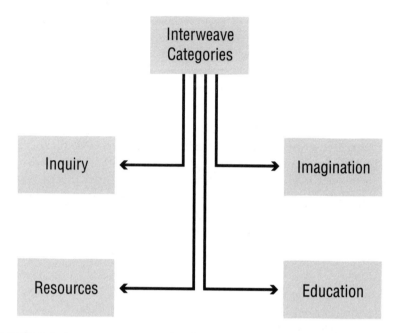

FIGURE 9.1 Interweave categories for jump-starting blocked processing.

- Open question (e.g., "Is that true?" or "Why did you do that?")
- Add a positive statement or ask, "Are you safe now?"
- "What happened next?"
- "What do you understand now?" or "What do you know to be true?"
  (Puts the pieces together in a coherent narrative.)
- "Look at the scene, what do you see?" (e.g., "Look at your mother's
  face, what do you notice?")

Socratic Method

In this method, which can take the form of a single question or a dialogue,
the therapists ask the clients simply worded questions that elicit an answer
from the memory network that they are desiring to link to the one that is
currently active (Shapiro, 1995, 2001). The questions the therapists ask lead
the clients to a logical conclusion. This method is quite powerful since it
enables clients to integrate what they already know in one memory network
but somehow don't know in another. It can be likened to merging two computer files.

A client who is processing a memory of being abused by her teenage brother is looping and stuck. She believes it is her fault. The therapist stops the BLS and asks her what is happening. She tells the therapist she is bad and is going to get in trouble.

Therapist: Who's responsible, a 3-year-old or a 15 year old?

Client: My brother is.

Therapist: Go with that. >>>>>>>>

Client: And my father is responsible for abusing my brother.

Therapist: Go with that. >>>>>>>

Case Examples of Socratic Interweaves

Mavis was a 35-year-old woman who was having difficulty getting over the end of a relationship. She just couldn't seem to move on. In fact, even though they had broken up over a year before, she was still wearing a bracelet her partner gave her. She was confused about why she was having such a hard time letting go of him. She knew he wasn't good for her; he did not treat her with love and respect. During an EMDR session targeting the end of the relationship she became stuck. She could not imagine letting go of him. In using the Socratic interweave in this case, I want to help her link memory networks that weren't linking on their own with the BLS.

Therapist: Is there anyone else in your life who treats you the way he does?

Mavis: No. (*She has a stunned look on her face.*)

Therapist: Go with that. >>>>>>>

Mavis: I finally understand the reality of how he wasn't there for me. >>>>>>> (*She is silent for several minutes.*) I imagined letting him go.

In the following session she told me that she removed the bracelet he had given her and tossed it into the ocean. It had become a handcuff, and now she was free.

In another case, the client was a woman in her late 40s who was processing guilt and distress she felt about an extramarital affair she had ended several years before about which she had never told her husband. She was stuck looping in the guilt and self-punishment. The blocking belief was "I need to hold on to this."

Therapist: Does your guilt and self-punishment bring you closer to your family?

Client: No.

Therapist: Go with that. >>>>>>

Client: *(She had an important realization.)* Keeping it keeps me at a distance from them. I can let go of it. *(By the end of the session she had let go of the guilt and felt a great deal of relief.)*

Case Example: Socratic Interweave With the Issue of Responsibility

Connie's processing had become stuck because she was feeling responsible for her teenage cousin's abuse of her when she was 6 years old.

Therapist: Who was responsible? *(I am checking to see if the NC has shifted.)*

Connie: I'm not sure who was responsible.

The NC had not fully shifted so I did another inquiry interweave. I knew she could empathize with her little daughter, Jill, and would not blame her for any abuse.

Therapist: If he had done this to your daughter, Connie, would she be responsible? Would it be her fault?

Connie: No.

Therapist: Go with that. >>>>>>

Connie: I can see the two of us again, but I'm *here* and not *there*.

Therapist: Who was responsible for the abuse? *(I am checking to see if the NC has changed.)*

Connie: *He was* responsible. *(She said this strongly and clearly.)*

Therapist: Are *you* bad because of what *he* did?

Connie: No. >>>>>

Case Example: Socratic Interweave for Dissociative States

It is common for clients who are processing traumas from accidents, surgeries, or childhood abuse to leave their bodies. Sometimes this is a memory of dissociating at the time of the trauma. An interweave that I have found very useful for these situations is to say to the client: "It wasn't safe to be in your body then. Is it safe to be in your body now?" If the client says yes, say, "Go with that" and do BLS. In my experience this links the present sense of safety with the past and the client comes into his or her body in a new way. If the client responds no, ask, "What do you need to be safe?" Continue from there, addressing safety needs.

Mary was processing the memory of nearly bleeding to death after a tonsillectomy at age 10. She described floating out of her body, a beautiful white light filled with love and joy, and an angel that was with her. After hearing a voice tell her it was not her time, she found herself coming back into a painful body, her throat on fire. During a break in the processing she reported feeling "floaty," like she wasn't fully back in her body. I asked her, "Is it safe to be in your body now?" She said yes. I told her to go with that. She then reported feeling back in her body, the "floaty" feeling gone.

Another interweave I have used for clients with dissociative experiences is one I have used for clients who have had near-death experiences and are stuck with the negative cognition "I'm not supposed to be here." These clients report blissful out-of-body experiences and have not fully come back in, hovering just outside themselves. They often resist being in the world, feeling like they no longer belong here. In these cases I have asked the client, "Is it true that you are not supposed to be here?" and then added BLS while he or she inquired. In every case clients have come back with a strong "yes," often to their surprise, and subsequently experienced a feeling of coming more fully into the body.

Case Example: Socratic Interweave for Grief and Loss

Clients who are processing the loss of a loved one often get stuck and loop with the belief that if they let go of their grief they are in some way betraying their loved one. I have found the following Socratic interweaves helpful in these cases.

Therapist: Do you need grief to prove love?
Client: No.
Therapist: Go with that. >>>>>

Or

Therapist: If you let go of the pain bond, what bond will you have?
Client: A love bond.
Therapist: Go with that. >>>>>>

Or

Therapist: Would you want your daughter to be bound to you by grief?
Client: No.
Therapist: Go with that. >>>>>>>

Or

Therapist: What would your husband want?
Client: He would want me to be happy.
Therapist: Go with that. >>>>>> Would he want you to not let go?
Client: No.
Therapists: Go with that. >>>>>>

Case Example: Using Socratic Interweave with Numbness

The client is stuck and not feeling. He reports feeling numb.

Therapist: If you could feel, what would you feel?
Client: Anger!
Therapist: Go with that. >>>>>>>

Case Example: Using Socratic Interweave to Link and Sort Associative Strands

Zena, who I described in the *EMDR in the Treatment of Adults Abused as Children* (Parnell, 1999), was processing a flashback memory that was new and distressing to her. In this session I used inquiry interweaves to help her move through the negative belief about herself being bad. At this point we are in the middle of the session, and she is processing a memory that has emerged in which she is on a bed with an older neighbor boy.

Zena: We're lying down on his bed and watching TV. He used to rub my back while we watched TV. . . . I liked that, it felt good. >>>>> We did stuff. (*She becomes quiet.*)

Therapist: What's happening now?

Zena: It's confusing. . . . I liked him, but I didn't want him to touch me. >>>>> I'm a bad girl. (*Her child-self is judging her harshly, creating a strongly held NC.*)

Therapist: Why do you believe you're a bad girl? (*I am trying to ascertain the origins of this belief so that I can craft an interweave.*)

Zena: 'Cause I like him and like being around him and I like some of the things he does and sometimes not other stuff. . . . I liked him but didn't want the touching. . . . I had a crush on him. . . . I guess I was in love with him. . . . We laughed together and watched TV together

Therapist: So you wanted love and attention from him but you didn't want the sexual attention? (*I am using a Socratic interweave to help her sort the confusing strands.*)

Zena: Yes. >>>>> I'm still there. (*She means in the image.*) He would rub my back and kiss me and it felt good. I really liked the attention. Being the youngest in my family, I never got much of that. (*She is realizing why her child self craved attention.*) >>>>> I'm not in the house anymore. It was confusing. I thought I must have been a bad girl because I wanted to see him. I just wanted to be with him. . . . I didn't want him to touch me. I didn't go there for sex. >>>>> (*She has an insight that changes her view of responsibility for what happened between them.*) He was the one who was bad. He knew it was wrong. . . . He told me not to tell!

At this point we were at the end of our time. She went to her safe place and connected with her child self. She felt calm and in a good place.

"I'm Confused"

This technique is used to link information that the clients know but do not have access to at the point they are in the processing (Shapiro, 1995, 2001). For example, many adults abused as children blame themselves for the abuse and feel angry with their child self. If during a session a client is stuck feeling angry with the 3-year-old child self who was abused by an uncle, the therapist might say the following: "I'm confused. A 3-year-old is responsible for the behavior of a 40-year-old?" If the client says, "No, that's not true, my uncle was responsible," the therapist then says, "Think about that," and does a set of BLS to link the information.

"What If Your Child Did It?"

With this technique the therapist tries to elicit empathy for the child self that the client is blaming (Shapiro, 1995, 2001). If the therapist knows the client has a daughter, niece, or other loved child, the therapist seeks to have the client think about the beloved child with sympathy, which then transfers the sympathy and understanding for her own child self. For example, if you know your client has a 6-year-old daughter and the stuck part is the client blaming the 6-year-old child self for the abuse, you could ask, "If this were your daughter Mary, would it be her fault?" If the client says no and means it, then you follow with a set of BLS.

Therapists can use variations on this theme by asking, "If this were your friend, what would you say?" For example, in the situation where a client was in a battering relationship and looping around guilt about leaving her husband, the therapist could ask, "If this were your friend, what would you tell her?"

Open Question

Sometimes it is helpful when clients are looping or stuck to inquire as to the reasons for their behavior or actions. I always assume there was a good reason for what they did; they are just not in contact with it. I might ask, "So why *did* you do_____?" The question is posed with curiosity and respect. It's an open question, different from the typical Socratic method, which usually guides the client to an answer that is obvious to the therapist. In the case of the open question, the therapist does not necessarily know what the client will come up with, but trusts that information will be revealed that will enable the processing to get back on track.

Case Example: The Use of an Open Question Interweave with a Battered Woman Looping with an NC

The client was an attractive, well-educated woman in her 50s who was still suffering from the end of a tumultuous marriage. She had been married for years to a violent, unstable man who terrified her. At the time of the session she was divorced but had to share custody of her daughter with him. She was processing the memory of his threatening her with a gun. She was stuck and looping around anger at herself for not doing more to stop him. "I should have called the police." Her tone was harsh, full of self-condemnation. Because I knew her to be a competent, intelligent woman, I believed there was good reason for her actions, but she was not in contact with that information. I asked her a question to help her weave in the reasons she had acted as she had. The question I posed to her was in a tone that communicated curiosity and respect, not criticism.

Therapist: Why didn't you call the police or ask for help?
Client: Because I was afraid to antagonize my husband.

Therapist: Go with that. >>>>>>>

Client: He was too dangerous. (*As a result of this interweave she realized that she had done what she had to do to survive.*) But I regret that I didn't call the police after things had calmed down.

Therapist: What would you do differently now?

Client: I'd call the police after I was safe.

Therapist: Imagine that. >>>>>>>

She felt relieved and the processing progressed.

Case Example: Using an Open Question Interweave for a Self-Blaming Rape Victim

The client was a 45-year-old woman who came to see me suffering from anxiety, depression, and low self-esteem. She hardly left her house and was overly dependent on her husband. She attributed her symptoms to a rape when she was an 18-year-old college student. She told me she had been walking to her college campus, her arms loaded with books, when a man she had never seen before drove up and offered her a ride. Though her gut advised against it, she got into the car. Instead of driving to her dorm, he took her to a deserted place and raped her. During a session in which we targeted the rape, she began to loop with anger at herself, saying, "I should never have gotten into the car." I realized that there was a reason she had overruled her gut, but did not know what it was.

Therapist: (*With a tone of curiosity I posed the question to her.*) Why *did* you get into the car? Who was the 18-year-old girl who got in the car? >>>>>>>>>>>> (*Long set of BLS.*)

Client: (*She has several important realizations about herself that bring compassion and understanding.*) She was naïve. She was taught to never hurt anyone's feelings. Her father was a minister and he was having an affair. Everyone pretended it wasn't happening. Her whole life up to that time set her up to get in that car.

Therapist: When you return to the original picture, what comes up now?

Client: I'm not getting into the car!

Therapist: Go with that. >>>>>>>>>>

Case Example: Sorting Using an Open Question

The client was a young woman working on a memory of being sexually abused by her grandfather who molested her from ages 4 to 8 during times he babysat for her. He was someone she was connected to yet who also hurt her. During a session in which she was processing an abuse incident, she looped in fear. Interweaves were done with her being rescued from the situation or leaving. Yet whenever she thought about the incident, she saw herself returning to her grandfather. Despite what she knew about him, her child self wanted to be with him. Full of self-hate and condemnation, she was furious with her child self's behavior. She was stuck. In order to help sort out threads that were tangled, I asked her an open question.

Therapist: Why *do* you return to your grandfather?

Client: Because he pays attention to me.

Therapist: Go with that. >>>>>>>>

Client: No one else pays attention to me.

Therapist: Did you want the touching?

Client: No.

Therapist: Go with that. >>>>>>>>>

Therapist: Who can give you the right kind of attention? (*I am bringing in a resource figure who is appropriate.*)

Client: My husband.

Therapist: Imagine that. >>>>>>

With these interweaves I was attempting to tease out the threads of association that had become entangled, separating the threads of complicity. It was important to separate out what she wanted. Often perpetrators choose needy children and get them to believe they are complicit in the abuse— "You wanted it."—when what the child really wanted was love and attention, not sex.

Add a Positive Statement or Ask "Are You Safe Now?"

For some clients, adding positive statements like "It's over," or asking "Are you safe now?" helps them calm down and pull out of looping. For example, a client is looping with a high level of affect while processing a car accident in which he was struck by a truck on the freeway, causing him to lose control and hit the center divider. His belief is "I'm going to die." The therapist can ask, "Are you safe now?" or "Did you survive?" When he answers yes, the therapist says, "Go with that" and adds BLS.

Focus on the Outcome, "What Happened Next?"

It can be helpful for some clients who are looping or stuck to focus on the outcome of the traumatic experience—the fact that they did survive. Sometimes when a traumatic event has been quite shocking, the person becomes stuck in the "I'm going to die" moment. It can appear in the processing like a broken record repeating over and over, stuck in the same place. In these cases I have found it helpful to *remind the client of the next thing that happened after the moment of terror.* It is like picking up the arm of the record player and placing it on the next groove of the record.

For example, Juanita had grown up in a Latin American country that had bullfights. When she was 3 years old, she was at the fair with her grandmother and a bull escaped from his enclosure and rampaged through the fairgrounds, terrorizing the people. In her memory, she suddenly found herself looking up into the angry red eyes of a giant bull about to gore her. In the next moment her grandmother whisked her away from the bull and pulled her under a table to safety. As this client processed this 10 SUDS memory, she remembered many other things that happened that day, but whenever she brought up the original picture it was still a 10 SUDS with the bull staring down into her 3-year-old's eyes. It just would not budge. I finally asked her, "What happened next?" She recounted the scene when her grandmother pulled her away from the bull to safety. I told her, "Focus on that." As she moved her eyes back and forth she imagined that scene. After the set of eye movements she said that the scene had progressed and connected to the scenes of safety, and her grandmother's love for her. When we checked the target image with the bull, it had gone down to a 0 SUDS.

"What Do You Understand Now? Or What Do You Know Now to Be True?"

In this interweave the therapist asks the client to explain what she understands or knows to be true. As she does this, the therapists uses BLS. This interweave helps the client sort out what is true from what is not and to create a cohesive narrative. It helps link the pieces together that heretofore have been fragmented.

Case Example: What Do You Know to Be True?

Betsy was a 38-year-old woman who had a history of severe sexual and physical abuse. She had many intact memories of abuse as well as symptoms and memory fragments she did not understand. Throughout her life, Betsy's mother accused her of being a liar, causing her to doubt her own perceptions and reality. Throughout her childhood her mother told her and others that Betsy was crazy. Even though she had long since cut off relations with her mother, she still chronically doubted herself. As a child Betsy remembered seeing her mother do something and then hearing her mother tell her that it never happened. It became apparent to me that Betsy had memory networks that were unintegrated and fragmented. She had memories of what she saw and experienced as well as memories of being told that her perceptions were not accurate. During one session when she was looping and confused about what was real, I asked her to tell me, "What do you know to be true?" We added BLS and she spoke out loud. She began to give an account of what she saw and heard as a child, including her mother blatantly lying to her aunt on the phone. She then had the realization, "My mom was the liar! I perceived things accurately. She lied all the time!" After this the threads began to sort themselves out. She had a series of memories of her mother lying. We used this interweave of "What do you know to be true?" often when she became confused, the threads entangled.

"Look at the Scene. What Do You See? What Do You Understand?"

This is an interweave that can shift the client's attention, bringing in information from a broader perspective. Often clients will spontaneously do this, but when they don't, this interweave can be helpful to get the processing back on track.

Case Example: "What Do You See?"

The client, a 52-year-old high school teacher, was hurt by her first boyfriend who stood her up for the prom. The incident devastated her, affecting how she viewed herself in relationships all her life. When processing this memory she began to loop around the distress she felt with the NC, "I'm unworthy of love." It struck me that she had based her self-esteem as a woman on how an adolescent boy treated her.

Therapist: Can you look at the face of the boy who hurt you and tell me what you see?

Client: He's so young! And he has red hair and pimples. He's not even that good looking. I let that kid affect how I feel about myself? (*She laughed.*)

Therapist: Go with that. >>>>>>>

Client: I feel relieved. As a high school teacher I know how young and ignorant high school boys are. I can't believe I let it affect me so much.

Her SUDS was a 0, and we installed her PC, "I am lovable."

Resources

During the preparation phase of treatment, therapists and clients have identified outer resources—people in the clients' life they identified as nurturing or protective of them in their current life or from the past. These resources can include the therapist, friends, lovers, partners, relatives, teachers, clergy people, or pets. They have also identified inner resources—nurturing, protective, or wise figures from their own psyche that can be summoned when needed. These can include the adult self, inner adviser, or wise self, spiritual or religious figures, and power animals.

Inner and outer resources are brought in when clients are looping and are unable to naturally connect with these resources. These resources can be called upon to nurture, protect, rescue, or explain. A commonly used inner resource is the *adult self* who is deliberately brought in to protect or nurture the child self if the adult self is not coming in automatically to help the child. Korn, Rozelle, and Weir (2004) recommends installing the resources that the clients will need specific to the memory that will be targeted. For example, if you are going to work on abuse memory from the time the clients were 3, you can ask the clients what resources their child self will need to work on that memory. Then install nurturer, protector, wise figures, and so on. This does not work so well for clients who don't know what the target memory will be at the beginning of the session, for example, in the case of clients who are bridging to find the target, beginning with a dream, or other symptom. Also, sometimes clients will begin in one memory and find themselves in an earlier memory that is more charged. For these clients I like to at least have a safe place and nurturing and protector figures named that we can call on if necessary.

When clients are looping or stuck I will often ask, "What do you need? Or what does the child need?" When the clients respond, I will say, "Imagine that," and add BLS to link it in. If the clients respond with "I don't know," I will begin to offer suggestions. I might ask if they need someone to protect them, nurture them, or explain something to them. Then I will ask, "Who can do that for you?" If again they cannot come up with a response, I will offer suggestions, some of which will come from the resources we installed earlier or I remember from their history taking. I believe it is always best to first ask the clients before offering suggestions. In this way you are pulling the information from their memory network. This is experienced as empowering. If the clients cannot answer easily, then I offer suggestions. Do not assume what the clients need. I have often been mistaken in my assumptions.

Don't be too quick to rescue the clients. It is a powerful and healing experience to go through the feelings fully, riding the waves. Even though they are painful, clients move through them and gain confidence in their ability to tolerate strong affect. For many people, what is important is that they come to what is true for them, even if it is a painful truth, and then feel the feelings associated with the understanding. For example, many children who are abused or neglected believe it is their fault, that their parents are really loving and good. They spend their lives repeating a pattern of involvement with abusive or neglectful partners. When the clients can see and experience through EMDR that their mother did not take care of them, did not love them, they can feel the grief associated with that understanding and move on. The pattern can be broken in the present. Accept the facts, grieve, and move on. At this point if the clients are stuck in the grief and looping, the therapists can ask, "What does the child need?"

Resource Interweave Sequencing

1. The client is looping and stuck. For example, the client is processing a childhood abuse memory of being locked in a closet. She is looping at a high level of affect.

2. The therapist asks the client what is happening.

3. The client responds. For example, she says, "I'm trapped and I can't get out."

4. The therapist asks, "What do you need?" or "What does the child need?"

5. The client responds to the therapist's inquiry. "I need someone to get me out of here."

6. The therapist asks, "Who can do that?"

7. The client responds with the needed information. "My friend Julie can do it."

8. The therapist instructs the client to imagine that, or go with that, and adds BLS to process and link in this information.

If when the therapists ask the clients what they need, and they say they don't know, then the therapists can provide suggestions. "Do you need help? Do you need someone to comfort you? Do you need protection?" When the clients say yes to any of the suggestions, the therapists either follow with another question, e.g., "Who could do that?" or says "Go with that." The principle is to ask the clients first, then offer suggestions. It much more empowering for clients to find solutions on their own. Don't assume what the clients need. Ask first.

Also don't assume which resources the clients need. Just because clients installed certain resources in the beginning of the session or treatment doesn't mean these are the resources they will need in their interweaves. Often, when asked, clients will come up with resources they had never thought of before. If they can't think of any resources to bring in and they are blocked in some way, too caught in the helplessness of the childhood memory network, the therapists can offer the resources the clients installed. "Can your protector figure come in to help you?" At this point it can feel like throwing ropes out to a drowning person. You hope that they will find one that will work, grab hold of it, and get pulled to safety.

Case Examples: Bringing In an Inner Resource

Estelle was processing a memory of being 7 years old and trying to learn to ride a bike. She was sad and helpless. Her NC was "I can't do it." During her processing she linked to several related memories of being over her head and not getting the help she needed to learn. When she returned to the original picture it had not changed. "I'm still alone and can't ride the bike."

Therapist: What does the child need?

Estelle: Someone to help her.

Therapist: Who could do that?

Estelle: My adult self.

Therapist: Go with that. >>>>>

Estelle: My adult self helped the child by putting the bike on grass, not gravel. She is patient with her and having fun. She's good with her. I can do it!

In another example, a 45-year-old woman who had been severely molested as a child began to have dreams in which a wolf appeared during our EMDR therapy. This wolf became an important ally in the work. Whenever she would become overwhelmed or stuck during the processing, we would call on him to protect the little girl from the perpetrators. Her SUDS would typically go from a 10 to a 0 and we would install the image of him scaring away the perpetrators and nurturing the little girl who snuggled on his back. She would say to herself, "I am safe now," as she did the BLS with the imagery. She would even summon his presence before going to sleep at night, which gave her more peaceful sleep.

Bringing In Resources for Family Members

Clients who as children felt responsible for taking care of family members will sometimes get stuck and loop. They need to get out of the family, but can't because of their feeling of loyalty or responsibility. Very young children can feel it is their job to take care of their mother and siblings. They love their family, but it is more than they can do to care for their needs. An interweave I have found helpful is to bring in resources for the other family members. I might ask, "What did your mother need?"

Client: She needed someone to help her.

Therapist: Who could do that?

Client: A nanny

Therapist: Imagine that. >>>>>>>>

In another case:

Therapist: What did your mother need?

Client: She needed someone to teach her how to be a parent.

Therapist: Who could do that?

Client: My friend Jane.

Therapist: Imagine that. >>>>>>>>

In another case the client had an angry, abusive sister who she loved but was terrified of.

Therapist: What does your sister need?

Client: Someone to love her and set limits with her.

Therapist: Who could do that?

Client: You, the therapist could do that.

Therapist: Imagine that. >>>>>>>>

Imagination

With imagination interweaves therapists and clients collaborate to come up with creative solutions to problems that are blocking the processing. When clients are looping and stuck, therapists stop the BLS and ask what's happening. If it is a dilemma that the clients see no solution for within the memory itself, the therapists can give the clients permission to do or say whatever the clients would like in their imagination. Imagination interweaves can be used to link as well as sort networks. Sometimes clients will say, "I wish I could have done _____." When I hear this I will ask, "Would you like to imagine doing _____?" If the client says yes, I will say, "Imagine that," and add BLS. For example, the client might say, "I wish I could tell my father what a jerk he is, take my child out of there, and never come back." I would say, "Would you like to imagine that?" and add BLS.

Sometimes clients will resist using imagination interweaves. "I can't do that, or it's not real so it has no validity." I will agree with them that we cannot change the past, but add that we *can* change how the past is stored in our nervous system. I encourage them to explore with their imagination. "Play with the scene. You will not forget what really happened." The following are interweaves that fall within this category. The imagination interweave includes metaphor/analogy and "let's pretend" described by Shapiro (1995, 2001), as well as others that I have found to be useful.

Case Example: Imagination Interweave with Dentist Trauma

I used an imagination interweave with Julianne, a client who had been traumatized by a cruel dentist, a case I describe in *Transforming Trauma: EMDR* (Parnell, 1997a). In one session while processing a traumatic experience with the dentist, she was looping at a high level of affect. She sobbed and said she wanted to get out of there but was trapped. "No one is going to help me so I might as well be resigned to being a victim. I had to be helpless and be hurt and be good." She was rageful, but her child self was stuck in helplessness and couldn't express her angry feelings. I stopped her and asked her what she would like to do.

Julianne: I would love to have my adult self join my child self and trash the dentist's office. I want to stab the dentist with his needles and kill him with his equipment. Then I want to throw his body out the window, along with the box of rubber animals he gave me as prizes after his torture treatments.

Therapist: Imagine that. >>>>>>>>

Julianne: My body doesn't have to defend itself against the dentist anymore.

But Julianne, who had been having difficulty with her husband sexually because she unconsciously linked him with the dentist, quickly associated to her relationship with her husband. "There's no way out of the marriage. I have to keep letting him penetrate me. There was a way out with my boyfriends." I realized that being penetrated by needles in her mouth was linked to penetration by her husband's penis. Her husband, who as a maturing man was becoming heavier and hairier—and thus like the dentist—made Julianne fearful of being hurt and trapped. Prior to marriage, she had been able to leave boyfriends, but with marriage and children escape was much more difficult. "I can't get out of here! The person who could rescue me is the one who's doing it to me, and there's no way out," she cried.

She was looping again. I saw that another interweave was necessary. She needed to disassociate her husband from the dentist.

Therapist: Can you imagine your husband rescuing the little girl from the dentist?

Client: Yes! I know he would.

Therapist: Imagine that. >>>>>>

She spoke aloud with the BLS. "He came into the office very diplomatically and asked him (the dentist) three times to stop it. He told the little girl, 'We're getting out of here,' picked her up, and left. He then pushed a button and exploded the dentist in his office. He told the little girl that he would take her out and buy her a real nice present, not some stupid rubber animals."

Julianne felt "great!" after that and talked about how she could choose whether to make love with her husband. We included the eye movements to install that new understanding. Afterward, she stated firmly, "I don't have to be a victim in sexual relationships."

Case Example: Imagination Interweave with Birth and Development

Margot came to see me because she was unhappy with her personal and professional life. She told me that she kept choosing men who were incapable of intimacy. A large woman who was gruff and distant, she wanted me to help her in just a few sessions. In taking her history I learned that she was not welcomed into the world by her mother with whom she never formed an attachment. "My mother was cold. She didn't know what to do with me." She did, however, form a bond with her father, a warm, kind man who wanted children. Despite her aloofness, Margot was able to easily develop and install resources and processed without difficulty. During one EMDR session she went back to the time she was born and brought home from the hospital. She said, "My mother won't look at me. She puts me in the crib and walks away. I feel so totally alone." She told me she could smell the flowers and remembered the wallpaper in the room. She began to loop around feeling completely cut off and unloved. "There's no one to gaze at me . . . to appreciate me. I wish I had a different mother."

Therapist: Would you like a different mother?

Margot: Yes!

Therapist: Who would you like as a mother?

Margot: Meryl Streep. She would understand how to gaze at me with interest and love. But I want her from the beginning. I want to feel wanted.

Therapist: Would you like to imagine that you were in her womb, that she carried you lovingly inside and then gave birth to you?

Margot: I like that idea!

Therapist: Imagine that. >>>>>>>>>

Margot talked as she experienced the BLS. She told me that she was happy in Meryl Streep's womb. She felt loved and cared for. When she imagined being born, she saw her looking at her and she took that in. She told me she also brought her father who, along with Meryl, cared for her. She worked through the scene that she had before with her mother, but this time with Meryl Streep as her mother, loving and nurturing her. At the end of a long set, she reported feeling good.

Therapist: Would you like to imagine what it would be like to have Meryl Streep as your mother throughout your childhood?

Margot: Yes, that would be good.

Therapist: Okay, imagine that. >>>>>>>>>>

At the close of the session Margot reported a SUDS of 0, her PC "I am worthy of love." After only a few months of EMDR during which we used creative imaginal interweaves, she completed her work with me. She felt better about herself, her work, and her potential for intimacy.

Case Example: Imagination Interweave for Grief and Loss

I will often offer the possibility for clients who are processing the death of a loved one to do in imagination what they could not do at the time of the death. Many people will have things they were not able to say at the time. Perhaps they didn't get a chance to say good-bye. With clients processing grief and loss, even if they have reached a SUDS of 0, I will ask them if there is anything they would like to say to their loved one. If they say yes, I say imagine that and add BLS.

Therapist: Is there anything you would like to say to your father that you didn't get to say then?

Client: Yes.

Therapist: Imagine saying that. >>>>>>

"Knowing What You Know Now, What Would You
Do Differently Now?"

This imagination interweave comes up during processing when clients say they feel stuck in regret that they didn't do or say something. Often it is something they could not have done at the time because they didn't have the information or the perspective they now have. When this comes up I ask the clients, "Knowing what you know now, what would you do differently?" When they tell me what it is, I say, "Imagine that," and add BLS.

Case Example: Client Who Had a Traumatic Abortion as a Teen Drug Addict

Marlene was processing a memory of having an abortion when she was a troubled teen. Alienated from her family and acting out in a way she was ashamed of, she had become pregnant. Because of feeling shame and guilt, she did not tell any friends or family about her situation. Instead she relied on her drug-addicted boyfriend to support her, who, of course, let her down. During the reprocessing of the trauma she began to loop feeling guilt, trauma, and anger. She was angry with herself for relying on her boyfriend and not getting the help she needed. "I didn't include others. I don't include others. I didn't tell people. There were people who could have helped."

Therapist: Knowing what you know now, what would you do differently?

Client: I'd get the education about the procedure, so I would know what to expect. I was shocked at how painful it was. Education would have helped me a lot. I would also bring in my best friend for support. I wouldn't have my boyfriend involved at all.

Therapist: Imagine that. >>>>>>>>>>.

After that set she felt a great deal of relief. She remembered that 10 years later she did tell her parents. They accepted it without condemning her in the least. She felt the guilt and shame she had carried release with her tears. She recognized the support she had in the present with her loving husband. With a broader perspective she realized more fully that her adolescence was a rough period of time for her. She felt compassion for her young self.

Case Example: Imagination Interweave with a Child Tricked into Sexual Abuse Situation

Bernadette had a history of sexual abuse by her mother. In this session she was processing a memory from early childhood in which she was tricked into getting physically close to her mother who abused her. She is looping with a high level of distress, upset at being deceived.

Therapist: Knowing what you know now, what would you do differently?

Client: I wouldn't go near her. I'd run away.

Therapist: Imagine that. >>>>>>>>

She felt relief. She would not be tricked again. The processing continued back on track.

Expression of Forbidden Impulses

For many clients who have been abused as children, strong emotions are locked deep inside because at the time of the abuse it was not safe to express these feelings. The inhibited expression of emotion can manifest as tightness in the throat or jaw and can block the processing. With EMDR, clients are encouraged to allow the angry thoughts and feelings to be expressed in whatever way is arising for them in their imaginations. The full expression of anger frees up energy that has been blocked and has reinforced the feeling of being powerless. With BLS, clients who have been horribly hurt and shamed tell the perpetrators how they feel about what they have done to them. When the clients fully express anger and rage at the perpetrator in the safety of the therapist's office, they feel a sense of empowerment and freedom from fear. The anger is then cleared from the system, in many cases eliminating the desire for revenge or the need for actual confrontation.

Between the ages of 5 and 10 Bonnie had been sexually abused by her father. She was a quiet, introverted child who felt quite helpless in her family. In our EMDR sessions she felt tremendous rage toward her father. Her child self would get a bat and beat her father bloody as her adult self restrained him so he couldn't escape. She released her child self completely and expressed the rage she could not safely express as a child. As a result of being allowed to fully express her rage, albeit in her imagination, she experienced increased openness, playfulness, and empowerment. Consequently, she reestablished a relationship with her elderly father and she saw him once a year for short visits.

In a case I describe in *Extending EMDR* (Parnell, 2004), a client who was suffering from postpartum depression was afraid of knives because she had images of stabbing her baby. I encouraged her to "imagine stabbing your baby." At the end of the set she began to laugh. She told me that the knife turned into a rubber knife and her baby just kept laughing at her. "I can't kill my baby," she said. She then said she was afraid of killing herself with the knife. I told her to imagine that, and tapped on her knees. She reported having a profound spiritual experience, peace that she was yearning for.

Metaphor, Stories, and Analogy

Metaphors, stories, and analogies can be very helpful in unblocking stuck processing. Often the therapists can use images that have come spontaneously from the clients during the processing to use in an interweave. These metaphors often take the form of images that are dreamlike in symbolism and can be very powerful.

Use of the Split Screen for Sorting

Another method for sorting networks that are causing clients to loop is the use of a split screen. The notion of using the split screen as an interweave was first introduced by Martinez (1991). With the split screen clients can either imagine both parts on either side of an imaginary screen, or they can draw the two sides using art materials. Drawing enables clients to take the confusion and externalize it, allowing them to see it more objectively. I have found drawing very useful in helping clients to sort networks that have become entangled.

Case Example: Split-Screen Interweave with Sexual Abuse Client Confusing Her Husband With Her Father, the Perpetrator

Adults sexually abused as children often confuse their partners with their perpetrators. The use of the split screen can help clients differentiate between the two. As I mentioned earlier, EMDR can be used to differentiate networks that do not go together. Clients who are abused by a man may fear all men, having difficulty distinguishing between men who are safe from men who are unsafe. In one case the client, a 28-year-old medical student married to an artist who was sensitive and gentle, was processing the memory of making love with her husband when she began to loop, her father's face superimposed over his. When I stopped the BLS she told me what was causing the looping. I asked her if she could imagine a split screen, with her father's face on the one side, and her husband's on the other. I then asked her to notice, as we did the BLS, "What is the same, and what is different between the two?"

At the end of the set she looked at me calmly and said, "At first they looked the same, they both were men, they both had passion in their eyes, but my husband looked loving and kind, and my father scary. They are not the same." We did more BLS and the processing continued. After that session she reported being more comfortable making love with her husband, her father's face no longer superimposed over his.

Case Example: Using Drawing to Enhance the Split-Screen Interweave

Betty came to see me suffering from anxiety and phobias. During the course of therapy it was revealed that she had been physically abused, and possibly sexually abused by family members. What's more, her mother had an undiagnosed psychotic disorder with symptoms of paranoia, compulsivity, and bizarre behavior. At home she was perpetually anxious and fearful, avoiding her violent brothers as much as she could. In contrast to her demeanor at home, as soon as she was out the door she became a different person: confident, smart, and capable. At school and with friends she thrived. Betty survived by spending as much time as she could outside of the home. She never revealed to anyone the terror she lived with on a daily basis at home, coping by compartmentalizing her life, keeping the pieces separate.

During one EMDR session during which we were working on an incident from her childhood, Betty began to loop. I stopped the eye movements and asked her what was happening. She explained that she was confused. Apparently, in order to survive her chaotic childhood, she had created compartments for two versions of her family and family members. In one she kept a representation of an ideal family, a family that was close-knit and caring. In the other she had the real family, one that was violent, chaotic, and abusive. I asked Betty if she could draw the two family representations on a piece of paper. We would divide the page in half. On one side she would draw the ideal family, and on the other her real family, the way they really were. At first she resisted drawing. "I can't draw," she complained. I coaxed her, by putting a piece of paper in front of her with markers and saying, "You can draw stick figures if you want. It doesn't matter what it looks like. What is most important is that you get something on the page." She then set to work.

What she drew with stick figures was quite helpful to her and to me, revealing the split she had created internally. The ideal family was close together and orderly; mother, father, and children assembled in the order of their ages. The real family was dominated by a gigantic father, dark and menacing. Family members were scattered on the page. After viewing the drawing together, I asked Betty to hold both images in her mind while she did a long set of eye movements. At the end she reported an integrated view of her family, the confusion she had reported earlier gone. She told me that it was helpful for her. And even though she resisted drawing, she understood now that it helped her see things she might not otherwise have seen. It got the confusion on the page and out of her. In subsequent sessions, we used this interweave to sort ideal mother from real mother and then ideal father from real father. She also began to use this interweave on her own between sessions, something she decided to do on her own without my suggesting it. When she became confused about something, she would draw it and add BLS. This became a useful tool for her.

The Two-Hand Interweave

The two-hand interweave, developed by Robin Shapiro (2005), is much like the split-screen interweave. It can be used to sort or to integrate networks. She recommends using it to differentiate events, feelings, cognitions, and ego states from the past from those in the present. The following is the protocol:

1. The client anchors one conflicting feeling, thought, choice, belief, or ego state in one hand.
2. The client anchors another feeling, thought, choice, belief, or ego state in the other hand.
3. The therapist begins BLS, or the client can alternate opening and closing hands.
4. If there is distress in one or both of the choices, it is cleared with the standard protocol. After the clearing is complete, both hands are rechecked.

After the BLS the therapist asks the client, "What difference do you notice?"

For example the client from the case mentioned above could be asked to hold her husband in one hand and her father in the other and then "go with that" as she received BLS. Then the therapist would ask, "What do you get now?" If she said, "My husband loves me and my father wants to hurt me," the therapist would say, "Go with that," and add more BLS, continuing on with the processing.

For case examples and more information on the use of this interweave read the chapter "Two-Hand Interweave" in *EMDR Solutions* (Shapiro, 2005).

Safe Place or Conflict-Free Image

There are times when the safe place can be used as an interweave. In these cases, the clients don't go there for a break to rest, but rather, the sense of safety in the present is linked in with BLS. At other times, if it doesn't facilitate the continuation of the processing to resolution, going to the safe place would not technically be considered an interweave.

I have found that clients who have been multiply abused or traumatized as children will want to imagine bringing their child selves to a place of safety surrounded by resource figures. This is actually linking in the fact that they are safe now and the past is the past. I will often close sessions with these clients by asking them to imagine taking their child self out of the house where the abuse occurred and bringing them to someplace safe. Sometimes they imagine bringing the child into my office with me and their adult self. Some clients imagine bringing their child to their present home where they feel safe and have adult resources. In this way clients integrate the past with the present. I will do this interweave, even if the session is complete, with clients who have had multiple abuse incidents over time in the same situation. The reason for this is that the memory network often remains activated even though one incident has been reprocessed. Feeder memories can begin to surface, creating distress for the client. By rescuing, or removing the child from the old situation, the incident reprocessed in the session feels more complete. Though more bad things happen in that house, for now, the one bad incident has been completed and the child is safe in the present. It is like one scene from a movie is over, you have put the VCR on pause, and you are taking a break in the here and now.

Education

With the education interweave therapists introduce new information to the clients that is not in the system. For many people from dysfunctional families information about appropriate behavior may not have been learned. The therapists in these cases may offer information about the way in which healthy family members interact with one another. In other cases the therapists may have more technical information that the clients don't have that can be used in an interweave. For example, a man who had been molested as a child had a compulsive need to clean himself. He showered several times a day because he never felt clean. The therapist asked him if he knew that all of the cells in his body had been replaced and that none of the old ones remained from the time of the molestation. When he thought about that with the eye movements, he felt a sense of relief. Later he reported that the need to compulsively clean himself had disappeared.

Clients sexually abused as children typically believe that they are bad if their bodies experienced pleasure during the abuse. When this came up with a client and she could not shift the NC because neither the child nor the adult had any information to the contrary, I did an education interweave. I told her, "It is normal for the body to experience pleasure when it is touched a certain way. Just like if you stub your toe or bump your knee, the body responds with pain, certain kinds of touch make you feel pleasure. What he did was wrong, bad. You are not bad for your body's natural response."

Both the child and the adult needed this information because it was not in the system. Her SUDS went down and her PC became "My body responded in a normal way. He was bad for doing what he did to me." She felt great relief from the guilt and shame associated with the abuse memories and her body's responses to the stimulation. The perpetrator had told her repeatedly that she was bad because of her sexual stimulation. The interweave helped to deprogram this negative and harmful message.

Case Example: Education Interweave for Grief and Loss

The client was looping over feeling bad that her mother died when she left the room to have a break.

Therapist: Did you know that it is hard for people to let go into death when their loved ones are in the room? Because of the attachment it is difficult for them to let go. This is a very common phenomenon. Hospice workers are very familiar with this.

When the client understands and accepts the statement, say "Go with that," and add BLS.

USING INTERWEAVES TO CLOSE SESSIONS

It is important to become more active with interweaves toward the end of sessions in order to have a more complete closure. I have found that EMDR therapists are often too cautious and don't use interweaves for closure as they could. I rarely leave clients above a SUDS of 2 or 3. Instead, I begin to ask questions and link networks more actively as we are running low on time. For example, I might ask a client still stuck in a house where she was being abused, "What does the child need?" She might respond, "She needs to get out of there." I would then ask, "Who can get her out of there?" When she responds, "My dragon can do it," I would say, "Go with that" and add the BLS. Adults traumatized as children often need interweaves to help close them. These can include interweaves of rescue, nurturing, or linking networks.

CASES THAT USE MANY DIFFERENT INTERWEAVES

The following are a series of case examples that illustrate how to employ a variety of interweaves together to aid in processing.

Case Example: Using Imagination Interweaves, Resource Interweaves, and Education Interweaves

Kendra, whom I described in *Transforming Trauma: EMDR* (Parnell, 1997a), was referred to me by a colleague who had been seeing her in individual therapy over 4 years. A successful businesswoman in her mid-40s, she was married and had young children. Despite the years of therapy, she continued to be plagued by symptoms of depression and guilt that she had failed to do something important. She reported feeling like there was a cloud of doom hanging over her. She suffered from nightmares and was fearful of windows, which she would close and lock compulsively. She had severe anxiety and panic attacks.

Kendra believed she knew the cause of her symptoms. When she was 3 years old her 19-month-old brother Billy died suddenly of pneumonia. But instead of telling her the truth, her mother told her that Peter Pan had come through the window and had taken her brother to Never-Never Land where he would be a little boy forever. But this story did not comfort her at all. Instead it terrified her, fueling her child's imagination with images of dangerous pirates, man-eating crocodiles, and other awful dangers. She identified with Wendy, the big sister whose job it was to find her brother and bring him safely back home. She remembered gazing out of the window of their sixth-story apartment, desperate to get her brother back, but feeling a failure because she didn't know how to fly. As small children will, she became obsessed with the Peter Pan story, demanding that her mother read it to her night after night.

Making matters worse, 24 hours after Billy's death Kendra's mother removed all trace of him. His nursery was dismantled, his clothes disposed of, and all photographs of him removed. It was as if she erased his existence. "I never got to say good-bye to him," she told me sadly. Later, in her adolescence, Kendra's father died suddenly. Her mother removed all traces of him too and moved to another state.

In one session we installed a safe place and nurturing and protector figures. She installed her adult self as one of the nurturers. We decided I would tap on her knees for the BLS (she wanted the physical contact). She liked long sets of knee tapping during which she would speak aloud.

We began with the image that was most disturbing to her, "the image of my brother going out the window with some man. I don't know who it is. All I see is a back. No face." As she was speaking, her voice changed, becoming high-pitched like that of a small child. She clutched a pillow to her chest, feeling vulnerable and afraid. Her negative cognition was "I'm not safe."

As I tapped on her knees she spoke intermittently, telling me about how she had lost her father too very suddenly. She puzzled about how anyone could get up to the sixth floor, how unsafe she felt. During several sets she processed sadness, fear, and confusion. Then she seemed stuck. She could not sort out the story her mother told her as a child from the story she now knew to be true. An image of a man in the window lifting Billy up in his arms came to Kendra.

Kendra: I know my dad took him but my mom is telling me something else. (*The 3-year-old is struggling to make sense out of bits and pieces of conflicting information. Her adult and child memory networks were tangled up. More calmly, but tearful, she continued.*) I know it's my dad because I can hear him. I know something's wrong. I know Billy's gone but I don't know what that means. It doesn't make any sense. My dad wouldn't leave with Billy and never bring him back. That's why my mother's story makes sense. (*She still sounds confused, looping.*) But, the man in the window looks like my father . . . but my dad wouldn't do that—he loves Billy.

At this point I stopped tapping. She talked some more about her confusion. I wanted to separate the child and adult networks. I believed a resource interweave was needed. Since I knew that Kendra had a clear understanding of what happened in her adult network, and she was a kind, loving mother to her own children, I asked her if her adult self could explain what really happened to her child self. When she answered yes, I began tapping on her knees as she spoke out loud to her 3-year-old self. She used a soft, gentle voice, using language a small child would understand. >>>>>>>>>>

Kendra: Something really sad has happened. Billy was much sicker that we realized, and when we put him to bed last night his cold got really bad. He stopped breathing, and we didn't know it until we went in this morning. We all have a body and a soul. His body is gone, but his soul is still alive. We can't bring him back. We will miss him a lot, and we will all be sad for a long time, but you didn't have anything to do with it and no one could have stopped it.

When I stopped the tapping and checked in with her, she said she was relieved. But then sadness showed in her eyes. When I asked her what was happening, she told me that she was sad that she had not gotten to say good-bye to him. I decided to do an imagination interweave.

Therapist: Would you like to imagine saying good-bye to him?

Kendra: Yes, and I'd like my daddy to go with me.

Therapist: Okay, imagine that. >>>>>>> (*Suddenly she opened her eyes and asked me to stop.*) What's happening?

Kendra: I can't go in there.

Therapist: Why not?

Kendra: Because he's blue. He's blue like a blueberry!

I was stunned. What was this about? I had no clue. Flying by the seat of my pants I decided to try an education interweave to see if it would help.

Therapist: Oh, I don't think he's blue. I think he just looks like he's sleeping.

Kendra: (*She looked at me relieved.*) Okay. But I want something to remember him by. (*All of his things had been removed after his death.*)

Here I offered another imagination interweave.

Therapist: What would you like? (*She took a few moments and checked in with the 3-year-old, then responded.*)

Kendra: Yes, I'd like to have one of his blankets because it's something I can hold on to. And it smells like him. I also want my daddy to go with me.

Therapist: Okay, imagine that. >>>>>>>>>>>

She told me that Billy looked peaceful in his crib, as if he were asleep. Crying, she said, "Good-bye Billy, I'll miss you a lot, and now I'm all alone." After crying and processing for a few minutes, she stopped. She said she felt relieved. We continued processing and doing some more interweaves until, when we returned to the original picture, she said she felt much better, her SUDS a 0. "The story doesn't make any sense. It was just a story." She told me the image now looked two-dimensional, like painted cardboard or a shadow. "My brother died of pneumonia and I didn't have any closure." When I asked her what she believed about herself now, she answered, "I'm safe as anybody else. The odds of someone coming through the window are pretty slim." We installed the PC, then did a body scan and debriefed.

The following week she reported feeling much better. She was waking up happy, her nightmares were gone, and she felt joyful and calmer. We continued with two more sessions before she felt she had completed the piece of work for which she had sought treatment.

Case Example: Using Multiple Interweaves With a Client With Issues of Neglect Triggered in a Group Setting

Pauline told me that she had a lifelong belief, "I don't belong," that was recently triggered while in a group of people. "I feel outside, peripheral. I feel vulnerable and easily humiliated like I'm not enough." Pauline was adopted when she was 8 days old. A week after her adoption, her adopted parents adopted another baby a few days younger than she. Two years later they adopted yet another baby. Her sister, who was close to her in age, was hard to soothe. She screamed and cried a lot. Pauline said that her sister's screaming was terrible for her because they shared a bedroom and playpen.

Pauline easily installed resources. Her safe place was a high mountain meadow. She had several nurturing figures, including her grandmother, her mother, an aunt, and a friend. Her protectors were a bear and a dragon.

Pauline did not have any specific memories associated with the feeling triggered in the group. I decided to bridge back from the NC, "I don't belong."

Therapist: Close your eyes and go inside. Say to yourself, "I don't belong." What emotions do you feel?

Pauline: I feel empty . . . angry, inadequate.

Therapist: What do you notice in your body?

Pauline: I feel something here. (*She touches the area of her solar plexus.*) It feels empty. I also feel my teeth rattling, and my jaw giving. The backside of my body feels numb.

Therapist: Trace it back in time. Let whatever comes up come up without censoring it. (*She closes her eyes and is quiet for a few moments.*)

Pauline: I'm playing with some children. I feel different. I'm light like I want to fly away. I'm hovering above everyone.

Therapist: How old are you?

Pauline: I'm about 8.

Therapist: Trace it back farther in time. Let whatever comes up come up. Go back as far as you can. (*She is quiet for a time, then begins to speak.*)

Pauline: I want out of here! Out of this room this playpen, this noise.

Therapist: What picture do you have?

Pauline: I'm in a bedroom. There are cribs on two walls. I'm against the long wall in the crib. It is late afternoon. Light is filtering in. I'm lying on my back. I have a bottle. I'm holding my bottle. My sister is not there. (*I now began to tap on her knees.*)

Soon she was in the memory of her sister screaming. This went on for a while. Then she said she couldn't stand it. She was looping.

Therapist: What does the child need?
Pauline: She needs Grandma to hold her.
Therapist: Imagine that. >>>>>>

She felt better, but then she continued to feel distressed by the sound of her sister's screams.

Therapist: What do you need?
Pauline: I need my own room.
Therapist: Imagine getting your own room
Pauline: But that's cheating . . .
Therapist: It's okay to cheat with this situation. (*Meaning you don't have to do things literally.*)
Pauline: Ok. >>>>>>>>>
Pauline: I feel much better in my own room. When I was older I did have my own room. They should have given it to me sooner. >>>>>>>

She has another memory in which she is in a playpen with her sister. Her sister is scratching her legs. She is moving her legs.

Pauline: I'd like to kick her.
Therapist: Would you like to do that now? If it's okay with you, I'll tap on your shoulders and you can kick.
Pauline: Okay. (*She begins to kick hard with her legs while I tap on her shoulders.*)
Therapist: What's happening now?
Pauline: That felt good. I feel much better.

She processed other memories from her childhood related to her sister and not being seen. After a while I asked her to return to the bedroom. This is the bedroom that was separate from her sister.

Pauline: I feel an enormous space beneath me. *(At this point time was running out on the session. I needed to become more active with interweaves.)*

Therapist: What does the child need?

Pauline: I want my mama.

Therapist: Imagine that.

Pauline: She's so overwhelmed! *(She cries and feels compassion for her mother who had three babies to care for.)* It's too much for her. I want to bring in help. *(She then brings in aunts.)* My mother would never ask for help. She would do it all herself. I'm like that too. *(This is big insight for her.)*

Therapist: Let's return to the scene in the bedroom. *(I don't force her back to the scene with her sister.)* What comes up now?

Pauline: It's not disturbing to me.

Therapist: On a scale from 0 to 10, how would you rate it now?

Pauline: It's a 0.

Therapist: What do you believe about yourself now?

Pauline: There is plenty of love to go around.

Therapist: Hold the belief with the picture. *(I installed the PC.)* >>>>>>

Pauline: I can ask for help if I need to.

After the body scan she reported that she still had some tingling in her back and arms. We ended with safe place, nurturers, and putting the body sensations in a container.

Session with High Intensity and Blocked Processing That Required Several Interweave Attempts Before Finding One That Worked

Sometimes it takes several attempts to find the interweave that will help the client move out of the looping. The following case from *EMDR in the Treatment of Adults Abused as Children* (Parnell, 1999) demonstrates how the therapist sometimes needs to try and fail several times before finding the "right" interweave. This session also demonstrates the installation of resources at the beginning of the session, the use of the safe place in the middle so the client can take a break, and the use of imagination and resource interweaves.

The session was a very intensive session with Alice, a 40-year-old nurse, early in the middle phase of EMDR therapy. In this session, she was processing being abused by her grandmother, who held Alice underwater in the bathtub and locked her in a closet. A number of interweaves and interventions were unsuccessful in lowering the very high level of disturbance that she was looping in. I finally found one that worked—I brought myself and her adult self to rescue her child self.

Alice came to the session feeling scared, anxious, and agitated, and did not know why. We began the session by doing a guided imagery of going down the stairs to her safe place. I asked her child self how old she was, and she replied, "Five years old"; she was "scared," and her breathing accelerated. "What are you afraid of?" I asked. She replied in a child's voice, "I'm afraid of Grandma."

I asked her to imagine a protective boundary around herself and her child that made them safe. Alice was silent for a while and then told me that she had imagined a force field like the one in *Star Trek* movies, which was invisible but nothing could get through it. I then asked her to imagine her child self with her in the safe place surrounded by that force field. After a while, she told me that Little Alice liked being held and liked hugs. I told her to give little Alice exactly what she needed. When she had the feelings of safety and comfort strongly in her body and mind, I installed these feelings with eye movements. I told the child self that she could call on Big Alice to be there for her if she needed her and that they could go to the safe place in the force field together if she wanted to.

Alice seemed to feel comfortable with those instructions and was ready to bring up the memory we had worked on the week before that was associated with not feeling safe with Grandma; the memory was of Grandma giving little Alice a bath. The NC was, "I'm different, I'm not like everybody, and that's bad. I'm stupid. It's bad to be different from everybody else." She was feeling scared and agitated. Her body began to squirm. >>>>>

Alice: She's mad at me . . . she says that the clothes I had on were from her and I got them all dirty. >>>>> She's really mad and hitting me with her hand on my face. . . . She doesn't like it when I cry, she says I'm a baby . . . *there's places for babies. (She is getting more agitated, wringing her hands, her breathing accelerated.)* >>>>> I'm someplace in the bathroom but not the bathtub . . . someplace scary . . . someplace small. *(She has become very upset and frightened. She is overwhelmed. She is looping and the SUDS is not reducing with the eye movements. She tells me she wants to go to the safe place for a rest.)*

Therapist: Imagine Big Alice taking Little Alice to the safe place. The force field is around the safe place. You are safe now. You can put the scary stuff in a file folder in my office and we can get it later.

She imagined the adult and child selves playing together in a fun place and calmed during the imagery. I told her that she could return to the scary memory if and when she wanted to and continue the processing. After 10 to 15 minutes, she was ready to return to the bathroom scene. >>>>>

Alice: I'm in a closet on the wall up high. She would put me in there when I was bad . . . and I was small and I couldn't get out. I could die in there and nobody would know I was in there. . . . I have to wait for her to come back and let me out.

I asked her questions for clarification. Alice is quite upset again.

Alice: She leaves her in there a long time . . . (*Her adult self is speaking about her child self, but then changes to a child's voice in the first person.*) It's small and dark in there . . . I can't call for help or it will make her madder. >>>>> (*She is getting more upset, very agitated, breathing rapidly, wringing her hands.*) I'm still in there. . . . I can't move. . . . Grandma says the closet on the wall can move and can go down. . . . If I cry she'll make it go down. . . . Then it would be really dark there. . . . I can't cry or move! >>>>> I'm still in there. I don't want to be in there anymore! If I have to stay there any longer I just want to die! (*She is very upset and looping. She is stuck in the closet and not getting out.*) >>>>>

Therapist: Say what you need to say. (*I try an expression of forbidden impulses interweave, giving her permission to express verbally unspoken words.*) >>>>>

Alice: I'm still in there I don't want to be in there anymore. I want to get out! (*She remains extremely upset. My interweave did not work.*)

Therapist: Go with, "I want to get out."

Alice: I'm still in there. I can't get out! (*She is frantic, and panicking.*)

Therapist: (*I decide to try a Socratic interweave, reminding her that she did eventually get out of the closet, and did survive.*) You did eventually get out of the closet, didn't you?

Alice: Yes.

Therapist: Think about that. >>>>>

Alice: (*She's still extremely upset. The interweave did not work!*) I'm still there! Get me out! (*She is pleading with me for help.*)

At this point my instincts took over and I used resources interweave, bringing in myself and Alice's adult self to rescue the child self from the confines of the closet.

Therapist: >>>>>> (*I told her the following as I kept her eyes moving.*) I come into the bathroom along with Big Alice and I break open the closet with an ax and get Little Alice out of the closet. We hold her. . . . You are safe and protected. . . . I then take the ax and destroy the closet, so that you can never be put back in there again. . . . Big Alice and I protect you from Grandma. . . . (*Her distress has dropped, her breathing is calming down, and she is no longer writhing in the chair and wringing her hands. This interweave has worked!*) . . . Big Alice and I take Little Alice to the safe place and put the force field around us. >>>>>

Alice: I feel the force field. . . . I feel safe and protected. >>>>>

Therapist: (*I installed the PC, "I am safe and protected now."*)

Alice: The closet is gone, you destroyed it. It's smashed into a million little pieces. >>>>> We're both in the force field and we're happy.

By this time Alice had completely calmed. The new image of the destroyed closet had replaced the old one with her trapped inside, and she felt confident that Little Alice could never be put back in there again. She felt deeply moved by my rescue of her and my demonstrated protectiveness of her. Her SUDS was down to a 0, and she was peaceful. This session deepened the trust between us and gave her new confidence that I would be able to find a way to get her out of the places of terror, even if it meant my coming in and saving her myself. Over the next couple of years of EMDR processing the old image of the closet never returned, and when she thought of the incident she would see the image of the destroyed closet.

As you can see, I did not know what was happening or exactly what to do. I kept offering her suggestions that did not work. Eventually, I found one that did. I believe it is most important for the therapist not to panic when interweaves are not taking; rather, keep trying different things until one *does* take. It is the client who provides the feedback. If an interweave works, the processing begins to move again, or the SUDS drops. If I hadn't been able to find an interweave that worked, I could have asked her to return to the safe place to calm down and feel safe.

Doing EMDR with highly traumatized clients who are looping can often feel like you are groping in the dark for a key that will unlock the door. I have learned over time to keep trying different keys and eventually I find the one that opens the door.

PART IV

CLINICAL APPLICATIONS

10

WORKING WITH PHOBIAS

EMDR CAN EFFECTIVELY treat phobias (de Jongh, Ten Broeke, & Renssen, 1999; Shapiro, 1999). I have had many successes treating phobic clients.
In this chapter I will review the standard EMDR protocol for simple and
process phobias and then provide some tips and case examples.

Shapiro divided phobias into two classes, simple and process. "A simple
phobia is defined as a fear of an object (e.g., a spider) that is circumscribed
and independent of the client's actions. The fear is generated by the sight
of the object and is independent of further participation" (1995, 2001, p.
227). These phobias usually require fewer steps to treat. A process phobia
is more complex, requiring more steps to treat it. A process phobia is fear
of a situation that involves the active participation of the client. For instance,
a phobia of driving across a bridge requires that the client get in a car, drive
to the bridge, drive across the bridge, and continue to the destination. Shapiro explained that in order to clear a process phobia, all of the significant
parts of the experience must be targeted and reprocessed. In addition, this
is also true for some simple phobias if the client must interact with the feared
object in daily life (e.g., the client's new boyfriend has a pet snake and she
has to see it on a regular basis.)

Shapiro delineated the following steps for both kinds of phobias (1995,
p. 223, 2001).

1. *Teach the client self-control techniques to handle the fear of fear.* These can include safe place and other resource installations. Techniques from somatic
experiencing can also be used, such as pendulating and finding a safe place
in the body. Deep belly breathing and grounding exercises can be taught.

2. *Target and reprocess one or more of the following:*

a. *Antecedent/ancillary events that contribute to the phobia.* These can be incidents that are linked by content to the phobia, such as dog bite leading

to fear of dogs, or they can be incidents that are linked somatically, emotionally, or cognitively, e.g., fear of spiders linked to being touched at night against her will by someone creepy.

b. *The first time the fear was experienced.* This information can be gathered through the history taking, or through bridging back.

c. *The most disturbing experiences.* As you take a history of the phobia, listen for the most disturbing instances. You may or may not need to target each one, depending on the generalization effect. But you will want to note what they are and go back and check to see if they are cleared.

d. *The most recent time the fear was experienced.* For example, when was the most recent time she was afraid of a dog?

e. *Reprocess any associated stimuli.* What are the triggers for the fear? For example, the sight of a spiderweb or any crawling bug?

f. *The physical sensations or other manifestations of fear, including hyperventilation.* Sometimes physical sensations associated with fear will trigger a panic reaction, such as being out of breath or sweating. Target and reprocess these if necessary.

3. *Incorporate a positive template for fear-free future action.* Have the client imagine seeing a spider in a safe way.

4. *Make a contract for action.* The client has to actually meet the feared object or do the feared thing.

5. *Run a mental videotape of the full sequence and reprocess the disturbance.* This step is usually included for process phobias such as fear of flying or driving, but can also be used for simple phobias when the client must participate with the feared object.

For example, Have the client imagine getting in the car, driving to the bridge, driving across the bridge, and successfully arriving at her destination. You want to be sure to include all of the parts to the phobia. If associated pieces are not reprocessed, they may prevent the phobia from resolving.

6. *Reprocess targets that are revealed between sessions.* When the client returns, ask what came up for her during the week. Target any new memories, associations, or blocks to accomplishing her goal. Reevaluation is a crucial step to phobia work. Client feedback guides the work.

When I work with a client who has a phobia I take a thorough history of the problem to find out as much about it as possible. For example, from Gloria, a client with a fear of spiders, I wanted to know how long she had been afraid of spiders. Was she afraid of all spiders, little ones as well as big ones? Did her fear include other bugs? When did the fear start? Was there a precipitating incident? What had she done to try to treat this problem?

Had she ever done any therapy? You also want to know how the phobia is currently affecting the client's life. In Gloria's case she avoided traveling and always checked places she stayed for spiders.

Ask for the earliest experience of the fear and the worst experiences. Make a list of the fearful experiences and arrange them chronologically. Although Shapiro (1995, 2001) recommended targeting the fearful experiences chronologically, I have found that sometimes it is better to begin with the experience that has the most charge. Korn, Rozelle, and Weir (2004) also reported that it is best to work with the most charged memory first in order to get the strongest generalization effect through the memory network. I have found that if you can find the strongest, most representative experience of the fear, you will need fewer sessions. I have had success clearing many phobias in one EMDR session.

Also key to the most successful resolution of a phobia is to find the memories that are linked to the *symptoms*. The best targets are often found from bridging back from a recent charged experience of the phobia, or an experience the client can recall that has significant charge. For example, John had a phobia of having blood drawn. If he even saw a needle he would feel faint. He had had the phobia as long as he could remember and had no idea where it came from. I asked him if he could recall an experience when he had his blood drawn and he felt the fear. He said he could. We homed in on the most charged part of that memory with the emotions of fear, body sensations of light-headedness, and the belief, "I'm going to die," and bridged back. What came up for him was a memory of being bitten on the finger by his pet hamster when he was 8 years old. He was very surprised at the link. As he looked at his bloody finger he thought that the hamster had bitten it off. We targeted and reprocessed this memory using the standard protocol to a 0 SUDS and installed the PC "I'm safe." He then imagined having blood drawn in the future with no difficulty. He felt relaxed and at ease, with some discomfort that was normal for anyone who has his blood drawn.

Therapists are most successful at treating phobias with EMDR when the etiology is connected to discrete traumatic incidents. A client who was bitten by a dog and as a result develops a fear of dogs is likely to be helped with EMDR. However, phobias that are symbolic or multicausal can take longer to treat. For example, in the San Francisco Bay Area where I practice, many people have bridge phobias. In my experience, these phobias often do not develop from a traumatic experience on a bridge. For some clients the fear is associated with wide-open spaces. They may have the same fear on open roads such as in the desert. These clients may not be fully in their bodies as they drive, a problem that triggers a panic reaction. One client was afraid to drive across the bridge because the bridge represented separation from her family, something she was not yet ready to do. Fear of flying often has nothing to do with a trauma on a plane, or may not even be associated with flying. For many it has to do with letting go of control, trusting someone else with their life, being in a small cramped space, or even the body sensations that the movement of the plane stimulates. People who were traumatized as children may have many phobias; they don't feel safe in the world. In these cases, it can take a long time to treat the phobias. I have had several clients whose fear of spiders was linked to childhood sexual abuse.

As is true in working with traumatic experiences in general, it is important to get all of the pieces that are associated with the fear. Feedback from clients about what gets in the way of their doing the feared thing provides information about where next to focus. There are no failures, just new information to direct the next target.

Case Example: Simple Phobia of Cockroaches

Bob sought EMDR to treat a phobia of cockroaches. He told me he had a distinct memory of when it began. He said that he was 13 years old and living in the Middle East with his parents. "One night I was hungry and went to the kitchen to get something to eat. When I turned on the light I was shocked to see that the floor was covered with cockroaches that all quickly scurried away. I think I stepped on one with my bare feet but I'm not sure if it is a memory or a fear of doing that."

In preparation for EMDR processing we installed a safe place, a nurturer figure, and a protector. He had no difficulty installing these resources. When he brought up his safe place, he could readily calm himself down. He was ready to begin EMDR. He chose tapping on his knees as the form of BLS he preferred.

He told me that the most disturbing picture was seeing the cockroaches in the kitchen and stepping on one. "I was so afraid I froze. I was afraid they would eat me." His NC was "I'm helpless," and the PC was, "I can stay calm," which he rated a VoC of 1. His emotions were disgust, fear, and panic, his SUDS 9. He told me he felt the disturbance in his chest, stomach, and feet. "I feel the crunch."

After I asked him to bring up the image in the kitchen, the feelings in his body, the emotions of fear and disgust, and say to himself, "I'm helpless," I began to tap on his knees. Very soon his breathing became heavy, peaked, and then decreased in intensity.

Therapist: What's happening now?

Bob: They disappear under the kitchen furniture. I don't know where they go. I'm curious.

Therapist: Go with that. >>>>>>>>

Bob: I imagine I can put on shoes and turn on the light in the hall to warn them so it will scare them and I won't step on them.

Therapist: Go with that. >>>>>>>>>

Bob: My mother is making goulash. She puts the paprika in and it is full of baby cockroaches. The goulash is moving. (*He is visibly upset. I do a long set of BLS until his breathing relaxes.*)

Bob: She cleans everything. It's better. But I'm still scared. (*He puts his hand on his stomach. At this point he seemed to be stuck in the fear. I do an interweave based on safety.*)

Therapist: I'm confused. Are cockroaches dangerous?

Bob: No, I know they aren't.

Therapist: Go with that. >>>>>>>> (*Bob takes a big relieving breath. His body relaxes.*)

Bob: I feel relief. They run because they are afraid of *me*. I'm dangerous to them. (*He laughs.*)

Therapist: Go back to the original picture when you walk into the kitchen. What comes up for you now?

Bob: It's less disturbing. But now I don't like it that they are looking at me.

Therapist: Go with that. >>>>>>>>

Bob: I am having a memory of my parents looking at me like I'm a bug. They are laughing at me, putting me down. (*He has opened up another associated memory.*)

Therapist: Go with that. >>>>>>>>>>

Bob: I can't do anything about it. I'm stuck. I can't defend myself. (*At this point he seems stuck again, needing an interweave.*)

Therapist: What do you need?

Bob: I need to be a few years older. Then I could say something to them.

Therapist: Imagine that. >>>>>>>>>

Bob: I feel much better. I feel some sadness. I loved my parents. They are gone now. I feel closer to them. (*He seemed to be opening up a new network. I wanted to refocus him on the phobia.*)

Therapist: Go back to the scene in the kitchen. What comes up now?

Bob: It doesn't feel disturbing to me.

Therapist: On a scale from 0 to 10, where 0 is no disturbance or neutral and 10 is the highest disturbance, how disturbing does it feel to you now?

Bob: It's a 0.

Therapist: What do you believe about yourself now?

Bob: I'm whole, okay.

Bob rated the VOC a 7, which we installed. Then I did a future pace with him.

Therapist: Imagine yourself in the future with cockroaches.

Bob: Yes, I can do that. >>>>>>>>>

He did it without a problem. He did a body scan reporting sweaty palms, but a calm body.

When we debriefed I told him that he needed to test the work by seeing cockroaches. He told me that he would need to possibly go on a vacation to a warm tropical place. "I'll suggest it to my wife as a therapy need."

Case Example: Fear of Acupuncture Needles

Ned sought EMDR because he was afraid of acupuncture. Specifically, he was afraid of needles in the backs of his legs. When I asked him what it was about the needles that bothered him, he told me it was "the fear of someone landing on them and pushing them in. Needles in the front are not a problem." I inquired if he remembered the first time he had this fear.

"Yes, I remember getting a shot in the butt when I was around five," he replied. "I fought very hard against the doctor."

During the preparation phase we installed a safe place, which was his meditation cushion, his close friend as a nurturing figure, and his adult self as his protector. He chose a flowing river as the metaphor he wanted to use to create distance. An easy rapport developed between us and he had good ego strength. This problem seemed distinct and workable as long as we could find the best target. Because the earliest memory of the fear did not clearly fit with his symptoms, I decided to use the bridging technique to find the target.

Therapist: Think of a time recently when you had this fear of acupuncture needles. What picture represents the worst part?

Ned: Lying on my stomach, needles in my legs, with the fear someone will land on me and break them.

Therapist: What emotions do you feel?

Ned: Fear, sweating. I don't dare move. There is tension in my stomach and tension in my neck.

Therapist: What do you believe about yourself?

Ned: I'm helpless

Therapist: Trace it back in time. Let whatever comes up come up without censoring it. (*Ned closed his eyes and was silent for a few minutes.*)

Ned: I was standing and I see my mother leave for the hospital. I see her driving away with my father. It would be a long time until I would see her again.

Therapist: How old are you? (*I am trying to orient to time.*)

Ned: Maybe 3 years old.

From here we developed the target. The picture was his mother driving away. He felt sad and alone, with a hole in his stomach. He said that the space feels different around his body. The NC was "I'm going to die." The PC was, "I can survive." The VoC a 2, the SUDS 8. >>>>>>>>

Ned: I feel angry. They are lying to me. I feel so sad and alone. The memory feels linked to the shot in butt, during which I fought. >>>>>>> I had other memories of dogs scaring me, bullies after school. (*I'm not sure where he is with regard to the original target so I ask him to return and check it.*) The scene with my mother doesn't bother me anymore.

He rated it a 0 SUDS. He told me he believed he was okay. We installed that PC. Then I asked him to check the memory of getting the shot in the butt. He told me that it was less distressing, a SUDS of 3. He still felt angry. We began BLS.

Ned: It feels stuck. I still feel the same. (*I believe he needs an interweave.*)

Therapist: What do you need?

Ned: Someone to explain to me what is happening, maybe demonstrate giving a shot on a tomato.

Therapist: Imagine that. >>>>>>>> *(I could see his face relax as he did the BLS.)*

When I checked in with him he reported that the SUDS had gone down to a 0. The PC was "I have control," which he rated a VoC 7 and we installed.

I then asked him bring up the memory of having acupuncture needles on the back of his legs. What came up now?

Ned: I'm worried about the needles causing nerve damage. *(At this point I believed he needed an education interweave.)*
Therapist: What information do you have about that?

When he thought about my question he realized he had not asked enough questions of the acupuncturist and that he could do that now.

Ned: I can get the information I need to make an informed decision about my safety.
Therapist: Imagine doing that. >>>>>>>

After the BLS he was much more relaxed. When I asked him what came up now when he thought of having acupuncture, he told me that it didn't feel disturbing. He rated it a 0 SUDS. His PC was, "I can ask questions, I have choices," which we installed. After the body scan he told me he felt good. During the debriefing he said that he realized that the phobia linked to all three of the memories he processed. His not being able to give the information he needed was associated with the feeling of fear and helplessness. He now needed to have acupuncture and see how he did. Any problems or fears that should arise associated with it we could work on in future sessions.

Case Example: Fear of Crowds

Paula's presenting problem was claustrophobia. We spent time exploring the issue before focusing on a target.

Therapist: What specifically are you afraid of?
Paula: I'm afraid of crowds. I avoid crowds.
Therapist: What is it about crowds that bothers you?

Paula: I'm afraid someone will take up my space, my air.

Therapist: What was the worst experience of this claustrophobia you have had?

Paula: I had a panic attack on a plane 20 years ago. I couldn't breathe. I got up and went to the galley in order to compose myself.

Therapist: Are there any other experiences that are important? What was the earliest one you can recall?

Paula: When I was 8 I woke up from anesthesia during a tonsillectomy. They forcefully tied me down. It was terrible.

At this point I had a number of ways I could begin to target this issue. I chose to go in on the panic on the plane, which was very charged, and bridge back from there. I was not convinced that any of the memories she had provided me were the essential links to the phobia. I thought that by bridging back we could find a better target that would be the most connected to the symptom of claustrophobia.

Therapist: Close your eyes and go inside. Bring up the panic on the plane. What picture represents the worst part of that incident?

Paula: I was sitting next to the window.

Therapist: What emotions do you feel?

Paula: Panic.

Therapist: What do you notice in your body?

Paula: I feel tense. My hands are sweating. I feel tense here. (*She points to her solar plexus.*)

Therapist: What do you believe about yourself?

Paula: I'm weak, I'm not enough.

Therapist: Good. Now trace it back in time. Let whatever comes up come up without censoring it. (*She is silent for a few moments.*)

Paula: I'm in fifth grade at a new school. I felt very out of place. I felt awful. I didn't fit in. I had no one to talk to. (*It is interesting to note that the memory that came up was different from, and seemingly unrelated to, the memories the client had brought up in the beginning. I tend to trust the memory that comes up for clients when they bridge back, even when it is not obvious how it is linked to the symptoms. Usually as the client processes, the connections become apparent.*)

Therapist: What picture represents the worst part?

Paula: I'm standing alone in the playground. All the girls are jocks. I'm feeling out of place.

Therapist: What emotions do you feel?

Paula: Lonely, angry.

Therapist: Where do you feel it in your body?

Paula: In my chest.

She reported a SUDS of 6. Her NC was, "I'm not good enough." I did not ask for the PC or VoC because I didn't want to take her out of the experience and have to reactivate the memory network. She was in the scene and it was lit up.

She processed this memory down to a 0 SUDS, ending with a PC, "I am good enough," which we installed. We then returned to the image on the plane. She reported that she no longer felt distress on the plane. I asked her to imagine flying, which she was able to imagine with ease. We added BLS as she imagined flying. I then asked her to imagine herself in the future in crowds. She had no difficulty imagining these things and I added BLS.

It is interesting to note that in this case her claustrophobia did not link to the surgery experience. It did not even come up as she processed. Her claustrophobia was more of a social phobia.

Case Example: Finding a Target by Bridging Back From a Representational Image of the Feared Object

Claudia sought EMDR treatment for her phobia of pigeons. "I was terrified of the pigeons at St. Mark's Square in Venice." Flapping birds were especially disturbing to her. She couldn't tolerate the sight of a bird that was injured after striking a window when it flapped around afterward. "Ever since I was a child I haven't been able to tolerate touching a bird." She couldn't recall ever having had a traumatic experience with a bird. She had no idea where her fear came from. She could not come up with any specific incidents. She feared the possibility of an encounter with a bird. In order to find the historical link to the phobia I decided to bridge back from her worst imagined scenario.

Claudia could easily install resources. Her safe place was a tropical island, her nurturing figure was a wise and compassionate man, and her protector was a guardian angel. We installed each of these resources one at a time. She chose watching a movie as a metaphor to create distance. After installing the resources, we bridged back from a highly charged imaginary image.

Therapist: Close your eyes and go inside. When you think of this fear of birds, what picture is most disturbing to you?

Claudia: A flapping bird near my face. The worst part is the feathers touching me.

Therapist: What emotions do you feel?

Claudia: Fear.

Therapist: Where do you feel that in your body?

Claudia: I feel hot, I'm breathing fast. My heart is beating rapidly. My palms are sweating.

Therapist: What do you believe about yourself?

Claudia: I'm helpless.

Therapist: Bring up the picture, emotions, and body sensations, and trace it back in time. Let whatever happens happen without censoring it.

Claudia: I'm 4 years old and having an operation to remove my tonsils and adenoids. They are putting a mask over my face for the anesthesia. I was helpless and forced to do this.

Therapist: What picture represents the worst part of this?

Claudia: I'm lying down on my back and I'm fixed in place. I see faces and people are in the back. I can't move. The mask is coming down on my face.

Therapist: What negative belief do you have about yourself?

Claudia: I'm helpless.

Therapist: What would you like to believe about yourself?

Claudia: I can be strong and make choices.

Her VoC was 1.5, emotions "I'm scared, helpless," SUDS 8.

Therapist: What do you notice in your body?

Claudia: There's pressure on my chest. I can't get enough air. There's tension in my arm and my whole body.

At this point I began to tap on her knees and she began to reprocess the memory of the surgery. Claudia processed somatically, with very little imagery. After one long set she said that there was an empty whiteness that was frightening to her. At that point I directed her to return to the image of the mask we started with and tell me what came up for her.

Claudia: It feels less charged.

Therapist: Go with that. >>>>>>>

Claudia: I feel like I'm stuck in a black box. I can't hear my mother. I can't tell who is who. I feel like I am merged with her. If I break out I will kill her, but if I make myself small I hurt myself. *(I believe she is processing a memory of being in her mother's womb prior to her birth. I'm not sure where this is going, or if it is relevant to the presenting symptoms, so I ask her to return to the original picture.)*

Claudia: It feels less charged. I have a sense of disappearing inside.

Therapist: Go with that. >>>>>>>

Claudia brought up a new memory that involved a rape. She said she disappeared inside to deal with it. She began to loop, saying that she needed help. I could see that an interweave was needed.

Therapist: Would you like to imagine getting help?

Claudia: Yes. I can bring in my wise man and my angel to help me. >>>>>> *(As she imagined this, her face and body relaxed.)* I feel much better.

Therapist: Can you return to the original picture of the mask over your face? What comes up now?

Claudia: It's not charged.

She rated it a SUDS 0. Her PC was, "I got through it okay." Her VoC was 7. We installed her PC. I then asked her to return to the image of the bird we began with. What came up now when she brought it up? She told me that it felt okay, it didn't bother her at all. "I'm okay" we installed with that picture too. We then checked all of the previously scary scenarios with birds. When she told me they were not charged, I told her "Go with that," and tapped on her knees as she imagined them. Then we did a future pace. I asked her to imagine herself in the future at St. Mark's Square with the pigeons. What came up for her now?

Claudia: I'm afraid of stepping on them.

Therapist: Go with that. >>>>>> *(She smiled and laughed.)*

Claudia: The pigeons parted like the sea did for Moses. They go someplace else. I still don't want to touch them, but I feel okay.

We installed "I'm okay" with that picture, did a body scan, which she reported to be clear, closed, and debriefed. She would let me know what came up for her during the week and she realized that in order to test the work she would need to be in contact with pigeons. She felt ready and able to do that. She could see now that her phobia had nothing to do with birds at all. It had been linked to several other memories primarily through the body sensations and emotions. She now had insights and felt free from the effects of these experiences.

Case Example: Process Fear of Flying

Abby came in to see me because she had a fear of flying. She was an outgoing, active woman in her 30s, and this fear was limiting her life. She told me that she loved to travel but that she was so afraid of flying that she would have to take enough sedatives to knock her out for the duration of the flight and that she would feel the aftereffects of the drugs into her trip. She wanted to be able to travel for her job, but the fear was limiting what she could do.

When I asked her how long she had been afraid of flying, she told me that it was since she was in her teens. She had been with a group of students overseas when, on the return flight to the United States, one of the plane's engines failed, causing the plane to plummet several thousand feet before the auxiliary engine kicked in and kept them from crashing. After making an emergency landing the group was put on another plane and made it safely to the States. But then came the most dramatic part of the story. She told me that the group landed in the southern part of the state and had to take another flight to the Bay Area. The whole group was so traumatized from their experience that they decided to take a bus. But Abby was determined to get back in the saddle, so she took a flight instead. Then, shortly before they were due to land, the pilot came on the intercom and announced that they were having difficulty with their electrical system, and directed everyone to get into crash position because they were not certain the landing gear would come down. She was terrified. Fortunately, the electrical system did work and the landing gear came down. But after that experience she couldn't fly without the use of drugs.

I asked her what she had tried in the past to treat this fear. She had done several years of talk therapy, she told me, cognitive-behavioral therapy, and United Airline's fear of flying program. She did all of United's program except fly. Nothing had helped her. To my astonishment, she told me she had even taken flying lessons and learned to fly an airplane. She could fly as long as she could see the pilot or copilot on the plane herself. It was large commercial airplanes that triggered her phobia.

We installed a safe place and nurturing and protector figures. She could practice evoking the resources well. I decided we needed to target the incident on the plane and reprocess it first since it was obviously linked to the phobia.

We began with the worst part of the incident on the plane. She said it was when the engine quit and the plane plummeted. The image was sitting in her seat, hearing the screams of other passengers. The NC was "I'm powerless." The PC was "I can have control." The VoC was 1, emotions terror, SUDS 10, and the body sensations were in her stomach. She felt her arms tense as she remembered gripping the armrests. As she processed the memory she experienced many intense waves of body sensations. Most of her processing was somatosensory. The experience of losing altitude has an intense effect on the body. So much of this experience was frozen there. After a while I asked her to return to the original image and tell me what came up. She told me that it didn't feel very charged. In order to make sure we had gotten all the pieces of that experience, I asked her to go back to the beginning of that incident, scan through, and look for any charge. She did that and indicated places that still held charge. I asked her to focus there, and did more BLS. She scanned through the incident several times until she reported that the whole thing had a 0 SUDS. We then installed the PC, "I survived," as she ran the whole incident through like a video. Her body scan was clear.

I asked her if she could imagine flying in the future. She said she thought she could, a short flight. I then directed her to imagine all the steps she could imagine taking to fly: packing her bags, driving to the airport, going through security, getting on the airplane, flying, and arriving safely. She ran through the whole thing feeling confident that she could do it. Finally, I told her that in order to test her work she would have to fly. She agreed to book a flight soon. She would call me with the results.

A couple of months went by and I did not hear from Abby. I began to wonder what had happened. Finally she called me. She told me that she had not flown on a large commercial airplane yet, just a smaller one around the Bay Area. I encouraged her to come in and we would see what was preventing her from accomplishing her goal. As we explored what was blocking her, she realized that she could not make the call for the reservation. In the past, making the phone call was fraught with anxiety. We checked the work from before to see if it had held, and it had. We then targeted making the reservation, focusing on an earlier charged memory. After we cleared that, she imagined making the phone call for a reservation followed by the rest of the steps, including a relaxing flight to a fun destination. Then she felt ready to make the flight. Not long after that she successfully took a 2-hour flight.

Case Example: Using the Bridging Technique to Find a Target for a Flying Phobia

Sofia was terrified of flying, which she avoided. A tall, robust woman in her 40s, her face became tense when she talked about her fear. When I asked her what it was about flying that frightened her, she told me it was the turbulence. Had she had any bad experiences on planes that she thought were linked to this fear? She didn't recall any. She had had the fear of turbulence as long as she could remember. There was no precipitating incident, no trauma associated with flying. I asked her what it was about the turbulence that was disturbing to her. "It's the feeling of being lifted off the ground and shaken," she said. This description was intriguing to me. I suspected it meant something, but I didn't know what it could be. We installed safe place, nurturing figures, and protectors. Despite her anxiety, she had good ego strength. There was an easy rapport between us.

Because there were no clear precipitating incidents associated with the phobia, I decided to bridge back to find a memory linked to the symptoms.

Therapist: Can you think of a time when you had the fear of turbulence?

Sofia: Yes, I was on a flight with my sister. We were sitting near the emergency exit. The plane began to shake and move up and down. I was terrified.

Therapist: Close your eyes and go inside. What part of the experience was most disturbing to you?

Sofia: The feeling of being lifted off the ground and shaken.

Therapist: What emotions do you feel?

Sofia: Terror.

Therapist: What do you feel in your body?

Sofia: I feel like I'm off the ground. My heart is racing.

Therapist: What do you believe about yourself?

Sofia: I'm going to die.

Therapist: Trace it back in time. Let whatever comes up come up without censoring it. Go back as far as you can. (*She is silent for a long time.*)

Sofia: I don't know if this is real. I have an image of a baby and a man is shaking her. I think it is my father. He was very abusive. I know he beat my mother when she was pregnant with me.

Therapist: What picture is the worst part for you?

Sofia: It's the image of the baby being lifted up and shaken.

Therapist: What emotions do you feel?

Sofia: Terror.

Therapist: What do you notice in your body?

Sofia: I feel pain in my neck. I feel like I am off the ground. I feel upset inside.

Therapist: What do you believe about yourself?

Sofia: I'm powerless.

She rated this image a SUDS 10. At this point I began to tap on her knees. I did not ask for the PC or VoC because I was concerned it would take her out of her experience and derail the processing. She was activated and ready to go.

Sofia processed this image with a great deal of intensity. She cried, rode the waves of terror, and expressed rage at her father. Images of sexual abuse also came up. At one point she stood up and punched her imagined father with her fists as I tapped on her back. When we returned to the image of the shaken baby, it had faded and the SUDS was a 0. We installed the PC, "I'm powerful." After that I asked her to return to the memory of turbulence on the flight with her sister. What came up now? She said it didn't feel disturbing to her. I told her to go with that and tapped on her knees. She said it felt fine, no problem. She was feeling powerful and in control.

Finally, I asked her to imagine taking a flight in the future, including all the preparations, reservations, packing, driving to the airport, security, flying (including turbulence), and landing safely. "Play it all through like a video." She did that as I tapped on her knees. At the end she said it felt great. "I can do it!" Her body scan was clear, and she felt energy coursing through her body in a good way. We debriefed. I told her she had to now test the work and fly. "Let me know how it goes and if there is anything that causes you anxiety," I told her.

Several months later she contacted me and told me that she had flown successfully without anxiety. She was happy to be free of the phobia that had limited her life. Our single EMDR session on this lifelong problem had done the job.

I am convinced that this work was successful as quickly as it was because we were able to find and reprocess the key incident that was linked to the symptom.

11

RECENT TRAUMAS AND CRITICAL INCIDENTS

EMDR IS EFFECTIVE in helping to heal the emotional and psychological effects of recent traumatic events. A recent trauma is defined as a trauma that occurred up to 3 months pretreatment. It seems that it takes 3 months for a trauma to be stored as long-term memory. Prior to 3 months the trauma is unintegrated, more fragmented, and stored as separate frames. EMDR can be used immediately following an incident; the protocol, however, differs from that of the standard protocol. In this chapter I will first present the protocol for recent traumatic events that Shapiro (1995, 2001) described in her text, followed by a modification that can be helpful with some clients.

PROTOCOL FOR RECENT TRAUMATIC EVENTS

With this protocol, each frame of the incident is targeted and reprocessed in order to get the most comprehensive treatment effect. If only the most disturbing part of the memory is targeted and reprocessed a generalization effect through the entire memory is not likely to occur. It is important to clear all the associated disturbance from all parts of the client's memory.

STEP #1: HISTORY-TAKING, PREPARATION, AND INSTALLATION OF RESOURCES

After the clients tell you why they have sought treatment, do the standard history taking and preparation that you would do with any other client. Be sure to install resources: safe place, nurturing and protector figures, and perhaps a wise/spiritual/inner adviser.

Case Example: John Witnesses a Murder-Suicide

John came into treatment because of a recent trauma that was extremely disturbing to him. He was having trouble sleeping and he couldn't get the images out of his mind. Two months before, a man shot and killed his wife outside his office and then turned the gun on himself. In the first session with John, he told me the story of what had occurred, I then took a history and installed resources. John had good ego strength and was functioning well. He could easily find a safe place and other resources. We both felt he would be ready to begin EMDR the following session.

STEP #2: NARRATIVE HISTORY OF THE EVENT

Ask clients to tell you what happened from beginning to end. It can be helpful to begin with what led up to the incident, or what they were doing before. For example, if your client had had a fight with her boyfriend before she got in her car and had an accident, you will want to know this. Also ask what happened after the incident. Did they go to the police? Was there a trial? What did they do to survive? The things that happen before and after a trauma can be associated with it and reminders can continue to trigger symptoms. You want to make sure to process all of this information.

John's Narrative

A lawyer with a successful practice, John was waiting in his office for his client to arrive when he heard a loud noise, like a firecracker or a gunshot. He looked out his office window and two floors below he looked into the eyes of a woman who had just been shot. "I knew immediately that she was dead." He saw a man slumped over who he believed was still alive. "I thought that someone was killing people." Immediately John got down on the floor. Then he got up and locked his door. He was worried that his client was in danger. A few minutes later his client banged on the door. John quickly let her in. To his horror, she had witnessed the shooting right in front of her. He held and comforted her. She told him that it had been a murder-suicide. As awful as it was, he was relieved that they were not in danger. Not long after that the police came and then the client left. Finally John went home.

STEP #3: TARGET THE WORST PART OF THE EVENT FIRST

After the clients have told you the story, ask them to tell you the *worst part* of the incident. "When you think of the shooting, what part is the worst for you?" Target this frame of the incident with the standard steps (picture, NC, PC, VoC, emotions, SUDS, and body sensations). Then begin the desensitization phase, reprocessing this frame. As you do, it may generalize into the other frames of the incident. From time to time return to most charged frame and check it. When it is down to a SUDS 0 or 1, install a PC that goes with that frame. A common PC is, "It's over."

In John's case, he said the worst part was when he looked out the window and saw the dead woman.

Therapist: What picture represents the worst part?

John: Looking down on her face. I looked in her eyes and knew that she was dead.

His NC was "I'm not safe," his PC, "I'm safe." He reported that the VOC was a 1. The emotions were horror and fear. The SUDS was 8, body sensations were accelerated heart rate, sensations in his hands, and the urge to bite his nails.

He processed this scene until he rated it a 0 SUDS. He installed the PC, "I'm safe."

STEP #4: TARGET THE FIRST DISTURBING SCENE

After the worst scene has been processed, ask the clients to close their eyes and go back to the beginning of the incident, scan through it, tell you when they come to the *first* part that is charged. Target and reprocess this frame.

Therapist: Close your eyes and go back to the beginning of this incident. Scan through it and tell me the first part that is disturbing to you.

John: The first disturbing part is when I heard the gunshot. It was so loud.

Therapist: What picture do you have?

John: I'm sitting at my desk.

Therapist: What do you believe about yourself?

John: I'm not safe.

Therapist: What emotions do you feel?

John: Fear, shock.

Shapiro (1995, 2001) recommended setting up the whole protocol on each frame, but I have found that it may be necessary to skip the PC and

VoC and SUDS if you are short on time or if it takes clients out of their experience. Reprocess this frame to a SUDS 0 or 1 and install a PC.

STEP #5: TARGET THE NEXT MOST DISTURBING SCENE

When the first disturbing frame is complete, go back to the beginning and ask the clients to scan through the incident and tell you the next thing that is charged. "The next thing that is charged was walking out of the building and seeing the bodies and blood." We targeted and reprocessed this frame and installed the PC, "I'm safe."

STEP #6: CONTINUE TO PROCESS EACH FRAME OF THE MEMORY CHRONOLOGICALLY

Continue targeting and reprocessing each frame, and installing a PC through the entire narrative. The last frame John identified was his client leaving. John looked out the window and saw detectives. He said that they looked like they were out of a movie. There was an ambulance and the gun and crime scene was cordoned off with tape. There was chalk around the gun and where the people had died. It seemed strange, like a movie, but also terrible. He knew he was no longer in danger. He targeted and reprocessed this scene to completion.

STEP #7: SCAN THROUGH THE ENTIRE EVENT LIKE A MOVIE, LOOKING FOR ANY CHARGE

If charge is identified ask the client to focus on it and add BLS.

Therapist: Close your eyes and go back to the beginning of the incident and scan through it like a movie. Open your eyes and tell me if you experience any charge.

John: The first thing that comes up is the sound of the sirens.

Therapist: Focus on that. >>>>>>>>>>

Therapist: What comes up now?

John: It went away, it faded.

Therapist: Okay, scan through it again. Let me know if you experience any charge.

John: I see the gun and blood on the ground. It is an enormous gun.

Therapist: Go with that. >>>>>>>>>>>

STEP #8: CONTINUE TO SCAN AND REPROCESS THROUGH THE EVENT UNTIL THE CLIENT REPORTS IT TO BE FREE OF CHARGE

John scanned through the scene several times, reprocessing hot spots when he found them. Finally he reported that there was no charge, a SUDS of 0.

STEP #9: INSTALL A PC WITH THE ENTIRE EVENT

Ask clients to scan through the entire incident as they repeat the PC.

Therapist: When you think of the shooting incident, what do you believe about yourself now?

John: It's over. I survived.

Therapist: I want you to scan through the entire incident from beginning to end as you repeat those words to yourself.

John: Okay. >>>>>>>>>>>>>

STEP #10: BUILD SELF-EFFICACY

This step is optional. Use BLS to reinforce moments of control, strength, and resolve, and for mental rehearsal (from Solomon, 1997).

STEP #11: DO A BODY SCAN AND CLOSURE

Ask clients to scan their body while they repeat the PC. If they report disturbance, you can use BLS to process or close depending upon what is safest for the clients at that time. Take time to close and debrief the session. You can work on any material that remains in the next session.

Solomon (1997) suggested that sometimes it is best to target traumatic moments chronologically. I believe this is the case when information in one frame is important to the frame that follows. For example, a police officer was distressed because he did not fire his gun at a suspect when he was in a life-threatening situation. The officer was stuck believing he failed as a cop. In this case he needed to process chronologically in order to see that the action he took in the situation was actually the best one.

Sometimes the incident has many parts to it, like chapters, and you can only process one chapter in a session. For example, a client who has had a serious car accident may need to process the accident in one session, the emergency medical care in a second one, and physical therapy in a third.

MODIFIED PROTOCOL FOR RECENT TRAUMATIC EVENTS

There are times when using this protocol is not in the best interests of the clients. Breaking the incident down and reprocessing it frame by frame is too time-consuming. The clients can feel very distressed and require immediate relief. I have found, as have many of my EMDR colleagues, that this protocol can be modified for some clients with an acute recent trauma.

STEP #1: HISTORY-TAKING, PREPARATION, AND INSTALLATION OF RESOURCES

The therapists follow the same procedure for assessment for appropriateness for EMDR as they would do for the standard protocol.

STEP #2: USE CONTINUOUS BLS AS THE CLIENTS PROVIDE THE NARRATIVE OF THE INCIDENT

Ask clients to give you a narrative of the event, but as they tell the story they receive BLS. Instruct clients to tell you what happened and to feel their feelings, but if they should start to associate to other memories, they are to signal you and return to the incident they were working on.

STEP #3: AFTER GOING THROUGH THE COMPLETE MEMORY ONCE WITH BLS, ASK CLIENTS TO RETURN AGAIN TO THE BEGINNING AND TELL YOU HOW DISTRESSING IT FEELS

They can rate their distress on the SUDS scale, or give you a verbal report. If it is still charged, focus on where the charge is and add BLS.

STEP #4: ASK CLIENTS TO SCAN THROUGH THE ENTIRE EVENT, LOOKING FOR CHARGE

When clients find a charged place, ask them to focus there and add BLS.

STEP #5: SCAN THROUGH UNTIL THE ENTIRE EVENT NO LONGER FEELS CHARGED

Take a SUDS on the entire incident.

STEP #6: WHEN CLIENTS REPORT A 0 SUDS, ASK FOR A PC THAT GOES WITH THE ENTIRE EVENT

Do BLS while the clients scan the entire incident from beginning to end with the PC.

STEP #7: DO A BODY SCAN AND CLOSE AND DEBRIEF THE SESSION

Be sure to leave enough time for closure. You may want to have clients use safe place and put any unfinished material in a container.

Case Example: Client Whose Dog Was Killed in Front of Her

A client I knew well and had done EMDR with in the past called me and said she wanted to see me immediately. She told me that she was unable to function since her dog had been run over by a car the week before. I scheduled to see her in a few days.

When Kelly arrived I was taken aback to see how distressed she was. Normally an outgoing, talkative woman, she was quiet and withdrawn. She told me that since her dog was killed she had been unable to sleep. Plagued by nightmares and images of him being killed, she felt frozen and grief-stricken and couldn't stop crying. She wanted EMDR as soon as possible to help alleviate her symptoms. We began by installing a safe place and nurturer and protector figures. Then I asked her to tell me what had happened. I was planning to do the standard protocol for recent traumatic events.

As she began to tell me her story, she became quite distressed. There was a lot of detail to her story. I began to become concerned that her narrative was taking too much time. I was worried that we would not have enough time to process the incident if we followed the protocol. I wanted to give her relief in this session. I did not want her to leave more distressed than she was when she came in.

For this reason, I asked her to hold the pulsers from the tac-audio scan in each of her hands and tell me the story of what happened from beginning to end. I told her that when she came to strong feelings or images, to stay with them and ride the waves. If the processing should connect to associated memories, she was to signal me and we would return to the incident. She agreed to this and we started at the beginning of the story. She spoke aloud for most of the time, stopping occasionally to go more fully into the feelings. At one point I told her that she did not have to give me the details if it

wasn't necessary for her. I was concerned about becoming vicariously traumatized myself.

She told me that she had gone grocery shopping with her new baby and
her dog, a rambunctious young beagle. Just as she was getting her baby out
of the car seat, the dog jumped out of the car and took off. Before she could
stop him, he was hit by a car in the parking lot. It was a horrifying sight.
At this place I urged her to stay with the feelings a bit more before she
proceeded with the narrative. She rode the waves of emotion and sobbed as
she processed. After the wave, I stopped the BLS and checked in. Then she
continued with the narrative and BLS. At one point she signaled me that she
was having some childhood memories come up. I stopped the BLS and directed her to return to the incident. The next scene she processed was the
most disturbing to her. She was torn between attending to her baby and her
injured dog. We spent longer on this scene, allowing her time to clear the
images, smells, sounds, and other sensory information.

At the end of the narrative I asked her to go back to the very beginning
and tell me where she experienced any charge. She told me that she had
some charge around the moment of seeing her dog hit. She was still feeling
sad about that and there was still a feeling of shock. I directed her to focus
on that and we began more continuous BLS. After she felt complete with
that part, I again asked her to return to the beginning and scan through the
incident and tell me where she experienced any charge. She closed her eyes
for a moment and reported some feelings in her stomach. As she focused
there, we did more BLS until it felt clear to her. We continued to return to
the beginning, scanning through and focusing on the hot spots with BLS
until she no longer reported feeling any charge. I then asked her to rate the
entire incident on a scale from 0 to 10. She said it was a 0. I asked her what
she believed about herself when she thought of the whole incident. "It's
over," she replied. I directed her to play the movie of the incident from
beginning to end with the belief as she began the BLS. She did a body scan,
reporting that her body felt relaxed and open. "I'm no longer frozen." We
debriefed the session and set up a follow-up appointment.

The next week when she came in, she reported that she felt significant
relief. She was no longer haunted by the disturbing images and was not
crying anymore. She felt sad, but not traumatized. In fact, she told me that
after she left my office she had stopped by the Humane Society and found
a new dog. She could hardly believe that the trauma and loss had cleared
so quickly. She told me it felt like it had happened a year ago instead of
just 2 weeks before. When we checked in with the incident itself, there was
still some charge on key scenes. In just a few minutes we were able to target

and reprocess those scenes until she reported a 0 SUDS with the entire incident. As she processed, she was able to remember happy memories with her dog. Instead of feeling the loss, she now had more access to the good memories, which she cherished. She left my office with a smile on her face and a sense of a positive future with her new dog.

I have used this protocol employing continuous BLS with the narrative many times now, as have EMDR colleagues, with excellent results. It is important to keep the clients focused on the incident being processed. If clients should associate to earlier memories, simply redirect them to the target incident. It is also very important that you *reprocess all the pieces of the incident*. For that reason I ask clients to scan from beginning to end several times until they report little or no charge. The reevaluation is also important in determining whether there are other pieces to reprocess. Ask your clients how they did following the session. From their dreams, insights, associations, triggers, and emotions, you will be able to target places that might cause symptoms.

USING THE RECENT TRAUMATIC EVENTS PROTOCOL WITH CRITICAL INCIDENTS

I have found in some cases that when I target and attempt to reprocess traumatic incidents that happened in the distant past, a generalization effect through the entire incident does not occur. The incident remains in frames as if they were separate incidents. Sometimes I can predict that this will happen and I automatically use the recent traumatic events protocol, but other times I do not and realize after the clients have begun to work that they are not moving beyond the initial part of the narrative. For example, one woman was processing a car accident that happened 30 years before in which her brother was killed. She had been experiencing survivor guilt, which kept her from living fully and enjoying her life. After hearing the story of what happened, we targeted when she discovered her brother's lifeless body beneath the car, the worst part of the incident. When she became stuck and looped, believing she should have been the one to die, I asked her to return to the beginning of the incident and find the *first* disturbing moment. I felt we needed to process the incident chronologically because the beginning of the incident would provide her with important pieces of information. Indeed, when she processed the first scene, she realized that it was her brother who asked her to sit by the door so she could get out of the car first. He had chosen to sit in the middle seat from which he was subsequently ejected. After processing that scene, we continued with the rest of the incident, frame by frame, including the scene in the hospital and the funeral.

Frequently with *critical incident traumas* you need to use the recent traumatic events protocol. Solomon (1996) defined a critical incident as "any situation beyond the realm of a person's usual experience that overwhelms his or her sense of vulnerability and/or lack of control over the situation." Solomon contended that many types of situations can be critical incidents. What seems to be key is the person's perception of vulnerability and ability to control the situation. These incidents can include major traumas such as accidents, rapes, combat, and assaults.

What seems to happen in the aftermath of a critical incident is that the person becomes stuck in the moment of vulnerability. What remains uninte-grated are the moments that follow, during which the person took some sort of action. When EMDR is used, including each of the frames, the moments of action taken are integrated into the whole and the person feels a sense of efficacy and power.

Solomon (1997) recommended reprocessing critical incidents frame by frame, targeting them chronologically or beginning with the most disturbing scene. Clients are asked to close their eyes and to scan the entire incident for anxious moments that are reprocessed. When clients no longer report charge, they are asked for a PC that applies to the entire incident. Next, they are asked to scan through the entire incident and think of the PC while receiving BLS. Finally, in order to build self-efficacy, BLS is used to reinforce moments of control, strength, and resolve, and for mental rehearsal. Solo-mon stressed the importance of follow-up.

Case Example: Critical Incident Trauma Client Kidnapped and Raped

Megan was a short, slender brunette in her late 20s. She came to see me because she was suffering from the effects of a traumatic kidnapping and rape 3 years before. She told me that she had been with a group of students in the jungles of Central America when a native man with a gun burst into their lodge and kidnapped her. In our first sessions she told me the story of what had happened. I took a general history and installed resources. She had good ego strength and had had no previous traumas. This event had been extremely shocking to her sense of self and safety in the world. The narrative seemed to have several parts to it. I wasn't sure in the beginning just what the different parts were, but I knew that there was a part where she was kidnapped, one in which she was raped, another in which she got help, and another when she had to return for a trial. I made a mental note that we needed to include all of these frames in order to complete the work.

We began by targeting the part that was most disturbing to her, when the man pointed the gun at her and grabbed her. The NC was "I'm helpless," the SUDS a 10. She processed this part rapidly, including the installation of a PC, "I'm powerful," but I could tell from what she was reporting that she had not processed the entire incident. For that reason, I instructed her to return to the beginning and tell me the first thing that was disturbing to her. She identified a scene in which the man fired the gun and the native people who worked in the kitchen jumped out of the window. I could tell that this was another of what Solomon (1997) called an "oh shit" moment, a moment of vulnerability awareness. The NC was "I'm going to die," the SUDS was a 10. She processed this scene quickly and installed the PC, "I survived." I again asked her to return to the beginning and scan through the incident and tell me the next part that was disturbing to her. The next scene she identified was in the boat that they took down the river. After the gun-man forced her into the small boat, he ordered her to start the outboard motor. Megan told me that she was in such terror that her body would not obey her commands. Her arms were like rubber bands and she did not have sufficient strength or control to pull the cord to start the motor. Her NC, to my surprise, was, "I'm incompetent." She felt fear and shame. She pro-cessed this scene, which included the terrifying journey down the river—but not the rape—to a 0 SUDS and installed the PC, "I'm powerful."

I then asked her to tell me the next scene that was disturbing to her. She identified the rape in the jungle, which she also processed to a 0 SUDS and PC.

By this time we were getting low on time. I realized that even though there was more to do, this was all we could accomplish for this session. I asked her to go back to the beginning and scan through the scenes we had done and tell me if she experienced any charge. When she signaled me that there was charge in a place, I instructed her to focus on that and did more BLS. We passed through the scenes several times until she reported that it felt clear. I asked her what she believed about herself now when she thought about the incident. She told me, "I'm powerful." I asked her to repeat those words to herself as she scanned the scenes she had processed with BLS. With a broad smile on her face, she told me she felt good. I told her that we would continue to work on the other parts next time and we debriefed the session. When she stood up to leave she told me, "I feel taller!"

In subsequent sessions we worked on other scenes that also needed to be processed frame by frame. We also targeted residual body sensations. Most of the trauma had been cleared in the first session.

12

CARE FOR THE CAREGIVER

A QUESTION THAT I AM frequently asked at the end of my trainings is, "How do you take care of yourself when you see so many traumatized clients?" As psychotherapists specializing in the treatment of trauma, we have all had the experience of giving too much time and energy to our work and clients, leaving us feeling tired and depleted. This is especially prevalent since 9/11, when the world has been in such upheaval. How do we resource our clients when we are also feeling stressed by world events? Overworking can lead to depression, exhaustion, health problems, and burnout. In this state we find that we are not able to help anyone, not even ourselves. In order to take care of ourselves while we help others, I subscribe to the "airlines" model of self-care, which means first providing for our own needs before attending to the needs of others.

SUGGESTIONS FOR THERAPIST SELF-CARE

Following are a number of suggestions for ways you can care for yourself. Remember, you have to be resourced yourself before you can be a resource to others. What advice would you give a close friend who was working as hard as you are?

BALANCE THE KINDS OF CLIENTS IN YOUR PRACTICE

Try to work with a range of different clients. We have a finite amount of energy to work with. Ask yourself, "How much energy does each of your clients take?" Clients who are chronically depressed, clients with complex PTSD or Axis II diagnoses, tend to take more energy from their therapists over a prolonged period of time. Even if you are very good at working with difficult clients, try not to overload your practice with them. Balance your practice with less demanding clients who don't have a lot of transference. It helps to have clients in your practice who are getting better. Focused, time-limited EMDR therapy doing performance-enhancement work such as helping to prepare for test-taking or speaking can be fun and rewarding. Successes give you energy.

If you find that you are working too much with challenging clients, examine your own beliefs. Do you deserve to be happy? Is your self-worth tied to how many hours or how self-sacrificing you have been? Who would you be if you didn't work so hard?

Sadly, it took a life-threatening illness to get a dear friend of mine to slow down and let go of her challenging clients. When she was forced to retire because of her illness she was relieved, yet she regretted that she hadn't done it earlier. She believed in the end that she had allowed her clients to drain her life force.

TAKE BREAKS

It is important to pace yourself and take regular breaks from your practice. *Don't wait until you are exhausted before you take a vacation.* American culture rewards hard workers. We believe we are good people if we work hard. We tend to overwork and then pay the price. I advise scheduling regular breaks. I need to take a week off every 6 weeks. If I go longer than that, I begin to feel depleted. Find what works for you. Those of us in independent practice are often afraid that we won't have enough money if we take breaks. Is that really true? Check up for yourself. How much is your life worth? We underestimate the physical and emotional cost of our work, especially if we work with highly traumatized people. You should be an example of balance and health for your clients. If you are grumpy and depleted, what are you teaching your clients?

Take vacations, but also take breaks during the day. Go for a walk, have lunch with a friend, go to the gym. Build in physical exercise and pleasure.

EAT A HEALTHY DIET, EXERCISE REGULARLY, GET A MASSAGE

What advice do you give your clients? Take care of yourself. Don't skip meals so that you can see 5 clients in a row. Eat regularly. Keep yourself fueled to get through the day. Pace yourself. Eat healthy, balanced meals. Watch your caffeine intake. Make sure you get regular exercise. Yoga can also be restorative. Walk, run, bike, play. Get outside and into nature. Restore yourself with things you love. When you begin to feel depleted, get a massage. Bodywork is a wonderful way to restore balance and to help clear some of the residue from the work with clients.

CREATIVITY AND PLEASURE

Find creative outlets for yourself. Painting, writing, music, dance, and cooking are some possibilities. Expand beyond a therapist identity. Find things that bring you pleasure. What makes you happy? Nobody wants to work with a grim therapist. Get into nature. Take up a new sport or one you have done in the past. Lose yourself in a good novel.

MEDITATION

Meditation is an excellent way to help with balance and peace. As I mentioned earlier in this book, Vipassana meditation is helpful in many ways. It helps you develop concentration and the ability to focus and be present. Meditation helps with relaxation and stress reduction. Over time you become more centered and present. It helps with self-acceptance and disidentification with the thoughts, feelings, and body sensations that arise in the mind. Self-constructs are seen as mind-body phenomena that pass through. You see that neither your clients nor you can be defined by this changing phenomenon. As you practice Vipassana meditation, you develop the courage to look and be with difficult thoughts and feelings. Compassion for self and others increases. Over time, the mind becomes silent and spacious. In this silent space, without interference from the judging mind, intuition comes through as well as creativity. You experience more equanimity and balance and an increased ability to be with whatever life brings.

Silent retreats that are 8 days or longer are an excellent way to deepen this practice. It can be helpful to find a group of people and sit together on a regular basis. It can be helpful to begin and end the day with meditation, and to sit for a few minutes before your more difficult clients arrive to center yourself.

USING BLS TO RESOURCE YOURSELF

I have found it helpful to use BLS to clear myself of traumatic residue from my clients. For many clients who are multiply traumatized, it is difficult for them to arrive at a SUDS 0 because of feeder memories. In these cases I often find myself drained or carrying unprocessed feelings in my own body. I will use BLS to clear any images, body sensations, or emotions related to the clients' work. For years I have used a tac-audio scan for this. You can also tap on your knees or do the butterfly hug. I focus on any images, emotions, body sensations, or cognitions I might have from the day's work, and then turn on the machine, leaving it on continuously. I allow my mind and body to move the blocked energy through, focusing on whatever is arising in my awareness. I find that after 10 to 30 minutes I fall asleep and awake refreshed. Some people may prefer shorter sets. If you find yourself processing old memories that feel overwhelming, stop the BLS. You can return to your body sensations, imagine your safe place, or bring in other resources. Keep in mind that BLS can activate earlier unprocessed material so be careful. Find what works for you. In this way you can keep clearing your clients' trauma from your system and not be vicariously traumatized. If the clients' material stimulates countertransference, then it might be better to find an EMDR therapist who can do the work to clear your material.

You can also use resource installation for yourself. If you feel a need for renewal, you can imagine your safe place and add BLS. You can install images of nurturing, protector, wise, and spiritual figures. You can install an inner adviser. For trouble sleeping, imagine your safe place along with any resource figures and tap. Use the resource work for yourself.

HOW TO BE THE BEST EMDR THERAPIST

To be successful with EMDR, you must have good clinical skills, an ability to develop rapport with clients, an understanding of psychological development, and an understanding of the effects of trauma. You must be comfortable with high levels of affect and be able to attune to clients. You must also know how to listen to and trust your own intuition. The best EMDR therapists are good listeners and are at ease not knowing what is happening or what will emerge next. They are comfortable with what Alan Watts (1951) called the "wisdom of insecurity."

EMDR therapists should be well-grounded, spacious, and attuned to the client. In this way you are present, and yet your consciousness is open, allowing whatever is arising for the clients to be there without fear or judgment. This is very much the quality of consciousness that is cultivated by Vipassana meditation practitioners. You trust the process that is unfolding. You are confident that whatever is arising in the clients' awareness is okay just as it is. In this way you communicate to the clients that it is safe to open to and trust the EMDR process. The clients become more open and curious about information that comes up in sessions as well as outside of sessions. Questions such as "I wonder what this is about?" Or "Where did this come from?" arise instead of punitive beliefs like, "I'm a bad person for acting or thinking this way."

To be proficient in EMDR, you must be familiar with the EMDR protocols and procedures. To do that you should immerse yourself in them. Use EMDR often, read the literature, and practice as much as you can. After the initial training you might pair up with a colleague and exchange sessions for a while, providing feedback to each other. Get consultation, individual and group. Join or organize peer consultation groups where you can practice or consult on cases. Work toward certification. Go to trainings, workshops, and conferences. Join an EMDR online discussion group. Repeat trainings. Attend trainings by a different trainer.

One of the best ways to learn EMDR well is to get your own EMDR therapy. In this way you will clear issues in your own life that might impede your ability to be present with your clients. Therapists who have not done their own work often stop their clients from working through traumas they have not gotten through themselves, impeding their healing because of their own limitations. You can also work on any countertransference issues with EMDR. Receiving your own EMDR therapy also helps you understand from the inside out what your clients experience. You will understand why it is important to ride through abreactions without stopping, why it is annoying to the clients when therapists talk or interpret. It also gives you confidence in the method. After doing your own work, you can ask your clients to go to places that you have also gone, letting them know confidently that they can get through it.

Last, I want to encourage you to use your skills and your artistry, trust yourself, and make EMDR your own. Find your unique expression and integration of this marvelous healing method. Open to the mystery and trust clients' expression of their unfolding. In this way you will be continuously renewed by your work and your clients will become free from their suffering.

APPENDIX 1: EMDR PROCEDURES AND CHECKLISTS

EMDR PROCEDURAL STEPS CHECKLIST

1. Explain trauma theory and EMDR
2. Explain EMDR Session
3. Establish type of BLS
4. Establish signal for "stop" and "keep going"
5. Establish metaphor
6. Install safe place, comfortable place, or conflict-free image
7. Install nurturing figures, protector figures, and other resources
8. Identify issue or memory
9. Identify picture
10. Ask for the NC
11. Ask for the PC
12. Ascertain VoC rating (on a scale of 1–7)
13. Identify emotions
14. Ascertain SUDS rating (on a scale of 0–10)
15. Locate and identify body sensations
16. Desensitize to SUDS (0 or 1)
17. Identify PC
18. Ascertain VoC rating (6 or 7)
19. Install PC
20. Perform a body scan
21. Close
22. Debrief

SAMPLE VIGNETTE OF THE PROCEDURAL STEPS (assessment phase)

1. Target Memory

Therapist: What old memory would you like to work on today?
Client: When I was 10 my family left me at a gas station while I was using the restroom. Ten minutes later they came back and got me.

2. Picture

Therapist: What picture represents the worst part of the incident?
Client: When I came out of the restroom and I realized they had gone.

3. NC

Therapist: When you bring up the picture, what do you believe about yourself now? or What negative belief do you have about yourself now?
Client: I'm unlovable.

4. PC

Therapist: When you bring up that picture or incident, what would you like to believe about yourself now?
Client: I'd like to believe I am lovable.

5. VoC

Therapist: When you bring up that picture of coming out of the restroom, how true does "I am lovable" feel to you now (on a gut level) from 1, completely false, to 7, completely true?
Client: About a 2.

6. Emotions

Therapist: When you bring up the picture and say to yourself, "I'm unlovable," what emotions do you feel?
Client: Shocked, scared, and a little sad.

7. SUDS

Therapist: On a scale from 0 to 10, where 0 is no disturbance or neutral and 10 is the worst disturbance you can imagine, how disturbing does that feel to you now?

Client: About a 5.

8. Location of Body Sensation

Therapist: Where do you feel the disturbance in your body?

Client: In my chest, legs, throat, and stomach.

9. Desensitization

Therapist: Now bring up the image, emotions, and body sensations and repeat to yourself, "I'm unlovable." When you have it let me know. (*Begin BLS.*)

MODIFIED EMDR PROCEDURAL STEPS CHECKLIST

1. Identify the problem, issue, or memory

2. Install or evoke safe place and resources for support (optional)

3. Identify an image or picture
   "What picture represents the worst part of the memory?"

4. Identify emotions
   "What emotions do you feel?"

5. Identify body sensations
   "What do you notice in your body?"

6. Identify NC
   "What do you believe about yourself?"

7. SUDS (optional: take if it is clinically useful to know, skip if it takes the client out of the process)
   "How disturbing does that feel to you now on a scale from 0 to 10 where 0 is no disturbance or neutral, and 10 is the most disturbance you can imagine?"

8. Desensitize
   "I'd like you to bring up the image, along with the emotions and body sensations and say to yourself (the NC, e.g., 'I'm powerless'). When you have it, let me know and I'll begin the bilateral stimulation."

9. Install the PC
   When the SUDS is 0 or 1 ask, "What do you believe about yourself now?" Skip the VoC. Install the PC.

10. Perform a body scan
    Omit if the SUDS is above a 0 or 1, or if you don't have time.

11. Close and debrief
    Be sure to do thorough closure (see Chapter 6). Always leave enough time to debrief.

SAMPLE VIGNETTE OF THE MODIFIED PROCEDURAL STEPS
(assessment phase)

1. Target Memory

Therapist: What old memory would you like to work on today?
Client: When I was ten my family left me at a gas station while I was using the restroom. Ten minutes later they came back and got me.

2. Picture

Therapist: What picture represents the worst part of the incident?
Client: When I came out of the restroom and I realized they had gone.

3. Emotions

Therapist: When you bring up the picture, what emotions do you feel?
Client: Shocked, scared, and a little sad.

4. Location of Body Sensation

Therapist: Where do you feel the disturbance in your body?
Client: In my chest, legs, throat, and stomach.

5. NC

Therapist: What do you believe about yourself now? or What negative belief do you have about yourself now?
Client: I'm unlovable.

(Note: if the client is visibly distressed and beginning to process, you can begin the BLS at this time. The SUDS can be taken later when the processing is winding down and the client is reporting that the charge has lifted. The positive cognition can be ascertained at the completion of the session when the SUDS is down.)

6. SUDS

Therapist: On a scale from 0 to 10, where 0 is no disturbance or neutral and 10 is the worst disturbance you can imagine, how disturbing does that feel to you now?
Client: About a 5.

7. If the memory network is activated, begin BLS to initiate desensitization phase.

CLINICAL SIGNS OF DISSOCIATIVE DISORDERS

Clinical signs that suggest to the therapist that the client may have a dissociative disorder (DID) (Puk, 1999):

1. **Somatic symptoms:**
   - headaches intractable to over-the-counter remedies
   - illnesses that physicians cannot account for that may be somatic memories

2. **Sleep problems:**
   - frequent nightmares or night terrors
   - sleepwalking

3. **Flashbacks:**
   - recent traumatic events, childhood events, multiple, serial PTSD → multiple personality disorder (MPD)

4. **Derealization and depersonalization:**
   - client does not feel like him/herself (e.g., smaller or larger)
   - client's surroundings do not look the same
   - client looks in mirror and sees something other than usual reflection
   - client "floats" above or alongside self
   - client describes life as dreamlike

5. **Schneiderian symptoms:**
   - frequently hearing voices in head, not externally (as in schizophrenia)
   - made feelings: feelings that come out of the blue without any way to explain them (schizophrenics usually do not show made feelings, they have flattened affect)
   - made thoughts and behaviors
   - MPD—full range of affect

6. **History of years of psychotherapy with little progress:**
   - clients with many different diagnoses over the years
   - multiple psychiatric hospitalizations with varying diagnoses
   - once diagnosis is made [MPD or dissociative disorder not otherwise specified (DDNOS)], there is usually a good prognosis for recovery
   - long-term treatment (usually averages from 6 to 9 years of traditional therapy)

7. Memory lapses:
- example: how one got to the store; finding unfamiliar items in house; or missing narrative history of life
- may be substance abuse, illness, depression/dementia
- a highly organized MPD system can fill in the blanks

If clients respond positively to these clinical signs, therapists may want to administer the DES or the SCID-D-R. When in doubt, refer clients or consult with clinicians who specialize in DID.*

---

* Reprinted with permission of Puk (1999).

QUICK ASSESSMENT FOR EMDR READINESS
IN AN OUTPATIENT SETTING

1. Do we have rapport? Do I feel I can work with this person?

2. Is he/she committed to safety and treatment?

3. Can clients handle high levels of affect? Can they install a safe place and other resources? Can they respond to guided visualizations?

4. How are clients currently functioning? Do the clients have supports, family, friends, community?

5. Do the clients have a medical condition that may require a physician consultation to assess safety issues with EMDR utilization?

6. Are the clients abusing drugs or alcohol? Do the clients have other self-harming behaviors?

7. Do the clients have a mental illness that would contraindicate the use of EMDR until they are stabilized? Do the clients need a medication evaluation?

8. Do the clients have DID?

9. Are the clients involved in an active legal case?

SUMMARY OF RESOURCES, COPING SKILLS, AND TECHNIQUES FOR CREATING DISTANCE AND/OR CONTAINMENT

Inner and Outer Resources

Safe place
Positive, conflict-free image
Nurturing figures
Protector figures
Adult self
Wise being
Spiritual resources
Inner adviser or wise self
Figures from books, stories, movies, TV, history, cartoon characters
Inner strength
Positive memories
Images from nature
Image of a positive goal state
Skill development, or a sense of mastery

Coping Skills

Relaxation stress reduction
Grounding skills
Mindfulness practices
Somatic therapies

Techniques

Distancing techniques
Creating an imaginal container

PROTOCOL FOR DEVELOPMENT OF THE POSITIVE, CONFLICT-FREE IMAGE*

1. Help the client identify the conflict-free image by asking questions such as
   - Where in your life do you feel wholly yourself?
   - What is an activity that all of you feels free to engage in?
   - When is a time when you do not have any of the difficulties you came here to resolve?

   For example, think of a time in your everyday life when your body feels most like just the way you want it to feel. You do not have any fear or anxiety. This should be a time when all of your energy is engaged in a positive manner and you experience only positive (or neutral) feelings about yourself or body.

2. Ask the client to select an image that represents a conflict-free area of functioning and evokes *completely* positive feelings. Install this image with the associated body sensations with BLS.

3. The client must be able to hold this image in a consistently positive manner and actually strengthen the image through the sets. If this does not happen, return to step #2.

4. Listen for and identify PCs that emerge.

5. Have the client practice using this technique between sessions to manage distressing affect related to his or her symptoms. For example, she may want to bring up the image before going to sleep, public speaking, and so on.

6. Use the conflict-free image as an interweave during the processing of negative material in the standard EMDR protocol for recent traumatic events. (This was described in Chapter 11.)

---

* Phillips (1997a, 1997b); reprinted with permission of Maggie Phillips, Ph.D.

LIST OF NEGATIVE AND POSITIVE COGNITIONS

Negative Cognitions	Positive Cognitions
I am a bad person.	I am a good person.
I am worthless (inadequate).	I am worthy; I am worthwhile.
I am shameful.	I am honorable.
I am not lovable.	I am lovable.
I am not good enough.	I am good enough.
I deserve only bad things.	I deserve good things.
I cannot be trusted.	I can be trusted.
I cannot trust myself.	I can trust myself.
I cannot trust my judgment.	I can trust my judgment.
I cannot succeed.	I can succeed.
I am not in control.	I am now in control.
I am powerless.	I have power.
I am weak.	I am strong.
I cannot protect myself.	I can protect myself.
I am stupid.	I have intelligence.
I am insignificant (unimportant).	I am significant (important).
I am a disappointment.	I am okay just the way I am.
I deserve to die.	I deserve to live.
I deserve to be miserable.	I deserve to be happy.
I am a failure.	I can succeed.
I have to be perfect.	I can be myself.
I am permanently damaged.	I can be healthy.
I am ugly.	I am fine as I am.
I should have done something.	I did the best I could.
I did something wrong.	I learned (can learn) from it.
I am in danger.	It's over; I am safe now.
I cannot stand it.	I can handle it.
I am not safe.	I am safe now.
I am bad.	I am okay as I am.
It's my fault.	It's not my fault.
I'm going to die.	I survived, I'm safe now.
I'm dead.	I'm alive.
I'm broken.	I'm beginning to heal.
There is something wrong with me.	I'm fine as I am.

SUMMARY OF WHAT TO DO IF THE PROCESSING IS LOOPING OR STUCK

1. Return to target
2. Look for blocking beliefs
    Safety
    Responsibility
    Choice/control
    Shame
3. Check for feeder memories
4. Address clients' fears
5. Look for blocking images
6. Look for blocking body sensations
7. Orient in time and place; check the senses ("What do you hear, smell, taste?")
8. Talk to the child self ("What do you need?")
9. Consult the Inner Adviser or Wise Self

SUMMARY OF NONINTERWEAVE STRATEGIES

1. Change the eye movement
2. Change the type of BLS
3. Alter the target
    Distancing techniques: Change the image to smaller, black and white, still photo, video, or form a protective barrier
    Hierarchy
    Change the sound
Create a container
Increase the sense of safety in the present
Return to a safe place or conflict-free image

IMPORTANT CONCEPTS FOR
ADAPTIVE INFORMATION PROCESSING

- Integrates memory networks
- Separates networks
- Develops of a coherent narrative
- Moves from psychological to objective memory
- Arrives at what is true
- Creates a broader perspective
- Clears the emotional charge

SUMMARY OF INTERWEAVE CATEGORIES AND SUBCATEGORIES

Inquiry Interweaves

- Socratic method
- "I'm confused."
- "What if your child/best friend/client/spouse, etc. did it?"
- Open question (e.g., "Is that true?" or "Why did you do that?")
- Add a positive statement or ask, "Are you safe now?"
- Focus on the outcome ("What happened next?")
- "What do you understand now?" or "What do you know to be true?"
- "Look at the scene, what do you see?" (e.g., "Look at your mother's face, what do you notice?")

Resource Interweaves

Nurturing figures, protector figures, wise figures, and others. Resources that can nurture, rescue, explain, or help in some way.

Imagination Interweaves

Expression of forbidden impulses
Metaphor, stories, and analogy
Split-screen, two-hand interweave
Safe place/conflict-free image

Education Interweaves

APPENDIX 2:
TRAUMA EXPOSURE AND CRISIS
INTERVENTION WITH CIPBS*

ABSTRACT:

CIPBS (Conflict Imagination Painting and Bilateral Stimulation) is a new, EMDR (Eye Movement Desensitization and Reprocessing, Shapiro) and KiP (Katathym imaginative Psychotherapie, Leuner) related approach for trauma exposure and crisis intervention that also includes basic elements of art therapy. CIPBS is a structured process, using symbolization and bilateral stimulation. It can be integrated in different therapeutic approaches and settings. The poster shows case examples of the application in different fields like psychooncology and childhood trauma and also some results of a pilot study.

INTRODUCTION:

Most of the new and effective methods used in trauma therapy, like EMDR and KiP include imagination, resource work and non-verbal elements. CIPBS is a structured procedure for trauma exposure and crisis intervention that combines tactile bilateral stimulation (like EMDR) with imagination and symbolization. This seems to unblock and accelerate information processing, integrate sensory, affective and cognitive elements and activate resources and self healing potentials. Distress is reduced rapidly, and spontaneus, creative solutions with deep emotional resonance arise. Psychotherapists trained in CIPBS report that trauma exposure with CIPBS is less distressing for patients than most other methods.

In a pilot study we tested different trauma focused interventions, including CIPBS, EMDR and CBT (Cognitive Behavior Therapy) in the treatment of breast cancer patients with PTSD symptoms.

---

* Poster presented at the VIII European Conference on Traumatic Stress, Berlin, Germany, May 22–25, 2003.

M E T H O D S :

Breast cancer patients in different settings of medical routine care were screened for PTSD symptoms by use of the BC-PASS (Breast Cancer- Psychosocial Assessment Screening Scale, Isermann et. al). If the critical score of Factor C: "Emotional Stress Reaction" was exceeded, they were randomly assigned to three treatment groups (2: Resource focused Cognitive Behavior Therapy; 3: Resource focused EMDR; 4: Resource focused EMDR and CIPBS. Post treatment testing was 3 months after pretest. As an additional group (group1) we included breast cancer patients of a specialized rehabilitation clinic (intense medical, psychological and physiotherapeutic aftercare) before and after a 3- or 4 week inpatient program. In each group 10 subjects were treated (N= 39: one dropout in group 2).

R E S U L T S :

All four groups showed pre-post improvements in reducing PTSD symptoms and depression. EMDR and EMDR+CIPBS was more effective than Standard Rehabilitation and CBT (p < .01). The combination of CIPBS and EMDR also tend to reduce symptoms of depression more effective than EMDR alone (p < .05).

C O N C L U S I O N :

The results of the pilot study show that psychotherapeutic interventions, especially EMDR and CIPBS, are effective in reducing PTSD symptoms and depression in breast cancer patients. Symptoms of depression were most reduced in the CIPBS + EMDR group. This corresponds with reports of psychotherapists working with CIPBS, indicating that CIPBS seems to allow a more gentle trauma exposure. This might be a result of the combination of imagination and symbolization of the trauma by painting. Further research is needed to explore the different effects.

T R E A T M E N T :   P R E - P O S T   M E A N S

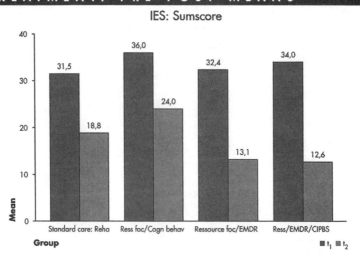

IES: Sumscore

Treatment: Pre-Post Means (con't)

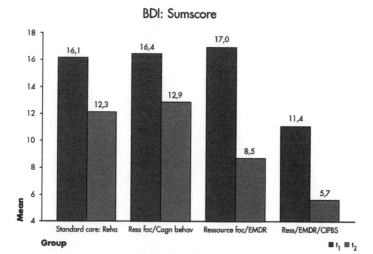

BDI: Sumscore

TABLE 1

Pre-treatment and post-treatment means (M) and standard deviations (s) for the two main outcome measures IES and BDI

Scale	Group	n	Age	Number of specific sessions	Pre M	s	Post M	s	Pre-post differences	Differences between groups (post)
IES Sumscore (15 items)	1: Standard Rehabilitation	10	50,2	5,3	31,5	14,19	18,8	11,73	p = .010	} n.s.
	2: Res. foc. Cognit. Behav.	9	54,7	4,9	36,0	11,41	24,0	11,01	p = .013	} p< .01
	3: Res. foc. EMDR	10	51,9	5,1	32,4	8,99	13,1	4,07	p < .000	} n.s.
	4: Res. foc. EMDR + CIPBS	10	49,6	5,1	34,0	6,41	12,6	10,10	p < .000	
		39	51,5	5,1	33,4	10,34	16,9	10,38		
BDI Sumscore	1: Standard Rehabilitation	10	50,2	5,3	16,1	9,29	12,3	9,47	p = .05	} n.s.
	2: Res. foc. Cognit. Behav.	9	54,7	4,9	16,4	8,04	12,1	4,04	n.s.	} p< .05
	3: Res. foc. EMDR	10	51,9	5,1	17,0	7,50	8,5	2,63	p < .01	} p< .05
	4: Res. foc. EMDR + CIPBS	10	49,6	5,1	11,4	5,48	5,7	2,31	p < .011	
		39	51,5	5,1	15,2	7,72	9,6	5,95		

CIPBS CASE EXAMPLES

Patient A, 39 years

Situation: Breast cancer patient developed fear of death a few weeks after the medical treatment

Safe place: Laying down on the grass and feeling the sunshine

1: SUD 9
5: SUD 0

1: I'm afraid I have almost no time to live
2: soon I will move to our new house
3: I'm not alone, I have my family
4: I'm making my way on a path
5: I see myself walking in the sunshine

Patient B, 48 years

Situation: Nightsweats triggered fear of relapse, one year after breast cancer surgery

Safe place: I'm protected by the rainbow

1: SUD 10
5: SUD 1-2

1: I'm afraid the nightsweats mean my cancer has returned
2: I just see the colour green
3: I'm surprised that I only see the colour orange
4: suddenly I see an island with a house on it
5: a happy fish with red lips comes up in the water, the fish needs water to live, I realized that the sweats are'nt necessarily a sign of danger

CIBPS Case Examples (con't)

Patient C, 30 years

Situation: The vomit of her partner's child triggered childhood trauma with vomit of her mother

Safe place: sitting relaxed in front of a hut on a swing with a striped awning, looking out at the ocean
1: SUD 10
5: SUD 1

1: the vomit makes me panic and feel very small and helpless

2: I feel grief and there is a lump in my throat

3: my stomach is constricted

4: I wish I could relax

5: I can't keep this relaxed state it keeps disappearing

6: I feel so sad that I keep loosing the relaxed state

7: I can choose how I view my life: I love nature, I appreciate my partner, I love beeing on the beach, I would like to have a dog, I love the sunshine, I can focus on the love in my life

REFERENCES

Acierno, R., Van Hasselt, V. B., Tremont, G., & Meuser, K.T. (1994). Review of validation and dissemination of eye-movement desentitization and reprocessing: A scientific and ethical dilemma. *Clinical Psychology Review, 14*, 287–299.

Artigas, L. A., Jarero, I., Mauer, M., Lopez Cano, T., & Alcal, N. (2000, September). *EMDR integrative treatment protocol and the butterfly hug.* Poster presented at the EMDRIA conference, Toronto, Ontario, Canada.

Baker, N., & McBride, B. (1991, August). *Clinical applications of EMDR in a law enforcement environment: Observations of the Psychological Service Unit of the L.A. County Sheriff's Department.* Paper presented at the Police Psychology (Division 18, Police & Public Safety Sub-Section) Mini-Convention at the annual convention of the American Psychological Association, San Francisco.

Bass, E., & Davis, L. (1988). *The courage to heal: A guide for women survivors of child sexual abuse.* New York: Harper & Row.

Bernstein, C., & Putnam, F. (1986). Development, reliability, and validity of a dissociation scale. *Journal of Nervous and Mental Disease, 174*, 727–735.

Blore, D. C. (1997). Use of EMDR to treat morbid jealousy: A case study. *British Journal of Nursing, 6*, 984–988.

Boel, J. (1999). The butterfly hug. *EMDRIA Newsletter, 4*(4), 11–13.

Bresler, D. E. (1986). *Free yourself from pain.* New York: Simon & Schuster.

Bresler, D. E. (1990). Meeting an inner adviser. In D. C. Hammond (Ed.), *Handbook of hypnotic suggestions and metaphors,* (pp. 318–320). New York: Norton.

Carlson, J. G., Chemtob, C. M., Rusnak, K., & Hedlund, N. L. (1996). Eye movement desensitization and reprocessing (EMDR) as treatment for combat PTSD. *Psychotherapy, 33*(1), 101–113.

Carlson, J. G., Chemtob, C. M., Rusnak, K., Hedlund, N. L., & Muraoka, M. Y. (1998). Eye movement dessensitization and reprocessing for combat-related posttraumatic stress disorder. *Journal of Traumatic Stress, 11*, 3–24.

Chambless, D. L., Baker, M. J., Baucom, D. H., Beutler, L. E., Calhoun, K. S., Crits-Christoph, P., et al. (1998). Update on empirically validated therapies. *The Clinical Psychologist, 51*, 3–16.

Chemtob, C. M., Nakashima, J., Hamada, & Carlson, J. G. (2002). Brief treatment for elementary school children with disaster-related PTSD: A field study. *Journal of Clinical Psychology, 58*, 99–102.

Chemtob, C. M., Tolin, D. F., van der Kolk, B. A., & Pitman, R. K. (2000). Eye movement desensitization and reprocessing. In E. B. Foa, T. M. Keane, & M. J. Friedman

(Eds.), *Effective treatments for PTSD: Practiced guidelines from the International Society for Traumatic Stress Studies* (pp. 139–155, 333–335). New York: Guilford Press.

Cocco, N., & Sharpe, L. (1993). An auditory variant of eye movement desensitization in a case of childhood posttraumatic stress disorder. *Journal of Behavioral Therapy & Experimental Psychiatry, 24,* 373–377.

Cohn, L. (1993a). Art psychotherapy and the new eye movement desensitization and reprocessing (EMD/R) method, an integrated approach. In E. Dishup (Ed.), *California art therapy trends* (pp. 275–290). Chicago: Magnolia Street Publisher.

Cohn, L. (1993b). *Art therapy and EMDR.* Workshop presentation at the EMDR Conference, Sunnyvale, CA.

Cohn, L. (2005). Personal communication.

Colleli, G. (2002). Personal communication.

Colelli, G. (2004). Personal communication.

Crabbe, B. (1996, Nov.) Can eye-movement therapy improve your riding? *Dressage Today,* 28–33.

Daniels, N., Lipke, H., Richardson, R., & Silver, S. (1992, October). *Vietnam veterans' treatment programs using eye movement desensitization and reprocessing.* Symposium presented at annual convention of the International Society for Traumatic Stress Studies, Los Angeles.

Davis, L. (1990). *The courage to heal workbook.* New York: Harper & Row.

De Jongh, A., & Ten Broeke, E. (1998). Treatment of choking phobia by targeting traumatic memories with EMDR: A case study. *Clinical Psychology and Psychotherapy, 5,* 264–269.

De Jongh, A., Ten Broeke, E., & Renssen, M. R. (1999). Treatment of specific phobias with eye movement desensitization and reprocessing (EMDR): Protocol, empirical status, and conceptual issues. *Journal of Anxiety Disorders, 13,* 69–85.

Diegelmann, C. (2003). Personal communication.

Diegelmann, C. (2006). Krisenintervention und Traumaexposition mit CIPBS (Conflict Imagination, Painting and Bilateral Stimulation). In S. Ditz, C. Diegelmann, & M. Isermann. (Eds.). *Psychoonkologie—Schwerpunkt Brustkrebs. Ein Handbuch fuer die aerztliche und psychotherapeutische Praxis* (pp. 264–286). Stuttgart: Kohlhammer.

Diegelmann, C., & Isermann, M. (2003, May). *Trauma exposure and crisis intervention with CIPBS.* Poster session presented at the VIII European Conference on Traumatic Stress, Berlin, Germany.

Diegelman, C. & Isermann, M. (2005). Personal communication.

Doctor, R. (1994, March). *Eye movement desensitization and reprocessing: A clinical and research examination with anxiety disorders.* Paper presented at the 14th annual meeting of the Anxiety Disorders Association of America, Santa Monica, CA.

Douglass, F. (1941). *The life and times of Frederick Douglass.* New York: Pathway Press.

Edmond, T., Rubin, A., & Wambach, K. G. (1999). The effectiveness of EMDR with adult female survivors of childhood abuse. *Social Work Research, 23,* 103–116.

Erickson, M. H., & Rossi, E. L. (1976). Two-level communication and the microdynamics of trance and suggestion. *American Journal of Clinical Hypnosis, 18,* 153–171.

Feske, U. (1998). Eye movement desensitization and reprocessing treatment for posttraumatic stress disorder. *Clinical Psychology: Science and Practric, 5,* 171–181.

Feske, U., & Goldstein, A. (1997). Eye movement desensitization and reprocessing treatment for panic disorder: A controlled outcome and partial dismantling study. *Journal of Consulting and Clinical Psychology, 65,* 1026–1035.

Foster, S., & Lendl, J. (1995). Eye movement desensitization and reprocessing: Four case studies of a new tool for executive coaching and restoring employee performance after setbacks. *Consulting Psychology Journal*, 48, 155–161.

Foster, S., & Lendl, J. (1996). Eye movement desensitization and reprocessing: Four case studies of a new tool for executive coaching and restoring employee performance after setbacks. *Consulting Psychology Journal: Practice and Research*, 48(3), 155–161.

Gendlin, E. (1981). *Focusing*. New York: Bantam Books.

Goldstein, J. (1976). *The experience of insight*. Boulder, CO: Shambala.

Goldstein, A., & Feske, U. (1994). Eye movement desensitization and reprocessing for panic disorder: A case series. *Journal of Anxiety Disorders*, 8, 351–362.

Goldstein, J. (1976). *The experience of insight*. Boulder, CO: Shambala.

Harner, M. (1980). *The way of the shaman*. New York: Bantam.

Hartung, J., Galvin, M., & Gallo, F. (2003). *Energy psychology & EMDR: Combining forces to optimize treatment*. New York: Norton.

Hebb, D. O. (1949). *The organization of behavior: A neuropsychological theory*. New York: Wiley.

Henry, S. L. (1996). Pathological gambling: Etiological considerations and treatment efficacy of eye movement desensitization/reprocessing. *Journal of Gambling Studies*, 12, 395–405.

Herbert, J. D., & Meuser, K. T. (1992). Eye movement desensitization: A critique of the evidence. *Journal of Behavior Therapy and Experimental Psychiatry*, 23, 169–174.

Herman, J. L. (1992). *Trauma and recovery*. New York: Basic Books.

Hyer, L. (1995). Use of EMDR in a "dementing" PTSD survivor. *Clinical Gerontologist*, 16, 70–73.

Kabat-Zinn, J. (1990). *Full catastrophe living: Using the wisdom of your body and mind to face stress, pain, and illness*. New York: Dell.

Kaplan, B. J., Simpson, J. S. A., Ferre, R. C., Gorman, C., McMullen, D., & Crawford, S. G. (2001). Effective mood stabilization in bipolar disorder with a chelated mineral supplement. *Journal of Clinical Psychiatry*, 62, 936–944.

Kaplan, B. J., Fisher, J. E., Crawford, S. G., Field, C. J., Kolb, B. (2004). Improved mood and behavior during treatment with a mineral-vitamin supplement: An open-label case series of children. *Journal of Child and Adolescent Psychopharmacology*, 14(1), 115–22.

Klein, J. (1988). *Who am I?* Longmead, Shaftesbury, Dorset, UK: Element Books.

Kleinknecht, R. (1993). Rapid treatment of blood and injection phobias with eye movement desensitization. *Journal of Behavior Therapy and Experimental Psychiatry*, 24, 211–217.

Kleinknecht, R. A., & Morgan, M. P. (1992). Treatment of post-traumatic stress disorder with eye movement desensitization and reprocessing. *Journal of Behavior Therapy and Experimental Psychiatry*, 23, 43–50.

Korn, D. (1997). *Clinical application of EMDR in treating survivors of sexual abuse*. Workshop presentation, EMDR International Association Conference, San Francisco.

Korn, D., Rozelle, D., & Weir, J. (2004). *Looking beyond the data: Clinical lessons learned from an EMDR treatment outcome study*. Session #321. EMDR International Association Conference, Montreal, Canada.

Kornfield, J. (1993). *A path with heart: A guide through the perils and promises of spiritual life*. New York: Bantam.

Leeds, A. M. (1997, July 13). *In the eye of the beholder: Reflections on shame, dissociation, and transference in complex posttraumatic stress and attachment related disorders. Principles of case formulation for EMDR treatment planning and the use of resource installation*. Unpublished paper presented at the EMDR International Association Conference, San Francisco.

Leeds, A. M. (1998). Lifting the burden of shame: Using EMDR resource installation to resolve a therapeutic impasse. In P. Manfield (Ed.), *Extending EMDR: A casebook of innovative applications* (pp. 256–281). New York: Norton.

Leeds, A. M., & Shapiro, F. (2000). EMDR and resource installation: Principles and procedures for enhancing current functioning and resolving traumatic experiences. In J. Carlson & L. Sperry (Eds.), *Brief therapy strategies with individuals and couples*. Phoenix, AZ: Zeig/Tucker.

Leeds, A., & Korn, D. (1998). *Clinical applications of EMDR in the treatment of adult survivors of childhood abuse and neglect*. Workshop presentation at the EMDR International Association Conference, Baltimore.

Lendl, J., & Foster, S. (1997). *EMDR performance enhancement for the workplace: A practioners' manual*. Self-published manual. Inquiries to: Sandra Foster, Ph.D., 220 Montgomery St., Suite 315, San Francisco, CA 94104. E-mail: samrolf@aol.com.

Levine, P. (1997). *Waking the tiger: Healing trauma*. Berkeley, CA: North Atlantic Books.

Levine, P. (1999). *Healing trauma: Restoring the wisdom of the body*. Boulder, CO: Sounds True.

Levine, S. (1987). *Healing into life and death*. New York: Anchor/Doubleday.

Linehan, M. (1993a). *Cognitive-behavioral treatment of the borderline personality disorder*. New York: Guilford Press.

Linehan, M. (1993b). *Skills training manual for treating borderline personality disorder*. New York: Guilford Press.

Lipke, H. (1994, August). *Survey of practitioners trained in eye movement desensitization and reprocessing*. Paper presented at the annual convention of the American Psychological Association, Los Angeles.

Lipke, H. (2000). *EMDR and psychotherapy integration*. Boca Raton, FL: CRC Press.

Lipke, H. (2005, September). *Getting past "You weren't there" EMDR and the combat veteran*. Plenary presentation at the conference on the EMDR International Association, Seattle, WA.

Lipke, H., & Botkin, A. (1992). Brief case studies of eye movement desensitization and reprocessing with chronic post-traumatic stress disorder. *Psychotherapy, 29*, 591–595.

Lohr, J. M., Kleinknecht, R. A., Conley, A. T., dal Cerro, S., Schmidt, J., & Sonntag, M. E. (1992). A methodological critique of the current status of eye movement desensitization (EMD). *Journal of Behavior Therapy and Experimental Psychiatry, 23*, 159–167.

Lovett, J. (1999). *Small wonders: Healing childhood trauma with EMDR*. New York: Free Press.

Marcus, S., Marquis, P., & Sakai, C. (1997). Controlled study of treatment of PTSD using EMDR in an HMO setting. *Psychotherapy, 34*, 307–315.

Marquis, J. (1991). A report on seventy-eight cases treated by eye movement desensitization. *Journal of Behavior Therapy and Experimental Psychiatry, 22*, 187–192.

Martinez, R. A. (1991). Innovative uses. *EMDR Network Newsletter, 1*, 5–6.

Maxfield, L., & Melnyk, W. T. (2000). Single-session treatment of test anxiety with eye movement desensitization and reprocessing (EMDR). *International Journal of Stress Management, 7*, 87–101.

McFarlane, A. C., Weber, D. L., & Clark, C. R. (1993). Abnormal stimulus processing in PTSD. *Biological Psychiatry, 34*, 311–320.

McNally, V. J., & Solomon, R. M. (1999, February). The FBI's critical incident stress management program. *FBI Law Enforcement Bulletin*, 20–26.

Miller, E. (1996). *Letting go of stress*. Source Cassette Learning Systems, Inc.

Myers, L. (2003). *Becoming whole: Writing your healing story*. San Diego: Silver Threads.

Nadler, W. (1996). EMDR: Rapid treatment of panic disorder. *International Journal of Psychiatry, 2*, 1–8.

O'Brien, E. (1993, November/December). Pushing the panic button. *Family Therapy Networker*, 75–83.

Ogden, P., Minton, K. & Pain, C. (2006). *Trauma and the body: A sensorimotor approach to psychotherapy.* New York: Norton.

Omaha, J. (2004). *Psychotherapeutic interventions for emotion regulation.* New York: Norton.

Page, A. C., & Crino, R. D. (1993). Eye-movement desensitization: A simple treatment for post-traumatic stress disorder? *Australian and New Zealand Journal of Psychiatry, 27,* 288–293.

Parnell, L. (1995–1998). *EMDR in the treatment of sexual abuse survivors.* EMDR Institute: Level II Specialty Presentations.

Parnell, L. (1996a). Eye movement desensitization and reprocessing (EMDR) and spiritual unfolding. *Journal of Transpersonal Psychology, 28,* 129–153.

Parnell, L. (1997a). *Transforming trauma: EMDR.* New York: Norton.

Parnell, L. (1997b, July). *Beyond recovery: EMDR and transpersonal experiences.* Paper presented at the conference of the EMDR International Association, San Francisco.

Parnell, L. (1998a, July). *Transforming sexual abuse trauma with EMDR.* Workshop presentation at the conference of the EMDR International Association, Baltimore.

Parnell, L. (1998b). Post-partum depression: Helping a new mother to bond. In P. Manfield (Ed.), *Extending EMDR: A casebook of innovative applications* (pp. 37–64). New York: Norton.

Parnell, L. (1999). *EMDR in the treatment of adults abused as children.* New York: Norton.

Parnell, L., & Cohn, L. (1995). *Innovations in the use of EMDR, imagery, and art.* EMDR regional network meeting, Sunnyvale, CA.

Pellicer, X. (1993). Eye movement desensitization treatment of a child's nightmares: A case report. *Journal of Behavior Therapy and Experimental Psychiatry, 24,* 73–75.

Perry, B. (2002, June). *Trauma memory and neurodevelopment: A proposed mechanism of action for EMDR.* Plenary session of the conference of the EMDR International Association,

Phillips, M. (1997a, July). *The importance of ego strengthening with EMDR.* Paper presented at the conference of the EMDR International Association, EMDRIA, San Francisco.

Phillips, M. (1997b, November). *The importance of ego strengthening with dissociative disorder patients.* Paper presented at the 14th international fall conference of the International Society for the Study of Dissociation, Montreal, Canada.

Phillips, M. (2000). *Finding the energy to heal: How EMDR, hypnosis, TFT, imagery, and body-focused therapy can help restore mind-body health.* New York: Norton.

Phillips, M. (2001, January/April). Potential contributions of hypnosis to ego-strengthening procedures in EMDR. *American Journal of Clinical Hypnosis, 43*(3–4), 247–262.

Phillips, M., & Frederick, C. (1995). *Healing the divided self.* New York: Norton.

Popky, A. J. (1997). *EMDR integrative addiction treatment model.* EMDR Institute, Level II Specialty Presentation, San Francisco.

Popky, A. J. (2005). DeTUR, an urge reduction protocol for addictions and dysfunctional behaviors. In R. Shapiro (Ed.), *EMDR solutions: Pathways to healing* (pp. 167–188). New York: Norton.

Popper, C. W. (2001). Do vitamins or minerals (apart from lithium) have mood-stabilizing effects? *Journal of Clinical Psychiatry, 62,* 933–935.

Puffer, M. K., Greenwald, R., & Elrod, D. E. (1998). A single-session EMDR study with twenty traumatized children and adolescents. *Traumatology, 3*(2).

Puk, G. (1991). Treating traumatic memories: A case report on the eye movement desensitization procedure. *Journal of Behavior Therapy and Experimental Psychiatry, 22,* 149–151.

Puk, G. (1999). Clinical signs of dissociative disorders. In F. Shapiro (Ed.), *EMDR Institute Manual.* Pacific Grove, CA: EMDR Institute.

Rossman, M. L. (1987). *Healing yourself: A step-by-step program for better health through imagery.* New York: Walker.

Rothbaum, B. O. (1997). A controlled study of eye movement desensitization and reprocessing for posttraumatic stress disordered sexual assault vicitms. *Bulletin of the Menniger Clinic, 61,* 317–334.

Salzberg, S. (1996). *Loving-kindness meditation—learning to love through insight meditation* (audio cassette). Boulder, CO: Sounds True.

Salzberg, S. (2002). *Loving-kindness: The revolutionary art of happiness.* Boston: Shambala.

Salzberg, S. (2005). *The force of kindness: Change your life with love and compassion.* Boulder, CO: Sounds True.

Salzberg, S., & Kabat-Zinn, J. (1997). *Loving-kindness: The revolutionary art of happiness.* Berkeley: Shambala.

Scheck, M. M., Schaeffer, J. A., & Gillette, C. S. (1998). Brief psychological intervention with traumatized young women: The efficacy of eye movement dessensitization and reprocessing. *Journal of Traumatic Stress, 11*(1), 25–44.

Schmidt, S. J. (2002). *Developmental needs meeting strategy for EMDR therapists.* San Antonio, Texas: DNMS Institute, LLC.

Schore, A. N. (1994). *Affect regulation and the origin of the self: The neurobiology of emotional development.* Hillsdale, NJ: Erlbaum.

Schore, A. N. (1998, January 31). *Memory, brain process and development, part I.* Understanding and Treating Trauma: Developmental and Neurobiological Approaches: Lifespan Learning Institute Conference, Los Angeles.

Shalev, A. Y., Friedman, M. J., Foa, E. B., & Keane, T. M. (2000). Integration and summary. In E. B. Foa, T. M. Keane, & M. J. Friedman (Eds.), *Effective treatments for PTSD: Practice guidelines from the International Society for Traumatic Stress Studies* (pp. 359–379). New York: Guilford Press.

Shapiro, F. (1989a). Efficacy of the eye movement desensitization procedure in the treatment of traumatic memories. *Journal of Traumatic Stress Studies, 2,* 199–223.

Shapiro, F. (1994). Alternative stimuli in the use of EMD(R). *Journal of Behavior Therapy and Experimental Psychiatry, 25,* 89.

Shapiro, F. (1995). *Eye movement desensitization and reprocessing.* New York: Guilford Press.

Shapiro, F. (1999). Eye movement desensitization and reprocessing (EMDR) and the anxiety disorders: Clinical and research implications of an integrated psychotherapy treatment. *Journal of Anxiety Disorders, 13,* 35–67.

Shapiro, F. (2001). *Eye movement desensitization and reprocessing: Basic principles, protocols, and procedures* (2nd ed.), New York: Guilford Press.

Shapiro, F., & Solomon, R. (1995). Eye movement desensitization and reprocessing: Neurocognitive information processing. In G. Everley & J. Mitchell (Eds.), *Critical incident stress management.* Elliot City, MD: Chevron.

Shapiro, F., Vogelmann-Sine, S., & Sine, L. (1994). Eye movement desensitization and reprocessing: Treating trauma and substance abuse. *Journal of Psychoactive Drugs, 26,* 379–391.

Shapiro, F. & Silk-Forrest, M. (1997). *EMDR.* New York: Basic Books.

Shapiro, R. (Ed.) (2005). *EMDR solutions: Pathways to healing.* New York: Norton.

Siegel, D. J. (1998, February). *Memory, brain process, and development, part II.* Understanding and Treating Trauma: Developmental and Neurobiological Approaches: Lifespan Learning Institute Conference, Los Angeles.

Siegel, D. J. (1999). *The developing mind: Toward a neurobiology of interpersonal experience.* New York: Guilford Press.

Siegel, D. J. (2002). The developing mind and the resolution of trauma: Some ideas about information processing and an interpersonal neurobiology of psychotherapy. In

F. Shapiro (Ed.), *EMDR as an integrative psychotherapy approach: Experts of diverse orientations explore the paradigm prism.* Washington, DC: American Psychological Association Press.

Siegel, D. J. (2001) Toward an interpersonal neurobiology of the developing mind: Attachment relationships, "mindsight," and neural integration. *Infant Mental Health Journal.* 22(1–2), 67–94

Silver, S. M., Brooks, A., & Obenchain, J. (1995). Eye movement desensitization and reprocessing treatment of Vietnam war veterans with PTSD: Comparative effects with biofeedback and relaxation training. *Journal of Traumatic Stress, 8,* 337–342.

Solomon, R. M. (1994, June). *Eye movement desensitization and reprocessing and treatment of grief.* Paper presented at the fourth international conference on Grief and Bereavement in Contemporary Society, Stockholm, Sweden.

Solomon, R. M. (1995, February). *Critical incident trauma: Lessons learned at Waco, Texas.* Paper presented at the Law Enforcement Psychology Conference, San Mateo, CA.

Solomon, R. M. (1996, June). *EMDR applications to critical incident stress management* (handout). Session 20. Paper presented at EMDR International Association Conference, Denver, CO.

Solomon, R. M. (1997, July). *The application of EMDR to critical incident trauma.* EMDR International Association Conference, San Francisco.

Solomon, R. M. (1998). Utilization of EMDR in crisis intervention. *Crisis Intervention, 4,* 239–246.

Solomon, R. M., & Kaufman, T. (1992, October). *Eye movement desensitization and reprocessing: An effective addition to critical incident treatment protocols.* Preliminary results presented at the annual conference of the International Society for Traumatic Stress Studies, Los Angeles.

Solomon R. M., & Kaufman, T. (1994, March). *Eye movement desensitization and reprocessing: An effective addition to critical incident treatment protocols.* Paper presented at the 14th annual meeting of the Anxiety Disorders Association of America, Santa Monica, CA.

Spector, J., & Read, J. (1999). The current status of eye movement desensitization and reprocessing (EMDR). *Clinical Psychology and Psychotherapy, 6,* 165–174.

Steinberg, M. (1994). *Structured interview for DSM-IV dissociative disorders—revised (SCID-D-R).* Washington, DC: American Psychiatric Press.

Steinberg, M. (1995). *Handbook for the assessment of dissociation: A clinical guide.* Washington, DC: American Psychiatric Press.

Taylor, C. (1991). *The inner child workbook.* Los Angeles: Tarcher.

Thomas, R., & Gafner, G. (1993). PTSD in an elderly male: Treatment with eye movement desensitization and reprocessing (EMDR). *Clinical Gerontologist, 14,* 57–59.

Thompson, J., Cohn, L., & Parnell, L. (1996, June). *Beyond the cognitive interweave: The use of dreams, art, and imagery in EMDR.* Paper presented at the conference of the EMDR International Association, Denver, CO.

Tinker, R., & Wilson, S. (1999). *Through the eyes of a child: EMDR with children.* New York: Norton.

Tinker, R., & Wilson, S. (2005). The phantom limb pain protocol. In R. Shapiro (Ed.), *EMDR solutions: Pathways to healing* (pp. 147–159). New York: Norton.

van der Kolk, B. A. (1994). The body keeps the score: Memory and the evolving psychobiology of posttraumatic stress. *Harvard Review Psychiatry, 1,* 253–265.

van der Kolk, B. A. (1996). The complexity of adaptation to trauma: Self-regulation, stimulus discrimination, and characterological development. In B. van der Kolk, A. C. McFarlane, & L. Weisaeth (Eds.), *Traumatic stress* (pp. 182–213). New York: Guilford Press.

van der Kolk, B. A. (1998, January 31). *Social and neurobiological dimensions of the compulsion to forget and re-enact trauma.* Understanding and Treating Trauma: Developmental and Neurobiological Approaches Lifespan Learning Institute Conference, Los Angeles.

van der Kolk, B. A., Burbridge, J.A., & Suzuki, J. (1997). The psychobiology of traumatic memory: Clinical implications of neuroimaging studies. In R. Yehuda & A. C. McFarlane (Eds.), *Annals of the New York Academy of Sciences (Vol. 821): Psychobiology of posttraumatic stress disorder.* New York: New York Academy of Sciences.

van der Kolk, B. A., McFarlane, A. C., & Weisaeth, L. (Eds.) (1996). *Traumatic stress.* New York: Guilford Press.

Van Etten, M. L., & Taylor, S. (1998). Comparative efficacy of treatments for posttraumatic stress disorder: A meta-analysis. *Clinical Psychology and Psychotherapy, 5,* 126–144.

Waller, S., Mulick, P., & Spates, C. (2000). *A meta-analysis of leading psychological interventions for PTSD: The effect of selected moderator variables.* Paper presented at the third world conference of the International Society of Traumatic Stress Studies, Melbourne, Australia.

Watkins, J. G. (1971). The affect bridge: A hypnoanalytic technique. *International Journal of Clinical and Experimental Hypnosis, 19,* 21–27.

Watkins, J. G. (1990). Watkin's affect or somatic bridge. In D. C. Hammond (Ed.), *Handbook of hypnotic suggestions and metaphors* (pp. 523–524). New York: Norton.

Watts, A. (1951). *The wisdom of insecurity: A message for an age of anxiety.* New York: Pantheon Books.

White, G. D. (1998). Trauma treatment training for Bosnian and Croatian mental health workers. *American Journal of Orthopsychiatry, 63,* 58–62.

Wildwind, L. (1993,). *Chronic depression.* Workshop presentation a the conference of the EMDR, Sunnyvale, CA.

Wilson, S. A., Becker, L. A., & Tinker, R. H. (1995). Eye movement desensitization and reprocessing (EMDR) method treatment for psychologically traumatized individuals. *Journal of Consulting and Clinical Psychology, 63,* 928–937.

Wilson, S. A., Becker, L. A., & Tinker, R. H. (1997). Fifteen-month follow-up of eye movement desensitization and reprocessing (EMDR) treatment for PTSD and psyschological trauma. *Journal of Consulting and Clinical Psychology, 65,* 1047–1056.

Wolpe, J. (1991). *The practice of behavior therapy* (4th ed.). New York: Pergamon.

Wolpe, J., & Abrams, J. (1991). Post-traumatic stress disorder overcome by eye movement desensitization: A case report. *Journal of Behavior Therapy and Experimental Psychiatry, 22,* 39–43.

Young, W. (1995). EMDR: Its use in resolving the trauma caused by the loss of a war buddy. *American Journal of Psychotherapy, 49,* 282–291.

INDEX

abreactions
    case example, 227–29
    characteristics, 224–25, 226
    client preparation for, 225, 226
    inhibition of emotion in, 227
    risk, 224
    therapeutic response, 225–26, 227
    therapeutic significance, 224
accelerated information processing, 5–6
activated memories, 150
adaptive information processing, 6–7, 34, 251–
    53, 337
addiction, 20, 34, 110
adjunctive EMDR, 77–78
adolescent development, 51–52
adult ego state, 11
adulthood, developmental history, 52
adult-self–child-self relationship, 94–98,
    221–22
allies
    fictional characters, 101
    inner adviser, 99–101
    nurturing figures, 90–94
    protector figures, 84, 90–91, 94
    spiritual figures, 98–99
    wise being figure, 98
amygdala, 16–17
anesthesia, 54
anger problems, 175–77
antidepressant medications, 55, 64
anxiety
    treatment case example, 129–35
    treatment protocol, 121–23
art therapy
    closing incomplete session, 218–19
    to enhance split-screen interweave, 277–78
    in pacing treatment, 76
    between session, 144–45, 223
    target development, 184–87

assessment
    in adjunctive EMDR, 77–78
    affect tolerance, 60–61
    child-self–adult-self relationship, 94–95,
        96–97
    client artwork, 184–85
    client commitment to healing, 60
    client commitment to safety, 59
    client readiness for treatment, 57–65, 332
    dissociative disorders, 63
    EMDR protocol, 27, 28–29
    medical health, 61–62
    modified EMDR procedures, 329
    self-harm behaviors, 63
    social supports, 61
    for target development, 123–24
    therapeutic progress, 140–41, 246
    in three-phase trauma therapy model, 35
    see also history taking; reevaluation of therapy
        gains
attachment, developmental history, 51
attentional processes. see bare attention; dual
    focus of attention

bare attention, 112–13
benziodiazepines, 54–55
Bernstein, C., 63
between-session activities
    artwork, 144, 184
    homework exercises, 223
    journal writing, 143–45
    reevaluation in therapy, 140
    resource utilization, 105–6
between-session stress
    assessment of client readiness for therapy,
        60–61
    pace of treatment and, 74–76, 77
    preparing client at close of session, 32, 213,
        222–23

bilateral stimulation
    abreaction during processing, 225
    changing, to release blocked processing, 249
    client self-soothing, 82
    in desensitization, 203–4
    devices for, 69–70
    forms of, 14, 37, 68–70
    to install positive cognitions, 31–32
    to install safe place, 84–85, 86–87
    introduction in therapy, 29–30
    mechanism of EMDR action, 13
    neurological impairment and, 62
    in resources installation, 34, 81–82, 106–7
    speed and number, 30
    symbol for, in case examples, 23
    tapping on knees or hands, 70
    therapist self-care, 322–23
    see also eye movements
bipolar disorder, 64
birth trauma, 48
blocked processing
    application of interweaves, 33–34
    blocking beliefs as source of, 239–42
    body sensations as source of, 245–46
    causes, 238
    characteristics, 236–37
    client fear as source of, 243–44
    client self-blame as source of, 240
    contacting child self to release, 247–48
    feeder memories in, 242–43
    feelings of shame as source of, 241–42
    images as source of, 244–45
    introducing EMDR to release, 66
    noninterweave strategies to release, 248–51,
        336
    outcome-focus to release, 265
    positive statements to unblock, 264–65
    powerlessness beliefs as source of, 240–41
    recognizing, 237–38
    return to target to release, 238–39
    safety beliefs, 240
    sensory awareness to release, 246–47
    signs of release, 246
    steps for intervention with, 237, 336
    temporal awareness to release, 246
    see also interweaves; loops, cognitive or emo-
        tional
body memory, 202–3
    without visual memory, 233–35
body safe place, 115
body scan
    EMDR protocol and procedure, 32, 202–3,
        211–12
    omitting during close of session, 213–14
    purpose, 32, 115

recent trauma intervention, 313
    in target development, 152–53
borderline personality disorder, 54
breathing exercises
    grounding skills, 111, 220–21
    insight meditation, 113
bridging technique
    case examples, 157–67, 169–70, 171–77,
        178–82, 183–84, 307–8
    emotion-focused, 174–77
    goals, 122, 155
    indications, 154–55
    with negative cognitions, 182–84
    with physical sensations, 177–82
    with problematic behaviors, 170–74
    from symptom, issue, or current problem,
        155–57
    from symptom of insomnia, 167–68
    with transference issues, 168–70
Broca's area, 17
butterfly hug, 82, 323

caffeine, 56–57
cancer patients, 198
case examples, 23
case formulation
    case examples, 120–21, 126–35
    clinical significance, 119
    complex cases, 136–39
    for current anxiety and behavior, 121–23
    distress about moving, 127–29
    fear of dying, 126–27
    guidelines, 119, 120
    preparation for examination, 129–35
    target development, 122
chaining of trauma memories, 235–36
change processes
    accelerated information processing, 5–6
    adaptive information processing, 6–7
    artwork as record of, 185–86
    charged memories in, 116, 122
    client commitment to healing, 60
    client's innate wisdom in, 6–7, 10
    closure session in therapy, 32–33
    complex cases, 135–36
    deconditioning limbic system, 18
    ego state integration, 11
    emotional processing, 246
    fear of, 244
    felt sense of truth in, 9–10, 253
    generalization effects, 122, 123, 124, 149
    incomplete session, 212–15
    insights gained between sessions, 146
    installation of positive cognitions, 31–32
    interweave action, 251

journal record, 145
mechanism of EMDR action, 13–14, 252–53
memory network integration, 11–12, 18, 252
objective forgiveness, 8–9
resource development and installation, 34
signs of progress, 140–41, 246
signs of progress during desensitization, 206, 207
somatic sensations, 246
speed of processing, 205
transforming psychological memory to objective memory, 7–8
see also blocked processing
channels of association, 5–6, 10, 208
charged memories
  EMDR processing, 207–8, 209
  phobia intervention, 295
  recent trauma intervention, 312–13, 314
  role of distancing interventions, 116
  trauma representation image, 122, 194
child abuse
  child's feelings of shame after, 241–42
  child's powerlessness beliefs after, 240–41
  child's self-blame for, 240
  EMDR effectivemess, 119
  forms of bilateral stimulation and, 70
  history taking, 52–53
  inhibition of emotional expression related to, 275–76
  need for resource development and installation, 80
  network differentiation issues, 277
  risk of abreactions in processing, 224
  severity of effects, 53
child ego state, 11
  to release blocked processing, 247–48
childhood
  developmental history, 51
  medical treatment experiences as trauma, 54
children
  contraindications to negative cognition, 198
  modification of EMDR procedures for, 39, 43
child-self–adult-self relationship, 94–98
  loving-kindness meditation, 221–22
CIPBS, 186
closing incomplete session, 32–33
  causes of incompleteness, 212
  containing unfinished material, 217–18
  goals, 212–13
  interweaves for, 214–15, 237–38, 254, 281
  loving-kindness meditation, 219–22
  positive cognition installation, 215–16
  procedure, 32
  steps, 213–14
  subjective units of disturbance and, 237–38

use of art, 218–19
use of imagery, 216–18
closing session
  debriefing, 212
  preparing client for between-session experiences, 212, 222–23
  recent trauma intervention, 313–14, 315
  see also closing incomplete session
cognitive-behavioral therapy, EMDR and, 66
Colelli, G., 198
complex cases, 135–36
  case examples, 136–39
  EMDR effectiveness, 119
  history taking, 48
  modified EMDR protocols and procedures for, 43–44
  target development, 149
  therapeutic goals, 135
conflict-free images
  examples, 88, 89–90
  in interweaves, 279–80
  protocol for development, 334
  purpose, 34, 88–89
  to unblock processing, 251
conflict imagination, painting, and bilateral stimulation, 186
contact lenses, 68
contract, therapeutic, 49, 294
countertransference
  in abreaction response, 226
  therapist resistance to EMDR and, 73
critical incident intervention, 317–19

debriefing, 212
depression, 55, 63
desensitization
  bilateral stimulation in, 203–4
  communication during, 205–6, 207, 208–9
  dissociation during, 206
  EMDR procedure, 203–11
  EMDR protocol, 29–31
  emotional functioning in, 206
  processing channels of association, 208
  processing styles, 204–5, 207
  signs of progress, 206, 207
  subjective units of disturbance during, 209–10
  therapeutic purpose, 203
  therapist stance during, 203, 206
development
  adolescence, 51–52
  adulthood, 52
  birth and early infancy, 51
  history taking, 50–52
  memory, 15

devices for bilateral stimulation, 69–70
Diegelmann, C., 39, 186, 198
diet and nutrition
    assessment, 56–57
    therapist self-care, 321
dissociation
    client experience in, 229
    during desensitization, 206
    risk, 229
    sleepiness as manifestation of, 232
    Socratic interweaves for, 258–59
    therapeutic response, 229–31
dissociative disorders
    clinical signs, 330–31
    considerations before commencing EMDR,
        53–54, 63
    manifestations in therapy, 231
distancing techniques, 116–17, 333
    to control arousal, 60
    indications, 117
    to unblock processing, 249
    use of metaphors, 70–71
Douglass, F., 101
dreams
    EMDR and, 13–14, 146
    as targets, 146, 187–89
drumming, 14
dual focus of attention
    clinical significance, 30
    during desensitization, 205–6
    handling abreactions in processing, 227
    handling dissociation during processing, 229
    in meditation, 112

eating behaviors, 172–74
eating meditation, 114–15
ecologically appropriate emotions, 7
education interweaves, 280–81
ego states
    as memory networks, 11
    therapy goals, 11, 252
ego strengthening
    client preparation for therapy, 79–80
    clinical significance, 79
    development of inner strength, 101–3
    grounding skills for, 110–11
    relaxation/stress reduction skills for, 110
    somatic psychotherapy techniques, 115
    thought field therapy techniques, 116
    in three-phase trauma therapy model, 35
    see also resource development and installation
EMDR in the Treatment of Adults Abused as Children
        (Parnell), 119, 154–55, 199
emotional functioning
    abreactions in processing, 224–29
    affective resonance of negative cognition, 197

affect tolerance, 60–61
assessment phase of EMDR, 29
bridging from emotions, 174–77
communication of feeling, 17
considerations before commencing EMDR,
    60–61
in desensitization, 206
desensitization processing styles, 204
ecologically appropriate emotions, 7
during EMDR session, 201
imaginal container for affect management,
    117–18
inhibition of emotional expression related to
    child abuse, 275–76
neurophysiology of trauma, 16
in target development, 152
EMPowerplus, 55
enemas, 54
exercise, 56–57
explicit memory
    development, 15
    trauma effects, 16
Eye Movement Desensitization and Reprocessing (Sha-
        piro), 81
eye movements
    changing, to release blocked processing,
        248
    client resistance to, 69
    contraindications, 69
    duration of, 30
    introduction in therapy, 30
    limitations, 69
    machines for directing, 68–69
    mechanism of EMDR action, 13–14
    seizure disorders and, 62
    speed, 30
    technical development of EMDR, 18–19,
        21–22
    therapeutic technique, 68, 69

fears
    of dying, 126–27
    as source of blocked processing, 243–44
    see also phobias
feeder memories, 242–43
felt sense
    integration of neuronetworks, 12
    treatment goals, 253
    of truth, 9–10
fictional characters, 101
fictional images, 196
fight-flight response, 16–17
firefighters, 198
flashbacks as target, 153–54, 195
floatback technique, 122. see also bridging tech-
    nique

forgiveness, objective, 8–9
Foster, S., 34
frequency of sessions, 74, 143

Goldstein, J., 112–13
grief
    education interweave for, 281
    EMDR effectiveness, 19
    imagination interweave for, 274
    Socratic interweaves for, 259–60
grounding skills, 110–11, 220–21
guided imagery, 35, 76
    for between-session stress, 222–23
    relaxation techniques, 110

Hakomi therapy, 115
headphones, 69–70
heartbeat, 14
Hebb, D. O., 10
hippocampus, 14, 15–17
history taking
    child abuse experience, 52–53
    client's perceptions, 48
    client spirituality, 56
    complex trauma, 48
    developmental history, 50–52
    establishing therapeutic relationship in, 27,
        49–50
    forms for, 50
    goals, 27, 47–49, 50–51
    health behaviors, 56–57
    identification of client resources, 55–56
    mental health treatment, 53–55
    multiple trauma client, 150
    pace, 50
    phobia intervention, 294–95
    recent trauma intervention, 309–10, 314
    symptom focus, 49
    trauma history, 52
homework, 223
hyperarousal, 60
    neurophysiology, 16
hypnotherapy, 35

images, trauma representation
    client difficulties with, 42
    composite image, 194–95
    containing unfinished material at close of ses-
        sion, 217–18
    development in EMDR session, 29, 193–95
    distancing techniques, 116–17
    from fiction, 196
    flashback images, 195
    fragmented image, 195
    imaginal container for affect management,
        117–18

imagined images, 195
    miniaturization, 218
    negative future images, 196
    noninterweave techniques to unblock pro-
        cessing, 249–50
    as source of blocked processing, 244–45
    stimulation of memory network, 37
    target development, 151, 302–5
    therapeutic purpose, 197
    trigger images, 195
    from vicarious traumatization, 195–96
imaginal container, 117–18
    techniques to unblock processing, 250
imaginal target images, 195
imagination interweaves, 337
    application, 271
    case examples, 271–76, 277–78
    client resistance to, 271
    metaphors, stories, and analogies in,
        276
    split screen technique to sort networks,
        276–78
    two-handed, 278–79
implicit memory, 15
incomplete session. see closing incomplete ses-
    sion
indications for EMDR, 4, 19–20, 119
infantile amnesia, 15
information processing
    development, 15
    EMDR goals, 5–7, 252–53, 337
    trauma effects, 3–5, 15–18
    see also adaptive information processing
informed consent, 68
inner adviser, 99–101
    to release blocked processing, 248
inner strength, 101–3
inquiry interweaves, 337
    definition, 255
    mechanism of action, 255
    Socratic type, 255–61
    subcategories, 255–56
insights gained between sessions, 146
insomnia, bridging from symptom of, 167–
    68
installation of positive cognitions, 31–32,
    211
installation of resources. see resource develop-
    ment and installation
integrated treatment, 35, 65, 66
interpersonal relationships
    considerations before commencing EMDR,
        59, 61
    developmental history, 51–52
    identification of client resources, 55–56
    trauma effects, 5

interweaves
    application, 33–34, 254–55
    based on client perceptions, 265–67
    categories, 255. *see also* specific category, 337
    client collaboration in use of, 253
    client self-blame interventions, 261–62
    for closing incomplete session, 214–15,
        237–38, 254, 281
    common errors in application, 254
    definition, 12
    education type, 280–81
    finding effective interweave, 287–90
    guidelines, 254
    handling abreactions, 226
    imagination type, 271–80
    "I'm confused" technique, 261
    indications, 251, 253
    mechanism of action, 251
    open question type, 262–64
    purpose, 33
    resource type, 267–71
    safe place in, 279–80
    split screen technique, 276–77
    technical evolution, 21–22
    therapist's difficulty in finding, 73
    timing of intervention, 254
    to unblock blocked processing, 251
    use of multiple interweave types, 281–87
introducing EMDR to clients, 29–30, 65–67

journals, 143–45

Kidd, S. M., 93
Klein, J., 220
Korn, D., 49, 64, 106, 149–50, 267, 295
Kwan Yin, 98–99

language, trauma effects, 17, 18
Leeds, A., 34, 106
legal issues, 64
Lendl, J., 34
length of session, 74, 76–77, 120
length of treatment, 67
Levine, P., 115
Life and Times of Frederick Douglass, The (Douglass), 101
light stream visualization, 110
limbic system, 16
    clinical significance, 17
    treatment goals, 18
Linehan, M., 111–12
location of body sensation, 29
loops, cognitive or emotional
    characteristics, 33, 236
    manifestations, 237
    see also blocked processing

Lovett, J., 39, 198
loving-kindness meditation, 219–22

Mahler, M., 157, 161
Mahoney, M., 39
major ("big T") trauma, 4
mandalas, 144
Martinez, R. A., 277
mechanism of EMDR action, 13–14, 252–53
medical health
    assessment, 54–55, 61
    avoidance of medical care, 61
    considerations before starting EMDR, 62
    medical treatment as source of trauma, 54
    therapist self-care, 321–22
meditation, 30, 56
    eating meditation, 114–15
    loving-kindness, 219–22
    therapist self-care, 322
    Vipassana, 112–14, 322
    walking meditation, 114
memory
    activated, 150
    body memory without visual memory,
        233–35
    body sensations in evocation of, 202–3
    chaining, 235–36
    of complex trauma, 43
    EMDR outcomes, 6, 7–8
    emergence of new, between sessions, 146
    feeder memories, 242–43
    hemispheric processing, 15, 16
    multiple trauma client, 150
    normal development, 15
    recent trauma, 309
    representative traumatic incident, 149
    trauma effects, 4, 15–16
    see also charged memories; images, trauma representation; target development
memory networks
    clinical significance, 10–11
    definition, 10
    differentiation, 13, 277
    EMDR action, 252–53
    Socratic interweaves to integrate, 255
    split screen technique to sort, 276–78
    stimulation, 37
    treatment goals, 11–13, 18
    see also memory; target development
metaphors
    imagination interweaves, 276
metaphors, to create distance, 70–71
migraines, 69
mindfulness practices, 111–13. *see also* meditation
minor ("small t") trauma, 4

mitrovalve prolapse, 61
modified EMDR procedures
  checklist, 43, 328
  for complex trauma, 43–44
  to develop negative cognitions, 198
  to develop positive cognitions, 199
  indications, 40, 41–42
  omitting steps, 42
  rationale, 39, 40–41, 43
  for recent trauma, 314–17
  sample vignette, 329
  subjective units of disturbance scale, 202
  use of safe place, 44
movement as resource, 104–5
movement therapy, 35
multiple trauma client
  memory chaining, 235–36
  three-pronged protocol, 149–50
music, 104

narcotics, 55
narrative construction
  memory network integration and, 252
  recent trauma intervention, 310
  treatment goals, 12, 252
nature images, 105
negative cognition
  affective resonance, 197
  bridging from, 182–84
  client difficulties with, 39, 42
  contraindications, 198
  definition, 197
  development in EMDR, 197–98
  examples, 335
  modification of EMDR procedure, 43, 198
  omitting from EMDR procedure, 39, 42, 198
  qualities, 197–98, 199–200
  target development, 151–52
  therapeutic application, 29
neuronetworks. see memory networks
neurophysiology
  development of positive images, 88–89
  mechanism of EMDR action, 14
  memory networks, 10–11
  neurological impairment and bilateral stimulation, 62
  resource development and installation, 81
  synaptic pruning, 16, 81
  trauma experience, 14–18
nightmares, 4
  as targets, 188
nodes, 10
  targets as, 28
numbness during therapy, 233, 260
nurturing figures, 90–94, 116

objective forgiveness, 8–9
objective memory, 7–8, 252–53
observing, 31, 112–13
Omaha, J., 117–18
open question interweave, 262–64
outcomes research
  EMDR, 19, 20–21
  posttraumatic stress disorder, 149–50

pace of treatment, 74–77, 120, 143
panic disorder, 19, 61
Parnell, L., 34
performance anxiety, 20
perpetrators, objective forgiveness, 9
Perry, B., 14
phantom limb pain, 19
pharmacotherapy, EMDR and, 54–55, 63–64
Phillips, M., 89, 102
phobias
  EMDR efficacy, 19, 293, 295
  history taking, 294–95
  self-control techniques, 293
  symbolic, 295–96
  target development, 154, 293–94, 295
  therapeutic procedure, 293–94
  therapy case examples, 296–308
physical symptoms
  body memory without visual memory, 233–35
  body sensations as source of blocked processing, 245–46
  bridging from, 177–82
  considerations before commencing EMDR, 61–62
  location of body sensations, 29
  memory networks and, 10–11
  numbness during therapy, 233
  trauma effects, 3
Popky, A. J., 34
positive cognition
  client difficulties with, 40, 42
  at close of session, 215–16
  contraindications, 199
  development in EMDR session, 199, 334
  examples, 335
  installation, 31–32, 211
  instilling safety at end of session, 38
  obstacles to installation, 32
  qualities, 198–99, 200
  recent trauma intervention, 311–12, 313, 315
  therapeutic application, 29, 199
positive memories, 88–89, 103–4
positive statements, 264–65
posttraumatic stress disorder
  assessing client readiness for therapy, 60, 62, 64–65

posttraumatic stress disorder (*continued*)
  case formulation case example, 120–21
  cognitive symptoms, 17–18
  EMDR efficacy, 19, 20, 21
  neurophysiology, 16
  outcome research, 149–50
  symptoms, 4
preparation phase of EMDR
  in adjunctive EMDR, 77–78
  assessment of client readiness, 57–65
  child-self–adult-self relationship assessment,
    94–95, 96–97
  clinical significance, 79
  development of coping skills in, 110–16
  ego strengthening, 79–80
  establishing metaphors to create distance,
    70–71
  goals, 27–28, 119–20
  introducing EMDR to clients, 29–30, 65–
    67
  recent trauma intervention, 309–10
  resource development and installation, 34,
    80–82
  therapeutic container, 57, 64
  in three-phase trauma therapy model, 35
procedural steps
  body scan, 211–12
  checklist, 325
  closing normal session, 212
  conflict-free image development, 334
  desensitization, 203–11
  identifying location of body sensations,
    202–3
  identifying presenting issue, 193
  image creation, 193–97
  interweave application, 254–55
  negative cognition development, 197–98
  phobia intervention, 293–94
  positive cognition development, 198–99,
    334
  positive cognition installation, 211, 215–16
  readiness for EMDR session, 193
  resource installation or evocation, 193
  sample vignette, 326–27
  speed of processing, 205
  subjective units of disturbance scale, 201–2
  validity of cognitions scale, 200–201
  see also closing incomplete session
procrastination, 171–72
projective identification, in therapist, 73
protector figures, 84, 90–91, 94, 116
protocols and procedures
  adjunctive EMDR, 77–78
  amenability to modification, 36
  application of interweaves, 33–34
  bridging technique, 156–57

critical incident intervention, 317–19
for current anxiety and behavior, 121–23
essential protocol elements, 36–39
explaining to client, 65–67
indications for modification, 42
integrated therapy with EMDR, 35
making modifications to, 39–42, 43
pace of treatment, 74–77, 120
phases, 27–33
procedural steps, 193, 325–27
readiness for EMDR session, 193
for recent trauma, 309–14
resource development and installation, 81,
  106–7
three-phase model, 34–35, 149–50
for treating complex trauma, 43–44
using dreams as targets, 187–88
see also modified EMDR procedures; procedural steps
psychoanalytic therapy, EMDR and, 66
Psychological Birth of the Human Infant (Mahler), 157, 161
psychological memory, transformation to objective memory, 7–8, 252–53
psychotic disorders, 63–64

recent trauma intervention
  critical incident intervention, 317–19
  indications, 309
  modified protocol, 314–17
  standard protocol, 309–14
  target development, 310–12
reevaluation of therapy gains
  behavioral shifts, 145
  client functioning, 143
  client insights, 146
  client journal, 143–45
  dream review, 146
  emergence of new memories, 146
  pace of treatment, 143
  procedure, 33, 140
  purpose, 33, 143
  signs of progress, 140–41
  symptom review, 145
  system changes, 146–47
  target change, 147
relaxation exercises
  after incomplete session, 214
  for ego strengthening, 110
  in establishing safe place, 84, 85–86
REM sleep, 13–14
resistance to therapy
  client's, 73–74
  imagination interweaves, 271
  therapist's, 71–73, 74
  see also blocked processing

resource development and installation
  assessing client readiness for therapy,
    60
  beginning EMDR session, 193
  child-self–adult-self relationship, 94–98
  common therapist errors, 254
  definition, 34, 80
  distancing techniques, 104
  establishing safe place, 83–85
  fictional characters, 101
  focus on specific challenge, 106–7
  goals, 34, 80–81
  images of nature, 105
  inner adviser, 99–101
  inner strength, 101–3
  neurophysiology, 81
  nurturing and protector figures, 90–94
  positive goal state, 105
  positive images, 88–90
  positive memories, 103–4
  recent trauma intervention, 309–10, 314
  resource interweaves and, 269
  sense of mastery, 105
  between session activities, 105–6
  session closing, 216–18
  spiritual resources, 98–99
  techniques, 34, 81–82, 106–10
  therapeutic significance, 80, 106
  therapist self-care, 323
  use of movement, 104–5
  use of music in, 104
resource interweaves, 337
  application, 267–68
  case examples, 269–71
  sequencing, 268–69
response flexibility, 12–13
responsibility issues as source of blocked pro-
    cessing, 240, 258
rhythm, 14

saccades, 30, 34
safe object/person, 88
safe place, 28, 34
  applications, 82
  assessing client readiness for therapy, 60,
    82–83
  in body, 115
  cue word, 85
  drawing, 84
  establishing, 82–85
  guided relaxation to, 84, 85–86
  inability to develop, 87–89
  in interweaves, 279–80
  in Modified EMDR Procedure, 44
  script, 86–87
  to unblock processing, 251

safety
  blocking beliefs related to, 240
  considerations before commencing EMDR,
    59
  end of session, 38–39, 212, 214–15, 216
  increasing sense of, to unblock processing,
    250
  interweaves to address, 253
  therapeutic environment, 37
  therapeutic relationship and, 57–58
  see also safe place
sand tray therapy, 35, 76
Schmidt, S. J., 91–92, 98, 99
Schore, A. N., 16, 81
Secret Life of Bees (Kidd), 93
seizure disorders, 62, 69
self concept
  adult self as nurturing figure, 91–92
  assessment, 48
  building self-efficacy beliefs in intervention
    with recent trauma, 313, 318, 319
  child as family caretaker, 270
  coherence in, 12
  control and powerlessness beliefs, 240–41
  development, 15
  feelings of shame as source of blocked pro-
    cessing, 241–42
  memory networks in, 11
  psychological memory, 7–8
  self-blame for abuse, 240, 261–62, 263
  sense of mastery, 105
  target development, 182–84
  trauma effects, 3, 4
self-control techniques, 60
self-harm behaviors, considerations before com-
    mencing EMDR, 59, 63
sensorimotor therapy, 35, 115
sensory awareness to release blocked process-
    ing, 246–47
sexual abuse clients, 119
  body memories, 202–3
  body memory without visual memory,
    233–35
  pace of treatment, 75
  tactile stimulation, 70
sexuality and sexual behavior
  considerations before commencing EMDR, 59
  developmental history, 52
shame
  interweaves to address, 253
  as source of blocked processing, 241–42
  sources of, 241
Shapiro, F., 3, 4, 7, 10, 14, 18–19, 21–22, 27,
    35, 36, 37, 41, 60, 62, 63, 68, 76, 81, 82,
    85, 121, 140, 149, 198, 199, 200, 224,
    251, 293, 295, 309, 311

Shapiro, R., 278
sibling relationships, 51
Siegel, D. J., 12–13, 252
single-incident trauma, target development, 148–49
single photon emission computed tomography, 15
sleep
    EMDR mechanism and, 13–14
    see also dreams
sleepiness during therapy, 231–33
social support assessment, 61
Socratic interweaves, 255–61
Solomon, R. M., 313, 318, 319
somatic experiencing, 35, 76
somatic psychotherapy, ego strengthening techniques, 115
spirituality
    assessment, 56
    resource development, 98–99
    spiritual core self, 98
    three-phase trauma therapy model, 35
split-screen interweave, 276–78
Steinberg, M., 63
stopping processing, signal for, 27–28, 68, 120, 208–9
stress reduction skills, 110
subjective units of disturbance scale, 29, 31
    client difficulties with, 41, 42, 202
    closing session, 237–38
    during desensitization, 209–10
    EMDR procedure, 201–2
    recent trauma intervention, 311–12, 313, 314–15
substance use, considerations before commencing EMDR, 59, 62–63
suicidal behavior/ideation, 59
support groups, 61
symbolic action, 218
symptom-focused approach
    bridging technique, 154–55
    rationale, 49, 142–43
    reevaluating therapy, 140, 145
    in target development, 49, 122
synaptic pruning, 16, 81

tac-audio, 23
tactile stimulation, 23, 69–70
talk during EMDR, 30, 205–6, 207, 208–9, 254
    handling dissociation during processing, 230, 231
talk therapy
    integrated therapy with EMDR, 35, 65, 66
    limitations, 17
    in three-phase trauma therapy model, 35

target development
    alterations to target to unblock processing, 249–50
    in assessment phase of therapy, 28
    beginning EMDR session, 193
    body awareness in, 152–53
    chronological approach, 122, 123–24
    client difficulty in, 151
    clinical significance, 28–29, 148
    dreams and nightmares as targets, 187–89
    EMDR goals, 5
    emotional functioning in, 152
    flashbacks, 153–54, 195
    history taking for, 27
    image for, 151
    mapping, 120, 123, 124
    memory charge, 122
    modification of EMDR procedures, 41–42, 151
    multiple trauma cases, 149, 150
    negative cognitions in, 151–52
    phobia intervention, 293–94, 295
    recent trauma intervention, 310–12
    reevaluation, 140, 147
    representative traumatic incident, 149
    schematics, 125, 127
    selection, 122–24, 142
    single-incident traumas, 148–49
    symptom-focused approach, 49, 122
    techniques, 151–53
    triggers, 153, 195
    use of art in, 184–87
    see also bridging technique; images, trauma representation
temporal awareness
    activation of trauma memory, 16
    memory development, 15
    qualities of negative cognition, 197–98
    to release blocked processing, 246
    validity of cognition scale, 200–201
therapeutic relationship
    in adjunctive EMDR, 77
    client fear of, 243
    as client resource, 58
    clinical significance, 39, 50, 58
    desensitization procedure, 203
    EMDR procedures interfering with, 39, 40
    EMDR requirements, 57–59
    goals, 50
    handling abreactions, 225–26
    in history-taking phase, 27, 49–50
    preparation for EMDR processing, 28
    safety in, 37
    therapist as nurturing figure, 90–94
    trust in, 57–58, 59

therapist factors
  for EMDR proficiency, 323–24
  failure to process to completion, 7
  resistance to EMDR, 71–73
  trust in process, 6
therapist self-care
  bilateral stimulation, 322–23
  client mix, 320–21
  creative expression for, 322
  health behaviors, 321–22
  meditation, 322
  pace of practice, 321
  rationale, 320
thought field therapy, 35, 116
three-phase trauma therapy model, 34–35,
  149–50
Tinker, R., 38–39
transference
  bridging back from, 168–70
  clinical significance, 66
  EMDR in psychodynamic psychotherapy,
  66
Transforming Trauma: EMDR (Parnell), 9, 62
transitional objects, 222–23
trauma effects
  communication skills, 17, 18
  generalization, 13, 252
  history taking, 52–53
  information processing, 3–5, 15–18
  interpersonal functioning, 5
  lack of engagement, 17
  limitations of talk therapy, 17
  memory networks, 12
  memory processes, 4, 15–16
  neurophysiological, 14–18

outcome-focus to release blocked processing,
  265
self-beliefs, 3, 4
synaptic pruning, 81
Traumatic Stress (van der Kolk et al.), 14–15
triggers as targets, 153, 195
trust
  in client, 59, 73
  in therapeutic process, 6, 7, 73
  in therapist, 57–58
truth
  client perception of, after EMDR, 7
  felt sense of, as EMDR outcome, 9–10
  interweaves based on client perception of,
  265–66
two-handed interweave, 278–79

validity of cognition scale, 29
  client difficulties with, 40–41, 42
  EMDR procedure, 200–201
van der Kolk, B. A., 14–15, 18
vicarious traumatization, 195–96
Vipassana meditation, 112–14, 322

walking meditation, 114
Watts, A., 323
Wildwind, L., 34
Wilson, S., 20
wisdom, inherent, 6–7, 10
wise being figure, 98
wise self. see inner adviser
witness awareness, 112
Wolpe, J., 29, 201, 249

yoga, 14, 110–11